The Hessians

Mercenaries from Hessen-Kassel in the
American Revolution

The Hessians

Mercenaries from Hessen-Kassel in the American Revolution

RODNEY ATWOOD

CAMBRIDGE UNIVERSITY PRESS

Cambridge

London   New York   New Rochelle
Melbourne   Sydney

Published by the Press Syndicate of the University of Cambridge
The Pitt Building, Trumpington Street, Cambridge CB2 1RP
32 East 57th Street, New York, NY 10022, USA
296 Beaconsfield Parade, Middle Park, Melbourne 3206, Australia

First published 1980

Printed in the United States of America
Typeset by Interprint Ltd., Malta
Printed and bound by Halliday Lithograph Corporation,
West Hanover, Mass

Library of Congress Cataloguing in Publication Data
Atwood, Rodney.
    The Hessians.
    Bibliography: p.
    Includes index.
    1. United States – History – Revolution,
1775–1783 – German mercenaries.   I. Title.
E268.A89   973.3′42   79-20150
ISBN 0 521 22884 0

Contents

List of maps		*page* vii
Acknowledgements		viii
Abbreviations		ix
Note on German ranks and currency		xi
Introduction		1
1	The German soldier trade	7
2	The Hessians go to America	22
3	The victories of 1776	58
4	The Battle of Trenton	84
5	The campaigns of 1777–81	117
6	Anglo-Hessian relations	144
7	The Hessian view of the American Revolution	158
8	Hessian plundering	171
9	Hessian desertion	184
10	Recruiting in Germany	207
11	The impact of the war on Hessen	216
12	Conclusion	234

Appendices

A	Hessians mustered into British service 1776–82	254
B	Hessian casualities in America	255
C	Calculation of total Hessians remaining in America	256
D	German auxiliaries as a proportion of British strength in America	257

Contents

Appendices – contd.

E Hessian battalions and *Jägercorps* serving in America   258

Bibliography   266
Index   277

Maps

———

1 Hessen-Kassel *c*. 1762. Based on Anton
Friedrich Büsching's, *A New System of
Geography*, vol. v. (London, 1762).   *page* 9
2 New York City and its environs, 1776. From
George F. Scheer and Hugh F. Rankin, *Rebels
and Redcoats*, p. 144.   67
3 New Jersey, 'Cockpit of the Revolution'. From
George F. Scheer and Hugh F. Rankin, *Rebels
and Redcoats*, p. 205.   85
4 The Battle of Trenton, 26 December
1776. Based on a map by Andrew
Wiederholdt in the Wilhelmshöher
Kriegskartensammlung at Staatsarchiv
Marburg.   94
5 Operations round Philadelphia, 177. From
George F. Scheer and Hugh F. Rankin, *Rebels
and Redcoats*, p. 231.   121
6 The assault on Fort Redbank, 22 October
1777. Based on a map by Lt. Wolff of the
Hessian artillery in the Wilhelmshöher
Kriegskartensammlung at Staatsarchiv
Marburg.   125

Acknowledgements

For their help and hospitality in the course of my work I am indebted to Dr Tim Blanning of Sydney Sussex College, Cambridge; Drs Heinz and Christa Stoffregen of Marburg; Dr G. B. Ferguson of the Nova Scotia Provincial Archives; Herr Colin C. Hoffman of Bonn; Dr W. Mueller of Stadtarchiv, Bayreuth, for making available to me a photostat of Feilitzsch's journal; the Goethe-Institut, London; the staffs of the various archives who helped me directly or who sent me material, particularly Dr Erika Kunz of the Murhardsche Bibliothek, Kassel, and Dr Auerbach and Dr Eckhardt of Staatsarchiv Marburg.

Without travel and study grants from the Department of Education and Science and the German Academic Exchange Service, I would not have been able to do my research in German archives.

Lady Lucas of the Old Manor, Wonston, Winchester kindly allowed me to use the papers of the Lucas Collection in the Bedford County Record Office.

Dr Jonathan Steinberg of Trinity Hall, Cambridge gave me much encouragement.

I am particularly grateful to Professor Jack Pole of St Catherine's College, Oxford, for his many wise observations and for helping me to find a publisher; and to Dr Joachim Fischer of Stadtarchiv, Frankfurt-am-Main for commenting on my manuscript and giving me the benefit of his encyclopaedic knowledge of German mercenaries in the American Revolution.

Abbreviations

—————

Add. MSS.   Additional Manuscripts in the British Library

AHR   *American Historical Review*

Bardeleben   Heinrich von Bardeleben, 'Tagebuch eines Hessischen Offiziers, Heinrich von Bardeleben', Julius Göbell, ed., *DAGeschBl*, XXVII–XXVIII (1927–8), pp. 7–119

DAGeschBl   *Deutsche-Amerikanische Geschichtsblätter/German-American Historical Review*. Yearbook of the German-American historical society of Illinois

Dinklage   LB Kassel. 4° Ms. hass. 186, Tagebuch des Obrist Lieutenants von Dinklage 1776–84

Feilitzsch   Stadtarchiv Bayreuth. Ms. 100, Tagebuch des mark-gräflichen Jäger-leutnants Carl Philipp von Feilitzsch März 1777 bis Juni 1780

Hessenland   *Hessenland: Zeitschrift für Hessische Geschichte und Landeskunde*. Kassel, 1888–1943

HMC   Historical Manuscripts Commission of Great Britain

Jungkenn   Jungkenn papers in the William L. Clements Library, Ann Arbor, Michigan. The numbers indicate volume and item

Kümmel   StaMarburg. Kirchenbuch von hess. Truppenteilen a. d. amerik. Feldzüge 1776–83: Abschrift B: Tagebuch des Pfarrers Kümmel Feldprediger bei den Fürstlich Hessischen Regimenter von Huyn und von Bunau

LB Kassel   Murhardsche Bibliothek der Stadt Kassel und Landesbibliothek

Malsburg   StaMarburg 12.11 I Ba 18$\frac{1}{2}$. Tagebuch meines Vaters des damaligen Capitains, späterhin Oberstlieutenant und ritterschaftlichen Ober Einnehmers des adeligen Stifts Kaufungen

ix

	Friedrich von der Malsburg aus dem Hause Escheburg
Mitteilungen	*Mitteilungen an die Mitglieder des Vereins für hessische Geschichte und Landeskunde.* Kassel, 1865–1934
Münchhausen	StaHannover 52 III Nr. 29. Diarium (Briefe) des als Adjutant des englischen Generals Sir William Howe am Nordamerikanischen Freiheitskriege teilnehmenden Hauptmanns Friedrich v. Münchhausen an seinen Bruder Wilhelm v. M., Geh. Kriegsrat in Hannover 1776–8. (In five bundles or fasces: the first two bundles being his letters, the last three his commentary upon Howe's *Narrative* in the form of footnotes. Where possible I give the number of his footnote as well as fasc: and folio.)
NGFKW	*Nachrichten der Gesellschaft für Familienkunde in Kurhessen und Waldeck.*
PMHB	*Pennsylvania Magazine of History and Biography.*
Reuber	Stadtarchiv Frankfurt-am-Main. Depositum Adolf Reuber Nr. 1. Tagebuch des Grenadiers Johannes Reuber
Sta	Staatsarchiv
WMQ	*William and Mary Quarterly*

Citations from documents in the Public Record Office follow the practice used there in ordering documents; thus, AO: Accounts Office, CO: Colonial Office, FO: Foreign Office, SP: State Papers, T: Treasury, and WO: War Office.

Note on German ranks and currency

The German *Unteroffizier* is translated by the English abbreviation 'NCO' (non-commissioned officer).

A *Stabskapitain* is not a staff captain, but a senior subaltern commanding a company in the absence of its chief, and is translated by the contemporary English equivalent 'captain-lieutenant'.

A *Stabsoffizier* is a 'field officer', i.e. a major, lieutenant-colonel, or colonel.

I usually omit the German prefix 'von' once I have initially identified the person, unless using the name in a proper title, for example, Grenadier Battalion von Minnigerode. Thus the commander of the second Hessian division, once identified as Wilhelm, Freiherr von Knyphausen, is called 'Knyphausen', not 'von Knyphausen'.

German currency is usually given in *taler, albus,* and *heller,* this being the practice in the Hessian *Kriegspfennigzahlamt* accounts. In Hessen before 1819, 1 *taler* = 32 *albus* and 1 *albus* = 12 *heller* or 9 *pfennigs.* The British Treasury reckoned $£1 = 5\frac{5}{6}$ *taler.*

Introduction

The hiring of auxiliary troops by great powers in the eighteenth century marks a transitional stage in the history of western warfare, from the feudal levy to the modern conscript army. Auxiliary contingents then served in the armies of all great powers (except Russia) in the wars of that century. International jurists of the time, attempting to draw limits to destructive warfare by applying Natural Law to human affairs, recognized the practice of one prince sending aid to another at war, in the form of troops, in exchange for moneys called subsidies. They distinguished between such troops, called auxiliaries (*Hilfstruppen*), and mercenaries, who were individuals who enlisted in foreign military service in return for a certain sum of money and certain conditions, such as a limit on the length of their service.

The study of the Hessen-Kassel corps enables us to see one of these auxiliary contingents in detail: its personnel, training, discipline, recruiting practices, organization, and the difficulty of its working as part of a foreign (British) army composed of men speaking a different language and with different political traditions. Both the Hessian corps and the British army included within their ranks mercenaries, i.e. foreigners who had enlisted for pay, but properly neither of them could be called mercenary.[1]

The Hessians are particularly interesting, not merely because their princes were the most successful, and later infamous, at hiring out auxiliaries; but also because they confronted in America a new society and new ideals of liberalism and patriotism which were to make the hiring of troops for pay anachronistic. The Hessian corps – indeed, all six German corps hired out to the British in that war, all collectively and incorrectly known as the 'Hessians' – are the best-known case of such an auxiliary contingent. Nearly every American schoolboy learns of Washington's defeat of the Hessians

---

[1] By common usage, however, the Hessians have been called mercenaries. In this work I refer to them as both auxiliaries and mercenaries.

1

at Trenton. It is doubtful if anyone save the specialist knows of Duke Karl Eugen's Württemberg contingent at Leuthen or the Brunswickers who served Venice against the Turks in the 1660s. This is not because the hiring of the Hessians was in any way exceptional for the time, but is due to the subsequent importance of the United States in world affairs and its role as an ideal for European liberals. The era of the American and French Revolutions marked a profound transformation of European public opinion. Subsequently, every aspect of the Hessians – the morality of the subsidy treaties, recruiting, desertion rates, their performance in war, their princes' private lives – became a subject of historical, and indeed political, debate in Germany.[2]

German historians of the last century, whether Prussian nationalists like Heinrich von Treitschke (a Saxon who transferred his xenophobic Germanism to Prussia) or liberal nationalists like Friedrich Kapp, had nothing but contempt for any German state north of Austria, save Prussia. In the eyes of these historians princes like Friedrich II of Hessen-Kassel were condemned because they were neither liberals nor nationalists. Yet both of these policies would create a national unified Germany; the princes could scarcely be expected to commit political suicide by preparing for their extinction.

The views of these German historians were uncritically adopted by their British and American counterparts like Sir George Otto Trevelyan and G.P. Gooch, while Bancroft was a friend of Kapp, who stayed in New York during political exile. To these historians the princes' crime was not merely to have trafficked in the blood of their subjects, but also to have opposed the realization of the liberal democratic state, the highest form of human government.

Study of the little German states has more recently shown that the ideals of benevolent rule carried out on a large scale by enlightened despots in Austria, Prussia, and Russia were also brought to fruition in legislation in the little principalities. American military historians writing of the revolution and the Hessians' participation remain ignorant of these developments. Friedrich of Hessen-Kassel established the first Foundling Hospital in Germany and the first museum on the continent open to the public, yet all we know of him from the standard histories is that he had one hundred bastards: a fact of dubious authenticity, in

---

[2] For the use made of the 'Hessians' by various interested parties, see H. D. Schmidt, 'The Hessian Mercenaries, the career of a political cliché', *History*, XLIII (1958), pp. 207–12.

Introduction

contemporary sources attributable only to the gossipy Wraxall. Friedrich was supposedly motivated only by sordid lust, his family life non-existent. Yet in February 1783, the hour of Britain's and Hessen's defeat, it was not of his troops or of subsidy arrears that Friedrich wrote to George III, but of being reunited with his sons:

> Knowing well how much [Your Majesty] interests himself in my affairs, I take the liberty of informing [you] of a domestic event of which no one could appreciate better the happiness to be enjoyed than a Monarch who knows so well what it is to be a father. My love for my sons, conspiring with the sentiments which they carry for me, has caused me to traverse the barrier which was to be found raised between us since their childhood, and at this moment I have the comfort of having all three with me.[3]

George Forster, present at the announcement of the happy event, wrote, 'So many cried for joy, that all the soldiers under arms on the drill square were in tears, as the Landgraf proclaimed his eldest son General of all the Hessian troops. He himself cried at length, and so did all the princes.'[4]

Of this Kapp and Treitschke take no cognizance. Complementary to their contempt for Friedrich of Hessen is admiration for Frederick the Great of Prussia as (of course) a precursor of German national greatness. Frederick supposedly despised the Hessians, thought Washington a great general, and took a keen interest in America's independence. A careful reading of Frederick's *Political Correspondence*, rather than what he wrote for Voltaire's consumption, shows the fallacy of these views. Yet Edward J. Lowell, the only English-speaking historian to write a book on the Hessians, appropriated Kapp's viewpoint.

Aside from histories animated by the partisanship of German nationalism, publications on the Hessians fall into three categories. First are the articles of dilletante like the *Zolldirektor* August Woringer of Kassel, Major General von Eisentraut, Pastor Junghans, and Otto Gerland in *Hessenland* and other periodicals, unknown to American military historians of the revolution. Often they had access to documents no longer available to us, sometimes belonging to their families; thus, although they are ignorant of American history, their work is still valuable.

Second are the strictly military German works, such as regimental histories. These too are unknown to Americans, with one

---

[3] SP81/196, Friedrich of Hessen to George III, 15 February 1783.
[4] Johann George Forster, *Briefwechsel*, I (Leipzig, 1829), p. 320.

exception: Max von Eelking's book on the auxiliaries, translated into English by J. G. Rosengarten, a German-American born in Kassel. Eelking's work is typical of others in this category: meticulous research in German documents, with a soldier's keen eye brought to bear on battles and skirmishes, but a very uncritical use of these sources and only trifling knowledge of American ones such as Sparks' edition of Washington's letters.

Third are the published journals and extracts of letters, such as those which appeared in Professor Schlözer's contemporary *Briefwechsel* at Gottingen. Those in English are better known to Americans, but one of the best, Bardeleben's, written by an intelligent subaltern in the 1776 campaign, is never mentioned. Yet the original is in America.

The best known of these published journals are the two volumes edited by Professor Uhlendorf, using the von Jungkenn papers at Ann Arbor, Michigan. Yet even Uhlendorf, with his meticulous scholarship, relied on Kapp for his account of the subsidy treaties in his introduction to the Baurmeister letters. The counterblast against Kapp, by Philip Losch, is unknown in America. For American historians, the time-worn books of Eelking (in Rosengarten's translation), Kapp and Lowell remain the only works on the German troops. Recently however a very good book has appeared on the Ansbach-Bayreuth troops, by Erhard Städtler, and two on the Hessians, one in English, by Ernst Kipping.

More important than the published material are the manuscript collections. First of these is that in Marburg, covering not only the Hessian military effort in all aspects, but also the organization of Hessen-Kassel as a state supporting an auxiliary corps. Journals in the *Murhardsche Bibliothek* in Kassel supplement the Marburg material.

Other German archives contain valuable material. Hannover has the reports of Electoral officers on the Hessian troop movements and also the important journal of Friedrich von Münchhausen, whose comments upon Sir William Howe's *Narrative* throw much light on the battles of Trenton and Redbank. Münchhausen's journal has been published in an English translation by Ernst Kipping with notes by Sam Smith, but they have omitted his commentary on Howe's *Narrative*, the most interesting part. Wolfenbüttel has the letters of Hessian officers to another auxiliary general, Riedesel, who with his wife is the subject of several biographies. Bamberg has letters of Ansbach-Bayreuth officers on the war.

Introduction

Journals of Hessian soldiers are relatively few (unlike those of their officers), and that of Grenadier Johannes Reuber, bits of which appear in translation in some books, is extremely valuable. A copy sold at Sotheby's for over £3,000 to a New York bookshop recently. With the help of Dr Joachim Fischer I was able to use a 'copy' in Frankfurt.[5]

With the exception of the von Jungkenn papers, Bardeleben's journal, and some letters of Captains Friedrich von Stamford and Johann Ewald to the Misses Van Horne of Boundbrook, New Jersey, the various German journals held in American archives are copies made by Bancroft and others, from originals in Germany.

The Colonial Office papers in the Public Record Office include reports of British officers who mustered the Hessian troops. The Hessian claim for 'extraordinaries' in the Audit Office and Treasury papers contains valuable information. Reports of British representatives in Germany, in the State Papers, throw light on negotiations, troop movements in Germany, and the soldier business in general.

In the British Museum, the letters of Frederick Haldimand, a Swiss in the British army in Canada, tell us about the Germans who served under him.

A reference in Ira. D. Gruber's book on the Howe brothers led me to two documents in the Bedford Record Office. The journal of Admiral Sir George Collier in the National Maritime Museum at Greenwich throws amusing light upon the character of General von Heister, the first Hessian commander.

Another reference, in Horst Dippel's excellent dissertation on German political opinion and the revolution, led me to obtain a photostat copy of Simon Louis du Ry's letter from the *Burgerbibliothek* in Bern, purportedly proving vast Hessian desertion (it doesn't).

So many British and American journals and collections of letters have been published describing the war and throwing credit or discredit onto the Hessians, that I can only mention the main ones here: on the American side, Washington's correspondence, Force's *American Archives*, Commager and Morris's *Spirit of 'Seventy-Six*,

---

[5] Reuber's original is in Kassel. To anyone unacquainted with Kasseler dialect it is almost impossible to read. Reuber, an intelligent but only partly educated private soldier, rendered phonetically into German any foreign words he heard: thus for the English 'man o' war' he wrote *Manuahr*. Reuber made two copies of the original himself for his sons. One of these is in Frankfurt, the other is presumably that sold at Sotheby's. There is also a copy by Bancroft in the New York Public Library.

The Hessians

Heath's *Memoirs*, and Frank Moore's collection of contemporary newspaper articles; on the British, the journals of Frederick Mackenzie, Archibald Robertson, and Ambrose Serle, and the letters of Sir Henry Clinton, Lord Rawdon, and Lieutenant Hale of the 45th have been especially valuable.[6]

I have attempted throughout to describe events as the Hessians saw and described them, without, I hope, being uncritical of their errors and misconceptions. I believe my study of the Hessians is the first to bring together the material in such a variety of sources, particularly British and German. A balanced view of the Hessians has too long been frustrated on the one hand by the emotional issues, first of German nationalism, and then of 'blood money' and 'trade in human beings', and on the other simply by ignorance of German conditions and source material. Even the British officer who mustered and inspected the Hessian auxiliaries in America thought, mistakenly, that Britain was to pay the Hessian Landgraf £5 for every dead man and a proportion for the wounded and disabled.[7] An American historian put this misconception into the language of the consumer public: 'every time an American bullet went home, the prince's cash register rang up a sale'.[8] The hiring of troops was simply a stage in the development of western armies originating at a time when the concept of the Rights of Man was unknown. It was in the American Revolution that the practice first came under attack, from partisans of American liberty.

[6] For these works and others, the reader is referred to the bibliography (for Hale's letters, see under W. H. Wilkin).

[7] HMC: *Report on American MSS. in the Royal Institution of Great Britain* (4 vols. London and Dublin, 1904–9), I, p. 100, Sir George Osborne to Capt. Mackenzie, 30 March 1777.

[8] John C. Miller, *Triumph of Freedom 1775–1783* (Boston, 1948), pp. 12–13.

1

The German soldier trade

By the late eighteenth century, German writers had long boasted of the warlike character of their people. A Hessian officer returned from America wrote:

Historians of all ages and peoples combine on this very point, that they portray the Germans as a very pugnacious and warloving people. Even envy of the meanest sort has never disputed their reputation for valour; it is woven into the spirit of the nation and stems from its very origin. . . . This warlike spirit still prevails amongst the people into our present age; it is the distinguishing feature of their character.[1]

Non-Germans were not quite so flattering of the role Teutonic arms played in the wars of the time. The French military writer Guibert was not alone when he spoke of the 'mania of all these little [German] sovereigns to have battlements and troops'. A contemporary English travel book described Germany as 'the *officina gentium*, the great nursery of the North, from which swarms of men have been drawn in all ages'.[2] This warlike character took the form, not of a German bid for European domination, for Germany itself was divided into a multiplicity of states; but of Germans providing trained contingents for the armies of the great powers, in return for pay.

This commerce in soldiers went back to the break up of the Mediaeval German Empire. The feudal levy had ceased to turn out, but there was no bureaucratic state apparatus for raising, equipping, paying, and maintaining men, nor for collecting taxes to support them. Kings and princes turned to 'military enterprisers' who, in return for cash per head, the right to keep booty and to

---

[1] Friedrich, Frieherr von der Lith, 'Feldzug der Hessen nach Amerika', *Ephemeriden über Aufklarung, Litteratur, und Kunst* (Marburg, 1785), II, p. 4. See also Samuel Pufendorf, *An Introduction to the History of the Principal Kingdoms and States of Europe* (London, 1697), pp. 301–2.

[2] G. A. H. Guibert, *Journal d'un Voyage en Allemagne fait en 1773* (2 vols. Paris, 1803), I, p. 121; Thomas Nugent, *Travels through Germany* (2 vols. London, 1768), I, p. 136; Robert Jackson, *A View of the Formation, Discipline and Economy of Armies* (3rd ed., London, 1845), p. 103.

traffic in arms and equipment as well as men, raised levies of troops. The soldiers were recruited from uprooted people who had mainly drifted into towns, who, in the old phrase 'took their skins into the market' and enlisted in return for bounty money (*Handgeld*). The heyday of the military enterpriser was the Thirty Years War, the arch-practitioner, of course, Wallenstein. He raised an army of 100,000 men, nominally under the emperor, but actually under the command of Wallenstein and his mercenary captains. With this horde he made war profitable, both by raising men and quartering them over areas from which he could exact *Kontribution*. For every Wallenstein, there were hundreds of small scale operators. Some were successful, received titles and became millionaires from their profits and booty; even more met with violent deaths.[3]

These independent military enterprisers were gradually driven from the market by the princes, who supplanted them. The princes, unlike private contractors, did not have to offer bounty money to attract recruits. They merely called up their farm boys to fill out the ranks at the exercise season and in time of war. Thus they could underbid their rivals. For the period roughly 1660–1760, there was almost constant war or threat of war amongst England, France, Austria, and the Netherlands. The demand for troops was frequent, but intermittent. Even the strongest states were financially unable to keep permanently under arms as many troops as were needed in war. It was easier to pay retainers to the German princes, who were willing to keep soldiers ready 'on call', as it were, for their paymaster. The German princes, by keeping outsized armies, helped to save themselves being swallowed up by the bigger powers, as the latter were interested in the princes' survival as a source of manpower.[4]

By the time of the American war, the private enterpriser was almost gone. Even the princes themselves were finding times difficult: two of the bidders for contracts to supply troops to the British, Bavaria and Württemberg, failed because state bankruptcy prevented them keeping regiments in a state of readiness.[5] Of those

[3] Fritz Redlich, *The German Military Enterpriser and his Work Force: a Study in European Economic and Social History* I and II (Vierteljahrschrift für Sozial- und Wirtschaftsgeschichte, nrs. 47 and 48, Wiesbaden, 1964–5). Redlich's little-known work discusses military entrepreneurship as a form of nascent capitalism.

[4] Ibid, II, p. 89.

[5] SP81/186, Sir William Faucitt to the Earl of Suffolk, 7 and 17 Feb. 1777 (both marked 'Private'); Friedrich Kapp, *Der Soldatenhandel deutscher Fürsten nach Amerika* (Berlin, 1864), pp. 105–6, 127–30.

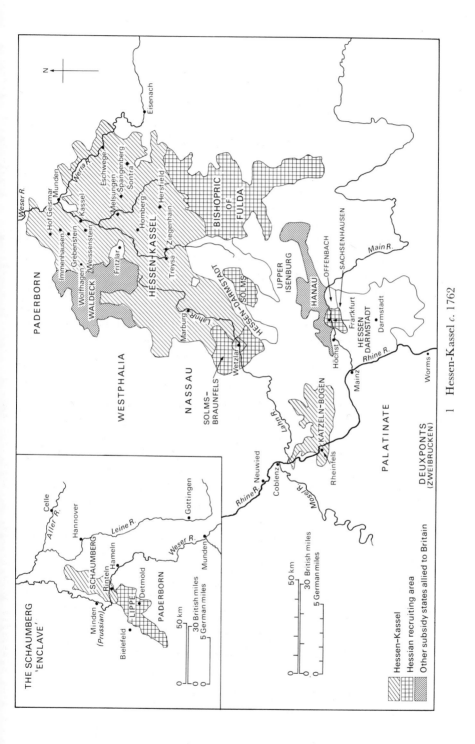

1 Hessen-Kassel c. 1762

Map labels:

THE SCHAUMBERG 'ENCLAVE'

Celle
Aller R.
Hannover
Leine R.
Göttingen
SCHAUMBERG
Minden (Prussian)
Rinteln
Hameln
LIPPE
Detmold
Bielefeld
PADERBORN
Weser R.
Munden
50 km
30 British miles
5 German miles

Eisenach
Weser R.
Hof Geismar
Munden
Immenhausen
Grebenstein
Wolfhagen
Weissenstein
WALDECK
Fritzlar
Werra R.
Eschwege
Spangenberg
Sontra
Kassel
Melsungen
Homberg
Treysa
Ziegenhain
Hersfeld
HESSEN-KASSEL
BISHOPRIC OF FULDA
PADERBORN
WESTPHALIA
Marburg
Lahn R.
HESSEN-DARMSTADT
HESSEN-SOLMS
UPPER ISENBURG
NASSAU
SOLMS-BRAUNFELS
Wetzlar
OFFENBACH
SACHSENHAUSEN
HANAU
Frankfurt
Höchst
Main R.
HESSEN DARMSTADT
Darmstadt
Mainz
Rhine R.
Worms
KATZELN-BOGEN
Rheinfels
Lahn R.
Neuwied
Coblenz
Rhine R.
Mosel R.
PALATINATE
DEUXPONTS (ZWEIBRUCKEN)

50 km
30 British miles
5 German miles

Hessen-Kassel
Hessian recruiting area
Other subsidy states allied to Britain

9

who actually did send contingents to America, the Duke of Braunschweig-Wolfenbüttel in particular only just saved himself from the abyss of financial ruin.[6]

The fate of the Hannoverian Colonel Albrecht von Scheither is illustrative of the fate of the individual military enterpriser. Scheither, who had served with distinction as a leader of light troops in the Seven Years War, contracted in the summer of 1775 to provide some 2,000 recruits from Germany for British regiments in America. If he collected these successfully, he was to provide another 2,000. He was to be paid £10 a head, from which to cover the costs of subordinate recruiters, travel and subsistence expenses and bounty, and to draw his profit. A British colonel, Faucitt, was to inspect the recruits and reject those unfit for service.[7]

Scheither was unable to make a worthwhile profit. He had increasing competition, first from Prussian, Austrian, and Dutch East India Company recruiters, then from the other princes with whom Britain concluded troop contracts early in 1776, and even from the 60th Regiment (the 'Royal Americans'), whose recruiters were active throughout Hannover and along the Rhine.[8] From November 1775 to the end of September 1776, Scheither managed to gather 1,738 men acceptable to Faucitt, while another 113 deserted and 161 were rejected.[9] Some of those rejected were of very dubious quality: one, for example, had an epileptic fit en route to the embarkation point. Scheither, despite his expertise in recruiting, declined to attempt to gather the second 2,000. He would be left with no profit if he had to offer bounties to compete with recruiters of other German states.[10] As a comment on the recruiting practices of the time, when a batch of fifty of the rejected were brought back from Portsmouth and disembarked near Hamburg, other recruiting officers descended like vultures to pick

---

[6] Karl Ehlers, 'Der Soldatenverkauf Karl Wilhelm Ferdinands von Braunschweig', *Niedersachsen*, XXXI (July–Dec., 1926), pp. 603–4.

[7] StaHannover 47 II Nr. 114, fols. 7–21 and 48; Sir John Fortescue, ed., *The Correspondence of George III from 1760 to December 1783* (6 vols. London, 1928), III, nrs. 1716, 1759, 1762–3. Scheither, in the old tradition of military enterprisers, hoped at first to raise a corps which he would command.

[8] StaHannover 47 II Nr. 114, fol. 106, Scheither to Faucitt, 19 Feb. 1776; 41 v Nr. 3, Major John Savage to Field Marshall Sporken, 20 Jan. 1776; *Politische Correspondenz Friedrich's des Grossen* (46 vols. Berlin, 1879–1939), XXXVII, p. 346.

[9] StaHannover 47 II Nr. 114, fol. 111. The final total supplied was 1867. WO4/99, fol. 198, Barrington to John Robinson, 3 Mar., 1777.

[10] StaHannover 47 II Nr. 114, fols. 104 and 106, Scheither to Faucitt, 28, Jan. and 19 Feb., 1776.

them up. Emanuel Mathias, British representative in the Hanse ports, happily informed Lord Suffolk, 'Some of them, I hear, have since fallen into the Hands of the Brunswick Officers, who are here on the Recruiting Service, and the others into those of the Kidnappers employed by the Dutch East India Company, so that We have luckily got rid of them all.'[11]

In 1781 the British East India Company sought to raise two regiments in Germany, each of 1,000 men, for its own service. Faucitt was ordered to consider the problem and went straight to Scheither as the great expert in the field. Scheither busied himself with the new plan, but within a month the British government decided to shelve his scheme as too expensive and disreputable, George III raising the men as two Hannoverian regiments in his capacity as Elector. This marked the end of the private military enterpriser in Germany. As Faucitt wrote to Lord Stormont, no one could raise troops in Germany except under the protection and auspices of some German prince who would permit depots to be formed within his dominions to hold and train recruits.[12]

Even under the auspices of a prince, a military dealer could find the commerce in soldiers a risky business. At the end of 1770 Colonel Felix Frederick, acting on behalf of the Duke of Württemberg who, finding the expense of a standing army too great for his finances, wished to dispose of his soldiers profitably, contracted with the British East India Company to supply 1,000 recruits. To show the quality of his wares, Frederick agreed to bring over a sample of 100 by March 1771, at the price of £7 each to cover costs. After severe difficulty, losing several to the 'crimps' of the Dutch East India Company, he landed his men at Gravesend on 14 April 1771, but company officials reneged on the agreement, having failed to get a bill for a new regiment through Parliament. They refused to reimburse Frederick his expenses.[13]

More certain of a return were the mainly Catholic princes of southern Germany. The Regiments of Royal Allemand, Royal Nassau, Royal Bavière, Royal Anhalt, Royal Alsace and Royal Deuxponts in the army of His Majesty the King of France, composed of Germans mainly from Bavaria and the Palatinate,

---

[11] SP82/95, fol. 52, 5 March, 1776.
[12] SP81/194, Stormont to Faucitt, 6 and 27 April, 25 May, 1781; Faucitt to Stormont, 17 April and 11 May, 1781.
[13] Add. MS. 23680 Nr. 1. The Case of Colonel Felix Frederick with the East India Company; *Journals of the House of Commons*, XXXII, p. 349 (23 April, 1771).

brought a steady income to these princes.[14] The variety of small states promoted competition among them to produce the best troops for foreign service, and indeed it may be true, as one Hessian officer wrote, that if Germany had been united, there would not have been such a common interest and pride in the army; for Germans would soon have thought of overseas conquests, and time devoted to the study of shipping, the compass and navigation would have meant less attention to the military manual and troop evolutions.[15]

Among the little principalities, one in particular gained a special reputation for its warlike character: Hessen-Kassel, whose people were descended from the ancient warrior Catti. Of all the princes who let out troops for hire, those of Hessen-Kassel were the most successful, and eventually incurred the greatest odium. Hessen had become Calvinist in 1605, and fought consistently on the Protestant side in the Thirty Years War.[16] Armies were ceaselessly marching across the land or quartered in its town. The longer the struggle lasted, the more of the people were under arms. And when the Hessian troops were finally disbanded at the war's end, the White Regiment[17] of General Geyso and some other bodies of men were kept on as three *Schlosscompagnies* to guard the Landgraf's palace. These units were to form the nucleus of the Hessian Guards, the core of the Hessian army.[18] Hessen had received subsidies for fighting in the war, and the countryside, which was generally poor, had been wasted. Thus it was not illogical to look on the army as a source of income. In Germany there was a centuries old tradition that troops had to pay for their own upkeep.[19]

To take this course was the decision of the Landgraf Karl (1670–1730). The European power struggle in the century following 1660 facilitated the soldier business, for the great powers, without modern resources to conscript and maintain armies, turned to princes like Karl, who had a steadily growing force. By 1676 the original three companies had grown to eighteen of foot and five of

[14] Redlich, *The German Military Enterpriser*, II, p. 98.

[15] Bernhard Wilhelm Wiederholdt, 'Über den kriegerischen Charakter der Deutschen und die Vorzüge des deutschen Militärs', *Neue Bellona*, III (1802), part ii, pp. 67–8.

[16] The lands of Luther's protector Philip the Magnanimous were divided amongst his four sons: the larger slices were Hessen-Kassel and Hessen-Darmstadt, the latter remaining Lutheran but generally siding with the emperor on political issues.

[17] Hessian regiments were then named for the colour of their banners. Later they adopted the more common practice of being named for their colonels or chiefs.

[18] Maximilian, Freiherr von Ditfurth, *Das Kurhessische Leibgarde-Regiment* (Kassel, 1882), p. 1.

[19] Redlich, *The German Military Enterpriser*, II, pp. 89–90.

horse. Karl, however, did not initiate the new phase in the soldier business; namely, the leasing of standing troops by a prince himself at peace to another state at war. This was done by Duke Johann Friedrich of Braunschweig, hiring three regiments to the Republic of Venice in the 1660s.[20] Karl of Hessen concluded the first agreement of the Hessian soldier trade with Christian V of Denmark in 1677. Hessen sent ten 'compagnies' of sixteen men each at twenty talers a man. The 3,200 talers thus paid were used by Karl to equip his troops, for from the very beginning the country's revenues were insufficient to support the army alone.[21]

Nearly half of those Hessians who went failed to return with their regiments in 1679, and the flags of the Regiments von Hornumb and Ufm Keller still adorn the Ridderholms Church in Stockholm. Well might von Stamford, historian of the Hessian army, write, 'This first expedition of the fighting men of the Hessian standing army was a forbidding prelude to the sacrifice of valiant men, which was to happen so often in subsequent times.'[22]

In that same year Hessen profited from the war in another way: Brandenburgers and Danes paid to be quartered there during the winter.

In 1687 Hessen-Kassel and Hessen-Darmstadt sent troops in the service of Venice to seize Morea from the Turks. The Regiment Prinz Karl was specially formed in Hersfeld in April 1687 of 1,000 men drawn from recruits and from other units, for each of whom Venice paid fifty talers. This expedition was even more costly than the Danish one. Of the 1,000 only 191 returned; of 1,000 Darmstadters only 184. Yet Negroponte was taken and the terrible Turk thrown back.[23]

Under the military arrangements of the German Empire, Hessen was to contribute troops to the Upper Rhine Circle. Karl, however, began to develop his army as that of a self-contained state.[24] To increase this army he continued to obtain revenues from

---

[20] Ibid, p. 95.
[21] Karl Demandt, *Geschichte des Landes Hessen* (2nd edn., Kassel, 1972), p. 268. Karl's precise motives may be described in the first biography of him to appear, by Dr Philippi of StaMarburg, just published. I have as yet been unable to consult it.
[22] Quoted in ibid.
[23] W. Sunkel, *Geschichte des 2. hessischen Infanterie-Regiments Nr. 88* (Berlin, 1876), p. 7; August Roeschen, 'Hessische Offiziere', *Hessenland*, III (1889), p. 151. It is notable that the price increased with the distance.
[24] Hans-Georg Boehme, 'Zur Wehrverfassung in Hessen-Kassel im 18. Jahrhundert', *Hessisches Jahrbuch für Landesgeschichte*, I (1951), p. 206.

subsidies, and although Hessen was landlocked her best customers were maritime powers, the Venetians, Holland and England. In 1688 by the Concert of Magdeburg some 3,400 Hessians took service under William of Orange, freeing Dutch troops for the expedition to England.[25] Karl's troops distinguished themselves in the Wars of the Grand Alliance (1688–97) and Spanish Succession (1701–14) against Louis XIV. Although hiring soldiers was profitable to the Hessian ruling house, the princes shared the perils of war with their subjects. Five of Karl's sons were in the field, and two of them fell in battle: Karl at Liège in 1702 and Ludwig at Ramillies in 1706.[26] A corps of 10,000 Hessians crossed the Alps and served with Prince Eugene in 1706–7 and thereafter in the Netherlands.[27] Despite various bribes offered by the French, Karl remained loyal to the allied powers. This was not solely for financial reasons. One notable consistency of the Landgrafs' policy was to hire their troops exclusively to Protestant powers, for the Hessians remained stern Calvinists.

After the treaty of Utrecht ended the wars of Louis XIV, Karl's son Friedrich, married to the sister of Charles XII of Sweden, led an auxiliary corps of 6,000 Hessians into Swedish service, but the intercession of Prussia and Britain prevented them reaching the battlefields of Pomerania.[28] George I of England made a new agreement to secure the services of 12,000 Hessians to protect his throne against the Pretender.[29] When Britain joined the Quadruple Alliance in 1726, she once again hired the soldiers of Hessen to fulfil her continental obligations. By a treaty of 1727 she paid an annual retainer of £125,000 to have first call on the Hessians' services.[30] Britain was rapidly becoming the Landgrafs' best customer. For the first time the term *Soldatenhandel* was applied to the Hessian princes' dealings.[31] By 1731 the Hessians had become such an established part of British foreign policy that Horatio, first Baron Walpole, dubbed them 'the Triarii of Great Britain, her last Resort in all Cases, both in Peace and War; both at Home and

[25] *Memoirs of the House and Dominions of Hesse Cassel* (London, 1740), p. 24.
[26] Ibid, p. 25.
[27] Max Braubach, *Die Bedeutung der Subsidien für die Politik im spanischen Erbfolgekrieg* (Bonn, 1923), pp. 155–8.
[28] Friedrich Wilhelm Strieder, *Grundlage zur Militär-Geschichte des Landgräflich Hessischen Corps* (Kassel, 1798), pp. 20–1.
[29] W. C. Perry, 'On the Employment of Mercenaries in Ancient and Modern Times', *The Nineteenth Century*, LXI (1907), p. 328.
[30] Strieder, *Grundlage zur Militär-Geschichte*, p. 21.
[31] Demandt, *Geschichte des Landes Hessen*, p. 271.

Abroad; howsoever ally'd, or wheresoever distress'd!'[32] Objections to hiring the Hessians were not made against subsidy treaties in themselves; they were grounded on expediency: against the cost, against introducing foreigners into the kingdom, against sacrificing Britain's interests for those of the Despicable Electorate.[33] Lord Strange was one amongst many who said it was contrary to the law of the Empire, for the Hessians might find themselves at war with their sovereign, the Emperor.[34] He might as well have saved his breath. In 1731, a time when Britain was at peace, Sir Robert Walpole obtained a vote of £241,259 1s 3d for keeping 12,094 Hessians in readiness for British service.[35] Nor was the Emperor likely to condemn the commerce in soldiers. He was a customer, and most of his theoretical subjects were in the market like Hessen. It was scarcely surprising that the learned professors of Württemberg, Rostock, and Helmstedt all proved conclusively in their theses that the princes had the legal right to aid foreign powers and that German fighting men were permitted by the law of the Empire to go into their service.[36]

In actual practice all British ministries resorted in wartime to employing mercenaries. The arguments in favour of hiring the Hessians were that as trained troops they could be ready much more quickly than Britain could recruit and train men; that Hessen's geographic location put her close to any probable seat of war; and most compelling of all, but one never admitted, that Britain's own military establishment at the beginning of any war did not inspire confidence.[37] The most eloquent example of Britain's eighteenth-century dependence upon continental mercenaries is Pitt, who condemned paying subsidies in violent speeches for years and voted against the treaties of 1755 with Russia and Hessen-Kassel. Yet during the Seven Years War he paid out subsidies not only to Frederick of Prussia, but also to maintain 'His

---

[32] Horatio, first Baron Walpole, *The Case of the Hessian Forces in the Pay of Great Britain* (London, 1731), p. 39. *Triarii*, Roman soldiers in the third and last rank of a legion, were also called *Subsidia* as they were usually drawn from Rome's allies.

[33] HMC: *The Manuscripts of the Earl of Carlisle preserved at Castle Howard* (London, 1897), p. 81.

[34] William Cobbett, *The Parliamentary History of England from the Earliest Period to the Year 1803.* (36 vols. London, 1806–20), XI, p. 1013 (debate in December 1742).

[35] *Journals of the House of Commons*, XXI, p. 769.

[36] Philipp Losch, *Soldatenhandel: Mit einem Verzeichnis der Hessen-Kasselischen Subsidienverträge und einer Bibliographie* (Kassel, 1933), pp. 15–20 and p. 24. See below, pp. 22–3.

[37] HMC: *Carlisle MSS.*, p. 81; Samuel Martin, *Deliberate Thoughts on the System of our late Treaties with Hesse-Cassel and Russia in regard to Hanover* (London, 1756), p. 23; *House and Dominions of Hesse Cassel*, p. 55; Corelli Barnett, *Britain and Her Army: a Military, Political and Social Survey* (Penguin Books, 1974), p. 236.

The Hessians

Brittanic Majesty's Army in Germany', an army composed mainly of Hessians, Hannoverians, and Brunswickers; and at the end of the war he boasted that he had conquered America in Germany.[38] The Landgraf Karl died in 1730. His eldest son Friedrich, then King of Sweden, and nominally Landgraf, was a gallant warrior and lover, but politically insignificant.[39] His brother Wilhelm, Statthalter of Hessen and de facto ruler, continued his father's policy. His aims were to enrich Hessen's military chest with British subsidies, maintain the traditional alliance with Protestant Prussia, already re-affirmed once in a treaty of 1714, and obtain possession of the County of Hanau, promised to Hessen by a treaty of 1648, whenever the existing ruling house should expire. In the War of the Austrian Succession Wilhelm was thrown into a dilemma, for his paymaster Britain was opposed to Prussia and allied with the Catholic Habsburgs, who had not recognized Kassel's right to Hanau and supported a Darmstadt claim instead. A corps of 6,000 Hessians was already serving in British pay when in 1744 Wilhelm supported Karl VII, Bavarian candidate for the Imperial crown, in return for the promise of an Electorship and territorial gains.[40] His support included 6,000 men for Karl's army. Similarly Wilhelm reaffirmed the treaty of alliance with Prussia in 1744.

Thus there occurred the extraordinary spectacle of Hessian troops at war simultaneously on both sides: in British pay garrisoning fortresses in the Low Countries and in the Bavarian army in southern Germany. A secret clause in theory prevented the two contingents facing each other on the battlefield.[41] Nevertheless, the double agreement caused bad feeling later, not least because the treaty with Bavaria included a 'blood money' clause: for every dead man Wilhelm was to receive 36 florins, for a dead horse 112 florins and 30 krone, and for a dead horse and rider together 150 florins. Three wounded were to count as one dead.[42] It was just as well that the Bavarians were defeated, Karl VII died, and the Hessian corps in Bavaria was saved from captivity by a speedy declaration of neutrality. They were still interned in Ingolstadt for

---

[38] Sir Reginald Savory, *His Britannic Majesty's Army in Germany during the Seven Years War* (Oxford, 1966), preface, p. viii.

[39] Wolf von Both and Hans Vogel, *Landgraf Wilhelm VIII von Hessen-Kassel* (Munich, 1964), pp. 14–20. Wilhelm succeeded to the Landgraviate in 1751.

[40] Either secularized church lands and the territory of the Bishop of Mainz lying within Hessen, or four imperial cities including Frankfurt-am-Main. Demandt, *Geschichte des Landes Hessen*, p. 275.

[41] Josef Sauer, *Finanzgeschäfte der Landgrafen von Hessen-Kassel* (Fulda, 1930), p. 7.

[42] Demandt, *Geschichte des Landes Hessen*, pp. 274–5.

The German soldier trade

six weeks before being allowed to return to Hessen. In 1745 Wilhelm renewed the British subsidy treaty, so that henceforth Hessians were available only to England.[43] This apparent double-dealing shocked later historians, but it was nothing extraordinary in the age of cabinet diplomacy, and when Wilhelm died in 1760 Frederick of Prussia wrote to his successor, 'Germany has lost its most valuable prince, his land a father, and I my truest friend.'[44]

The Hessian soldiers, composed of a larger proportion of natives than the armies of most German princes, was as good as any other of its time. Karl VII of Bavaria, visiting Hessians in his service in October, 1744, noted in his diary, 'The fine appearance and smartness of these troops cannot be surpassed . . . one could not see better.'[45] On many battlefields the Hessians 'held the sum of things for pay': at Rocoux (11 October 1746) against the French 'the Hessian Regiment of Mansbach, having stood their ground to the last . . refused quarter, so that few of them escaped'.[46] In both 1745 and 1756 Hessian troops were brought to Britain to repel threatened French and Scottish invasions. Guibert, seeing Hessians and Hannoverians garrisoned at Hanau in 1773 wrote, 'Le bataillon Hessois, surtout, m'a paru beau et bien tenu.'[47]

In the Seven Years War the British alliance cost Hessen dearly. In 1756 the French army under Richelieu broke into Germany, and, defeating the Duke of Cumberland at Hastenbeck, occupied Hessen, making it a theatre of war for the succeeding five campaigns. The French imposed heavy contributions. A tribute of 850,000 talers was demanded in 1757 in an attempt to break the alliance with Britain. Since this failed of its purpose, 500,000 more were demanded each year from 1759 to 1761. A smaller sum was levied in 1762.[48] In addition the French requisitioned grain for their soldiers and hay for their animals.[49] Both the main towns, Kassel and Marburg, were besieged, taken, and retaken many times. Marburg's famous *Elisabethkirche*, a centre of pilgrimage before the Reformation, was used as a granary by the occupying

---

[43] Ibid, p. 274. Wilhelm actually obtained possession of Hanau in 1736 when the ruling line died out, but not Imperial recognition.
[44] Quoted in Losch, *Soldatenhandel*, p. 21. Frederick's letters to his ministers demonstrate his esteem for Wilhelm as a statesman. *Politische Correspondenz*, XV, pp. 47, 54–5, 69–70; XIX, p. 62.
[45] Quoted in Both and Vogel, *Landgraf Wilhelm VIII*, p. 77.
[46] *The Gentleman's Magazine*, XVI (1746), pp. 540–1.
[47] Guibert, *Journal d'un Voyage en Allemagne*, I, p. 116.
[48] Sauer, *Finanzgeschäfte der Landgrafen*, p. 17.
[49] Both and Vogel, *Landgraf Wilhelm VIII*, p. 123.

17

The Hessians

French army. The ancient town changed hands fifteen times, the castle on the heights above, seven times.[50]

The effect of a prolonged war in Hessen, with French levies and British subsidies, was to make the Landgraf more independent of the Hessian Parliament (or, more accurately, Estates), the *Landstände*, which was burdened with making good the losses to the country out of its own sources of revenue. The subsidies, however, flowed into the war treasury (*Kriegskasse*), which the Landgraf's officials controlled and administered. Thus the Landgraf became rich while the *Landstände* lost the traditional power of the purse over their sovereign.[51] A British military historian notes, 'It was a curious fact that the British Parliament in its reluctance to create a large British army, for fear of military power in the hands of the monarch, helped German princes in their struggle against their own Parliaments by making it possible and profitable for the princes to maintain large forces on hire to the British.'[52]

The Hessian corps fought throughout the campaigns of the Seven Years War. Ferdinand of Brunswick, commander of 'His Britannic Majesty's Army in Germany', regarded them as more able to withstand the hardships of war than any other contingent.[53] Despite its name this army contained more Hannoverians and Hessians than British troops, who only appeared in September, 1758. Of total strength in 1760 of 90,000, some 37,800 were Hannoverians, 24,400 Hessians, 22,000 British, 9,500 Brunswickers, and there were some lesser contingents.[54] Yet it succeeded in tying down double its number of French troops, a service of inestimable value both to British conquests overseas and to Frederick of Prussia in his struggle against a European coalition. When Frederick heard of the conclusion of an Anglo-Hessian subsidy treaty for additional men in early 1759 he wrote to his minister in London, 'C'est avec bien de la satisfaction que j'ai appris par votre rapport ordinaire du 16 de ce mois la conclusion du nouveau traité de subside avec le cour de Hesse.' In both 1759 and 1778 Frederick regarded Hessen-Kassel as having an essential role in the defence of his western flank.[55]

---

[50] Ingeborg Schnack, *Marburg: Bilder einen alten Stadt* (Darmstadt, 1961), pp. 381 and 388.
[51] Sauer, *Finanzgeschäfte der Landgräfen*, pp. 17–19; F. L. Carsten, *Princes and Parliaments in Germany* (Oxford, 1959), p. 183.
[52] Barnett, *Britain and her Army*, p. 142.
[53] Savory, *His Britannic Majesty's Army*, p. 454.
[54] Ibid., pp. 202–3.
[55] *Politische Correspondenz Friedrich's*, XVIII, p. 51 (30 Jan., 1759); *Politische Testamente Friedrichs des Grossen* (Berlin, 1920), pp. 248–9.

The German soldier trade

With the fighting going on in Hessan, Hessian soldiers were sorely tempted to make off home to see how wives and sweethearts, or livestock and crops, were faring. In 1762 some 111 cavalry and 2,196 infantrymen deserted out of a contingent of 24,000.[56] The strain of maintaining this large corps fell heavily on the small state. By August 1761 the Landgraf informed Colonel Clavering, British representative at his court, that it would be impracticable to get more recruits if the war continued for another year. Recruiting officers sent to Hamburg, Lübeck and Bremen picked up only deserters and vagabonds, who were no sooner enlisted than they deserted again. The corps could hardly be kept up to strength until the Landgraf was once again master of his own country.[57] Hessian subalterns and rank and file for the last campaign were sixteen- and seventeen-year-olds.[58]

This mainly German army, by tying down French strength, enabled Britain to conquer her first empire overseas. British subsidies were well spent. By contrast the French who paid for the Duke of Württemberg's corps to serve with the Imperial Army against Prussia got a rabble. Duke Karl Eugen had introduced Prussian recruiting methods to enlist his troops, and in spring and summer of 1757 thousands of young men were forcibly pressed into service. Badly trained and brutally treated, they deserted in droves and were routed by Frederick of Prussia at Leuthen. Only about 1,900 of some 6,000 returned to Württemberg months later.[59]

The hardiness of the Hessian folk fitted them to endure the rigours of military service. A young German traveller noted in the 1780s that the men were stout and strongly built, and matched the country, which was rough and wild, abounding in woods and hills.[60] The air was cold but wholesome, the food not luxurious but nourishing.[61] Not only were the young Hessians of sturdy limb, but from early years they were mentally prepared for the soldier's life:

For many years the Hessian knows that he is born to be a soldier; from his youth he hears of nothing else. The farmer who bears arms tells the son his adventures, and the lad, eager to tread in the footsteps of the elder, trains his feeble arms early

[56] Savory, *His Britannic Majesty's Army*, p. 455.
[57] SP81/165, Clavering to Bute, 4 August and 13 October, 1761.
[58] J. Ewald, *Belehrungen über den Krieg, besonders den kleinen Krieg* (Schleswig, 1800–3), III, p. 266.
[59] Carsten, *Princes and Parliaments*, p. 137.
[60] Johann Caspar Riesbeck, *Travels through Germany in a Series of Letters written in German by the Baron Riesbeck* (3 vols. London, 1787), III, p. 149.
[61] *Encyclopaedia Britannica* (2nd edn. Edinburgh, 1780), V, p. 3628; *House and Dominions of Hesse Cassel*, p. 55. The most complete description of contemporary Hessen is in Anton Friedrich Büsching, *Erdbeschreibung*, VII (Hamburg, 1790), pp. 78–149 and 250–2.

to the use of formidable weapons; so when he has reached the size necessary to take a place in the valiant ranks, he is quickly formed into a soldier.[62]

Proportionately the Hessian army was the largest in Germany. In 1730, in peacetime, some 14,000 men were under arms, roughly one in every nineteen of the population of a quarter million. Prussia had only one of every twenty-three of her people under arms.[63] One commentator felt this was too many:

The people of this country are numerous and warlike, being disciplin'd and train'd, perhaps more than what is for the good of the Country. The Prince might employ them a great deal better in making them labour the ground, and take to useful trades.[64]

The Landgrafs would have denied this. The army was the country's greatest source of revenue, its 'Peru' as Wilhelm VIII called it.[65] Although the chief tax in Hessen was the military *Kontribution*, internal revenues alone could not pay for such forces. *Kriegskasse* accounts for 1742, a good year for subsidies but one in which a corps had to be maintained in the field, show that without subsidies from Britain of 933,000 talers, the state would have had a deficit of 445,000. With those subsidies it had a surplus even greater, 488,000 talers.[66] In the years from 1730 to .1750 the subsidy payments totalled some 8.3 million talers (£1.25 millions). The total revenue in taxes in that period was not much over 20 million talers.[67]

Despite the country's warlike constitution, the transition from the old-fashioned levy of armed men to a modern state army, financed by taxes collected by bureaucrats and recruited systematically, was only gradual. Throughout the first half of the eighteenth century, the old duties of the Hessian farmer to quarter both horse and man and to provide them with sustenance were commuted into cash payments which were used to build barracks. The requirement to provide horses and wagons for the army's train also became a cash duty called *Heerwagengelder*. The obligation to provide haulage for the transport, *Vorspanndienst*, was only reckoned as a set payment after it proved too much of a burden in the Seven

---

[62] Friedrich Justinian, Freiherr von Günderode, *Briefe eines Reisenden über den gegenwärtigen Zustand von Cassel* (Frankfurt and Leipzig, 1781), p. 151.
[63] Both and Vogel, *Landgraf Wilhelm VIII*, p. 63.
[64] *House and Dominions of Hesse Cassel*, p. 55.
[65] '*Ce Corps de troupes fait notre Perou, en le perdant nous perdrons tous nos resources.*' Wilhelm to August Moritz von Donop, his minister in Munich, 7 April, 1745, quoted in Both and Vogel, p. 215 n. 188.
[66] Ibid., p. 42.
[67] Ibid.

Years War. After this war Hessian troops were supplied for the first time, not directly by farmers in kind, but by magazines erected on the model of the French ones seen in Hessen.

The feudal obligation of certain parties to provide horse and weapons became submerged in the more universal requirement of military service. In 1762 the new Landgraf Friedrich II divided Hessen on the Prussian model into recruiting cantons, one for each regiment. Recruiting by violence was forbidden and large elements of the population were exempted, either by paying taxes or by profession, from being called up. Certain towns like Kassel, Marburg, and Ziegenhain were exempt from the cantons, although the artillery and the Guards regiments could draw volunteers from them. Propertied farmers, apprentices, salt workers, miners, domestic servants, students, and other important workers and taxpayers were also exempt, very much in accord with mercantilist principles of preserving vital elements of the population. Otherwise the names of all 'strong and straight-limbed' young men aged sixteen to thirty, not under 5 feet 6 inches, or 5 feet 4 inches if still growing, were enrolled on lists, kept by the local bailiffs, as available recruits for military service. The young men were to present themselves yearly at Easter and the lists kept up to date. Thus by the end of the Seven Years War the Landgraf, by converting the traditional duties of his subjects, had obliged everyone to support the army, either by actual service or by paying taxes.[68] When the Swiss historian Müller visited Kassel, he wrote, 'Before I came to Hessen, I scarce knew what a military people were. Nearly all peasants have served: thus in every village there are men of fine stature, manly form and bearing, and everywhere they talk of war: for in this century the Hessians have not only fought against the French in Germany, but even in Sicily and the Peloponnesus, and in Hungary under the great Eugene, and now in the New World.'[69]

---

[68] Boehme, 'Zur Wehrverfassung in Hessen-Kassel', pp. 207–9; Sta-Marburg 12. nr. 8539, Die Einrichtung der Werbe-Cantons. Boehme writes that the only step remaining to complete the transition from feudal host to conscript army was acceptance of the universal obligation of citizens to bear arms. In 1802 a Hessian officer wrote, 'All subjects of a country enjoy its protection, and are thereby without exception under an obligation to defend it. This is the universal maxim for every state.' Adam Ludwig Ochs, 'Das hessische Militär. Eine Skizze', *Neue Bellona*, II (1802), part iii, p. 203.

[69] Johannes von Müller, *Sämmtliche Werke* (27 vols. in 15. Tübingen, 1810–19), XIV p. 232 (letter dated September 1781).

2

The Hessians go to America

THE TREATY OF 1776

By 1776 the hiring of military corps in return for subsidies, by one state from another, was accepted in international law as well as practice. In 1758 the jurist Emer de Vattel defined auxiliaries thus:

> When a sovereign, without taking a direct part in a war carried on by another sovereign, merely sends him help in the form of troops or vessels of war, these troops or vessels are called auxiliaries.
>
> Auxiliary troops serve the prince to whom they are sent, in accordance with the orders of their sovereign. If they are sent to him without any conditions or restrictions they will be at his service equally for offensive or defensive war, and will be under obedience to him with respect to the duties they are to perform.

A subsidy was either money paid by one sovereign to another to aid the latter in war or 'a sum of money which one sovereign annually pays to another in recompense for a body of troops which the latter furnishes him in his wars, or holds ready at his service'. Agreements for such troops were 'treaties of subsidy'. To establish the morality and legality of such treaties, Vattel laid down the principle that aid could be given to a nation waging a just war, but not to one in an unjust war.[1]

Johann Friedrich Eisenhard, teacher of constitutional law at Helmstedt University, stated in a treatise of 1760 that the right of princes to make such treaties was found in the Treaty of Westphalia and that a prince could do so without the concurrence of his parliament (*Stände*). The only proviso was that such troops must not be engaged by the emperor's enemies.[2]

---

[1] Emer de Vattel, *The Law of Nations or the Principles of Natural Law applied to the Conduct and to the Affairs of Nations and of Sovereigns* (The Classics of International Law. Washington, DC, 1916. Translation of the 1758 edn), pp. 261–2.

[2] Gert Brauer, *Die hannoversch-englischen Subsidienverträge 1702–1748* (Untersuchungen zur deutschen Staats- und Rechtsgeschichte, new series, vol. I. Aalen, 1962), pp. 91–2. Eisenhard's work, published at Frankfurt and Leipzig in 1760, was entitled *Abhandlung von dem Rechte der Stände des Heiliges Römisches Reichs auswärtigen Mächten Kriegs-Völcker zu überlassen, wie auch von der Ausübung dieses Rechts nach den Reichsgesetzen und demjenigen was solchen ueberlassenen Kriegsvölckern gebühret.*

The Hessians go to America

Johann Jacob Moser writing in 1752 on the rights of peoples in wartime accepted the practice of hiring auxiliaries.[3] Christian Wolff, a great spokesman for Natural Law, included a section on subsidy treaties in his major work *Jus Gentium*:

Aids, or also auxiliary troops, or simply auxiliaries are defined as troops, both foot and horse, which one nation, not engaged in the war, sends to another nation carrying on war. In our native vernacular they are called Hülfs-Völcker [helpers].

Subsidies to-day are defined as moneys, which are paid to a nation carrying on war by another nation, not engaged in the war, so that the nation can pay the expense of military service ... also we have among us moneys with this name which are paid by a nation waging war to another for auxiliaries. You might also call these subsidy moneys.

Those are called treaties of war which are entered into for the purpose of war, as for auxiliaries, subsidies, and anything else which has to do with war.[4]

Stated here in theory is what Britain did in the Seven Years War; namely, paid subsidies to Frederick of Prussia to enable him to sustain his war effort against Austria and Russia, and paid subsidies to Hessen-Kassel, Braunschweig and the rest for auxiliaries to fight against the French.

Both Vattel and Wolff defined mercenaries, as distinct from auxiliaries, as foreigners who voluntarily enrolled themselves as soldiers for a certain time, certain provisions, and a certain sum of money. Thus the Hessians of whom we are dealing were, strictly speaking, auxiliaries and not mercenaries. According to Wolff, it was allowed, and indeed proper by Natural Law, to send auxiliaries and subsidies to a nation carrying on a just war.[5]

When the British government resolved to use force against the American colonists, it was almost inevitable that they should turn to foreign troops. The British army was too small to subdue the colonies. Existing regiments were under strength, and recruits could not be found in time.[6] Scheither's scheme to raise men in Germany met with limited success. Nor would the King allow noblemen to raise new regiments or permit any corps of foreigners to be incorporated within the British establishment.[7]

All British wars in that century had been fought by contracting with continental princes. The officers in America expected this to

---

[3] Johann Jacob Moser, *Grundsätze des europäischen Völckerrechts in Kriegszeiten* (Tubingen, 1752), pp. 206 and 210.

[4] Christian Wolff, *Jus Gentium Methodo Scientifica Pertractatum* (The Classics of International Law. Oxford, 1934. Translation of the 1764 edn), pp. 336–7.

[5] Ibid., pp. 337–8.

[6] Fortescue, *Correspondence of George III*, III, nr. 1699.

[7] Ibid., nrs. 1702 and 1773.

happen. Gage recommended hiring foreigners.[8] Captain William Glanville Evelyn of the 4th (King's Own) wrote to his cousin that the assistance of foreign troops would be highly politic and of these Russians were 'the most eligible, not only as being good soldiers, but by their not having any connections in this country, and from not understanding the language, they are less likely to be seduced by the artifice and intrigue of these holy hypocrits'.[9] Major General Henry Clinton also placed his bet on the Russians: 'We must be reinforced, not with Germans (I fear they will desert), [but with] . . . my friends the Russians. They have no language but their own; they cannot desert.'[10] But attempts to get 20,000 Russians from the Empress Catherine foundered, according to James Harris in Berlin through the instigation of Frederick of Prussia.[11] The Dutch having refused to permit their Scotch Brigade to serve outside Europe, the British once again turned to the little princes of Germany, who had already 'snuffed the cadaverous taint of lucrative war'.[12]

At the beginning of August 1775, reports of the battle on Breed's Hill appeared in German newspapers, and in that same month the Erbprinz[13] of Hessen-Kassel, the independent ruler of Hanau, wrote to George III offering troops.[14] The King's brother-in-law, the Erbprinz of Braunschweig-Wolfenbüttel, did the same in September on his father's behalf.[15] That same month Sir Joseph Yorke, British minister at the Hague, reported that Hessen-Kassel, Hessen-Darmstadt, Württemberg, Sachsen-Gotha, and Baden might furnish the numbers of soldiers wanted 'if proper measures are taken to treat with them'.[16] Hessen-Kassel, however, unlike

[8] HMC: *Report on the Manuscripts of the Earl of Dartmouth* (London, 1895), II, p. 226.

[9] G. D. Scull, ed., *Memoir and Journals of Captain W. Glanville Evelyn* (Boston, 1971), p. 77.

[10] Sir Henry Clinton, *The American Rebellion: Sir Henry Clinton's Narrative of his Campaigns, 1775–1782, with an Appendix of Original Documents.* William B. Willcox, ed. (New Haven, 1954), p. xvi n. 4.

[11] FO352/2, Harris to Suffolk, 9 Dec. 1775.

[12] The phrase is Burke's. Sir George Otto Trevelyan, *The American Revolution* (6 vols. London, 1899–1914), II, p. 43.

[13] Literally, the Hereditary Prince, i.e. the Landgraf's heir.

[14] SP84/547, 19 August 1775, enclosed in Yorke's letter to Suffolk, 25 August. Printed in Kapp, *Soldatenhandel*, p. 250.

[15] Fortescue, *Correspondence of George III*, III, nr. 1706.

[16] SP84/547, Yorke to Suffolk, 5 Sept. 1775. Printed in Kapp, *Soldatenhandel*, p. 243, but in such a manner as to give the false impression that Yorke had actually sounded out these princes. See also SP84/555, Suffolk to Yorke, 4 Mar. 1777, listing those princes actually approahced. Although two contemporary travel accounts state that Faucitt made an offer to Hessen-Darmstadt and was refused, there is nothing to support this in the official correspondence in SP81/181–96. See *A Tour through Germany. Containing Full Directions for Travelling in that Interesting Country* (London, n.d.), p. 91 and Riesbeck, *Travels through Germany*, III, p. 195.

Braunschweig and Hanau, did not tender an offer, for the King thought as late as November that Hessen would decline British overtures.[17]

Thus Britain, rather than the German prince at Kassel, sought a contract. Colonel William Faucitt in Hannover embarking five Electoral battalions for Gibraltar and Minorca to free British manpower for America, and inspecting Scheither's recruits, was instructed to proceed to the courts of Braunschweig and Kassel to obtain as many men as possible: at the former, probably 3,000–4,000, at the latter possibly as many as 5,000. Because of the unusual nature of the service and the Germans' 'insuperable horror' of the sea voyage, Faucitt was to offer subsidies and levy money per man as generous as any previous treaty.[18]

Faucitt's vital mission was no secret: it was widely reported by German newspapers and ambassadors.[19] At Braunschweig Faucitt concluded the preliminaries of a treaty for 4,300 men. From there he proceeded quickly to Kassel and entered into negotiations with one of the Landgraf's ministers, Martin Ernst von Schlieffen, a man of considerable and varied talents, both soldier and patron of the arts. Schlieffen, much to Faucitt's surprise, said that some 10,000 or 12,000 men could be made available. By 20 December 1775 a draft treaty was drawn up and dispatched to London; and although final agreement was not reached until February, the treaty was back-dated then to 15 January giving the Landgraf additional subsidy from that date to speed the mobilization of his corps.[20]

Friedrich Kapp, the German liberal whose account of the negotiations is still the most comprehensive, depicted Faucitt as the dupe of the princes, a subaltern mentality unfit for the task set him.[21] Yet judged by the spirit and letter of his instructions, Faucitt was eminently successful. King and ministry wanted trained men quickly, to crush the rebellion. The German princes could apparently offer these men. 'As there is not common sense in protracting a war of this sort,' wrote Lord George Germain, Secretary of State for the Colonies, 'I should be for exerting the utmost force of

---

[17] Fortescue, *Correspondence of George III*, III, nr. 1769.

[18] SP81/181, Suffolk to Faucitt, 11 Nov. 1775. Originally the Brunswickers at least were going to remain in Ireland, freeing regiments on the Irish Establishment for service in America. The Irish Parliament reacted so unfavourably that the Germans all went to America.

[19] Alfred Kröger, *Geburt der USA: German Newspaper Accounts of the American Revolution 1763–1783* (Madison, Wisc., 1962), p. 119; *Politische Correspondenz Friedrich's*, XXXVII, p. 337.

[20] SP81/181, Faucitt to Suffolk, 20 Dec. 1775; SP81/182, Faucitt to Suffolk, 1 Feb. 1776.

[21] Kapp, *Soldatenhandel*, pp. 40–1.

this Kingdom to finish the rebellion in one campaign.'[22] In all wars in living memory the force of the Kingdom had included hired contingents. Lord Suffolk, Secretary for Northern Affairs, within whose department the negotiations fell, shared this uncompromising attitude, believing that Britain should 'exert every nerve to subdue this rebellion in the most Expeditious and effective Manner'.[23] Faucitt's instructions reflected this outlook. Timely acquisition of the troops, not limiting the expense, was the object in the present emergency: 'great activity is necessary, as the King is extremely anxious to be at Certainty one Way or another, as to the Possibility of obtaining Foreign Troops for America. And if they can be procured, to obtain them with the utmost expedition.' Generous sums were to be granted on the assumption that a sufficiently large force quickly assembled could crush the rebels in one campaign and then return to Europe at relatively low cost.[24]

Thus on financial points Faucitt yielded to Schlieffen's demands, including an outstanding hospital account from the previous war of £41,820 14s 5d. The historian Kapp regarded this as the ultimate in the Landgraf's perfidy, declaring that not a penny of it was actually owed. But it was nothing new for the British to be in arrears of payment and to pay up only when they needed the Hessians' services again. The testimony of Thomas Bishop, who examined the accounts, is worth quoting:

> I think myself obliged in justice to declare, that whenever I had an opportunity of examining and comparing the Number of Sick actually maintained in the Hospitals with those specified in the Reports ... I never found that the Number of Sick were mistated [sic] in any such reports, nor does it appear to me that the amount of the expenses of these hospitals is, upon the whole, greater than they would have been if they had been more immediately under the British Commissariat.'[25]

That the Landgraf thought the money owing is vouched for by his sending a representative, Captain Christian Moritz von Kutzleben, to London in October 1774, to seek payment. Kutzleben badgered

---

[22] Quoted in Piers Mackesy, *The War for America 1775–1783* (Cambridge, Mass., 1964), p. 55.

[23] Quoted in Ira D. Gruber, *The Howe Brothers and the American Revolution* (New York, 1972), p. 7. Marcus Cunliffe, *Soldiers and Civilians: The Martial Spirit in America 1775–1865* (London, 1969), p. 40, says that the hiring of 30,000 foreign troops, although no novelty, was on an unprecedented scale. In 1711 foreign troops in British pay or subsidy amounted to 201,000. Charles Clode, *The Military Forces of the Crown* (2 vols. London, 1869), I, p. 260.

[24] SP81/181, Suffolk to Faucitt, 11 Nov. 1775. See also Suffolk's speech in the Lords. *Parliamentary History*, XVIII, p. 1198.

[25] *Journals of the Commons*, XXXVI, p. 421.

the government throughout 1775, but although he reported a probable subsidy treaty with Britain, he was not sent to negotiate one and played no part in its completion.[26]

In return the British were getting troops reckoned 'as good, in all respects, as any in Europe',[27] and ready to march on 15 February, ample time, it was thought, to reach America for the summer campaign. The Hessian corps commander was instructed to co-operate to the best of his ability with the British.[28] Schlieffen did not fail to brag in his memoirs that he had negotiated the most financially advantageous Hessian treaty of the century; but he held the stronger cards. The Landgraf had both troops and a full treasury, the British had money but needed soldiers – 'Being easy in his circumstances [wrote Faucitt], and unincumbered with debt, he is not so tractable in affairs of this nature, as some other German princes might be.'[29] Suffolk and the King were pleased with Faucitt's success in obtaining troops, the former writing that His Majesty 'with regard to the activity and discretion of your [Faucitt's] conduct, is very fully satisfied'.[30]

The treaty[31] renewed all previous agreements, and, as was usual, pledged mutual aid in case one of the parties were attacked. The Landgraf provided a corps of four grenadier battalions,[32] fifteen infantry battalions, and two *Jäger* companies. Each battalion took two three-pounder regimental pieces and the requisite gunners. Once mustered into British service, the troops were to enjoy British pay and emoluments, free passage for mail, transport of invalids back to Germany, and similar medical care as the British troops but under their own doctors. Fearing that the soldiers would be cheated of a part of their wages, high by German standards, Faucitt got an undertaking from Schlieffen that the men would enjoy full pay. Both Faucitt and Suffolk felt that the knowledge of

---

[26] StaMarburg 300 Philippsruhe E11/6 vol. 1, fols. 68, 85, 99, and passim.
[27] SP81/182, Faucitt to Suffolk, 1 Jan. 1776.
[28] SP81/182, Faucitt to Suffolk, 28 Jan. and 1 Feb. 1776.
[29] Ibid., 1 Feb. 1776.
[30] Ibid., Suffolk to Faucitt, 12 Feb. 1776.
[31] F. G. Davenport and C. O. Paullin, *European Treaties having a bearing on the History of the United States and its Dependents* (Washington, DC, 1937), IV, pp. 118–22; *Journals of the Commons*, XXXV, pp. 571–5. The treaty was also published at the time in London and Frankfurt.
[32] Grenadier battalions were specially formed by brigading the flank companies of the other regiments together. A grenadier 'battalion' had four companies, an infantry 'regiment' five. Since each Hessian regiment going to America took only one battalion, the terms 'regiment' and 'battalion' are synonomous for our purposes, and with reference to the Hessian corps will be used interchangeably. See SP81/182, Faucitt to Suffolk, 28 Jan. 1776.

such benefits of British service were a sure guarantee against desertion.[33] The Hessian rank and file did receive full pay, the officers had some of theirs returned to Hessen, for their families' use in their absence.[34]

Outside Europe the corps could serve only in North America. The Landgraf was to provide necessary replacements for casualties each year at thirty crowns banco per man. If an entire unit were wiped out by pestilence, shipwreck, or other disaster, the King would pay for replacement. The Landgraf received an annual subsidy of 450,000 crowns, double the normal, to continue as usual one year after the service had ended.[35] The British also undertook to apprehend Hessian deserters in their domains, including Hannover, and Hessians were not to be permitted to settle in America without their prince's permission.

As time was essential – article III of the treaty stated specifically, 'in the present circumstances there is not time to be lost' – the Landgraf ordered some thirteen battalions, over 8,000 men, to be ready to march on 15 February at the latest, even before King and Parliament had accepted the treaty. This caused Faucitt some anxiety, for he feared the treaty might be rejected in London while the Hessians were still mobilizing. 'The Landgrave, however, perceiving my embrassment on this head, very generously put me out of my pain by telling me, that, if any insurmountable obstacle should prevent the Treaty's being concluded all that remained for Him to do in that case, was to countermand the march of His troops, in the same manner as he should a Field-day, which the sudden change of weather had rendered impracticable.'[36]

The treaties with Hessen-Kassel, Braunschweig-Wolfenbüttel, and Hessen-Hanau were debated in the Commons on 29 February 1776. In the Lords Richmond introduced a motion asking the King to countermand the march of the mercenaries. Liberal historians of the nineteenth century made much of the opposition rhetoric in these debates.[37] On nearly every previous occasion, however, such

[33] SP81/182, Suffolk to Faucitt, 2 Jan. 1776.
[34] CO5/93, Part II, fol. 489, Sir Geo. Osborne to Germain, 17 Aug. 1776; StaMarburg 13 Acc: 1930/5 Nr. 195, fol. 67, Landgraf's instruction to all battalions, 24 Jan. 1776.
[35] One crown banco was equal to 4s 9¾d.
[36] SP81/182, Faucitt to Suffolk, 14 Jan. 1776.
[37] For example, Trevelyan, *The American Revolution*, II, pp. 50–5; Kapp, *Soldatenhandel*, pp. 171–85; Edward J. Lowell, *The Hessians and the other German Auxilliaries of Great Britain in the Revolutionary War* (New York, 1884), pp. 27–36. The treaties were approved by a considerable margin, 242 votes to 88, in the Commons, and Richmond's motion rejected by 100 votes to 32 in the Lords.

treaties had been opposed, always in vain, on grounds of expense to the British taxpayer or sacrifice of Britain's interests for those of Hannover. Outside governing circles they were often unpopular, but they remained an essential part of British conduct of war from William III to the Younger Pitt. Of the 1755 treaties for hiring Russians and Hessians, for example, one gentleman wrote to the diplomat Charles Hanbury-Williams, 'You see, your treaties are approved by a large majority, not withstanding they were so much abused without doors.'[38]

So it was in 1776. The majority of Englishmen who counted politically thought the American colonies essential to Britain's greatness and that right was on her side. Carlisle expressed in the Lords a widely held view:

> If we should concede, so as to relinquish every substantial benefit which we might derive from our political sovereignty and commercial control over our colonies, what will be the probable consequence, but that this country, deprived of the advantages of an immense commerce, will gradually sink into obscurity and insignificance, and fall at length a prey to the first powerful and ambitious state, which may meditate a conquest of this island?[39]

And the historian Edward Gibbon wrote, 'I am more and more convinced that we have both the right and the power on our side, and though the effort may be accompanied with some melancholy circumstances, we are now arrived at the decisive moment of persevering or losing forever both our trade and Empire.'[40] Britain's defeat in America was followed, of course, by the rapid development of British industry, the elimination of France as a colonial rival, and maritime and commercial supremacy through-out the globe, making nonsense of Carlisle's fears; however, men conduct themselves by what they believe, and Carlisle and Gibbon were not granted insight into the future.

Once the British were bent on coercion, the use of mercenaries followed as a matter of course. Since the age of nationalism, the hiring of foreign auxiliaries has become distasteful. In 1776 it was standard practice. As Friedrich Karl von Moser wrote bitterly in his attack on blind obedience to princes, 'There is no great or small power in Europe, which does not count German lords and men

---

[38] *Parliamentary History*, XV, p. 660n. See also HMC: *Carlisle MSS.*, pp. 57, 70, and 81 for other debates on subsidy treaties.

[39] *Parliamentary History*, XVIII, p. 1200.

[40] Gibbon to Holroyd, 31 Jan. 1776, in J. E. Norton, ed., *Letters of Edward Gibbon* (2 vols. London, 1956), II, p. 58.

amongst its warriors.'[41] The opposition's arguments, often heard before, were outweighed by contemporary practice. Lord John Cavendish spoke of the Landgraf's avarice and called the financial provisions of the treaty unparalleled in their extravagance. In 1755 Chesterfield had styled the Landgraf (then Wilhelm VIII) 'full as good at making a bargain as any Jew in Europe'.[42] The actual cost of mercenaries in British pay in 1779 was less than it has been in 1760: £683,068 against £874,607.[43] Cavendish said that Britain was impoverished and humiliated by applying to two small German princes.[44] If true, she had been humiliated and impoverished since 1689 when she began the long series of wars against France. Richmond in the Lords said that the mercenaries would be introduced into the Kingdom to subvert the constitution.[45] This was an old bogey. Twice before Hessians had been in Britain to defend her, in 1745 and 1756. In 1776 they were not allowed to land; in 1784, on their return trip, quartered during the winter at Chatham, Portsmouth, and Dover, their exemplary conduct drew favourable conduct.[46] Richmond also argued that Britain would be obliged by the treaty of alliance to come to Hessen's aid if she were attacked. Nearly all the treaties had included the alliance article, a sop to the princes, 'pompous, high-sounding phrases', as Suffolk himself said, '. . . the true objects of those treaties is not so much to create an alliance, as to hire a body of troops, which the present rebellion in America has rendered necessary.'[47] It was claimed that the princes were breaking the law of the Holy Roman Empire, and might have to go to war with their own sovereign, the Emperor.[48] But jurists accepted that princes who hired out troops for subsidies were not necessarily belligerents themselves, thus in practice avoiding conflicts with the Emperor.[49] In the Seven Years War, when Kassel and Marburg were occupied by a French army, the Landgraf himself never formally declared war on France, the ally of the Habsburg.[50] In the American war Hessen was not formally a

---

[41] Friedrich Karl, Freiherr von Moser, *Politische Wahrheiten* (Zurich, 1796), p. 105.
[42] *Parliamentary History*, XV, p. 625n.
[43] *Journals of the Commons*, XXXVII, p. 21, and XV, pp. 957–62.
[44] *Parliamentary History*, XVIII, p. 1168.
[45] *Parliamentary History*, XVIII, p. 1190.
[46] *The St James Chronicle*, 1–3 April 1784, Extract of a letter from Chatham, 29 March quoted in StaMarburg 12.11 I Ba 16 (Journal of the Grenadier Battalion Platte), fols. 429–30.
[47] *Parliamentary History*, XVIII, p. 1198.
[48] Ibid., pp. 1169–70.
[49] Brauer, *Die hannoversch-englischen Subsidienverträge*, p. 92.
[50] Losch, *Soldatenhandel*, p. 2.

belligerent, and in 1780 the Landgraf visited Paris without trouble. He was lodged next to John Adams in the Hotel de Valois, all the local wags declaring that if Adams were authorized to open negotiations he could have from the Landgraf as many troops to fight on the American side as already were hired out against them.[51]

More substantial was the fear that hiring mercenaries would destroy all hope of reconciliation and encourage Americans to seek foreign aid. After the introduction of redcoats into Boston, the 'Massacre' of 5 March 1770, the 'Intolerable Acts', and Gage's attempt to seize arms at Concord, Americans, raised in the tradition that 'a free parliament and a standing army were absolutely incompatible',[52] saw the spectre of militarism destroying their rights as Englishmen. The employment of European mercenaries, men 'such as have neither property nor families to fight for, and who have no principle, either of honour, religion, public spirit, regard for liberty, or love of country',[53] realized their worst fears. It was a clear sign that the Ministry was relying on coercion, leaving no option but resistance. When he received news of the treaties, Richard Henry Lee of Virginia wrote to Landon Carter:

The infamous treaties with Hesse, Brunswick, etc. of which we have authentick copies and Material reply to Graftons motion leave not a doubt but that our enemies are determined upon the absolute conquest and subduction of North America. *It is not choice then but necessity that calls for Independence, as the only means by which foreign Alliances can be obtained*: and a proper Confederation by which internal peace and union may be secured. Contrary to our earnest, early, and repeated petitions for peace, liberty, and safety our enemies press us with war, threaten us with danger and Slavery. And this, not with her single force, but with the aid of Foreigners.[54]

The treaties certainly gave impetus to the movement in America for independence, but their influence on seeking foreign alliances should not be exaggerated. Before news of the treaties, the Committee of Secret Correspondence on 3 March 1776 instructed Silas Deane to sound out Vergennes, the French foreign minister, 'whether, if the Colonies should be forced to form themselves into an

---

[51] Lyman H. Butterfield, ed., *Adams Family Correspondence* (3 vols. Cambridge, Mass., 1973), III, p. 275.

[52] Don Higginbotham, *The War of American Independence* (New York, 1971), p. 15.

[53] *The Pennsylvania Evening Post*, 30 March 1776, quoted in Frank Moore, *Diary of the American Revolution from Newspapers and Original Documents* (2 vols. New York, 1860), I, pp. 213–4.

[54] Edmund C. Burnett, ed., *Letters of Members of the Continental Congress* (8 vols. Washington, DC, 1921–36), I, pp. 468–9. Italics original. Grafton's defeated motion would have halted troop movements and invited the Americans to present grievances.

independent state, France would probably acknowledge them as such, receive their ambassadors, enter into any treaty or alliance with them, for commerce or defence, or both?'[55]

A second sound objection, and one shared by British officers, was the possibility of the 17,000 mercenaries being greeted with open arms by their 150,000 countrymen already settled in the colonies, and joining them: 'they will most likely be offered lands and protection' said James Luttrell, 'These warlike transports we are to fit out may then be considered as good as the Palatine ships for peopling America with Germans.' In the event the German-Americans were not activists in the revolution; probably because of their pietist background they made small contribution in proportion to their numbers. But there were sufficient to aid in a policy of subverting the mercenaries.[56]

Perhaps the British government, representing a more open society than the despotisms of central Europe, should have been more solicitous for the fate of 'the devoted wretches thus purchased for the slaughter . . . mere mercenaries in the worst sense of the word', as Lord Camden described the German auxiliaries in the Lords.[57] But European powers had struggled throughout history for greatness and dominion, usually at the expense of the blood of their peoples. Britain as an island and maritime power was able, through subsidy treaties, to keep her own men employed at home in manufactures and farming,[58] while other armies bled themselves on the battlefield. One modern historian has argued that the secret of Britain's success was her ability to avoid such losses, and that her decline in the twentieth century came when she had to commit troops on the continent on a large scale.[59] In the Seven Years War such considerations triumphed. British statesmen believed that it

---

[55] Burnett, *Letters of Congress*, I, p. 376.

[56] *Parliamentary History*, XVIII, pp. 1178–9; Richard D. Brown, 'The Founding Fathers of 1776 and 1787: A Collective View', *WMQ*, 3rd series, XXXIII (1976), p. 468 and n. 12. See below, pp. 98–9, 186–7.

[57] *Parliamentary History*, XVIII, p. 1223.

[58] Shelbourne considered this to be government policy. Ibid., p. 1220. That such was the aim of eighteenth-century governments is shown by the words of the French war minister, Saint–Germain: 'in order to make up an army we must not destroy the nation: it would be destruction to a nation if it were deprived of its best elements. As things are, the army must inevitably consist of the scum of the people and of all those for whom society has no use.' Quoted in John U. Nef, *War and Human Progress* (New York, 1950), p. 306. Nef's theme is that involvement in war is detrimental to a nation's economic and cultural development.

[59] A. J. P. Taylor, *The Origins of the Second World War* (Penguin Books, 1964), pp. 15–16.

was better to give English money than English lives, that the subsidy policy was cheaper because industry and trade would still flourish and soon draw back the money paid abroad. Thus they paid out some £10,694,365 in subsidies, and by 1767 £418,270 of this had gone to Hessen-Kassel.[60]

Turning to Hessen, one can scarcely write it off as one historian does the smaller German states, as oppressive absolutisms 'sunk in tradition and narrow in political outlook'.[61] Friedrich II of Hessen-Kassel was an educated and cultured man, the typical small scale enlightened despot: an active reformer, reorganizing the administration of his state and its penal code, abolishing the death penalty for various crimes and the use of torture. To aid economic recovery after the Seven Years War, he established a Chamber of Commerce (*Commerziencollege*), a market in Kassel, a fire insurance scheme, and a fund to aid farming (*Landassistenzkasse*).[62] His court was a centre for artists and men of letters, not all mere sycophants. Jakob Mauvillon, military engineer and physiocrat, published a work favourable to the colonists while at the *Collegium Carolinum* in Kassel. Among Mauvillon's colleagues at the *Carolinum*, Christian Wilhelm Döhm produced the first German translation of Paine's *Common Sense*.[63] Friedrich founded a society for the study of antiquities, and promulgated a law for the preservation of ancient monuments in Hessen. His two great monuments were the first museum on the continent open to the public and the first Foundling Hospital in Germany. The arts which flourished around his court were looked on with disapproval by the dour Calvinists of Hessen,[64] but were no more artifical than today's symphony orchestras and provincial theatres supported by government subsidies. Rather than accept the nineteenth-century historians' jaundiced views of Friedrich, one would do better to turn to a balanced modern assessment: 'The typical prince of his time, both ambitious and irresolute, lacking outstanding talents and showing no great

[60] Carl William Eldon, *England's Subsidy Policy towards the Continental during the Seven Years War* (Philadelphia, 1938), pp. 69, 160, 162 and passim.

[61] M. S. Anderson, *Europe in the Eighteenth Century 1713–1783* (Norwich, 1961), p. 198.

[62] O. Berge, 'Die Innenpolitik des Landgrafen Friedrichs II von Hessen-Kassel' (unpublished dissertation, Mainz, 1952), passim.

[63] Horst Dippel, 'Deutschland und die amerikanische Revolution: Sozialgeschichtlichen Untersuchung zum politischen Bewusstsein im ausgehenden 18. Jahrhundert' (unpublished dissertation, Cologne, 1972), pp. 89 and 186–7.

[64] 'The inhabitants of Cassel, who are Calvinists, shew no great passion for dramatic entertainments.' John Moore, *A View of the Society and Manners in France, Switzerland and Germany* (2 vols. London, 1779), I, p. 48.

achievements, he cannot be compared with the great successes of enlightened despotism, but was better than many contemporaries, and above all better than the reputation which the writings of nationalist historians gave him.'[65]

Thus Friedrich moved in the mainstream of his time. Unlike his forebears, he had no religious attachment to Protestant Britain, having secretly converted to Catholicism in 1749, a step which caused much anxiety in London and Potsdam at his accession in 1760 in the midst of a war with Catholic France and Austria. Kassel was quickly occupied by Hannoverian troops; Colonel Clavering dispatched from London to spy on the Landgraf, offering bribes to his chief minister, August Moritz von Donop; and Frederick the Great sent Friedrich the baton of a Prussian field marshal to keep him to the cause.[66] Schlieffen defended the 1776 treaty on the grounds of family ties binding Hessen to Britain's Royal Family;[67] but although a number of senior Hessian officers felt this loyalty, the Landgraf had been estranged from his first wife, Mary, daughter of George II, since his conversion.[68]

Friedrich's motive was undoubtedly financial. His court of 325 people, his opera and ballet, the acquisition of works of art, the palace of Weissenstein – a building which the Hessian *Landstände* thought could be neither constructed nor maintained without ruining the country[69] – his other building, and his reforms all cost money; and although the treasury was well stocked with British subsidies from the last war, outstanding payments ceased in 1770. After that the wealthier war treasury (*Kriegskasse*) was repeatedly drawn on to aid the civil treasury (*Kammerkasse*) and for other expenditures, such as the purchase of 150,000 talers worth of foodstuff in the hunger year of 1772.[70] Between 1765 and 1771 some 935,000 talers passed from *Kriegskasse* to *Kammerkasse*, most of it being written off without repayment.[71] Despite the loans which the Landgraf's officials made at 4 per cent to other princes and

---

[65] *Biographisches Wörterbuch zur Deutschen Geschichte* (3 vols. Munich, 1975), I, p. 774.

[66] SP87/39, passim; *Politische Correspondenz Friedrich's*, XIX, pp. 89–90 and 186.

[67] Kapp, *Soldatenhandel*, p. 194.

[68] Georg Forster, *Briefwechsel*, I (Leipzig, 1829), pp. 351–2. Moore, *Society and Manners*, II, p. 44. Friedrich married again in 1773.

[69] Johann Bernouilli, *Jonas Apelblad's Beschreibung seiner Reise durch Ober- und Niedersachsen und Hessen* (Berlin and Leipzig, 1785), p. 311.

[70] Wolf von Both and Hans Vogel, *Landgraf Friedrich II von Hessen-Kassel* (Munich, 1973), p. 93.

[71] Ibid.

private individuals, a profitable business,[72] by 1775 the *Kriegskasse* holdings had fallen to 298,210 talers from two-and-a-half times that in 1772.[73] To carry out their programme of reform and aid to the arts, Friedrich and his ministers must have seen a new subsidy treaty as timely aid. Undoubtedly the Landgraf, an easily in-fluenced personality, was moved in this direction by Schlieffen, a man of undoubtedly high capacities and strong character.

Although, in Kapp's words, Friedrich had introduced 'system and method to the business' of the soldier commerce by dividing Hessen into recruiting cantons,[74] he was not a great military practitioner. Of four Landgrafs who negotiated treaties for the hiring of soldiers, he was responsible for the fewest: his grandfather Karl concluded eighteen, his father Wilhelm VIII eleven, and his son Wilhelm IX (later Elector Wilhelm I) six. Of Friedrich's two, the first in 1760 was a consequence of his father's adherence to England's cause in 1756.[75] He enjoyed playing at soldiers by drilling the first battalion of his Guards; having no special pavilion for the purpose like his cousin of Darmstadt, he used the dining room of his palace in bad weather.[76] But after he had been left frustrated and unemployed in the Seven Years War, his main interests moved to the court, various cultural pursuits, and his active reform programme. Unlike his father, he was of little importance in Germany politically, despite the advantage which the traditional alliance with Britain brought him.[77]

When Boswell visited Kassel, greatly mistrusting the Landgraf, the Minister of the local Huguenot church said of his sovereign, 'Sir, take my word for it that he is a good prince. He has had many misfortunes. He has been treated very severely.... He needs only sensible and clever people to guide him.'[78] These people Friedrich

---

[72] Sauer, *Finanzgeschäfte der Landgrafen*, pp. 24–9.
[73] StaMarburg, Kriegspfennigzahlamt, 12. nr. 8304 (1772), p. 449; and nr. 8310 (1775), p. 459.
[74] Kapp, *Soldatenhandel*, p. 59.
[75] Losch, *Soldatenhandel*, pp. 7–15.
[76] Moore, *Society and Manners*, II, p. 41.
[77] *Politische Testamente Friedrichs des Grossen*, p. 201.
[78] F. A. Pottle, ed., *Boswell on the Grand Tour: Germany and Switzerland 1764* (London, 1953), p. 150. Like other Englishmen, Boswell mistrusted the Landgraf because of his Catholic conversion. Boswell's description of his motive is typical; he attributed it to his 'attach-ment to a certain Countess of the Catholic religion, who insisted that His Highness should surrender his soul to her before she would give him up her body'. See also SP87/45, fol. 168, Clavering to Halifax, 19 May 1763: 'The Landgrave's Character is altogether Frivolous ... His Design of recovering the County of Hanau is ... to have it in His Power, being in the Neighbourhood of Frankfort, to see some old female Acquaintances, particularly one who had a great share in the change of his Religion.'

The Hessians

found in the 'Prussian junta' of Schlieffen, Friedrich von Jungkenn, and Dietrich-Wilhelm von Wakenitz, officers who had come from Prussian service to Hessen;[79] and it is quite probable that it was they who recommended to him that Hessen, a poor country whose great asset was its hardy fighting men, should follow traditional policy and hire them out for British gold. The opinion of posterity has been, however, that the subsidy treaty 'darkened extraordinarily the image of a court much involved artistically but of no consequence politically'.[80]

THE HESSIAN CORPS

These Hessian soldiers,,whose services had been purchased, who were fighting for hire, were uncouth in manners, low in morals, but well trained in military duties, and familiar with war and violence.[81]

To the British, speed was essential in concluding the treaty with Hessen. They granted the Landgraf numerous favourable terms, including back-dating the subsidy to 15 January, in order that he should set his corps in motion as quickly as possible.[82] Thirteen battalions of Lieutenant General Leopold von Heister's first division had already set out from Kassel, Ziegenhain, Wolfhagen, Rinteln, and their other stand-quarters, for embarkation at Bremerlehe on the North Sea, when Faucitt was informed that sufficient shipping was not yet ready and the march had to be countermanded.[83] As the regiments returned, rumours flew about Kassel that peace had been concluded with the colonists, causing dismay amongst the officers until the real cause became known. Simon Louis du Ry, the Landgraf's Huguenot architect, wrote that the mobilization of the Garrison Regiments in particular had brought about a marvellous promotion amongst the officers, and for them there could be no peace. 'The officers with fat bellies and old faces would have not a little trouble if there were no war', wrote du Ry.[84]

---

[79] The phrase is George Forster's. *Briefwechsel*, I, p. 320. For the talents and importance of the three former Prussians, see Günderode, *Briefe eines Reisenden*, pp. 204–6.

[80] Demandt, *Geschichte des Landes Hessen*, p. 282.

[81] William S. Stryker, *The Battles of Trenton and Princeton* (Boston and New York, 1898), p. 39.

[82] SP81/182, Faucitt to Suffolk, 14 January 1776.

[83] StaMarburg 4h.410. nr. 1, fols. 16 and 22, Faucitt to Major von Estorff, 14 and 15 Feb. 1776. Estorff was Hannoverian commissary for the Hessian march through the Electorate.

[84] Otto Gerland, 'Kasseler Tagesneuigkeiten aus dem 18. Jahrhundert', *Hessenland*, VII (1893), p. 72. In the Garrison Regiment von Huyn for example, of 22 combatant officers,

The Hessians go to America

Amongst the rank and file feelings were more mixed. The élite, the grenadier battalions of Colonel Karl Aemilius Ulrich von Donop, were longing to get at the enemy and the delay caused them mortal chagrin.[85] But others were less keen to be torn from loved ones to cross the terrible ocean. Lieutenant Heinrich von Bardeleben described a moving scene as the Regiment von Donop left Homberg on 25 February. 'Disconsolate mothers, lamenting wives and weeping children followed the regiment in crowds, and impressed on us most sensibly the whole of this sad scene.'[86]

Leaving their garrison towns in late February or early March the first division[87] moved by easy stages, with a rest every fourth or fifth day, through Hannoverian territory to cantonments around Bremerlehe. For many of the young soldiers this march itself, not to speak of the voyage to America, was a wholly new experience. Passing the river Wumme where the land known as *Geest* lay under water as far as the eye could see, the men of the Leib-Regiment thought the individual houses with their thatched roofs standing up above the flood were ships at sea.[88]

The second division under Lieutenant General Wilhelm, Freiherr von Knyphausen, composed largely of garrison regiments whose ranks were filled out specially for the expedition, assembled in February and March for kitting and training at Wolfhagen, Ziegenhain, and other military depots. They marched from Hessen in early May, reaching cantons around Bremerlehe and Ritzebüttel at the end of the month, and embarked in early June.[89] The grief of families at the garrison regiments' departure was at least as great as that for the first division. *Freikorporal* Georg Julius von Langenscharz of the Garrison Regiment von Stein, going with his

---

(Footnote continued)

18 had their commissions dated February–May 1776. StaMarburg 12. nr. 831. Rangier-Rollen des Regiments von Huyn.

[85] Hans Huth, 'Letters from a Hessian Mercenary', *PMHB*, LXII (1938), p. 492.

[86] Bardeleben, p. 12. The chief of Bardeleben's regiment was not that Donop who commanded the grenadiers in America, but Lieutenant General Wilhelm Henrich August von Donop, who remained in Hessen.

[87] Composed of the grenadier battalions Linsing, Block, and Minnigerode; the Field Regiments Leib, Erbprinz, Prinz Karl, Trumbach, Ditfurth, Donop, Mirbach, Lossberg, and Knyphausen; the *Landgrenadier* regiment Rall; one *Jäger* company; and an artillery detachment of two three-pounders and gunners for each battalion.

[88] Dinklage, fol. 4, 10 March, 1776.

[89] StaMarburg 12.11 I Ba 13 (Journal of the Garrison Regiment von Huyn), fols. 2–15; and ibid, 16 (Journal of the Grenadier Battalion Platte), fols. 1–23. The second division was composed of the Field Regiment von Wutginau, the grenadier battalion Koehler, the Garrison Regiments Stein, Wissenbach, Huyn, and Bunau; a *Jäger* company; and artillery as for the first division.

father, a captain in the same regiment, to America, later recalled
his mother's feelings upon receiving news of the impending departure: 'The grievous parting which here followed, when a wife said
to her husband, and a mother to her son, perhaps for the last time,
'Take care of yourself,' can only be felt and not described. The
moment was come, and I left my good mother, disconsolate in tears
and lamentation.'[90] It was a scene enacted many times across
Hessen. Soldier Valentin Asteroth of Treysa recorded that the
Garrison Regiment von Huyn marched from Ziegenhain amidst
the melancholy cries of many people.[91] To encourage the men of
Huyn's regiment on their great adventure, a representative of the
Kriegscollegium read the Articles of War, reminding them 'that the
soldier, when he is true to his Prince, does his duty bravely, and is
virtuous, forever occupies a place worthy of esteem in the society of
men'.[92]

The Landgraf may have given Faucitt the impression that
ordering out his corps for the American expedition was no more
trouble than organizing a military field day. It was in fact far more
complicated. Not only did orders have to be sent to regimental
chiefs for calling back the thirty men per company on leave, for
augmenting each company with four NCOs and fifteen privates,
for issuing of cartridges and exercising of the troops, for quarter-
masters to draw pay and forage money from the *Kriegskasse*, for the
formation of grenadier battalions from the flank companies of the
line regiments, for officers' spontoons to be bundled up and deposited at the arsenal in Kassel, for ordnance horses to bear to
Bremerlehe officers who were not taking their mounts to America
(only field officers, i.e. majors and above, took two horses abroad),
and for dates of departure and march routes. In addition all
regiments had to draw up lists of men who owned property or were
only sons, and thus not eligible for foreign service. They were to be
discharged into garrison regiments remaining behind, and their
place taken by new men capable of sustaining the fatigues of
campaign. The Landgraf ordered each departing regiment to
exchange twenty tall fellows from their musketeer and fusilier
companies for an equivalent number of trained soldiers in the
Guards, keeping the best looking for his drill parades. Able ser-

[90] LB Kassel 8° Ms. hass. 123, Heft 1, Langenscharz, Meine Militär Laufbahn und
Erlebnisse vom Jahr 1776 an, fol. 4, 5 May 1776.
[91] LB Kassel 8° Ms. hass. 227, Valentin Asteroth, Erinnerungen aus dem nordamerkanis-
chen Krieg 1776–84, fol. 3.
[92] StaMarburg 12.11 I Ba 13 (Journal of the Regiment von Huyn), fols. 4–5, 12 April 1776.

geant majors from field regiments were promoted to commissioned rank and transferred to the garrison regiments, as were men from field and dragoon regiments capable of serving as NCOs.[93] Additional staff – surgeons, chaplains, wagonmasters, *Auditeurs* – were taken on.[94] A field hospital with a staff of twenty-three, and quantities of bedding, surgical utensils, and medicine had to be fitted out.[95] The three artillery companies of 588 officers and men manning the guns of the various battalions were brought up to strength, only with great difficulty, by last minute recruiting.[96] The time being short, regimental chiefs were enjoined to use every effort to train the new soldiers in the short interval before the march, and for this purpose 9,000 practice cartridges were ordered for the recruits of each regiment.[97]

Three kinds of battalions were leaving for America: field regiments, garrison regiments, and grenadier battalions.[98] Field regiments were composed of professional servicemen enrolled for twenty-four years, mainly native Hessians although recruiting of sturdy foreigners was recommended.[99] But maintaining large forces in peacetime was a heavy burden on the treasury of a small state like Hessen, and also deprived agriculture of necessary labour. Therefore thirty of the ninety privates in each company were on furlough (*beurlaubt*) at a single time. These men were either pursuing trades as craftsmen, or helping in the fields on family farms or as hired labourers.[100] The same men were not always on furlough, but there was a constant coming and going, from military duty to civilian occupation and back again.[101] Since the regiments were stationed in the cantons from which they were recruited, nearly all

---

[93] StaMarburg 13 Acc: 1930/5 Nr. 195, Vorläufige Ordres wegen Augmentation des marschierenden Korps 23 Dec. 1775–30 Mar. 1776, passim. Those young men liable to foreign service were termed *abkömmlich*, those who were exempt for reasons of family, profession, or property-ownership of at least 250 talers' worth, *unabkömmlich*. Also see above, p. 21

[94] StaMarburg 12.11 I Ba 6 (Journal of the Regiment von Knyphausen), fols. 2–3.

[95] AO3/55/2 Nr. 16, Accounts of the Hessian Field Hospital.

[96] StaMarburg 13 Acc: 1930/5 Nr. 891, fol. 9, LtGen v. Gohr to the Landgraf, 8 March 1776.

[97] LB Kassel 2° Ms. hass. 247, Aktenstücke der Brigade von Mirbach, fol. 79, LtGen v. Gohr to MajGen v. Mirbach, 29 Jan. 1776.

[98] For 'battalion' and 'regiment' see above, p. 27 n. 32.

[99] Anon., 'Geworbene Ausländer unter den Hessen in Amerika', *Allgemeine Militär-Zeitung*, LXV (1890), p. 172.

[100] See for example StaMarburg 11 F 1 d, Leave pass to Fusilier Abraham Wiegand of Knyphausen's regiment, dated 25 May 1776, giving him a year's leave to pursue his profession as a shoemaker.

[101] Maximilian Freiherr von Ditfurth, *Die Hessen in den Feldzügen in der Champagne, am Maine und Rhein während der Jahre 1792, 1793 und 1794* (Marburg, 1881), p. 6.

the soldiers except foreign mercenaries were close to their family homes. Despite its size the Hessian army was very far from being a state within a state.[102]

Because of the numbers returned from leave and the new recruits, Hannoverian officers escorting the first division reported the number of new men as forty-nine per company. On every rest day they were furiously exercised in the manual of arms, and although the Hessian infantry manual and the Landgraf's instructions laid down that new men were to be treated with patience and forebearance, and taught their drill by association with soldiers of the old stock, these new men were frequently beaten when slow at the drill.[103] The first Hessian division included the best and most professional troops which the British acquired by their six subsidy treaties, yet it is clear that even these were not composed solely of veterans.

Moreover, the long-serving old-timers of these regiments were looking a little long in the tooth for the rigours of a difficult sea voyage and arduous campaigning. In an age when a soldier was old at forty, of thirty-five NCOs in Lossberg's regiment sixteen were over forty and ten over fifty.[104] In the Regiment von Knyphausen, one third of the sergeant majors and half of the other NCOs were forty or over.[105] The professional skills of these men would be no asset to the British if disease struck them down.

Yet the Hessian regiments included excellent material, 'fit for any service in the world', as Faucitt reported; steady under arms and with the air of soldiers. The younger men would grow into the trade, stiffened by the veterans. Seventeen-year-old Johannes Reuber of Rall's regiment was one who did. If Reuber's journal is a true reflection of his character, he was the ideal soldier: loyal, brave, enduring, never questioning the actions of his superiors.[106] Corporal Martin Appell, like Reuber of Rall's regiment, was

[102] Ochs, 'Das hessische Militär', p. 209 treats the subject of the merging of civilian and military in Hessen. Although referring to a later period, the Hessen military system had not changed in its essentials.

[103] StaHannover 41 v Nr. 24, fol. 28, report of LtGen. v. Walthausen, 19 Feb 1776; ibid, fol. 51, Muller's report, 24 Mar. 1776.

[104] StaMarburg 12. nr. 203, Rang-Liste und Rangier Rollen von dem hochlöbl: Fusilier Regiment ... Lossberg. This and other rolls give ages for April 1775, to which I have added one year.

[105] StaMarburg 11. nr. 398, Rang-Liste Regiments von Knyphausen.

[106] Johannes Reuber, 'Tagebuch des Grenadiers Johannes Reuber aus Niedervellmar vom amerikanischen Feldzug', F. W. Junghans, ed., *Hessenland*, VIII (1894), pp. 155–7, 167–8, and 183–6.

another such; he rose to sergeant major by 1778.[107] Another good and reliable soldier was Corporal Wilhelm Hartung, aged twenty-six, of Lossberg's regiment; his experience was one year's service in the Hannoverian cavalry and three years with the Hessians.[108] Sergeant Berthold Koch of the Regiment von Trumbach had been a soldier since his recruitment in 1742 at the age of fifteen; in the Seven Years War he had fought at Bergen and in the other battles in Hessen.[109]

The men were stout Calvinists, and observed at the very least the outward signs of religion: their children were baptized on board ship or in military garrison, they celebrated marriage with the women who accompanied them to America, and their children were raised in the Christian religion and confirmed.[110] Frequent references to God in their journals indicate a simple piety.

The Hannoverians praised in particular the grenadier battalions and the regiments of Knyphausen and Trumbach.[111] Only two regiments of the first division drew unfavourable comment: Lossberg's and Rall's. The former, garrisoned at Rinteln in an isolated enclave of Hessen, was composed in large part of deserters from the troops of surrounding states and the Prussian garrisons of Minden and Bielefeld. Of all the battalions, Lossberg's had the most deserters during the march, fifteen, more than half of the total of twenty-four in the first division. Heister ordered its commanding officer, Colonel Henrich Anton von Heringen, to investigate. Heringen reported that the chief cause was the rumour of a free pardon in Schaumberg.[112] The deserters, who were mostly married

---

[107] LB Kassel 4° Ms. hass. 293/3, Brief vom Soldat Martin Appell aus Breuna an seine Eltern.

[108] Robert Oakley Slagle, 'The von Lossberg Regiment: a Chronicle of Hessian Participation in the American Revolution' (unpublished dissertation, the American University, 1965), p. 85 n. 37.

[109] K. Rogge-Ludwig, 'Über Berthold Koch und seine Erlebnisse in amerikanischen Freiheitskrieg, 1776–1782', *Mitteilungen* (1876), part i, pp. 1–2.

[110] Kümmel, fols. 16–26; August Woringer, 'Protocoll der Amtshandlungen die der Feldprediger G. C. Cöster bei den beiden löblichen Regimentern von Donop und von Lossberg und andern verrichtet', *DAGeschBl*, XX–XXI (1920–1), pp. 280–304. In Linsing's grenadier battalion, for example, there were 483 men in the Reformed Church, twenty Lutherans and one Catholic. The odd twenty-one probably represent the foreign mercenary element.

[111] StaHannover 41 V Nr. 22, Estorff to Sporken, 26 Mar. 1776, and Bremer to Sporken, 9 April; ibid Nr. 23, Estorff to Sporken, 22 Mar. 1776.

[112] Rinteln was located in Schaumberg, a county geographically separate from the bulk of Hessen, which had fallen to the Landgraf when the ruling line died out in the seventeenth century. 'Count of Schaumberg' was amongst the Landgraf's titles.

men and thought because of this that they were exempt from foreign service, had on news of the supposed pardon set off for Schaumberg, where Heringen was confident they could be picked up again, since most would return to their wives and children. The wide dispersal of company cantons on overnight stops had made it difficult to prevent desertion. Heringen sent off a messenger to warn his chief, Lieutenant General August Henrich von Lossberg, at Rinteln, so he could have them picked up at the border. To the best of Heringen's knowledge, none of the Hessians had been picked up by the Prussian recruiters lurking hopefully.[113]

The Lossbergers carried a large number of supernumeraries (*Überkompletten*) in case of desertion, and were able to make up the vacancies through these and by recruiting foreign deserters on the march.[114] By April 12 the regiment was back up to strength, but on the 16th, the very morning of embarkation, a plot was discovered amongst five Lossbergers to desert. Three of the men were arrested, including the ringleader, a Hannoverian deserter born in Münster.[115] To prevent the escape of deserters, the Landgraf had arranged conventions for their return with Hannover, Braunschweig-Wolfenbüttel, Bückeburg, and Hildesheim; the Hannoverians patrolled actively, and notices were posted 'most seriously warning all His Majesty's subjects and Inhabitants of those Countries in the Electoral Dominions through which the Troops are to pass, against facilitating or promoting the least Desertion, at the same Time commanding the Magistrates, Bailiffs, and Officers of the Garrisons and Quarters of His Majesty's German Troops, to make it . . . an Object of their Attention to its being prevented and opposed'.[116] Such precautions were typical of the time: any large movements of troops was accompanied by the threat of desertion en masse, and a contemporary estimated that between a twelfth and a fifteenth of the Prussian army would desert on the march.[117] The good conduct and relatively low desertion of the Hessians were exemplary for the time.[118] Hannoverian reports

---

[113] StaMarburg 4h.410. nr. 1, fol. 137, 8 April 1776. Ibid, fols. 139–49, listing the deserters of Major von Hanstein's company, shows that the deserters were mostly long serving, with enlistment dates in the 1760s.
[114] StaHannover 41 v Nr. 24, Estorff's report, 12 April 1776.
[115] Ibid.
[116] LB Kassel 2° Ms. hass. 247, Aktenstücke der Brigade von Mirbach, fol. 42, the Landgraf to Mirbach, 9 Feb. 1776; SP82/95, fol. 46, Mathias to Suffolk, 16 Feb. 1776; StaHannover 41 v Nr. 30, Public Notice, 30 Jan. 1776.
[117] Hans Speier, 'Militarism in the Eighteenth Century', *Social Research*, III (1936), p. 317; Riesbeck, *Travels through Germany*, III, p. 17.
[118] StaHannover 41 v Nr. 24, fol. 64, Bremer to Sporken, 9 April 1776, for example.

pay tribute to the excellent Hessian discipline and absence of disorder.

The *Landgrenadier* Regiment Rall, by contrast, was formed not of hardened deserters but of callow farm lads. Although the soldiers wore grenadier caps and there were six axemen per company as in the grenadier battalions, Rall's was not formed of élite flank companies. Rather, it had originated in 1703 when the best men of the *Landmiliz* regiments were drawn together and called, rather logically, a land grenadier battalion. In 1760 when the *Landmiliz* became garrison regiments, the *Landgrenadier* became in effect one of the field regiments.[119] It still betrayed its origins in the militia: for accounting, its finances were reckoned with those of the garrison regiments; more of its men were furloughed than in the other field regiments; and the Hannoverians reported that its men were the smallest of the first division, the Landgraf having taken the best ones for his Guards.[120] Johannes Reuber, a typical soldier of Rall's, was seventeen years old and 5 feet 1 inch tall. Faucitt, mustering the Hessians into British service at Bremerlehe, reported this battalion as much inferior to any others he had then seen, because its peace establishment was much lower than the others and the number of recruits correspondingly greater. 'They are however in surprising forwardness; which is owing to the activity and cleverness of their Colonel, who is one of the best officers of his rank, in the Landgrave's army.'[121]

The last comment may strike us ironically, but Rall's unfitness for independent command became evident only on the day of his death. He had spent his life as a soldier, being born in the Regiment von Donop, and had participated as a volunteer in Gregory Orlov's campaigns against the Turks. While Rall was with the Russians, the Landgraf, delighted at such keenness to pursue his profession, advanced him to colonel and chief of the former Regiment von Mansbach.[122]

Perhaps the best field regiment was the Leib-Regiment ('The Princes Own'). Its chief was the Landgraf himself, so it was a favoured unit. Its men were taller and presumably better physical specimens than those of other units, and its ranks in peacetime

[119] Ditfurth, *Das Leibgarde-Regiment*, pp. 5–6.
[120] StaMarburg 12. nr. 8310, Kriegspfennigzahlamt (1775), fol. 234; 12. nr. 212, Rangier Rollen vom Gren: Regiment Rall; StaHannover 41 v Nr. 24, Bremer to Sporken, 9 April 1776.
[121] SP81/183, Faucitt to Suffolk, 12 April 1776.
[122] *Allgemeine Deutsche Biographie*, XXVII, pp. 191–3; StaMarburg 4h.409. nr. 2, Relationes vom Russ.-Turk. Krieg.

were nearer full strength.[123] Its colonel, Friedrich Wilhelm von Wurmb, was one of the best Hessian officers. Major Frederick Mackenzie of the Royal Welch Fusiliers wrote in June 1781, '[Wurmb] is clear headed and cool. He serves with zeal, and is attentive only to establish his Character as a Soldier and an honest man. The Regiment he commanded last is the best disciplined in the Hessian Corps.'[124]

The young soldiers of the second division drew no such encomiums, however. Garrison regiments were Hessian militia, who assembled each year for four weeks between sowing and hay harvest to exercise, first in companies and then as complete regiments. They were in no sense professional soldiers. Their weapons were kept in a *Waffensaal* in each village and hamlet, ready to be issued in peacetime, for they served as a local police against disorders. In wartime they were intended for home defence or, as their name indicates, garrison duties.[125] Their officers were elderly regulars, in large part men promoted from the ranks. Their NCOs were drawn from dragoon regiments remaining in Hessen and from field regiments. The private soldiers were raw farm lads, and their training in the frenzied weeks before they set off for America was hindered by the continual introduction of new men. The Landgraf had ordered the chiefs of garrison regiments to discharge all their *unabkömmlich*: those with farms of their own, skilled metal workers and miners, sons of widows, students, and others. There were many more of these in the garrison than field regiments, and each one discharged had to be replaced with a new draftee. The new men hindered the rest in the exercises already learnt. The garrison troops were not actually able to fire with live cartridges until 19 and 20 March, a month after they had been brought together and only some six weeks before they set off for America.[126]

On the march through Hannover they were drilled at every opportunity. Unlike the troops of the first division, amongst these young soldiers the Hannoverians noted a reluctance to depart for America. General von Wangenheim reported, 'the troops of this division are nearly all children; I am astonished to see them so

---

[123] StaMarburg 12. nr. 296, Rang-Liste Leib Infanterie Regiment.
[124] Frederick Mackenzie, *The Diary of . . . as an Officer of the Regiment of Royal Welch Fusiliers during the years 1775–1781* (2 vols. Cambridge, Mass., 1930), II, p. 551.
[125] Ditfurth, *Die Hessen in der Champagne*, p. 6; Günderode, *Briefe eines Reisenden*, pp. 153 and 159.
[126] StaMarburg 12.11 I Ba 16 (Journal of the Grenadier Battalion Platte), fols. 2–3.

small and so young; and there is a great difference ... from the officers and men of the other regiments of the first division however small they may have been'. Only Wutginau's, a field regiment, was composed of fully grown men.[127] Faucitt noted that there was hardly an individual amongst them who appeared to be above seventeen or eighteen years, but he insisted that they were 'stout, bony [sic], and well put together. Lads answering this description would not be refused in any service; to which I must add that they were all the Landgrave's own subjects also, and on that account less liable to objection.'[128] Their good behaviour on the march, however, was at least equal to the first division's. There was no misconduct whatsoever, except when an officer of Wissenbach's regiment treated a Hannoverian subject in Cadenburg with violence, whereupon Knyphausen energetically punished the offender. There was even less desertion than in the first division.[129]

The three artillery companies were also recruited specifically for the American expedition, their numbers filled only with some difficulty. They drew their men from towns like Kassel and Marburg, where there were fewer poor labourers available as recruits than in the countryside. Lieutenant General von Gohr requested that men on furlough from the dragoon regiments in the country be taken to complete the artillery. Friedrich insisted that Gohr discharge propertied gunners in exchange for *abkömmlich* and volunteers.[130]

The two *Jäger* companies were recruited from foresters and huntsmen, attracted by extra pay and bounties.[131] Their individual fieldcraft and marksmanship were reckoned to be of special importance in America. They were distinguished by wearing green uniforms to blend into the woods, the rest of the Hessian corps wearing dark blue with regimental facings.

---

[127] StaHannover 41 v Nr. 24, Niemeyer to Sporken, 12 and 15 May 1776; ibid, Walthausen's report, 19 Feb. 1776.

[128] SP81/186, Faucitt to Suffolk (Private), 22 Jan. 1777. The second of two letters of the same date, Faucitt's defence against criticisms made of his reports on the troops in 1776. Clearly the British did not obtain in this second division the trained professionals they had bargained for. The descriptions of these troops also contradicts the view, held by Trevelyan and others, that homespun American farmers defended themselves against legions of pipeclayed mercenaries. It was more a case of two bodies of agriculturalists, albeit from very different societies, facing one another.

[129] StaHannover 41 v Nr. 30, fols. 14, 21, and 31, Wangenheim's report, 12 May 1776; Niemeyer to Sporken, 15 and 22 May.

[130] StaMarburg 13 Acc: 1930/5 Nr. 891, fols. 9 and 10–11, Gohr to the Landgraf, 8 March 1776, and the reply, 9 March.

[131] Ferdinand Zwenger, 'Johann Ewald in hessischen Dienst', *Hessenland*, VII (1893), pp. 159–60.

The Hessians

Two engineers, Captains Pauli and Martin, served on the Hessian staff. There was no corps of sappers in the modern sense. Pauli was also chief of one of the artillery companies, but as his men were dispersed amongst the battalions under subaltern officers, he had no one to command. When Captain Martin died on campaign in America, Lt. de Girancourt was transferred from the artillery to take his place. Map making was an art rather widely practised in the Hessian corps, judging by the excellent maps left by Lieutenant Andreas Wiederholdt of Knyphausen's regiment.

The Hessian officers who commanded the corps were not drawn solely from the aristocracy. The Hessian nobility was too small to officer such a large force, and except in the Guards the majority of officers were commoners: in 1779 there were 174 aristocrats and 294 commoners.[132] There was also considerable promotion from the ranks. Of 150 new officers to fill out the corps, twenty-six were former soldiers, and others had been promoted in the past for distinguished conduct in the field. Lieutenant Colonel Hillebrand, second-in-command of the Garrison Regiment von Huyn, had been promoted from corporal to lieutenant by order of Wilhelm VIII for gallantry at Roermond in 1758. He had also been awarded twenty pistoles from the *Feldkriegskasse* to kit himself out as an officer.[133] Major Hinte of the Regiment von Donop, a Pomeranian, had entered Hessian service in 1741 as a sergeant.[134] Even the ennobling 'von' was not a true index of a man's origins: Lieutenant Colonel von Porbeck of Wissenbach's had been ennobled only in 1771 after long service.[135]

There were also *Freikorporals*, potential officers in today's terminology. In each company except the grenadiers an able youth selected for future promotion served in the ranks for three years, carrying the company ensign in battle, and was advanced to commissioned rank at the end of that period only if he proved worthy. In his first three months a Freikorporal would do guard duties with the private soldiers before becoming an NCO, thus learning drill and discipline. The regimental rolls show the Freikorporal was often the son of the company chief, Hillebrand's own son Carl serving in his father's company; but even this did not

---

[132] Carl Preser, 'Der angebliche Verkauf der Hessen nach Amerika', *Allgemeine Militär-Zeitung*, XLV (1890), p. 459.

[133] *Mitteilungen* (1885), pp. 59–60.

[134] Friedrich Wilhelm Strieder, *Grundlage zu einer hessischen Gelehrten und Schriftsteller Geschichte* (18 vols. Kassel, 1781–1819), XVIII, p. 434.

[135] Ibid, XVII, p. 33n.

guarantee promotion at the end of three years.[136] Considering that Carl Hillebrand was only thirteen years old and Georg von Langenscharz who went to America as Freikorporal of his father's company in the Garrison Regiment von Stein was only eleven, it is hardly surprising that the Landgraf wrote Heister a peremptory letter in May 1777, ordering that 'children' who could be of no use to their regiments were not to be promoted to officer rank.[137]

The officers were a mixture of coarseness and culture. Their training was mainly practical, and not until the period of the French revolutionary wars, when the Hessians were foremost in Germany in elaborating new tactical experiences into theory,[138] was there any serious study of the profession. Adam Ludwig Ochs, a brilliant Hessian leader who began his service in the American war, later wrote:

I remember still that in my early youth the officer class was distinguished by rough manners and a conduct that obliged one to tell funny tales or even wild escapades, in order to imply the very worst. Who could last longest at a drinking bout, who showed the most duelling cuts and had beaten the night watchman or some poor apprentice lad, was held to be a fine fellow, and whoever had cheated a Jew, was considered a genius. Cleverness and knowledge were almost entirely foreign, and should there be found here or there such a fellow, he had to conceal his studies and often swim with the stream. All these things were the former fashion of the time, lack of a better upbringing, and in part a mistaken ambition to distinguish oneself as a soldier in some particular way and to raise oneself above one's fellow men. Thanks be to Heaven and the good example of today, that this fashion has completely changed.[139]

Friedrich II, however, by introducing his officers to his court with its French etiquette, and by founding a cadet corps in 1778, had already begun to change boorishness into refinement.[140] More of the officers were being educated, by 1771 sixty-one officers, cadets, and Freikorporals studying languages, mathematics, and engineering under Jakob Mauvillon and others were at the *Collegium Carolinum* in Kassel.[141] Those going to America included men like

---

[136] W. Grotefend, 'Die Ergänzung des hessisches Offizierkorps zur Zeit Friedrichs II', *Hessenland*, XIV (1900), p. 3; StaMarburg 12. nr. 831, Rang-Liste vom Regiment von Huyn.

[137] StMarburg 4h.410. nr. 1, fol. 501, 13 May 1777.

[138] Peter Paret, *Yorck and the Era of Prussian Reform 1807–1815* (Princeton, 1966), p. 82.

[139] Ochs, 'Das hessische Militär', p. 24. Duelling was actually forbidden by the Landgraf, but two officers died in affrays in 1776, both causing inquiries to be held.

[140] Müller, *Sämmtliche Werke*, V, pp. 39 and 55; XIV, p. 186.

[141] Freiherr von Dalwigk zu Lichtenfels, *Geschichte der Waldeckischen und Kurhessischen Stammtruppen des Infanterie-Regiment von Wittich (3. Kurhessisches) Nr. 83 1681–1866* (Oldenburg, 1909), p. 336.

Captain August Eberhard von Dinklage of the Leib-Regiment, who was acqainted with Ossian and whose hobbies included anthropology and palaeontology.[142] Captain-Lieutenant Karl Ludwig von Dörnberg enlivened his journal with citation from Horace.[143] One young man joined the Hessian corps going to America to further his education. Bernard Wilhelm Wiederholdt, educated in law, mathematics, and languages at the *Collegium Carolinum*, had taken a clerk's position at the *Kriegs und Domänenkammer* after family difficulties – his father, a minor official in the Landgraf's lottery, had been caught dipping into the funds – obliged him to support his family, found this too dull.

> The career which I had entered upon seemed to me not quite fitted to my studies. I sought an opportunity to give them a better course, and found it in the outbreak of the American War. As I could not doubt, in consequence of this war, to open up for myself the chance of much greater activity in pursuing my studies and my knowledge of affairs; and I hoped, besides fulfilling my wishes in such a satisfactory manner, to acquire practice in war and knowledge of lands, peoples, and the world. So straight away I exchanged the pen for the sword, and became in 1776 an ensign in the Hessian Leib-Regiment.[144]

Both Adam Ludwig Ochs and Friedrich von der Lith also dropped their pens for a chance of adventure in the new world, the former leaving his theological studies to serve the *Jäger* as a *Fourier* in 1777, the latter giving up Mallebranche and Locke to join the Leib-Regiment in 1778.[145]

The officers greeted the war with enthusiasm. They were indifferent to the political issues and longing for active service. Cornet Carl Levin von Heister, son of the Hessian corps commander designate, and in his father's dragoon regiment – 'Disconsolate that I, because no cavalry were taking part in the expedition, was damned to rot yet longer in a tiny little town' – eagerly sought a place as an ADC.[146] Slow promotion and poverty combined with the boredom of garrison life to make the American expedition, despite its uncertainty and long sea voyage, very attractive. Friedrike von Wurmb, a Hessian noblewoman living in France, hearing that her brother Carl of Mirbach's regiment was

---

[142] Dinklage, fols. 5, 121, 179–80, and 188.

[143] Karl Ludwig von Dörnberg, *Tagebuchblätter eines hessischen Offiziers aus der Zeit der nordamerikanischen Unabhängigkeits-krieg* (2 vols. Pyritz, 1899–1900), I, p. 8.

[144] Strieder, *Hessischen Gelehrten Geschichte*, XVII, pp. 32–3.

[145] Ibid, XVIII, pp. 347–8 and 421.

[146] Carl Levin von Heister, 'Auszüge Aus dem Tagebuch eines vormaligen kurhessischen Offiziers üver den Nordamerikanischen Freiheitskriege, 1776 und 1777', *Zeitschrift für Kunst, Wissenschaft, und Geschichte des Krieges*, III (1828), pp. 224–5.

off to America, wrote with pleasure for his sake: 'When one in his profession advances so slowly as he does, one may neglect no opportunity to speed one's promotion. Besides, he is a pretty fellow and perhaps will find a wealthy wife over there: that is hardly a rare thing in that country.'[147]

Carl von Wurmb's promotion was no slower than that of other subalterns in the Hessian regiments. The officers of the Regiment von Knyphausen at Ziegenhain were considerably older than one would expect of an active service unit: excluding their chief, Knyphausen, of twenty-three combatant officers in April 1775, one was in his fifties, eight were in their forties, seven in their thirties, and only seven in their twenties. Among the subalterns Lieutenant Andreas Wiederholdt, described by one misinformed American historian as 'an intelligent and conceited young man',[148] was aged forty-three years six months and had twenty-four years service. He had been promoted from sergeant major in 1760, and had distinguished himself in an outpost fight near Kassel in 1762, without gaining further promotion.[149] Besides the aging subalterns, the Regimental Surgeon, Pausch, was forty-five and one of his mates, forty; Quartermaster Müller was fifty-two and had served thirty-one years.[150] Subalterns in the garrison regiments, recently promoted from the ranks, included such elderly figures as 2nd Lieutenant Claudius Flueck of Huyn's regiment, fifty-eight with thirty-seven years service, and 2nd Lieutenant Wilhelm Stippich of Wissenbach's, over sixty.[151] Certainly the Hessian officer corps, compared to the British or American, counted many years of valuable training experience in its junior ranks, but the age of many left them frail victims to sickness and hardship.

This age difference applied to generals as well as subalterns: Heister and Knyphausen, the Hessian divisional commanders, were both about sixty in 1776; Howe was fifty-two, Clinton and Cornwallis both thirty-eight, and Washington forty-four.

[147] C. M. von Hammer, *Friederike von Wurmb: ein Zeit- und Lebensbild vom Rokoko bis zu Napoleons Tagen* (Munich, 1929), p. 134.

[148] Leonard Lundin, *Cockpit of the Revolution: the War for Independence in New Jersey* (Princeton, 1940), p. 195.

[149] Information left by *Zolldirektor* August Woringer in the Murhardsche Bibliothek in Kassel; Ewald, *Belehrungen*, III, p. 130.

[150] StaMarburg 11. nr. 398.

[151] Ibid, 12. nrs. 831 and 858. Most of these elderly officers sought their release during the American war, Stippich, for example, in May 1778, then aged sixty-three with forty-four years service, submitting a testimonial of his inability to carry out his duties, requesting retirement and a pension. These were granted. Ibid, 4h.410. nr. 2, fol. 262.

The excellent pay in British service and the additional allowance of forage money, as well as America's reputation as a land where fortunes were made, increased the officers' eagerness to sail. Most were in financial straits. Heister took up his command, in his own words, 'with glad spirit', but pointing out his advanced age and many wounds surmised that he might not survive the new campaign and that his family, without means, would have to depend on charity. His representations did not fail to have their effect on the Landgraf, who promised a pension of 1,200 talers for his family in his absence and after his death, should he fall, and promised to pay his debts, said to amount to 6,000 or 8,000 talers. He was also shrewd enough to demand and receive a similar corp commander's allowance as the Prince of Ysenburg, who had taken the last Hessian corps abroad in English pay in 1756.[152] Knyphausen too, reminding his sovereign of the ardours of his making a campaign in his sixtieth year, asked for an allowance to purchase his kit and a pension for his wife, who could not possibly subsist in his absence with their trifling means.[153]

The senior officers of course had households and appearances to keep up, but they had the advantage of higher incomes from their posts as regimental and company chiefs. The distress of the junior officers was at least as great. Captain Johann Ewald wrote of low pay and debts contracted in peacetime in the 1770s. He often went to bed hungry and in winter had to forego a fire in his stove. Yet there was great esprit de corps amongst the officers, and Wurmb, Motz, Le Long and others often shared their ha'pennies with him in times of need.[154]

The infantry manual shows the problem to have been a considerable one. Officers were warned to live on their pay if they had no independent incomes. If an officer contracted a debt of more than eight talers, he was to be arrested and to do guard duty until the debt was paid off. The amount of the debt was to be paid, not to the creditor, but to the Karlshafen Military Hospital. The creditor himself was to be arrested and punished, since lending money to officers without the regimental chief's permission was an

---

[152] Gerland, 'Kasseler Tagesneuigkeiten', *Hessenland*, VII (1893), p. 71; StaMarburg 4h.410. nr. 1, fols. 10–11, Heister to the Landgraf, 23 Jan. 1776. Du Ry's gossipy letter may have exaggerated the old general's debts. His allowance was 741½ talers while on German soil, £180 monthly in British pay.

[153] StaMarburg 4h.410. nr. 1, fols. 12–13, Knyphausen to the Landgraf, 31 Jan. 1776.

[154] Zwenger, 'Johann Ewald in hessischen Dienst', *Hessenland*, VII (1893), p. 158. Ewald was then in the Leib-Regiment, the names he mentions were his fellow officers.

offence. The severity of the warning indicates that such debts were not uncommon.[155]

In a military drawn from such a small state, the officer corps was a closely knit one. The same names – Wurmb, Donop, Bardeleben, Buttlar, Eschwege – occur repeatedly on the regimental rolls. Sons followed fathers in their regiments, and married daughters of their father's military friends; for example, in the corps that went to America the Adjutant General, Baurmeister, counted a cousin, a nephew, and a brother-in-law.[156] This inbreeding was mitigated by the number of 'foreigners' who joined the Hessians: Colonel von Borck of Knyphausen's regiment was a Pomeranian, Captain Friedrich von Stamford of English stock came from Nassau-Saarbrucken, Ensign Friedrich von der Lith was from Ansbach, the Marquis d'Angelelli of Bologna transferred from Prussian service, and Captain Maximilian Michael O'Reilly was born in Dublin and like many Irish soldiers had been with the Austrians at Prague, Breslau, Hochkirchen. Under Friedrich II a good number of Frenchmen also took service. What they all seemed to have shared was an eagerness to go to war and make their fortunes. Fortunately, their prince was not averse to these aspirations. To Knyphausen he wrote in 1778 that, although he did not want officers abandoning the American campaign, if they had an opportunity of making a favourable marriage and their fortunes either in Germany or America, he would look favourably on requests for discharge.[157]

The first division to a strength of 8,647 was embarked by 12 April. Twenty-four deserters were recorded, but according to the Hannoverians there were a few more whose places had been made good by the supernumeraries carried by all Hessian regiments. The embarkation returns show that eleven had been recaptured or replaced, either by supernumeraries or by recruiting en route. The Lossbergers, had picked up a number including Johann Goebel, a Swede from Stockholm.[158]

---

[155] *Reglement vor die hessische Infanterie* (Kassel, 1767), p. 652. In peacetime an ensign's pay was 7 talers a month, a captain-lieutenant's 12, a lieutenant general's 50; however, prices in Hessen were low: 2 lb of bread cost 1 albus, 1 lb of beef 2 albus and 2 heller, 1 lb of pork 2 albus (1 taler = 32 albus, 1 albus = 12 heller. All prices 1767). Ditfurth, *Die Hessen in der Champagne*, p. 6; Both and Vogel, *Landgraf Friedrich II*, p. 124.

[156] Carl L. Baurmeister, *Revolution in America: Confidential Letters and Journals 1776–1784*, Bernard A. Uhlendorf, ed. and trans. (2nd edn, Westport, Conn., 1973), pp. 76 n. 82, 127, and 202 n. 68.

[157] StaMarburg 4h.410 nr. 2, fol. 249, 18 June 1778.

[158] Ibid, nr. 1, fol. 95. The return for the first division is in ibid, fol. 157, that for the second in SP81/185, dated 6 June 1776.

The second division numbering 4,327 was embarked on 6 June. Thus a total of 12,974 Hessians entered British service in 1776. The regiments were permitted to take six wives per company,[159] the numbers averaging about twenty per battalion. Despite .expectations of a rapid victory, some men had a premonition that they would be away a long time, and to secure female companionship in the perils ahead they quickly married before their regiments' departure.[160]

THE CROSSING TO AMERICA

The British made every effort to keep their auxiliaries comfortable and in good health on the voyage to America. A corps weakened and decimated by disease would be neither willing nor able to engage in the campaign which the King hoped would strike the rebellion its death blow. Because the total number embarked exceeded what was expected, the transports at Bremerlehe were insufficient to provide the allotted two tons per man, and there was some crowding. This was alleviated en route at Portsmouth, nearly every battalion receiving an extra ship.[161] Suffolk assured Heister, much concerned for his men on an unknown voyage, that the troops would be well provided for and have sufficient space for the Atlantic crossing.[162] Schlieffen and Colonel Sir George Osborne of the Guards, appointed muster-master to the Hessians, travelled around the fleet at Portsmouth on 28 April to see that the men were properly victualled and accommodated.[163] The battalions were issued with fresh meat to sweeten their tempers for the long sea voyage.[164]

Most of the journals, kept by officers, were unstinting in praise of the care taken for the Hessians' transportation. Friedrich Maurer, surgeon of the Regiment von Trumbach, wrote to his family that his cabin, although not large, was fine and comfortable. He and the Quartermaster slept soundly in hammocks, and his friend

---

[159] LB Kassel 2° Ms. hass. 247, Aktenstücke der Brigade von Mirbach, fol. 98, the Landgraf to Mirbach, 20 Jan. 2776.

[160] Kümmel, fol. 3. To help him deal with the problems of his new flock, Pastor Kümmel, who had been specially ordained with five colleagues for service with the Hessian corps, purchased a copy of Sterne's 'Inquiry into Human Nature'.

[161] StaMarburg 12.11 I Ba 5 (Journal of the Regiment von Donop), fols. 7–8; Bardeleben, p. 29; Dinklage, fols. 30–1.

[162] StaMarburg 4h.410. nr. 1, fol. 272, 28 April 1776.

[163] Dinklage, fol. 30.

[164] StaMarburg 12.11 I Ba 6 (Journal of the Regiment von Knyphausen), fol. 7.

Lieutenant Hoepfner in the neighbouring bunk was so bemused by this that he rocked Maurer to sleep as a diversion. The battalion commander, Colonel von Bischhausen, was pleased with the state of the men and the food.[165] The rations were good, at least until the food went 'off': four pounds of bread and four pints of beer per day shared amongst six men, and a varied diet of beef twice a week, pork and pease twice a week, oatmeal, flour, cheese, and raisins. A kettle was provided for cooking, and a large linen bag and cooking fat to make suet pudding, regarded as a treat by the sailors. Grenadier Reuber thought the food coarse but nourishing, Sunday being a good day when beef as well as pudding was issued.[166] For sleeping each man received a mattress and pillow stuffed with wool and two blankets. Weather permitting, these were aired on deck each morning. The ships were cleaned periodically with vinegar as an antiscorbutic. Strict regulations were enforced: no smoking below decks, no gambling, no hoarding or selling liquor.[167] Whenever possible the companies exercised on deck.

For use in America the Ordnance Department supplied blankets, watch coats, harnesses for packhorses, scythes with whetstones, water carriers and forage cords.[168] At Faucitt's suggestion all Hessian personnel were allowed to send letters home without charge provided they were marked 'Bureau General des Postes à London'. This gave the British an opportunity to spy on the mail and check the morale of their auxiliaries.[169]

The fleet left Bremerlehe on 16 April, reaching Portsmouth ten days later. It sailed again on 6 May, carrying a detachment of the British Guards as well as Hessians, in the hope of reaching America for the opening of the summer campaign. Howe was instructed to await their arrival before attacking New York.[170] But every effort made to hasten the Hessian first division to America was in vain. The voyage proved dismal and prolonged. Weather was mixed and

[165] Fritz Maurer, 'Brief eines Hessen aus der Zeit der englisch-nordamerikanischen Kriegs', *Hessenland*, XX (1906), pp. 48–50.

[166] Reuber, fols. 47–8.

[167] SP81/182, 'Orders and Instructions for a Regiment while on board ship', and 'General Instructions to be observed by troops at sea.' They turned their coats inside out to preserve their appearance from pitch and tar.

[168] The last item was for tying up bundles of hay and sticks. StaMarburg 4h.410. nr. 1, fol. 127, 30 Mar. 1776.

[169] StaMarburg 4h.410. nr. 1, fol. 151; SP81/181, Faucitt to Suffolk, March 4, 1776. See below, p. 110, n. 139

[170] CO5/93, fol. 119, Germain to Howe, 3 May 1776.

mostly unfavourable. A storm lasting from 26 to 30 May gave them their first taste of really bad weather. Approaching the Banks off Newfoundland on the night of 6/7 June, they encountered a fog so thick that a man could not see his hand before his face. On all the ships, bells rang and drums beat so that the fleet would stay together. Every half hour the commodore, Hotham, fired a cannon shot to be heard by stragglers. 'This unharmonic music, in a deeply gloomy night on the Ocean, made no pleasant impression on our hearing and spirits' wrote Dinklage.[171] On 22 June they were on the banks and saw a great quantity of sea birds of all varieties, swimming and flying, a school of whales spouting, and an iceberg. The next day they caught quantities of codfish, each one weighing fifteen to twenty pounds, a welcome addition to their diet.[172]

The transports were to have rendezvoused with Howe's army at Halifax, but Captain Sir George Collier in the *Rainbow* brought word on 7 July that Howe had landed on Staten Island and they were to steer for Sandy Hook.[173] The Hessians had to endure the last part of the voyage without taking on fresh water and provisions. By the end of July, the biscuits were rotting, the water foul, the beer at an end, the men had scurvy, the itch, and swollen legs. 'Heaven help us to see land soon', wrote Dinklage.[174] An uncontrollable host of rats ate the tents, uniforms, even cartridges, and especially the provisions. They gnawed their way through the casks.[175] The transports made their way only slowly in this part of the voyage, in calms and against contrary winds and currents.

In early August with no port in sight, tempers were wearing thin. On board the transport *Perry* a sailor threw a burning coal at a Hessian sentry; there was an altercation, and Major General Stirn administered fifteen strokes of the cane to the sailor. Commodore Hotham protested that a Hessian inflicted punishment on a British seaman. Heister replied that it was hardly surprising the men were at the end of their endurance:

it is easy to understand that a people like the Hessians, tired of being imprisoned for four or nearly five months (for there are some regiments amongst us who were

---

[171] Dinklage, fol. 58.
[172] Ibid, fols. 66–7.
[173] Heister, 'Tagebuch eines vormaligen kurhessischen Offiziers', p. 229.
[174] StaMarburg 4h.409. nr. 3, fol. 65; Dinklage, fol. 87.
[175] So reported Colonel Heringen. 'Einige Briefe aus dem amerikanischen Krieg', *Militär-Wochenblatt*, XVIII (1833), p. 4854.

embarked on March 23) and obliged to drink foul water and to eat mouldy biscuit and meat salted right through, without beer, cheese, and butter, cannot be in good humour.

The officers were impatient for the end of the voyage, having exhausted their personal food supplies and being obliged to share the common rations. The scurvy, the itch, and contagious fevers had taken hold among the companies on several vessels.[176]

Hotham wrote back, apologising for the length of the voyage, caused by the light airs and calms almost constant since Halifax.[177] Knowing the good humour of the mercenaries to be essential for the success of the coming campaign, he sent Heister refreshments with the personable captain of the *Rainbow*, Sir George Collier, to jolly the Hessian general along:

the Commodore [wrote Collier] beg'd of me to visit the old Veteran to comfort Him, which I did, having ordered a side of Mutton & some poultry to be put in the Boat, as I understand his fresh Provisions were exhausted – the old General receivd me in the Civilest manner he was capable of & obliged me to swallow repeated Potations of a very good Hock, to the Healths of our Sovereigns our Friends in Europe &c &c, this joind to the Musick of his Band which He called for exhilerated the old Gentleman's Spirits so much that He entirely forgot his Distresses, & Inconveniences & seemd perfectly Happy: I concluded my Visit rather sooner than I perhaps might have done fearing the Strength of his Hock which he pushed about without intermission.[178]

With libations and music, but also with considerable sickness, the Hessians completed their voyage. The day after Collier's visit they sighted Long Island, and on 12 August the weary transports anchored below Staten Island. Four vessels bearing a party under Colonel Block which had become separated had arrived four days earlier; and Major General Mirbach's detachment, left behind at Bremerlehe to await more shipping, made landfall at Sandy Hook the same day as the main party. They were received with the greatest consideration by the Howes, disembarked on 14 and 15 August, were given choice camp-sites and fresh beef. General Howe put a house at Heister's disposal for his own use.[179]

Landing did not ease the Hessians' sickness problems. After a

[176] StaMarburg 4h.410. nr. 1, fols. 352–3, 5 Aug. 1776.

[177] Ibid, fols. 354–5, Hotham to Heister, 5 Aug.

[178] National Maritime Museum, Greenwich. Journal 35. Ms. 0085, The Journal of Admiral Sir George Collier (pages unnumbered but this entry dated 23 Aug. 1776).

[179] StaMarburg 4h.409. nr. 3, fols. 70–2; 4h.410. nr. 1, fols. 347–50, Heister to the Landgraf, 15 Aug. 1776.

week ashore some seven to eight hundred men were down with fevers, diarrhoea and scurvy.[180] It is probable that in their weakened state the Hessians suffered from an overindulgence in unripe fruit, there being great quantities of apple trees on Staten Island.[181] And without baggage animals and carts, they exhausted themselves dragging their gear from landing beaches to camp-sites, and thence to new camp-sites on the island's far side. Stirn's brigade had to convey their impedimenta some seventeen miles on 19 August, and sick Hessians were lying along the whole route. Heister had to ask Howe for a reduction in their work load. The previous morning the troops had turned out at four o'clock, and stood five hours in pouring rain before the movement order was cancelled from lack of transport.[182] It was hardly surprising the sick rolls grew.

The second division's voyage was equally tedious and unpleasant. Sailing from Ritzebüttel[183] on 9 June, they were delayed in their arrival at Portsmouth by unfavourable winds until the 20th. They sailed again on 8 July accompanied by transports carrying the 16th Dragoons and the Waldeck Regiment. Captain Fielding in command of the convoy blamed the poor sailing of the Dutch and North German transports for the length of the voyage.[184] When the Hessians first caught sight of land on 16 October, Quartermaster Carl Bauer of Koehler's grenadiers wrote that it was doubtful 'if Columbus at the first glimpse of the New World had greater joy at his discovery than we did. To each man it seemed he had been given new life. The sick were brought forth from where they lay between decks to convince them of this new discovery.'[185]

Some fifteen men died in the crossing of the first division,[186] ten

---

[180] Collier's Journal. Collier asserts that there were only thirty sick when they landed, but every Hessian account refers to considerable illness before reaching land: 'the majority of people with scurvy or otherwise sick'. Bardeleben, p. 56, 11 Aug.

[181] E. H. Tatum, ed., *The American Journal of Ambrose Serle* (San Marino, Calif., 1940), p. 94.

[182] StaMarburg 4h.409. nr. 3, fol. 76; 4h.412. nr. 1 (Journal of the Regiment von Ditfurth), fols. 9–10.

[183] Ritzebüttel, belonging to the independent city of Hamburg, was advantageously situated on the south side of the mouth of the Elbe. Hamburg, which had a considerable trade with Britain, was only too happy to allow the embarkation of the second division to take place there. SP82/95, fols. 117 and 146–8, Mathias to Suffolk, 10 May and 11 June 1776.

[184] Fielding to Philip Stephens, 28 Oct. 1776, quoted in *Naval Records of the American Revolution*, William Ball Clark, ed. (7 vols. so far, Washington, DC, 1964–76), VI, p. 1439.

[185] StaMarburg 12.11 I Ba 16, fol. 87.

[186] According to the journal of MajGen. Mirbach's ADC, Lt. Schotten. L. von Danckelmann, 'Die Einschiffung und Überfahrt der hessischen Brigade von Mirbach nach Nordamerika in Jahre 1776', *Mitteilungen* (1881), part i, p. 2.

in the second, a larger proportion.[187] But at least these sons of Hessian farmers knew that comrades had gone before them, and had the satisfaction of hearing of a series of unbroken successes achieved before their landing.

[187] Ewald, 'Tagebuch', I, p. 6, quoted in Ernst Kipping, *Die Truppen von Hessen-Kassel im Amerikanischen Unabhängigkeitskrieg 1776–1783* (Darmstadt, 1965), p. 33. Sir George Osborne, however, reported the number of dead as 50, as did the Landgraf's minister Wittorf, writing to the Erbprinz of Hessen-Kassel. Possibly this included those who died shortly after landing and those of both divisions. CO5/93, Part III, fol. 501, Osborne to Germain, 29 Oct. 1776; StaMarburg 4h.413. nr. 4, fol. 54, Wittorf to the Erbprinz, 28 Dec. 1776.

3
The victories of 1776

Is it to be supposed that 50,000 men, composed of German mercenaries, Scotch jacobites, Irish papists, and the produce of your gaols, are to conquer America? are to subjugate three millions of free people, whose motto is 'Death or Liberty'?[1]

THE MERCENARIES ARRIVE

The German auxiliaries were an essential part of the British war plan for 1776. Without them the subjugation of the rebels would have been unthinkable.[2] And although British officers had spoken of the Americans in Parliament and elsewhere with contempt the opening of the war had not been auspicious for British arms. Lexington and Concord had revealed a deficiency in light infantry training, neglected since the last war.[3] After a costly victory on Breed's Hill, General William Howe's troops were hemmed within Boston; and the enemy's skilful occupation of Dorchester Heights commanding a part of Boston Harbour obliged Howe to evacuate the city. Rebel forces led by Montgomery and Arnold had taken all British posts in Canada save Quebec, and although an assault had been beaten off in a snowstorm early New Year's morn 1776, Sir Guy Carleton and his men remained beleaguered in the old city.[4] At the same time that the first Hessian division was slowly crossing the Atlantic, a blundering assault on Charleston by Clinton and commodore Peter Parker ended in dismal failure, leaving southern Loyalists isolated. Thoughtful officers like Clinton and Captain Frederick Mackenzie noted their army's shortcomings: badly trained, poorly disciplined,

---

[1] *The London Chronicle*, XL (1776), p. 48.
[2] Mackesy, *War for America*, p. 62.
[3] J. F. C. Fuller, *British Light Infantry in the Eighteenth Century* (London, 1925), p. 120.
[4] Although the Canadian expedition ended in failure and enormous losses for the Americans, the impression at the time in London and Berlin was that the rebels were within an inch of success, or had even taken Quebec. Mackesy, *War for America*, pp. 56–7; *Politische Correspondenz Friedrich's* XXXVII, pp. 309 and 489.

and ill led, many of the officers having no idea of their business.[5] At Breed's Hill, Clinton declared that never in thirty years in the army had he seen 'so great a want of order'.[6] Thus the arrival of the trained Hessians and Guards was looked for eagerly.[7]

The Americans had been informed by their agents and British sympathizers of the Hessians' impending arrival. As early as 30 September 1775, the *Constitutional Gazette* reported that 10,000 Hannoverians were to be recruited to repress the colonists, that they would be quartered at American expense, and after serving seven years in America would receive from twenty to fifty acres rent-free in perpetuity. So prolific were these Germans that by the year 1800 there would be no less than a million of them in the four New England provinces alone. The same paper reported more accurately in April and May 1776, that the ministry intended to have 17,000 Hessians, Brunswickers, Hannoverians and Waldeckers in America by spring; and that they had sent over to Germany to engage 1,000 men called *Jäger*, people brought up to the use of rifles in boar hunting. The ministry plumed themselves that the *Jäger* would be a complete match for American riflemen.[8]

America's British adherents advised that the Germans could easily be persuaded to desert, and Arthur Lee` reported from London on 7 April that, as the Landgraf of Hessen was a notoriously dishonest man, it was probable that the troops he furnished were the worst he had, so 'if proper offers are made to the Germans, they will desert in great numbers'. Congress began to implement such a plan in August.[9]

While American leaders looked on the Hessians with calculation, the local civilians regarded them with nothing less than sheer horror. The stories of Hannoverian military settlements in New England can have been only the tip of an iceberg of rumour and propaganda about the horrors of German mercenaries descending upon a defenceless people.[10] Numerous Hessian diarists later re-

[5] William B. Willcox, *Portrait of a General, Sir Henry Clinton in the War of Independence* (New York, 1964), pp. 80–1; Mackenzie, *Diary*, I, p. 92.

[6] Quoted in Willard M. Wallace, *Appeal to Arms: a Military History of the American Revolution* (New York, 1951), p. 42.

[7] Add. MS. 21680, fols. 115 and 139, Captain Francis Hutcheson to Frederick Haldimand, 27 May and 12 August 1776.

[8] Moore, *Diary of the Revolution*, I, pp. 144–5 and 233–4.

[9] *Naval Records of the American Revolution*, IV, p. 1020. See below, pp. 186–7.

[10] Philip Davidson, *Propaganda and the American Revolution 1763–1783* (Chapel Hill, 1941), p. 371.

ported with grim humour that the people saw them as cannibals who would eat up the little children.[11] On the other hand, the British encouraged Hessian animosity against the rebels, a task made easier by the Germans' unfriendly disposition toward a people who rebelled against their rightful king. With simplistic exactness, the Quartermaster of Lossberg's regiment summed up the political origins of the war in a single sentence: 'Because the inhabitants of North America, by the greatest rebellion, obliged their rightful sovereign, King George III of Great Britain, to take up arms against them, he engaged in English pay a corps of Hessian troops of 12,000 men.'[12] Even before embarkation, a Hannoverian officer reported, the Hessians hated the Americans and looked on them 'as people who had sneered at their German fatherland and through an excess of reason had thought to take advantage of their present king'. They were eager to match themselves against the rebels, with no doubts of the outcome. The Hannoverian, from his own observations, agreed with the Hessians.[13]

Before the battle of Long Island, the British told the Hessians to expect no quarter from the rebels. They were encouraged to be 'zealous for the service and inveterate against the rebels for the nameless cruelties our prisoners have experienced from them'. Ambrose Serle, Admiral Lord Howe's secretary, remarked that the injudicious abuse and menaces of the rebels against the Hessians, as well as the hope of plunder, 'have stimulated the Hessians to such a Degree, as by no means inclines them to shew Tenderness and Mercy'. American newspapers, with their exaggerated accounts of the brutality of these 'ugly devils', as they described the Hessians, hardly endeared the rebels to Britain's auxiliaries.[14]

While on Staten Island, however, the Hessians observed strict discipline, Heister on General Orders commanding his men to

---

[11] Kümmel, fol. 7; Dinklage, fol. 119; Karl Alexander, Freiherr Schenk zu Schweinsburg, 'Briefe eines hessischen Offiziers aus Amerika', *Hessenland*, XVI (1902), p. 292.

[12] StaMarburg 12.11 I Ba 2 (Journal of Lossberg's regiment), fol. 3.

[13] StaHannover 41 V Nr. 24, fol. 64, Bremer to Field Marshall Sporken, 9 April 1776.

[14] Heringen, 'Einige Briefe aus dem amerikanischen Krief', p. 4856; HMC: *Report on the MSS of His Grace the Duke of Rutland* (London, 1894), III, p. 6; Benjamin F. Stevens, ed., *Facsimiles of MSS. in European Archives Relating to America 1773–1783* (25 vols. London, 1889–1895), XXIV, nr. 2042. The reference to 'ugly devils' appeared in *Freeman's Journal*, 12 Nov. 1776. Moore, *Diary of the Revolution*, I, p. 327. American historians have noted the 'priming' of the Hessians by the British, for example Thomas W. Field, *The Battle of Long Island* (Brooklyn, 1869), p. 188. They have not so readily noted that their own newspapers served the same purpose.

look upon all inhabitants as loyal subjects of the crown.[15] Serle
heard with pleasure the Hessians' singing Psalms, and contrasted it
with the dissipated behaviour of his own army; but Lord Rawdon,
Clinton's ADC, remarked sardonically, 'They sing hymns as loud
as the Yankees, though it must be owned they have not the Godly
twang through the nose which distinguishes the faithful.' Rawdon
said the Hessians terrified the Americans, despised them, and were
eager to be at them. He expected a spirit of competition between
the two contingents, Hessian and British, to be beneficial for the
service.[16]

Within a week of landing, the Hessians were stricken with fevers,
diarrhoea, and scurvy, and Heister wanted to rest his corps. Howe
and his men were eager for action, however, and the precious
summer months were slipping by. Despite illness many Hessians
shared their eagerness. As soon as they were able the battalions
began drilling for imminent battle. They were instructed to form
line two deep rather than three, as better suited to American
conditions, and to adopt a looser order; the officers were to remove
their marks of distinction, which served as aiming points for
American riflemen, an instruction that was ignored in some battalions as a point of honour.[17] On 16 August the *Jäger* manoeuvred
before Howe using two *amusettes*, light guns specially provided by
the British.[18]

In Heister the British had already found a ticklish customer.
Having bought the Hessians' services at great expense, they not
unnaturally expected a return for their wages. British treatment of
the Hessians smacks of double-dealing on more than one occasion.
Suffolk, fearful that the Hessian generals would be too careful of
the preservation of their corps, asked Faucitt to offer Heister and
Knyphausen what was in effect a bribe if they finished the business
quickly. Faucitt was to assure them of the reliance which they
could place in the King's munificence, 'if they conduct the service
on which they are employed in a manner equal to His Majesty's
expectations, and do not suffer it to be impeded and interrupted
either by a partial and improper regard for the preservation of the
troops which they command, or by idle jealousies of each other and
of the British Commanders, or by a punctilious observation to the

[15] StaMarburg 4h.410 nr. 1, fol. 364, 16 Aug. 1776.
[16] Serle, *Journal*, p. 56; HMC: *Report on the MSS. of the late Reginald Rawdon Hastings* (London,
1934), III, pp. 169 and 176.
[17] Bardeleben, p. 58; Malsburg, fol. 44.
[18] StaMarburg 4h.409. nr. 3, fol. 73.

innumerable little points of etiquette which are always liable to arise, but are always easy to be avoided, if there is a disposition to avoid them.' Such marks of esteem were only '*to take place at the successful close of the business*'.[19] To their credit both Heister and Knyphausen refused to be tempted: Heister asked that any mark of royal approbation be transferred to his wife and numerous off-spring, Knyphausen replied with polite nothings.[20]

William Howe saw the Hessian generals as an incumbrance. He had written to Germain that it would have been much better to have had the troops with their captains and subalterns only and to attach them to the British corps. 'We must endeavour to gain all the Service we can from Troops, who, having but a relative interest in the cause, may be too apt to use their every means consistent with the Letter of their Engagements to avoid the Loss of Men.'[21] This suggestion, showing that Howe's expectation of Hessian hindrance was even greater than Suffolk's, completely ignored the esprit de corps in the Hessian battalions and the probable unwillingness of juniors to serve under foreigners instead of the commanders they knew and trusted.[22]

Howe's conviction that the Hessians were trying to avoid close combat became stronger as events proceeded. In the same letter he asked for the local rank of colonel for senior British lieutenant-colonels, to avoid the risk of their being commanded by foreigners.

Germain replied soothingly that the favourable reports he had had of the Hessian officers (from Faucitt via Suffolk) gave him every reason to expect that Howe would find them so well disposed to the service that there would be no call for the desired promotion, particularly as it might introduce jealousy and unrest among officers favourably disposed to the British cause.[23] Faucitt's reports on the Hessian commanders were forwarded by Germain to Howe, the latter promising to make good use of the information.[24]

Faucitt described Heister as near sixty years of age, of cheerful disposition, healthy and active. As for personal bravery, the

---

[19] SP81/182, Suffolk to Faucitt, 12 Feb. 1776 (Private and Secret). Original italics.
[20] SP81/183, Faucitt to Suffolk, 25 March 1776 (Private); SP81/185, Faucitt to Suffolk, 21 June 1776. See also Kapp, *Soldatenhandel*, p. 212. The Brunswicker, Riedesel, received a similar offer.
[21] CO5/93. Part I, fol. 140, 25 April 1776.
[22] For example, see Lt. v. Bardeleben's remarks on the kindnesses of his LtCol, Carl Philipp Heymel. Bardeleben, p. 20. Some of the younger officers, particularly Freikorporals, were serving in their fathers' battalions.
[23] CO5/93, Part II, fol. 183, Germain to Howe, 11 June 1776.
[24] Ibid, fol. 212, Howe to Germain, 8 June 1776.

Landgraf could not have picked an officer more distinguished for intrepid behaviour on various occasions. He had been wounded so often as to be quite lame in one leg. But his military intelligence was less impressive:

> I have heard no incomiums [sic] bestowed upon his military genius and talents: his particular Friends ... are silent upon that head ... The plan of operations in general, or any enterprise in particular ... must be fairly and clearly chalked down to him beforehand; so that little, or nothing, may remain with him but simply to see that the same is carried into execution.

Obviously no Marlborough or Frederick. He was also inclined to be vain of his experience and long service, and would expect to be treated with deference and attention. Faucitt recommended that the British commander follow 'the policy of offering up a little incense of this kind'.[25]

Heister had already proved difficult at Portsmouth, declining to sail with the main body of the first division until a detachment under Major-General von Mirbach, left behind at Bremerlehe, should catch up. He cited his sovereign's instructions that he should not allow the corps to become separated, and visits from Schlieffen, General Harvey, the adjutant general, and Colonel Sir George Osborne, muster-master to the Hessians, failed to move him until he received a direct order from the King. To the British, when every moment counted if the rebellion were to be crushed, this pettifogging attention to the letter of his instructions was maddening. Well might Osborne remark that Heister seemed 'obstinate and tenacious whenever his resolution is fixed'.[26]

Thus when Heister arrived off Sandy Hook, tired and dispirited from his voyage, the Howes and their entourage showed every kindness and consideration. Ambrose Serle wrote that the Hessian

---

[25] SP81/182, Faucitt to Suffolk, 1 Feb. 1776. Heister had been keen to serve, but because he spoke neither English nor French, it was suggested that Jakob Mauvillon, the military teacher and physiocrat at the *Collegium Carolinum*, be sent as his secretary. Mauvillon agreed if they would pay him 400 talers and his wife a pension of 330 talers in his absence. This was accepted, but then he went on to demand a place on the council of war, and that military operations should be carried out according to his plans. This proposal was laughed out of court, and Mauvillon, who had already defended the American position before independence was declared, missed his chance to go to America. He still fought the Americans in one sense: many of the young officers he trained went to America. See the letter of du Ry, the Landgrave's architect, in Gerland, 'Kasseler Tagesneuigkeiten aus dem 18. Jahrhundert', *Hessenland*, VII, pp. 71–2. Schlieffen was another candidate for the corps command, but was sent instead to London to coordinate the troops' movement.

[26] CO5/93, Part II, fol. 422, Osborne to Germain, 29 April 1776. The correspondence dealing with this contretemps is in ibid, fols. 418–22 and StaMarburg 4h.410. nr. 1, fols. 259–73.

commander and his fellows 'have been treated with the greatest
Deference, which (as might be expected with Germans) has made a
pleasing Impression upon their Temper and Conduct, and inclined
them as heartily in the Cause as the warmest among us could
desire'. Both Heister and Donop noted that Howe took all possible
pains to make their stay in America agreeable.[27] Heister told
Howe, nevertheless, that it was necessary to disembark all his men
as quickly as possible and rest them because of the sickness and
complaints of the voyage. The British Guards by contrast refused
to land, eager to be at the enemy.[28]

General Howe expressed great concern for Heister's sufferings,
and begged him to come ashore immediately and refresh his troops.
The best camp-sites were provided for the Hessians and fresh
provisions issued. This put Heister in good humour. Howe waited
on him repeatedly with offers of refreshment for the officers and
beef for the men, in the meantime giving orders for the crossing to
Long Island. Howe knew that, although Heister might be difficult
and the major-generals men of moderate capacity, he could expect
good service from the colonels: Lossberg, Bose, Wurmb, Loos, and
especially from Donop, Rall, and Minnigerode, the last three in
particular having not only served, but also distinguished themselves in the last war.[29] As preparations for the British descent on
Long Island went ahead, Heister, fearful of being left behind, came
to Howe and said the Hessians would soon be ready to march and
did not want to be left behind. Howe applauded his spirit, and by
flattery and by expressing fears that the Hessians were not sufficiently recovered, got Heister in perfect good humour and eager
for the enterprise.[30]

On 22 August the advanced corps of the army, 4,000 strong,
crossed to Long Island on specially constructed flatboats, covered
by small ships of the line, frigates, and bombs. With them went
Donop's *Jäger* and grenadiers, 'with muskets sloped and in column
of march; preserving the well-considered pomp of German discip-

---

[27] Stevens, *Facsimiles*, XXIV, nr. 2042, 5 Sept. 1776; StaMarburg 4h.410. nr. 1, fol. 363,
Heister to the Landgrave, 3 Sept. 1776; Huth, 'Letters from a Mercenary', p. 493.

[28] StaMarburg 4h.409. nr. 3, fol. 70, 13 Aug. 1776; Bedford Record Office, Lucas Collection
L29/213. The following account relies mainly on this item and the journal of Heister's
corps.

[29] SP81/183, Faucitt to Suffolk, 9 April 1776.

[30] Such was the account given by Germain in a later breakfast conversation. The journal of
Heister's corps supports it in most details, but the Lucas account says the British crossed
to Long Island followed later by the Hessians. In fact, Donop crossed with the advance
corps, and it is unlikely he would have done so without Heister's approval. Bedford
Record Office, Lucas Collection L29/213; StaMarburg 4h.409. nr. 3, fols. 70–80.

line on that salt water which few of them had ever smelt until they obtained manhood'.[31] The American picquet under Colonel Edward Hand withdrew, burning crops. The bulk of the British army followed that day, and Donop pushed forward with *Jäger* and light infantry to occupy the village of Flatbush. A sharp skirmish ensued the following day between the *Jäger* and American riflemen, who burnt houses on the edge of the village.[32] Captain Max O'Reilly of Block's battalion described the Hessians' first action:

> The whole coast was held by the fearful riflemen, to a strength of about 3,000 men. They have rifles, generally like the German, but of an extraordinary length; for 40 hours they fired on us, and Donop's *Jäger* crept about through the fields like Croats on their bellies. More than 2,000 shots, which they fired, had simply the effect of wounding 12 of our people and killing one *Jäger* ... Our battalion lay behind a hedge, in the hope of drawing them out into the open, but No! it did not come to a fight, and Minnigerode's battalion relieved us.... You can well imagine how our Hessian grenadiers gnash their teeth with eagerness, because they cannot rush on these rascals ... Day and night we heard nothing but the rifle fire from the immense forests, which lay like a half moon facing our camp and the English.[33]

On 25 August Heister landed with Mirbach's and Stirn's brigades, 4,000 men, and took post behind Donop's.

THE BATTLE OF LONG ISLAND

The Hessians with their elderly subalterns, creaking sergeant-majors and loyal, disciplined rank and file were about to be tested in battle for the first time on the American continent. They had both the strengths and weaknesses of eighteenth-century mercenaries. Amongst the former counted the good training of regimental officers, the loyalty and esprit de corps of veteran soldiers, and in particular the fieldcraft and marksmanship of the *Jäger*, volunteers every one. On the debit side, there was no senior officer of outstanding abilities: Heister and his subordinates were battle-scarred veterans and knew their trade, but they brought no special insight to the war, and the major-generals in particular were not only men of moderate abilities, but were soon to be too ill for active

---

[31] Trevelyan, *The American Revolution*, II, p. 271.
[32] StaMarburg 4h.413. nr. 4, fol. 19, letter of Donop's adjutant, Captain Wagner, 3 Sept. 1776; Peter Force, ed., *American Archives*: Fifth series, *Containing a Documentary History of the United States*, (3 vols. Washington, DC, 1848–53), I, pp. 1136–7, Sullivan to Washington, 23 Aug. 1776.
[33] Schweinsburg, 'Briefe eines hessischen Offiziers', p. 292.

campaigning. The Hessian field regiments, like the redcoats, put their trust not in marksmanship, but in the close-order volley and the bayonet charge.[34] In the section devoted to shooting in the Hessian infantry manual, exactness of drill, not accuracy of aim, is emphasized.[35] They marched at only seventy-five paces to the minute, except in the deployment of columns into line, for which the Landgraf had ordered the pace to be increased to a hundred and ten.[36] Most important, these carefully trained regulars were difficult to replace. Once battle and pestilence had thinned their ranks, the Hessian population of about 350,000 could not supply the necessary replacements.[37] Recruits drawn from the rest of Germany would have no particular loyalty to the Landgraf, nor interest in the British cause.

Yet in the late summer of that decisive year, it seemed these disadvantages would matter little. For political reasons, the American army chose to dispute with the Europeans the possession of New York and its environs, on ground that was not unlike the battlefields of Germany, when their best chance lay in withdrawal to the interior. Holding a line of picquets along the Heights of Guan running from east to west across western Long Island, they had neglected to cover the pass of Jamaica on their extreme left. On Clinton's suggestion, Howe passed his main corps of 10,000 men around this flank, while fixing the enemy in front with Heister's corps at Flatbush and General James Grant's at Gowanus Bay further west.[38]

Long Island is perhaps not a typical battle of the war, for the British had a crushing superiority, and the conduct of the American generals, unused to manoeuvring large bodies of men, was singularly inept. The stereotyped view of the war – the King's troops marching in close order, the Americans shooting from behind rocks, bushes and trees – was here reversed, as Lord Stirling led out the American regiments to reinforce their picquets. Colonel Joseph Reed reported,

---

[34] Mackesy, *The War for America*, p. 77.
[35] *Reglement vor die hessische Infanterie* (Kassel, 1767), pp. 48–51. This was based primarily, and indeed in part merely repeats, the Prussian manual of 1757. Each Hessian battalion was broken into ten *pelotons*, which fired in turn. By the time the last had fired, the first had reloaded, the aim being to maintain a constant flickering fire across the battalion front.
[36] StaMarburg 12.11 1 Ba 9 (Mirbach Regiment Order Book), fols. 15–16.
[37] Contemporary population estimates vary considerably. See Büsching, *Erdbeschreibung*, VII, p. 80.
[38] Clinton, *Narrative*, p. 41.

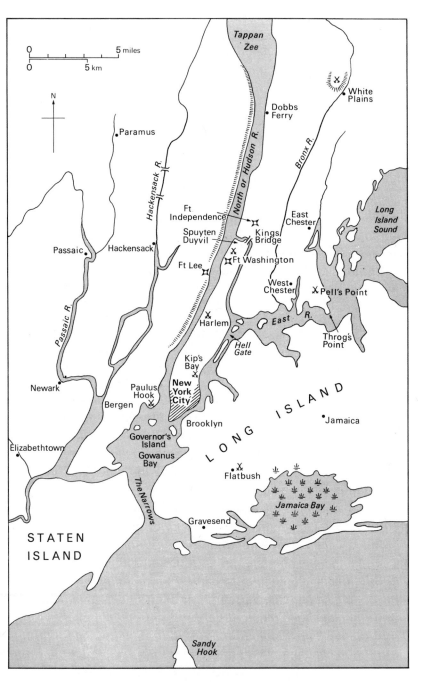

2 New York City and its environs, 1776

My Lord [Stirling], who loved discipline, made a mistake, which probably affected us a great deal; he would not suffer his regiments to break, but kept them in lines and on open ground. The enemy, on the other hand, possessed themselves of woods, fences, &c., and having the advantage of numbers, perhaps ten to one, our troops lost everything but honour.[39]

The Hessians did not enter battle in close and inflexible formations. A sketch map of Hessian dispositions at Flatbush shows that the advance was first made by small bodies of *Jäger* and grenadiers in skirmishing order, intermingled with three-pounder regimental pieces and amusettes.[40] When the main body followed, detachments of picked men from each battalion passed through the woods in open order, not, as Trevelyan says, as if crossing the *Friedrichsplatz* at Kassel on the Landgraf's birthday.[41] Only then was it that the regiments themselves advanced, scarcely firing a shot, but falling upon the Americans with the bayonet as they tried to reload.[42] Already broken by Howe's column on their left, they were an easy target. Some of them, so Hessian accounts relate, actually begged for mercy on bended knees. 'Their fear of the Hessian troops was ... indescribable,' reported Heister, 'in contrast, they offered the British much more opposition, but when they caught only a glimpse of a blue coat, they surrendered immediately and begged on their knees for their lives, so that I am surprised that the British troops have achieved so little against these people.'[43] Although Bardeleben did see some prisoners roughly handled, there cannot have been such a spitting of Americans to trees as rebel newspapers afterwards claimed, for they lost only 312 killed while 1,097 were captured.[44] The Hessians claimed 450 men and five guns as their share of the captives, while losing only two killed and twenty-six wounded of a total British loss of 377.[45]

---

[39] Force, *American Archives*, fifth series, I, p. 1231, Reed to William Livingston, 30 August 1776.

[40] StaMarburg 4h.410. nr. 1, fol. 377.

[41] Bardeleben, p. 60; Baurmeister, *Journals*, p. 36; Heringen, 'Einige Briefe aus dem amerikanischen Krieg', p. 4856; Trevelyan, *The American Revolution*, II, p. 279.

[42] HMC: *Hastings MSS.*, III, p. 182.

[43] StaMarburg 4h.410. nr. 1, fols. 361–2, Heister to the Landgraf, Sept. 3, 1776. The story of Americans begging for mercy is repeated by Bardeleben, Heringen, and an officer of the 42nd Highlanders, all eye-witnesses. *The London Chronicle*, XL (1776), p. 392.

[44] Bardeleben, p. 61; D. S. Freeman, *George Washington* (7 vols. New York, 1948–57), IV, p. 167n. The *Massachusetts Spy*, chief rebel propaganda organ in that state, published a letter purportedly from a British officer of Fraser's Highlanders (71st), asserting that the Hessians put to death all who fell into their hands. The letter is trotted out in every American account of the battle. Force, *American Archives*, Fifth series, I, pp. 1259–60; Field, *Battle of Long Island*, pp. 189–92.

[45] StaMarburg 4h.410. nr. 1, fol. 368; CO5/93, Part II, fol. 249. Thirteen of the casualties occurred in the days prior to the battle, an indication of the trifling resistance they encountered.

Except for the Maryland and Delaware regiments, fighting heroicly against hopeless odds, the American army dissolved into bodies of fugitives hiding in the woods or making for the defences at Brooklyn. This might have been the decisive moment of the war, and Heister's son claimed that the old general wanted to attack the American lines straight away.[46] Perhaps as an old soldier he possessed that sense of divining the temper of his troops and, knowing that their blood was up, thought that an attack must succeed. Had the British taken the American defences, that part of Washington's army on Long Island must have been destroyed, for there was insufficient shipping to get them all away in one embarkation. Instead Howe decided on regular siege approaches. On the night of 29/30 August, the Americans escaped by an evacuation as masterly as their previous arrangements had been incompetent. Admiral Lord Howe compounded his brother's error by not moving warships up the East River to block the escape.

The British were delighted with their auxiliaries' conduct in the battle. 'The Hessians behaved exceedingly well', wrote Captain Henry Duncan. Another officer ungrammatically reported, 'Nothing could behave better than the Hessians, and particularly their Jägers, or Riflemen, who are as much superior to those of the rebels as it is possible to imagine.' Captain Francis Hutcheson of the 60th thought the Hessians had acted with great coolness and resolution.[47]

The ease of their conquest was rather deceptive. The Hessians attributed the heavier British loss to a disorderly advance, but it was the British who had struck the main blow. Once the Hessians had penetrated through the wooded pass at Flatbush, they had little more to do than round up bodies of fugitives. It is possible that this misconceived contempt for American fighting capacities remained until the end of 1776, particularly with Colonel Rall whose regiment took two American colours.[48] Letters of Hessian officers at three levels of command – generals (Heister), field officers (Heringen), and subalterns (Bardeleben) – give no hint

---

[46] Heister, 'Tagebuch eines vormaligen hessischen Offiziers', p. 232. Captain von Münchhausen claimed there was an opening of 300 paces on one side of the American works. Münchhausen, fasc. 3, fol. 44.

[47] J. K. Laughton, ed., 'The Journal of Henry Duncan', *The Naval Miscellany*, I (Naval Records Society, 1902), p. 125; *The London Chronicle*, XL (1776), p. 358, 'Extract of a letter from an officer at New York, Sept. 6'; Add. MS. 21680, Hutcheson to Frederick Haldimand, 1 Sept. 1776. Faucitt benefited from the Hessians' success. Two days after dispatches announcing the victory reached London, he kissed the King's hand on being appointed Governor of Gravesend and Tilbury Forts. *London Chronicle*, XL, p. 358.

[48] StaMarburg 12.11 I Ba 3 (Journal of Rall's regiment), fol. 4.

that the writers were aware of how little they really had to do at Flatbush.

The Americans' ragged appearance increased the Hessians' contempt. Colonel Heringen noted the wretched state of American artillery and the length of time it took their riflemen to load. Captain Wagner, Donop's adjutant, wrote,

One encounters some pretty captains among the riflemen; one among others was a Palatine who supported himself in Pennsylvania with an inn, but he as well as his men had to help drag the captured cannons. Their clothing is a great mixture. A short smock of blue or white linen somewhat gathered at the sleeves. In short, what we have seen so far brings us little honour to fight against these.

Captain Max O'Reilly, who had seen the Americans melt away before the bayonets of his company, wrote rather too optimistically, 'After this day, I think, we shall hear no more of the riflemen, they have been exterminated from the face of the earth. . . . In short, our Hessians have thrown them into such terror and fear as can scarcely be believed.'[49]

This attitude seemed to be confirmed on 2 September when the American garrison of Governor's Island fled at the approach of ninety Hessians under Captain von Donop, leaving ten cannon so inadequately spiked that they were soon in use again.[50]

FROM NEW YORK TO WHITE PLAINS

Washington, torn between political and military considerations, scattered his forces about New York, Harlem, Kingsbridge, and along the shoreline, leaving himself widely vulnerable. Clinton urged Howe to strike boldly for Kingsbridge and cut off the enemy's line of retreat.[51] Howe instead made a less ambitious move. British batteries played on the enemy lines before New York to draw their attention. On the night of 14/15 September the advance corps, including Donop's *Jäger* and grenadiers, embarked on eighty-four flatboats, and crossed the East River the following morning to Kip's Bay, where Connecticut militia waited behind a defence that was 'nothing more than a ditch dug along the bank of the river with the dirt thrown out towards the water', according to one of their number, Private Joseph Plumb Martin.[52] From the

---

[49] Heringen, 'Einige Briefe aus dem amerikanischen Krieg', p. 4858; StaMarburg 4h.413. nr. 4, fol. 19, 3 Sept. 1776; Schweinsburg, 'Briefe eines hessischen Offiziers', p. 293.
[50] StaMarburg 4h.409. nr. 3, fol. 88.
[51] Clinton, *Narrative*, p. 44.
[52] Henry Steele Commager and Richard B. Morris, eds., *The Spirit of 'Seventy-Six: the Story of the American Revolution as told by Participants* (New York, 1967), p. 463.

boats, however, these works looked impressive. Rawdon, who was present, wrote, 'The Hessians, who were not used to this water business and who conceived that it must be exceedingly uncomfortable to be shot at whilst they were quite defenceless and jammed together so close, began to sing hymns immediately. Our men expressed their feelings as strongly, though in a different manner, by damning themselves and the enemy indiscriminately with wonderful fervency.'[53] Their anxiety was not without reason: at the landing at Throg's Neck in October, a leak in a boat carrying the Regiment Erbprinz was plugged with the water only two fingers' breadth from the gunwales.[54]

Fortunately for the attackers, when the covering ships of war showered the beaches with a storm of shot, the enemy quitted their lines and retired into a wood on the heights behind.[55] The spectacle of eighty-four assault boats, crammed with troops in the uniforms of three nations – English, Scots, and Hessians – drew enthusiastic comment from one Hessian officer at least.[56] As soon as the boats reached shallow water the men disembarked, formed promptly, and advanced into the woods. The companies of Captains O'Reilly and Eschwege of Block's battalion on the left wing encountered a body of several hundred rebel militia, who fired one volley and fled, hotly pursued, losing a lieutenant-colonel, five other officers, and forty-seven rank and file prisoners. The Hessians had three killed and fourteen wounded 'in exchange for the great satisfaction of having chased three battalions with two companies'.[57]

Washington was mortified at the flight of Private Joseph Plumb Martin and his comrades, but was unable to stop the fleeing rabble. Only lack of knowledge of the local terrain prevented Howe cutting off the whole force, thought Donop.[58] The Americans redeemed themselves the next morning, inflicting a check on the British light infantry at Harlem Heights. Both Donop and Major Baurmeister, Heister's adjutant general, attributed the salvation of the light infantry and Highlanders to Donop's rapid succours with

[53] HMC: *Hastings MSS.*, III, pp. 182–3.
[54] StaMarburg 4h.412. nr. 4, fol. 17.
[55] Ibid, 4h.413. nr. 4, fol. 97, Donop's account.
[56] Münchhausen, fasc. 2, fol. 67, letter of Capt. O'Reilly, 23 Sept. 1776.
[57] Ibid; StaMarburg 12.11 I Ba 14 (Journal of Block's battalion), fol. 4. Frederick Mackenzie wrote that he saw Hessian grenadiers bayoneting Americans as they tried to surrender; it may well be, as American riflemen were in the disconcerting habit of opening fire on Hessians who came up when they submitted, *Diary* I, p. 48; Ewald, *Belehrungen*, II, p. 140; Heringen, 'Einige Briefe', p. 4856.
[58] George Washington, *The Writings of* (39 vols. Washington, DC, 1931–44), VI, p. 95; StaMarburg 4h.413. nr. 4, fol. 97.

The Hessians

Jäger and a grenadier battalion. This is almost certainly an exaggeration of the Hessians' role: they lost only seven wounded, including Lieutenant Johann Hinrichs of the *Jäger*, who was nursed back to health by the widow of the Reverend John Ogilvie, owner of one of several large homes on Manhattan Island which Hinrichs protected against plundering.[59]

On 12 October another of Howe's cautious amphibious moves landed a force at Throg's Point up the East River, but the narrow neck of the peninsula was easily defended and the landing contained.[60] On 17 October the troops re-embarked and landed the next day at Pell's Point. Here they encountered Colonel John Glover's Marblehead Regiment,[61] fighting a gallant delaying action from behind stone walls, retiring in good order each time their flanks were threatened. From the reports of deserters, Glover claimed to have inflicted 800–1,000 casualties on Howe's army, and his biographer has presumed that these were mostly Hessians since they constituted three-quarters of the attacking force.[62] The numerous Hessian journals refute this claim. That of Heister's corps asserts that both British and American losses were considerable, but the Hessians themselves had scarcely any. The Regiment von Knyphausen, which executed the last of a number of flanking manoeuvres forcing Glover to retire, suffered only a few.[63] Here is the account of Lieutenant Andreas Wiederholdt, himself a participant:

As soon as we had been ferried across, which was done in Lord Howe's presence, we formed up immediately and marched towards the high ground, because in a wood close by the road, behind a so-called stone ridge, a battalion of riflemen lay concealed, and opened a heavy and unexpected fire on the English light infantry battalion, which marched at the head of the column, had proceeded carelessly,

[59] Baurmeister, *Journals*, p. 50; StaMarburg 4h.413. nr. 4, fol. 97; Roy W. Pettengill, *Letters from America 1776–1779: Being letters of Brunswick, Hessian and Waldeck Officers with the British Armies during the Revolution* (Cambridge, Mass., 1924), pp. 172–3. This is the second English translation of German mercenary letters appearing in Professor Schlözer's *Briefwechsel*, the most widely read German newsletter of the time. The first translation was W. L. Stone, *Letters of Brunswick and Hessian Officers during the American Revolution* (Albany, 1891).

[60] StaMarburg 4h.412. nr. 4, fol. 17.

[61] Glover came from Marblehead, near Salem, Mass. His regiment was composed of seamen.

[62] George A. Billias, *General John Glover and his Marblehead Mariners* (New York, 1960), pp. 110–23.

[63] StaMarburg 4h.409. nr. 3, fol. 126; ibid, 12.11 1 Ba 6 (Journal of Knyphausen's regiment), fol. 16. Lieut. Henry Stirke of the 10th Regiment described them as a grenadier battalion, an easy enough error as they wore fusilier caps. 'A British Officer's Revolutionary War Journal, 1776–1778', *Maryland Historical Magazine*, LVI (1961), pp. 160–1.

and had posted no flank patrols. [The riflemen] then ran off at full speed. But there was only one sergeant shot dead and two privates wounded by this fire. The enemy had dug in on the high ground facing us and greeted us with a number of cannon shots, but these had no effect because they flew wide. I skirmished with the enemy and they wounded one of my men, for which I sent one of them into the next world with my rifle. We camped here for the night, once again without tents. This area is called East Chester.[64]

This is no more boastful than Glover's exaggerated claims, and shows that the Marbleheaders' shooting was no more accurate than anyone else's in that war.[65]

Howe reached New Rochelle on 21 October. The next day the second Hessian division under Knyphausen with 670 Waldeckers disembarked from their transports and passed up the East River in flatboats. They were in high spirits at their landfall, and rowed up to Kingsbridge with drums beating, trumpets and fifes sounding and colours flying.[66] The Hessian ploughboys made a fine sight standing behind their old commander of forty-one years' service. Unlike Heister's men, those of the second division, although weakened by scurvy, were sent on active service before they could scarcely draw breath.

While the armies remained stationary, there was skirmishing by both sides. The newly arrived *Jäger* company under Captain Johann Ewald, one-eyed son of a postmaster, advanced rashly and narrowly escaped disaster in an engagement with Hand's Pennsylvanians.[67]

On 28 October Howe moved north again in two columns, led by *Jäger*. Heister's left-hand column was strung out on a bad road, with the English 2nd brigade and dragoons near the van, when they suddenly encountered the enemy drawn up on the heights at White Plains.[68] Only that morning Washington had sent forward Macdougall's brigade, including Haslet's excellent Delaware regi-

---

[64] Andreas Wiederholdt, 'Tagebuch des Capt. Wiederholdt von 7 October 1776 bis 7 December 1780', M. D. Learned and C. Grosse, eds., *Americana Germanica*, IV (1901), p. 19.

[65] Losses were roughly equal, American newspapers giving theirs as between thirty and forty, Strike the British as thirty-four. See Strike, as above, n. 63, and *Achives of the State of New Jersey*, W. S. Stryker, et al., eds., 2nd ser. (Trenton, NJ, 1901), I, pp. 217 and 219.

[66] Serle, *Journal*, p. 127.

[67] Malsburg, fol. 63; Washington, *Writings*, VI, p. 228 n. William Heath, *Memoirs of Major-General Heath* (New York, 1901), p. 16 gives Ewald's numbers as 250, twice his actual strength. He had four killed, three wounded. Ewald blamed his mistake on not knowing the ground. Johann Ewald, *Abhandlung über den kleinen Krieg* (Kassel, 1785), p. 78.

[68] Baurmeister, *Journals*, p. 63; Münchhausen, fasc. 3, fol. 69.

ment, to occupy outlying Chatterton Hill on his right.[69] The hill was a considerable obstacle, but not an insuperable one: 180 feet above the Bronx River and three-quarters of a mile long in an east-west direction. The top was cultivated and divided by stone walls, the south-east slope moderately steep and heavily wooded. At its foot lay the Bronx River.

As a preliminary to the action, Colonel Johann Rall on his own initiative promptly occupied ground at the base of a hill overlooking both armies' flanks; the former occupants, Spencer's New Englanders, retired rapidly over the Bronx.[70] Howe ordered two Hessian brigades to assault Chatterton Hill. Donop's however had to march from the extreme right wing to the extreme left to execute this attack, and never properly got into action.[71] The regiments of Prinz Karl, Ditfurth and Lossberg approached directly, supported by the Leib-Regiment, Rall's, and Knyphausen's. Reaching the Bronx stream, they found it too deep to wade, and hesitated. At that moment Brigadier General Alexander Leslie led two British battalions across a ford a short way downstream; they taunted the Hessians as they passed, bidding them stand out of the way, and charged uphill.[72] Had Leslie's men kept their momentum, they might have succeeded; but the officer leading them, carrying a fusil instead of the traditional spontoon, stopped to fire and then began to reload. The ranks following likewise halted under fire, and the impetus was lost.[73] They were thrust back with severe losses.

Then the Lossbergers crossed. A field of high grass before them was set alight so that the men had to carry their cartouche boxes on their heads. They were thrown back perhaps once, but pressed the assault.[74] Heringen had died of dysentery in September, and the regiment was led by Lieutenant Colonel Franziskus Scheffer. Scheffer, his second-in-command Major von Hanstein, and his company commanders Captains Altenbockum, Ries, Benning and Steding must have welded the odd assortment of deserters from Rinteln into a battle-worthy unit, for Cornwallis later testified that this regiment greatly distinguished itself at White Plains.[75]

[69] Caesar Rodney, *Letters to and from . . . 1756–1784*, C. H. Rydan, ed.(Philadelphia, 1933), p. 142.
[70] CO5/93, Part II, fol. 296, Howe to Germain, 30 Nov. 1776; H. B. Dawson, *Battles of the United States*, I (New York, 1858), p. 178. Malsburg, fol. 64.
[71] StaMarburg 12.11 I Ba 15 (Journal of Minnigerode's battalion), fol. 39.
[72] Bedford Record Office, Lucas Collection L29/213.
[73] Clinton, *Narrative*, pp. 51–2 and n. 27.
[74] StaMarburg 12.11 1 Ba 2 (Journal of Lossberg's regiment), fol. 41; Rodney, *Letters*, p. 143.
[75] StaMarburg 4h.411. nr. 1, fol. 149, 'Extract of the examination of LtGen the Earl Cornwallis before a Committee of the House of Commons upon Sir William Howe's

Meanwhile the regiments of Rall and Knyphausen also crossed, from the flanking position which Rall had taken up, the latter regiment led by Lieutenants Wiederholdt and Briede who were first into the water to animate their men. With British dragoons they struck the American flank. The militia and even three companies of Haslet's Delawares retreated in considerable disorder, the rest of the regiment retiring steadily.[76]

With the capture of Chatterton Hill, a dubious prize, the small battle ended. Even this little action provoked controversy, and since some of the British later thought the Hessians declined to attack, it is worth quoting from the letter of Captain Johann Caspar Ries of Lossberg's, his regiment having the lion's share of the fighting and the casualties:

Our Regiment and two English Regiments were ordered to scale the heights and dislodge the enemy. We advanced and found a little river before us, through which we had to wade, the water going into the cartouche pouches of most of the men. Scarcely were we through the water, than a rain of shot fell upon us, by which many were wounded. Besides that the left wing had to march through a wood that had been set alight, so that many men burnt the shoes on their feet. Notwithstanding all these difficulties, we scaled the heights and the enemy took to flight. Our regiment received 43 wounded.... After the enemy had been driven back everywhere, we scaled yet another hill, and then the whole army halted and remained in bivouac.[77]

Hessians and British assumed that the capture of Chatterton's Hill was a prelude to an assault upon the main position. Howe never made this attack, for a rainstorm on 31 October prevented an intended stroke, and then he turned south to a new target, one which was to yield great returns. Donop, however, thought an opportunity had been missed on the 28th, in not advancing Heister's division on the British left to cut off the retreat of Macdougall's brigade. He added, 'Genl Clinton's corps on the right had the village and the heights, both full of enemy, on their flank, and I believe that a general assault would have routed them.'[78] Donop believed Howe's intention was to penetrate into

(Footnote continued)
    papers.' (Knyphausen sent extracts bearing on the Hessian troops to his sovereign, taken from a printed copy of the proceedings.)
[76] Rodney, *Letters*, p. 143.
[77] StaMarburg 13 A 6 (Acc. 1930/5) Nr. 206, fol. 4, Extract Schreibens Capt. Joh: Casp: Ries, 19 Nov. 1776. Total Hessian losses were fifty-three killed and wounded. The figure of ninty-nine given by Fortescue includes all German losses 19–28 Oct. inclusive, among them thirteen Waldeckers not at White Plains and eight of Trumbach's captured by Gen. Hugh Mercer on Staten Island. CO5/93, Part II, fol. 303 gives a detailed return.
[78] StaMarburg 4h.413. nr. 4, fol. 98. Compare the comments of a young British officer in Mrs E. Stuart-Wortley, *A Prime Minister and his Son* (London, 1925), p. 88.

New England, an indication that the British commander kept his intentions well concealed from his German auxiliaries. It is also worth noting that relations between Howe and Clinton had already deteriorated so far that Lieutenant von Heister, the general's son and ADC, put Howe's failure to press the enemy down to bad blood between the two British generals.[79]

THE CAPTURE OF FORT WASHINGTON

The Americans' ready proclivity to raise earthworks at quick notice had worked advantages at Breed's Hill and Dorchester Heights. Such entrenchments as they threw up at New York were never before seen in an enemy's country, wrote a British officer.[80] But in inexperienced hands fortification was a two-edged weapon. Rawdon noted that the Americans were always adding to entrenchments which were often so extensive that they could not man half of them.[81] When mobility was often their greatest asset, their forts and fieldworks could too easily turn into traps. At Fort Washington and Charleston, American forces caught within their own defences suffered their two greatest defeats of the war.

Fort Washington and its counterpart across the Hudson, Fort Lee, were designed to prevent British vessels sailing upstream and cutting American communications. The former was also a threat to British control of Manhatten Island, and Howe had probably decided to turn against it before William Demont, adjutant of the 3rd Pennsylvanians, deserted to Lord Percy's camp, carrying with him plans of the fortress.[82] Washington's northward retreat had left the post isolated, but when Howe turned south on 5 November there was still sufficient time to evacuate the garrison, the attack not taking place until 16 November. By the 6th the Hessians were at Topp's Ferry on the Hudson, and Knyphausen had taken Fort Independence and secured a post on York Neck. By the 10th fascines had been made, and other preparations were going ahead,

---

[79] Heister, 'Tagebuch eines vormaligen hessischen Offiziers', p. 241.

[80] *The London Magazine, or Gentleman's Monthly Intelligencer*, XLV (1776), pp. 5023, 'Extract of a letter from an Officer under General Howe, dated Staten Island, July 12.' See also StaMarburg 12.11 1 Ba 15 (Journal of Minnigerode's battalion), fol. 17; Malsburg, fols. 49 and 69.

[81] Willcox, *Portrait of a General*, p. 55 n.2.

[82] The argument in Christopher Ward, *The War of the Revolution*, John Alden, ed. (2 vols. New York, 1952), II, p. 940 seems to dispose of Edward Delancey's claim that Demont's treachery caused Howe to revise his plans. Edward Floyd Delancey, 'Mount Washington and its Capture', *Magazine of American History*, I (1877), p. 79.

and Rall's brigade had been ordered to join Knyphausen at Kingsbridge.[83] These signs should have been clear to the Americans, but the commandant, Colonel Robert Magaw, believed he could hold the fort, as did Putnam and Greene. Washington himself at first wanted to withdraw the garrison, but allowed himself to be persuaded. Later he tried to conceal his part in the disaster.[84] The attack, set for 12 November, was delayed by heavy rains until the 16th. Of four assault forces, Knyphausen at his own request led the most important. Two lesser ones, Lord Percy's and Brigadier General Mathew's, struck from south and east respectively. The fourth, by the 42nd Highlanders, was intended as a feint across the Harlem River to Mathew's south.

Knyphausen had Rall's brigade, which had distinguished itself at White Plains, and Wutginau's regiment, but otherwise only garrison regiments, their ranks full of raw farm boys, and the Waldeckers of very indifferent quality. The troops were fortunate in their commander. Faucitt described him as extremely taciturn, but possessing one of the best reputations in the Hessian army. Galloway called him a truly great and gallant officer. The son of a soldier, he had begun his service in 1734. Now over sixty, he was still brave and active.[85]

At 7 a.m., to a salvo of artillery, the Hessians began their assault, Rall leading the right-hand column and Major General Martin Schmidt the left-hand. Knyphausen accompanied Schmidt's column, indicating his greater confidence in Rall. The columns broke through an abatis, waded a marsh, and began to climb, in places pulling themselves up by grasping the bushes. Then, incredibly, they were ordered to halt. Faulty British staff work had not allowed for low tide in the Harlem River, and Mathew's force were not yet across.[86] Under heavy fire, enduring casualties, the Hessians waited with mounting impatience.

Then at 10.30 a.m. another salvo signalled the attack. 'With an unabating firmness'[87] Knyphausen's men went forward, en-

---

[83] StaMarburg 12.11 1 Ba 6 (Journal of Knyphausen's regiment), fol. 21; Mackenzie, *Diary* I, p. 102; Wiederholdt 'Tagebuch', p. 22. Rall's brigade was actually Mirbach's, but as the latter was ill throughout 1776 Rall commanded it.

[84] Bernard Knollenberg, *Washington and the Revolution: a Reappraisal* (New York, 1941), pp. 13–19.

[85] CO5/139, fol. 331, Faucitt to Suffolk, 6 June 1776; Joseph Galloway, *Letters to a Nobleman on the Conduct of the War in the Middle Colonies* (London, 1780), p. 73; Friedrich, Frieherr von der Lith, 'Wilhelm, Freiherr von Knyphausen', *Hessische Denkwürdigkeiten*, III (1802), pp. 442–6.

[86] Stephen Kemble, *The Journals of Lieut.-Col. Stephen Kemble 1773–1789* (Boston, 1972), p. 99.

[87] *Heath, Memoirs*, p. 77.

couraged by their general, who tore down obstructions with his own hands, exposed to the fire like a common soldier, 'so that it is wonderful that he came off without being killed or wounded'.[88] Grenadier Reuber found the heights so steep, that when a comrade tumbled down, Reuber knew not whether he had been shot or lost his footing. Dragging themselves up over tangled thickets of beech trees, the columns became dispersed. As they neared the top, Rall rallied his men with shouts and the music of drums and hautbois: 'All those who are my grenadiers – forward march!'[89]

To facilitate Rall's advance, Knyphausen made a demonstration on the left. Rall, either by chance or good ground appreciation, led his column through a defile into which the American second battery could not fire. Although aided by the 42nd Highlanders turning their feint into a real attack, Rall's action was decisive, obliging Moses Rawlings' riflemen, many of their pieces fouled by repeated firing, to withdraw into the pentagonal redoubt at the centre of the defences. Only then could Knyphausen join Rall, fifty-five minutes after the second attack had started.[90] The riflemen within the redoubt were too cramped to offer an adequate defence. Having refused a summons the previous day, they could by eighteenth-century usage have been put to the bayonet, and one Loyalist argued that a Drogheda massacre would have shocked the rebels to submit.[91] The Hessians were extremely irritated at their losses, and had they taken the fort by storm, the carnage within the confined space would have been dreadful.[92] Instead, Rall and Knyphausen summoned the fort, sending forward Captain Hohenstein, an English-speaking officer of Koehler's battalion. Magaw's request for four hours to consider and free passage for the garrison was refused, and 2,818 officers and men marched out and laid down their arms before Knyphausen.

The capture of Fort Washington was the heaviest single blow to the American cause in the middle colonies. Washington wrote,

---

[88] Wiederholdt, 'Tagebuch' p. 23.
[89] Reuber, fol. 85.
[90] Heath, *Memoirs*, p. 77; CO5/93, Part II, fol. 300, Howe to Germain, 30 Nov. 1776; Henry Miller Lydenberg, ed., *Archibald Robertson, Lieutenant Colonel Royal Engineers: His Diaries and Sketches in America 1762–1780* (New York, 1930), p. 111. Not surprisingly, Sir John Fortescue, historian of the British army, attributed the success of the day to the attack of the 42nd. Hessian journals make only passing reference, if at all, to this.
[91] 'Eighteenth century usage' varied from place to place, but Frederick Mackenzie, usually a lenient observer, thought that 'they had no right to expect the humane treatment they received'. The Loyalist in question was Judge Thomas Jones of New York. Mackenzie, *Diary*, I, p. 110; Trevelyan, *The American Revolution*, II, p. 347 n. 1.
[92] Mackenzie, *Diary*, I, p. 110.

The victories of 1776

'The loss of such a number of Officers and Men, many of whom have been trained with more than common attention, will, I fear, be severely felt. But when that of the Arms and Accoutrements is added, much more so....'[93] Praise for the Hessians was high. Ambrose Serle declared, 'The Honor of the Day is imputed to Genl Kniphausen. The Hessians behaved with incomparable Steadiness and Spirit.' Sir George Osborne felt that no troops could have rendered more important service to the King, although Knyphausen's brigades were composed chiefly of recruits, drafts from militia and garrison regiments. One British officer with pardonable exaggeration wrote that Hannibal in his passage over the Alps could not have met with ground or difficulties more formidable than those the Hessians had to cross: 'They behaved with distinguished bravery.'[94] In Knyphausen's honour the fort was renamed for him. Another change of name, indicative of the run of success at the time, took place in New York, where the proprietor of an inn *The Golden Unicorn*, frequented by Hessian officers, renamed his establishment *The Landgrave of Hesse*.[95]

The consequences of the American disaster may be quickly summarized. With about 4,400 men Washington fell back to Newark, leaving detachments under Lee at White Plains and Heath in the Highlands. For once Howe acted with resolution in success, sending Cornwallis across the Hudson on 20 November with a corps including Donop's men. Scaling a steep escarpment six miles above Fort Lee, they only just failed to catch the American garrison which, warned of the British landing, quitted the post in such haste that they left camp kettles bubbling on fires. Donop's brigade reached the fort at 3 p.m., and promptly seized it with artillery and stores of all kinds.[96] Over one hundred stragglers were rounded up in the vicinity. Captured material in the two forts, Washington and Lee, totalled 146 cannon, 12,000 rounds, 2,800 muskets, 400,000 small arms cartridges, tents, entrenching tools, and 2,000 tons of the best wheat.[97]

At the same time, to secure an ice-free port, Clinton led an expedition of two British and two Hessian brigades to Rhode Island. As the Leib-Regiment, part of this force, marched towards

[93] Washington, *Writings*, VII, p. 287.
[94] Serle, *Journal*, p. 143; CO5/236, fol. 10, Osborne to Germain, 25 Nov. 1776; Force, *American Archives*, fifth series, III, p. 856.
[95] Malsburg, fols. 55 and 72.
[96] StaMarburg 4h.413. nr. 4, fol. 98, Donop's account; Kemble, *Journal* p. 101.
[97] Münchhausen, fasc. 2, fol. 9, 19–20 Nov. 1776; Bardeleben, pp. 83–4.

New York for embarkation, two of Howe's aides summoned Captain-Lieutenant Friedrich von Münchhausen to be the commander-in-chief's German ADC, to translate communications to the mercenaries.[98] On 8 December the troops occupied Newport without resistance. Those inhabitants who remained were mostly Loyalists or pacifist Quakers, but many others fled, according to Dinklage, because of the Hessians' terrible reputation 'so that they even believe we would eat up the little children'.[99]

Although tangential to our theme of the 1776 campaign, the Hessians' sojourn on Rhode Island is worthy of mention. The Germans particularly admired the beauty of the local women, and this admiration was reciprocated, for when the Leib-Regiment and Prinz Karl's embarked for New York the following May, Dinklage recorded, 'we saw at our departure numerous tears flowing everywhere, especially from the fair sex'. Clinton and his successor Lord Percy maintained good relations with the locals, and Percy was popular with his auxiliaries; on his departure for England in June 1777, the officers of Lossberg's brigade staged a concert for him. Hessian behaviour was exemplary, and when Newport was eventually evacuated in October 1779, Major General von Huyn was presented with a memorial from the inhabitants thanking him for the good conduct of his troops.[100]

Thus by early December 1776 a thoroughly successful campaign seemed to be nearing its close. Since the British landing on Long Island, the rebels had suffered an almost unbroken series of defeats; their deserters came in in large numbers, complaining of poor food, inadequate clothing, and disagreements in the rebel command.[101] The King's troops had captured 304 officers, 25 staff, and 4,101 soldiers.[102] No small part of these had fallen to the Hessians: 450 at Long Island, over 300 at the landing near New York, [103] and 2,800 at Fort Washington. General Charles Lee reckoned the effect of the loss of men and material at Forts Washington and Lee on

[98] Münchhausen, fasc. 2, fol. 3, 18 Nov. 1776.
[99] Dinklage, fol. 119, 4 Jan. 1776.
[100] LB Kassel 8° Ms. hass. 127, Valentin Asteroth, Erinnerungen aus dem nordamerikanischen Krieg 1776–1788, fols. 43–4; StaMarburg 12.11 1 Ba 10 (Journal of the Leib-Regiment), fol. 16; ibid 13 (Journal of the Garrison Regiment Huyn), fols. 50–1, 110–1; Dinklage, fol. 131, 18 May 1777; Kümmel, fol. 9.
[101] Makenzie, *Diary*, I, p. 95; Joseph Galloway, *The Examination of ... by a Committee of the House of Commons*, Thomas Balch, ed. (Boston, 1972), p. 14; Stevens, *Facsimiles*, XXIV, nr. 2043.
[102] StaMarburg 4h.414. nr. 4, fol. 50.
[103] CO5/93, Part II, fol. 275, Howe to Germain, 21 Sept. 1776.

American morale equal to 20,000 men.[104] Hessian losses were not slight; some 324 were killed and wounded at Fort Washington alone.[105] The mercenaries were earning their pay.

They were also adapting to new conditions. Having left their horses behind, all save a few senior officers and their ADCs were on foot to begin the campaign; an advantage, thought Lieutenant Heister, for the generals not having limitless numbers of messengers, their orders had to be firm and precise, not constantly changing.[106] Most officers and men marched with cartouche pouches slung loosely over their shoulders, so that greatcoats could be left open in the heat, carrying canteens filled with a mixture of rum and water. Detachments of volunteers had been formed in each regiment as flanking parties. Since fine watches and purses of gold coin were offered to these men, almost everyone had volunteered. The officers commanding these detachments had armed themselves with musket or rifle to replace their spontoons, which the Landgraf had ordered bundled up and deposited in the arsenal at Kassel before the regiments' departure.[107]

They had discovered that their equipment was unsuited to both climate and terrain. Their tall hats were knocked off in the forests, and regimental officers lamented that they did not have short-fitting linen uniforms like the British. By December many uniforms were in tatters.[108] On the practicality of the sword carried by Hessian soldiers, Ewald's comment is pointed: 'This is only a nuisance to the soldier while marching, increases costs, and gives opportunities for bad behaviour.'[109] The tents were useless: they leaked like sieves in the American downpour.[110] But for much of the campaign the troops went without them and bivouacked in the open. It was warm in the day, but quickly cooled at night, and the high incidence of dysentery was attributed to this temperature variation.[111] The outbreak of sickness was the only disquieting feature of the campaign, for the land was like a rich garden and

---

[104] John Alden, *General Charles Lee: Patriot or Traitor* (Baton Rouge, 1951), p. 280.
[105] StaMarburg 4h.413. nr. 4, fol. 31. This does not include Waldeckers.
[106] Heister, 'Tagebuch eines vormaligen kurhessischen Offiziers', p. 233.
[107] Ibid; Heringen, 'Einige Briefe aus dem amerikanischen Krieg', p. 4858; Wiederholdt, 'Tagebuch' p. 19; Friedrich von Lettow-Vorbeck, *Geschichte des Fusilier-Regiments von Gersdorff* ... (Marburg, 1913), p. 46; LB Kassel 2° Ms. hass. 247, Aktenstücke der Brigade von Mirbach, fol. 111, the Landgraf to Mirbach, 13 Jan. 1776.
[108] Heringen, 'Einige Briefe aus dem amerikanischen Krig', p. 4858; StaMarburg 4h.410. nr. 1, fol. 486, Heister to the Landgraf, 9 Feb. 1777.
[109] Ewald, *Abhandlung über den kleinen Krieg*, p. 20.
[110] StaMarburg 4h.409. nr. 3, fol. 77.
[111] Heister, 'Tagebuch eines vormaligen kurhessischen Offiziers', p. 234.

provisions were abundant. The men had plenty of beer and beef, pork and biscuit, and missed only the good rye bread of Hessen.[112] But virtually the whole corps was stricken with fevers. This was particularly serious among the more elderly senior officers. Heringen of Lossberg's regiment died on 23 September and was buried in the Lutheran graveyard at Brooklyn. His will directed that 400 thalers deposited in Rinteln be given to his regiment, and the money realized from the sale of his effects to his housekeeper to look after the children he had had by her.[113] The three major generals, Mirbach, Stirn, and Schmidt, were all *hors de combat*; a stroke had put Mirbach out of service for the whole campaign. Colonels commanded all their brigades. Colonel Carl von Bose of Ditfurth's was also ill, and Colonel Horn had to give up his command of Wissenbach's because of sickness.[114] It was expected, however, that the war would soon be over and the Hessians returning home.[115]

Old Heister reported to his sovereign that he was unimpressed with the newfangled ideas of the British. Although the Hessians had deployed in two ranks, the method proposed to him in August – that the men should not be closed up arm to arm, but somewhat more open – had not been employed by any battalion during the campaign. The grenadiers, who formed the advance corps of the army with the British grenadiers and light infantry, had fought just as the other regiments had done, with close ranks; but despite this, had suffered fewer losses than most units. From the other regiments, detachments had been sent ahead to skirmish, rendering excellent service on all occasions. But the main body of each regiment had followed at musket shot's distance, always closed up arm to arm. Only when the broken terrain and woods obliged them to, did they break ranks.[116]

Heister's claims for the traditional close order were not as absurd as they seem. A British officer, Sir Thomas Dilkes, writing of the advance of the Hessian grenadiers up the Connecticut road on 18 October, reported, 'The steady and regular advance of the Hessian grenadiers was, in comparison with the rapid movement of our

[112] Jungkenn 1:29, Col. v. Cochenhausen to Jungkenn, 17 March 1777.
[113] StaMarburg 4h.409. nr. 3, fol. 113, 25 August 1776.
[114] StaMarburg 4h.410. nr. 1, fol. 462, Heister to the Landgraf, 22 Sept. 1776. Bardeleben reported on 25 Sept. that he was virtually the only one in his battalion free from sickness; it continued thus into November. Dinklage was in bed the first three weeks of that month. Bardeleben, pp. 73 and 78; Dinklage, fol. 98.
[115] Münchhausen, fasc. 2, fol. 11.
[116] StaMarburg 4h.410. nr. 1, fol. 507, Heister to the Landgraf, 21 March 1777.

own men, uncommonly fine to see. The grenadiers besides ourselves sustained an animated march, which achieved its object, and
we took possession of the road.'[117]

All Hessian regiments used detachments of skirmishers, and the
use of such detachments rather than adopting open skirmishing
order in the line regiments was the major tactical innovation which
the Hessians adopted in America. Thus, although they adapted to
American warfare, they did not reject the groundwork on which
their system was based: the close order and regular movements
suited to their authoritarian discipline.[118]

[117] Kröger, *Geburt der USA*, p. 180. This is my own translation of the German. I have not
been able to find the original.
[118] The detachments are usually called *Pelotons*; sometimes the term *Flanquers* which better
describes their role is used. Such detachments had already been employed in Europe, by
the Duke of Bevern at Reichenbach in the Seven Years War. Ewald, *Belehrungen*, III, p.
321.

4

The Battle of Trenton

THE DEFEAT OF RALL

When a Regiment or Battalion is posted in a village, which is not far from the enemy, the Chief or Commander must immediately cause a Redoubt to be erected on a chosen spot or height, or where it is in some other way advantageous, which is large enough that the Regiment or Battalion has space for itself within.[1]

I did not think that all the Rebels in America would have taken that Brigade prisoners.[2]

The fall of Forts Washington and Lee was followed by Cornwallis's pursuit of Washington's fast dwindling army. The rebellion was collapsing in military failure. Nicholas Cresswell, an English traveller, noted the inability of rebel recruiters to get men by any means, although their bounty was £12.[3] On 25 November Cornwallis set off after Washington with the élite of the army, British grenadiers and light infantry, Hessian *Jäger* and grenadiers. On 28 November he entered Newark just as Washington's rearguard was leaving the town. For three days he pursued, and on 1 December approached Brunswick close on Washington's trail. Donop's corps posted itself on the high ground opposite the town, and receiving an enemy cannonade with only trifling loss, succeeded by the activity of the *Jäger* in preventing the rebels destroying entirely the bridge about half a league from the town. Washington was forced to yield up Brunswick and continue his retreat towards Princeton.

Both Donop and Minnigerode shortly afterward expressed their anger at the folly of Howe's orders halting Cornwallis at Brunswick. This was an opinion widely held by both British and Hessians.[4] Joseph Galloway, who with other leading Loyalists from Philadelphia, joined Howe's army near Hackensack, became so angry at the delay that he shouted that it was obvious Howe did

[1] *Reglement vor die hessische Infanterie*, p. 361.
[2] StaMarburg 4h.328. nr. 110, Grant to Donop, 27 Dec. 1776.
[3] *The Journal of Nicholas Cresswell 1774–1777* (London, 1925), p. 176.
[4] Münchhausen, fasc. 3, fol. 74, Note 7; Galloway, *Letters to a Nobleman*, p. 48.

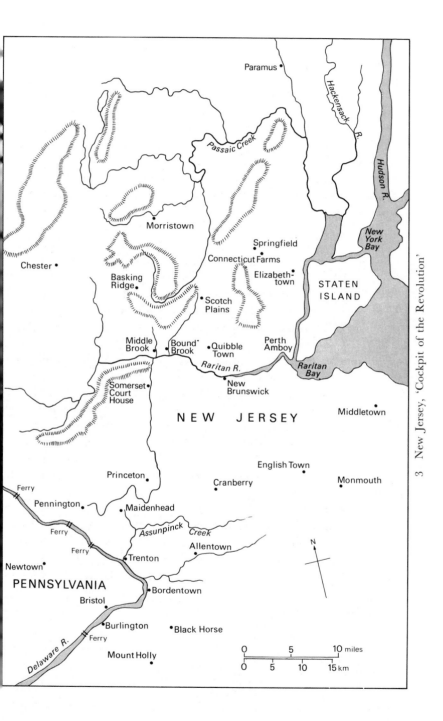

Paramus

Hackensack R.

Passaic Creek

Hudson R.

Morristown

Springfield

New York Bay

Chester

Connecticut Farms

Elizabeth-town

STATEN ISLAND

Basking Ridge

Scotch Plains

Middle Brook

Bound Brook

Quibble Town

Perth Amboy

Raritan R.

Raritan Bay

Somerset Court House

New Brunswick

NEW JERSEY

Middletown

Princeton

English Town

Cranberry

Monmouth

Ferry

Pennington

Maidenhead

Assunpinck Creek

Ferry

Ferry

Allentown

N

Newtown

Trenton

PENNSYLVANIA

Bordentown

Bristol

Burlington

Ferry

Black Horse

Delaware R.

Mount Holly

0   5   10 miles
0   5   10   15 km

3 New Jersey, 'Cockpit of the Revolution'

85

not wish to finish the war. Ewald, who was present, added, 'Everyone of sound judgement was inclined to have the same thoughts.'[5]

After an eight hour delay, sufficient to permit Washington's army to escape, the pursuit continued. At 3 p.m. on 8 December, Donop's advance guard came up with Washington's rear crossing the Delaware at Trenton. After an exchange of cannon fire, Washington crossed, leaving the British masters of Jersey. In Donop's opinion, had they possessed pontoons or landing craft, they would have been in Philadelphia in three days.[6] As it was, the Delaware proved the limit of their advance.

Washington's margin of escape was so narrow that Galloway, greatly chagrined at his escape, wrote that Howe had calculated with great accuracy the exact time for the enemy to make his retreat with impunity.[7] Although Washington had seized or destroyed all the boats his men could find, Galloway later testified that there were materials sufficient to build rafts or pontoons to ferry the corps across.[8] According to Howe's German ADC, Friedrich von Münchhausen, both Donop and Rall subsequently asked Howe for permission to advance upon Philadelphia, and both were ordered to hold their brigades in readiness, presumably to cross the Delaware when it froze.[9] Donop's account gives the impression that he was only awaiting the arrival of Koehler's grenadiers with the heavy artillery before continuing, not just to Burlington, which he had been unable to occupy, but on to Philadelphia. The city was at this time in a panic at the rumoured approach of the fearful Hessians, and Congress had abandoned the capital.[10]

The rapid collapse of the enemy position and the capture of General Charles Lee just before the end of the campaign left Howe in a better position than he had expected.[11] He was quite content, however, to retire to the pleasures of New York. Münchhausen, who saw him at close quarters for two campaigns and two winters,

[5] Ewald, 'Tagebuch', I, p. 60, quoted in Ernst Kipping, *The Hessian View of America 1776–1783* (Monmouth Beach, NJ, 1971), p. 23.

[6] StaMarburg 4h.413. nr. 4, fol. 98.

[7] *Letters to a Nobleman*, p. 48. This remark was plagiarised by Stedman.

[8] *The Examination of Joseph Galloway, Esq., by a Committee of the House of Commons* (Boston, 1972), p. 138.

[9] Münchhausen, fasc. 4, fol. 14, note 11.

[10] Stevens, *Facsimiles*, XIV, nr. 1397, Robt Morris to Silas Deane, 20 Dec. 1776/29 Jan. 1777; Add. MS. 34,413, fol. 153, letter from New York, 3 Jan. 1777.

[11] On 25 Sept. he reported to Germain that further progress in that campaign was doubtful. CO5/93, Part II, fol. 283.

wrote of him:

He is certainly ... basically an honourable man, cool headed, and possessed of personal bravery in the highest degree, and in addition, if he looks at a place, he sums it up with a sharp and accurate eye. Against that ... as soon as we have gone into winter quarters, he allows himself to be carried away with assemblies, concerts, balls &c &c, and above all the faro table, and goes to sleep, from which the belated opening of the campaign is a very natural consequence.[12]

Howe determined to leave a chain of posts across New Jersey to protect the Loyalists, who were coming in in vast numbers to swear loyalty to the King. This loyalty, like that shown to Congress under similar circumstances, was more apparent than real, dictated by the consideration of which army had the upper hand at a certain moment. Münchhausen attests to having written out thousands of protection papers in German, so that the auxiliary troops should not molest the loyal, and that many of these papers were subsequently found on the bodies of American soldiers slain in battle or captured.[13] Lieutenant Colonel Scheffer testified that various enemy officers came to Trenton to get protection papers, dined with Rall, and reconnoitred the garrison at close quarters.[14]

As Galloway observed,[15] of these Jersey posts the weakest were those closest to the enemy: Rall's brigade with a handful of *Jäger* and dragoons at Trenton, about 1,500 effectives; and Donop with three grenadier battalions, the 42nd Highlanders, and the *Jäger*, 1,800 effectives, at Bordentown and Black Horse. Further back were Major General Alexander Leslie at Princeton and General James Grant, overall commander in Jersey, at Brunswick. Donop was not happy with this arrangement. He did not consider Rall competent to hold an independent post. Rall, however, was held in high esteem by Howe, with whom he breakfasted on 14 December when the British commander-in-chief was at Trenton. Donop had wanted to have Rall's brigade under his command at Bordentown, and to have only an outpost of 150 men detached to Trenton doing duty there in rotation. Rall persuaded Howe to let him have a separate command as brigadier at Trenton.[16]

---

[12] Münchhausen, fasc. 3, fol. 73, note 6. Compare the opinions of Chas Lee, quoted in Troyer S. Anderson, *The Command of the Howe Brothers* (London, 1936), pp. 319–20, and Allan Maclean in Stuart-Wortley, *Prime Minister and Son*, pp. 105–6.

[13] Münchhausen, fasc. 3, fol. 74, note 8.

[14] StaMarburg 4h.328. nr. 112, fol. 74, Scheffer's testimony at New York, 24 Aug. 1778.

[15] *Letters to a Nobleman*, p. 52.

[16] Münchhausen, fasc. 3, fol. 76, Note 11. Slagle, 'The von Lossberg Regiment', (The American University, 1965), p. 68, says there is no documentary evidence that Rall asked

The Hessians

After the event, Howe claimed that Rall had disobeyed an order from him to build redoubts.[17] No such order came from Howe, as Münchhausen, who would have had to translate it into German, attests. Instead, on 14 December Rall demonstrated to Howe how he could take position on favourable ground near the edge of town and defeat any rebel attack without building defence works.[18]

Trenton was an open place with a number of roads coming in from a countryside that was well cleared of woodland with fields 'tolerably well laid out',[19] now covered with a blanket of snow and somewhat depopulated by the war.[20] Unless fieldworks were erected, it was defensible against surprise from any direction only through constant vigilance and active patrolling. That Rall and Howe thought otherwise shows their contempt for the rebel army. Donop, however, thought that Rall should erect redoubts for his artillery, and sent his engineer, Captain Pauli, to select a spot. With sure judgement Pauli picked the obvious place, the junction of the Princeton and Pennington roads with King and Queen Streets at the top end of the town.[21] Not only would a work here secure the garrison against surprise from the most likely direction, but guns in it could enfilade the streets in which defenders would have to form up. Rall never built this redoubt. Instead the cannons were placed uselessly in front of his headquarters.[22]

Rall did, however, attempt to counter surprise by active patrolling and by having one company under arms and one regiment

(Footnote continued)

for the post. Besides Münchhausen, Wiederholdt said so, as did the journal of Minnigerode's battalion. As Donop's second-in-command, Minnigerode was in a position to know. 'Tagebuch des Capt. Wiederholdt', p. 25; StaMarburg 12.11 I Ba 15, fol. 53.

[17] *The Narrative of Lieutenant General Sir William Howe* (London, 1780), p. 8.

[18] Münchhausen, fasc. 3, fol. 14, Note 11. Münchhausen's papers include in fasc. 4, fols. 76–7 a reply from an Englishman to a query of Münchhausen's. This Englishman was either Donop's ADC at the time or possibly Joseph Galloway, whose *Letters to a Nobleman* Münchhausen was acquainted with, and who says in his *Reply to the Observations ... of Howe*, (London, 1780), p. 93, that he advised Donop not to be drawn off to Mount Holly, and so presumably was with him at the time. Galloway made the point that it was incredible that Rall and Donop, if they had orders from Howe to erect redoubts, did not do so 'when their own safety and honour depended on their obedience'. If orders were sent to Donop in writing, why were they not produced at the inquiry, asks Galloway. Ibid, pp. 94–5. The English letter in Münchhausen says the order to build redoubts came from Donop, not Howe, to Rall.

[19] Cresswell, *Journal*, p. 264.

[20] Donop reported to Heister from Rariton Landing, 3 Dec. 1776, 'The majority of people in these parts have fled with all their bags and baggage (*mit Sack und Pack*), partly from rebellious inclinations, partly from fear of the Hessians whom they have had described to them as monsters (*Unmenschen*).' StaMarburg 4h.409. nr. 3, fols. 153–4.

[21] See map p. 94.

[22] Jungkenn 1:71, 'A true narrative of the surprise ... at Trenton' (by LtCol Scheffer).

fully dressed ready to turn out each night. There was an endless series of alarums and snipings, and the men got little sleep. One company, Captain Altenbockum's of Lossberg's, was under arms three nights in succession,[23] and the men of the regiment did not remove their cartouche pouches for eight days.[24] The consequence was an increasing sick list, so that Scheffer and Major Dechow of Knyphausen's wrote to Heister on December 17 that a mere hundred men per regiment were fit for duty, that the men suffered from cold and sickness, and disaster threatened.[25] The message did not reach Heister until it was too late.

Rall was an able battlefield leader, an inspiring commander under fire, as the journal of Grenadier Reuber of Rall's own regiment testifies.[26] Many adverse comments written about him came only after his disgrace. His adjutant, Lieutenant Piel, and Quartermaster Heusser of Lossberg's both testify to his courage, his convivial fellowship, his kindness to and popularity with his subordinates.[27] Ewald, no mean judge, wrote that many of those who criticised Rall after his death were not fit to have carried his sword.[28] Yet there is no doubt that at Trenton he proved himself unfit to command such a post in the face of the enemy. Wiederholdt described how Rall spurned the good advice of Major Dechow:

Not the least precaution was made, no rendezvous or alarm place was laid down in case of attack; Even less was it thought possible that we could be attacked. Major von Dechow offered a truly sensible proposal, to throw out some sort of defence work and take the cannon into it, so that everything would be prepared for an unforeseen event, and we could best defend ourselves: *Scheiszer bey Scheisz*! was the Colonel's reply: let them come: what defences [do we need]? We will go at them with the bayonet; Major von Dechow continued with this line of argument and said: Colonel, sir, it costs us nothing indeed; it may not help us, but it will not cause us any harm, and to undertake this work recommends itself to me. I would like to know, he [Rall] said to him, how and where I will make this work; he repeated his previous words, laughed out loud at both of us and went off. He thought the name of Rall was so frightening, and stronger than all the works of Vauban and Coehorn, on which no rebel would make an assult. – A clever

---

[23] Stryker, *Battles of Trenton and Princeton*, pp. 100–1.
[24] Jungkenn 1:71, 'A true narrative'.
[25] StaMarburg 4h.410. nr. 1, fol. 451.
[26] Reuber, fol. 85.
[27] LB Kassel 4° Ms. hass. 188, fols. 27–8; StaMarburg 12.11 I Ba 2 (Journal of the Regiment von Lossberg), fol. 50. But the similarity of these passages seems to indicate that the two men collaborated, or that Heusser's source was Piel.
[28] Ewald, *Belehrungen*, II, p. 132. The judgements of these Hessian officers are fairer than Galloway's, that Rall was 'Obstinate, passionate, and incessantly intoxicated with strong liquors'. *Letters to a Nobleman*, pp. 51–2.

man to command a corps, and even more than that, a fine fellow to defend a town![29]

It was never Heister's intention, any more than Donop's, that Rall, a fairly junior colonel, should command a brigade. It came about by force of circumstance: Rall's brigadier Mirbach had been ill since arriving in America, Colonel Carl von Bose who succeeded him also fell sick, Colonel Heringen of Lossberg's, senior to Rall, died of dysentery at Brooklyn, and Colonel Borck of Knyphausen's was convalescing from a wound at New York.[30] As Howe's defenders are quick to point out, the Hessians had done nothing before Trenton to merit a lack of confidence.[31] Rall's brigade had distinguished itself during the campaign of 1776, most particularly Lieutenant Colonel Franziskus Scheffer and the Lossbergers. Based on Heister's recommendation, the Landgraf decided to promote Scheffer to Heringen's vacancy as colonel and award him the order *Pour la vertu militaire*.[32] All three regiments had suffered heavy losses; the Lossbergers had forty-five casualties at White Plains and twenty-nine more at Fort Washington, where Knyphausen's lost sixty-eight men and Rall's forty-nine.[33] The battalions were under strength and many of the senior officers were either sick or convalescing from wounds, including Scheffer, Lieutenant Colonel Bretthauer of Rall's, and Major Dechow of Knyphausen's, twice wounded at Fort Washington, but who had to stay with the regiment because Colonel Borck had been taken to New York with a more serious wound.[34] With Rall in his cups and most of his senior officers sick, the brigade was in no state to repel the coming attack. Baurmeister recorded:

The day before [the battle], Colonel Rall wrote to Colonel von Donop that his brigade was extremely fatigued because of the miserable weather and continuous service and was in no condition to defend the post without relief and reinforce-

[29] Wiederholdt, 'Tagebuch', p. 24.
[30] StaMarburg 4h.410. nr. 1, fols. 589–94, Heister to the Landgraf, 14 July 1777. This is Heister's defence on being relieved of command, but is supported by details in the journal of his corps. In his letter recalling Heister, the Landgraf charged him with putting Rall, third most junior of the Hessian colonels, in charge of the brigade. Ibid, fol. 496, 7 April 1777.
[31] Anderson, *Command of the Howe Brothers*, p. 207.
[32] Alas for poor Scheffer! Friedrich, then in Rome, was greeted on his return to Kassel by news of Trenton, and Scheffer's award and promotion were suspended until the inquiry on Trenton was completed. StaMarburg 4h.410. nr. 1, fol. 459, Landgraf to Heister, 22 Feb. 1777; ibid, nr. 2, fol. 24, to Knyphausen, 22 Sept. 1777.
[33] StaMarburg 4h.413. nr. 4, fol. 31.
[34] Stryker, *Battles of Trenton and Princeton*, p. 156; StaMarburg 12.11 I Ba 6 (Journal of the Regiment von Knyphausen), fol. 23.

ments; that only two officers in his regiment were fit for duty; and that the other regiments had the same complaints, above all the gallant Regiment von Lossberg, which had suffered more than any other throughout the whole campaign.[35]

The contempt of Rall and Howe for the rebels was shared by General James Grant, commander of the scattered garrisons. The pug-like Laird of Ballindalloch had already declared himself in Parliament as to the worthlessness of the Americans as soldiers. Münchhausen commented that Grant, although much favoured by Howe, was unpopular with others, particularly the common soldiers, 'as they knew that if he had a good breakfast and evening meal, everything else was neglected'. One often found him surrounded by ducks and geese, which he had with him to supplement his table, 'standing out, because he was so short and fat'.[36] Grant refused to send Rall additional men, claiming he was behaving in a panicky manner; and to Donop he neglected to provide sufficient ammunition for his artillery, despite six written requests.[37] More foresight as to the coming stroke by the Americans may be credited to Donop and Rall than to Grant, despite language difficulties and Rall's neglect of spies. The British intelligence, based on reports of Loyalists, was good: there was a constant stream of information regarding the rebels' strength and intentions, much of it quite accurate.[38] If anything, there was an excess of intelligence: the locals told Rall and Donop almost daily of an impending attack.[39] But Grant sneered at the warnings from the Hessian colonels. Here is a typical selection of his replies to Donop:[40]

I can hardly believe that Washington would venture at this season of the year to pass the Delaware. (17 December)

it was making more of the rebels than they deserve. (21 December, referring to Rall's providing a strong escort for a messenger.)

The Rebels have neither shoes nor stockings, are in fact almost naked, starving for cold, without Blankets and very ill supplied with provisions. (21 December)

---

[35] Baurmeister, *Journals*, p. 78. I cannot find this letter in Marburg, but on 21 Dec. Rall wrote to Donop in similar vein: 'I am aware of my situation and three battalions are little enough to defend this place, as my honourable brother [officer] himself judges ... Redoubts I have not thrown out, as I have the enemy around me everywhere.' StaMarburg 4h.328. nr. 110, fol. 35a.

[36] Münchhausen, fasc. 3, fols. 78–9, note 11.

[37] Ibid. Donop had only 9 rounds per gun. StaMarburg 4h.409. nr. 3, fol. 169, Donop to Heister, 27 Dec. 1776.

[38] See the reports in StaMarburg 4h.328. nr. 110. Some of these are reproduced in Stryker, *Battles of Trenton and Princeton*, pp. 336–8.

[39] Münchhausen, fasc. 4, fol. 14, note 11.

[40] All quotes from StaMarburg 4h.328. nr. 110.

Tell the Colonel [Rall] he is safe. I will undertake to keep the peace in Jersey with a corporal's guard.

Only on Christmas Eve did Grant take notice of the gathering warnings to write a typically offhanded caution to Rall:

Washington has been informed that our Troops have marched into Winterquarters, and has been told that we are weak at Trenton and Princeton, and Lord Sterling expressed a wish to make an attack upon these two Places. I don't believe he will attempt it but be assured that my information is undoubtedly true, so I need not advise you, to be on your guard against an unexpected Attack at Trenton.

What seemed to be the attack occurred at twilight on Christmas evening, by about fifty Americans on the Pennington road. Rall himself led out a party to make sure they had been driven off. Inevitably vigilance relaxed after the awaited blow had fallen and been so slight. The weather was foul and the Hessians crowded back into their dismal quarters to enjoy the festive season as best they could. 'A pipe and a warm room are a German's delight,' wrote one traveller to Germany, 'The room cannot be too hot or too full of smoke.'[41] It was scarcely surprising that few wanted to do guard duty on Christmas night in snow and sleet. Major Dechow cancelled the normal dawn patrol for the following morning,[42] and Lieutenant Wiederholdt in command of the strengthened Pennington road picquet allowed his men after a night of ceaseless patrolling to take shelter in the guard hut.[43] Meanwhile, Donop foolishly allowed himself to be lured off to Mount Holly on 21 December, and remained there inactive.[44]

Thus when the attack fell it had the greatest of military advantages, surprise, against an enemy weakened by sickness, overconfidence, and the bad example of their commander, who led the libations.[45] Although the rebels were ragged, weakened, and ill equipped (except for artillery), they were conscious that if a blow were not struck soon, their cause was lost.[46] With grim resolve Washington's men crossed the Delaware 'in a storm of wind, hail, rain and snow',[47] and marched to the attack. Sullivan with the

---

[41] *The Journal of General Sir Martin Hunter* (Edinburgh, 1844), p. 187.

[42] Stryker, *Battles of Trenton and Princeton*, p. 145.

[43] Jungkenn 1:31, 'Copia eines Schreibens vom Lieutenant Wiederhold, April 15, 1777'.

[44] Ewald, *Belehrungen*, II, pp. 129–30.

[45] The Hessians were well supplied with rum, some of which the Americans drank after the fight, other casks were stove in. Force, *American Archives*, Fifth series, III, p. 1443.

[46] Washington, *Writings*, VI, p. 426n, Joseph Reed to Washington, 22 Dec. 1776.

[47] Rodney, *Letters*, p. 152. The oft told story of blood in the snow seems to have originated with Major James Wilkinson. Elisha Bostwick makes no mention of it in his memoirs.

brigades of St Clair, Glover and Sargent came down the road along the Delaware to cut off the Hessian retreat across the Assunpinck bridge, while Greene with Stephen, Mercer, and Lord Stirling emerged on the Pennington road just before eight o'clock. Wiederholdt's piquet fired a volley at the latter as they debouched from the woods, and withdrew in good order on Altenbockum's company which was on stand-by, and the orderly conduct of these detachments gained some time for the main body to form up, until Altenbockum fell wounded.[48] The troops assembled quickly, the Lossbergers, ominously, in a graveyard. But the battle was lost in the first few minutes when Captain Forrest's guns wheeled into position at the top of the town, where Captain Pauli had sited the redoubt that was never built. Rall was called by his adjutant, Piel, and appeared quickly (or slowly, depending upon whose account you read).[49] At first there was indecision; Washington noted from the Hessians' motions that they seemed uncertain how to act.[50] Typically Rall then attempted to lead his men in a bayonet attack up the main street. Three times before, the Americans had yielded to the Hessians' well-proven bayonets. Rall's order boomed forth again: 'Alle, was meine Grenadiers sein, vorwärts!'[51] The attack had gone only forty yards when it broke down under the fire of Forrest's guns, Rall's regiment in recoiling throwing part of the Lossbergers into disorder. A rush of the Americans led by William Washington and James Monroe captured the Rall Regiment three-pounders, whose inexperienced commander Lieutenant Engelhardt seems to have panicked. When Rall was shot down in a second attempt, his men and the Lossbergers fell back in considerable disorder into an orchard where they surrendered. 'It rained cannon balls and grapeshot here,' reported Lieutenant Colonel Scheffer, 'and snow, rain, and sleet came constantly into our faces. In short, none of our muskets would fire any longer.'[52]

Knyphausen's regiment formed up under Major Dechow on Queen Street, waited inactive. There were no standing orders on what action to take, no command from Rall, and Dechow like

---

[48] Heister sent his sovereign an eye-witness account received from John Barnes, a local sheriff, testifying that Altenbockum's men behaved well. StaMarburg 4h.410. nr. 1, fol. 488.

[49] Wiederholdt said he was slow to appear; Slagle, citing Piel as his authority, says he appeared quickly. Jungkenn 1:31; Slagle, 'The von Lossberg Regiment', p. 92.

[50] Washington, *Writings*, VI, p. 442.

[51] Reuber, fol. 90.

[52] Jungkenn 1:71, 'A true narrative of ... Trenton'. Stryker, *Battles of Trenton and Princeton*, p. 176 notes that one Hessian musket in twenty could fire at this point.

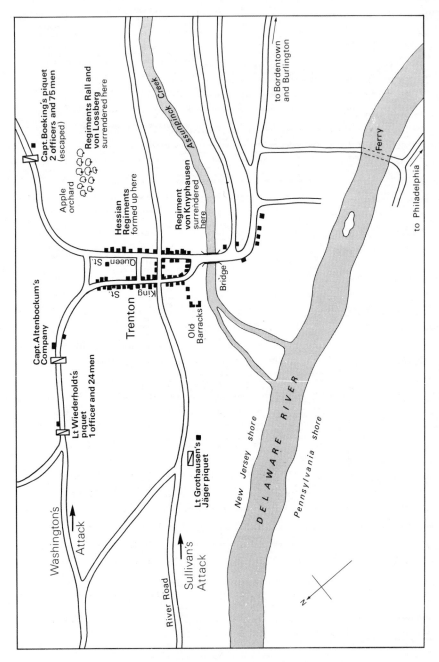

4 The Battle of Trenton, 26 December 1776

The Battle of Trenton

Grouchy at Waterloo failed to 'march to the sound of the guns'. When Wiederholdt with his piquet rejoined the regiment, he cried to Dechow in dismay, 'In God's name! why have we not occupied the [Assunpinck] bridge?'[53] The delay had been fatal. The regiment attempted to escape across the bridge, but their guns mired in a morass before they reached it. Dechow was mortally wounded in the hip, and the American brigades of Glover and St Clair surrounded them to complete the victory. Three officers and seventeen soldiers had been killed, and 919 prisoners taken.[54] The Americans had four killed and eight wounded.[55] Rall died of his wounds the evening after the battle, having supposedly discovered in his pocket a letter warning him of the coming attack. The note had been brought to Rall while he was in his cups the night before, and he had thrust it into his pocket without reading it.[56]

The affair hardly reflected the traditional honour of Hessian arms. The actual battle lasted only half to three quarters of an hour. A New England private summed up its brevity and completeness in his diary for 26 December:

This morning at 4 a'clock we set off with our Field Pieces and Marched 8 Miles to Trenton whare we ware Atacked by a Number of Hushing [Hessians] and we Toock 1000 of them besides killed some. Then we marched back and got to the River at Night and got over all the Hushing.[57]

How was it that 'three old established regiments, of a people who make war their profession',[58] had laid down their arms after inflicting only twelve casualties on the hitherto contemptible Americans? Demoralization by constant harassment and ceaseless duties, after an arduous campaign, and Rall's extraordinary failure to entrench at the head of the town greatly aided the well conducted American attack. However, the battle also reflected a failure of the Hessian tactical system. The regiments had turned out in reasonably good order, but they had formed up in their usual close ranks outside the town in the sleet and snow. Once

[53] Jungkenn 1:32, an account of the battle of Trenton by Andreas Wiederholdt.
[54] StaMarburg 4h.328. nr. 119; Washington, *Writings*, VI, p. 447, return of prisoners (including the wounded, among them Rall and Dechow, who both died of their wounds).
[55] Howard H. Peckham, ed., *The Toll of Independence: Engagements and Battle Casualties of the American Revolution* (Chicago and London, 1974), p. 27.
[56] Stryker, *Battles of Trenton and Princeton*, p. 192. My account is based largely on Stryker and the manuscript accounts of Scheffer, Matthaus, Wiederholdt, and Piel. A recent work, Samuel S. Smith's *The Battle of Trenton* (Monmouth Beach, NJ, 1965), makes good use of Hessian sources.
[57] Trevelyan, *The American Revolution*, III, p. 113 n. 1.
[58] *The Annual Register*, XX (1777), p. 17.

Altenbockum's company had been driven off and the Hessian guns taken, the Americans had moved into the town where musketeers and riflemen could dry their weapons and use them with impunity. The Hessians inflicted so few casualties because their muskets would not fire; and their system, which trained them to fight in close order, did not give them the flexibility to break up into small bodies of skirmishers who could have penetrated back into the town.[59]

Could the Hessians have adapted to a skirmishing order? As early as the battle of Long Island, detachments of volunteers had been drawn from the battalions to provide flanking parties.[60] But these, like the British light infantry, fought in a purely conventional manner; they represented no radical innovation, and were just as vulnerable to the fire of militia snipers as were the regiments themselves.[61] The Hessians also formed parties of volunteers from the regiments to serve as *Jäger* or chasseurs; Friedrich von der Malsburg commanded such a party against Sullivan's troops on Rhode Island in August, 1778, leading his men with such distinction that he won the order *Pour la vertu militaire*.[62] Another body of volunteers from eleven different battalions formed a *Jäger* company under Captain George Hanger, a British officer serving with the Hessians.[63] Neither of these detachments were proper *Jäger*, that is, woodsmen trained in the use of rifles. They were simply picked men from the field regiments, armed with musket and bayonet, and as such, like the grenadiers, a parasitic organization, drawing off the best men. Thus the American war forced no radical change on the European armies. 'The decisive innovation in infantry fighting ... the acceptance of open order tactics by the line infantry' had to await the French Revolutionary wars.[64]

---

[59] The failure of the Hessian weapons to fire was reported by Scheffer, Major Matthaus, and Piel. The failure of their tactical system did not emerge in the court martial, which was conducted under the impression that the Hessians were facing 7,000 to 8,000 Americans and that their only option was to retreat across the Assunpinck bridge. StaMarburg 4h.328. nr. 110, fols. 75 and 77; ibid, nr. 112, fol. 73; LB Kassel 4° Ms. hass. 188, fol. 26.

For a contemporary defence of Rall see *The London Evening Post*, 1–4 March 1777, letter from 'old England's and Col. Rall's friend', probably paid for or written by Kutzleben, the Hessian representative.

[60] Heringen, 'Einige Briefe aus dem amerikanischen Krieg', p. 4858.

[61] Ochs, *Betrachtungen*, pp. 30–1.

[62] StaMarburg 4h.415. nr. 5, fols. 159–66, extract of v.d. Malsburg's journal.

[63] T. H. Edsall, ed., *The Journal of Lt. John Charles Philip Von Krafft* (Collections of the New York Historical Society for the Year 1882. New York, 1883), pp. 56–7.

[64] Paret, *Yorck and Prussian Reform*, p. 37. See Peter Paret, 'Colonial Experience and European Military Reform at the End of the Eighteenth Century', *Institute of Historical Research*, XXXVII (1964), pp. 47–59.

The Battle of Trenton

Nor did American generals make any particular advance in this field. Except for Charles Lee, who advocated a more radical kind of guerrilla warfare,[65] Washington and his fellows sought to deploy their men in European lines, to teach them bayonet drill and to fire volleys in unison. The letters of Washington, Greene, and others are full of contempt for the militia.[66] Thus despite their failure at Trenton, the Hessians with their Frederician tactical system were not wholly unsuited to the war along the eastern seaboard, a war of pitched battles, sieges, and outposts not dissimilar to that in Europe.

The victorious Americans looked with curiosity on their prisoners, the dreaded Hessians. Sergeant Elisha Bostwick wrote:

I will make a few remarks as to the personal appearance of the Hessians. They are of Moderate Stature and rather broad Shoulders their limbs not of equal proportion light complexion with a blueish tinge hair cued as tight to the head as possible Sticking straight back like the handle of an iron Skillet. Their uniforms blue with black facings,[67] brass drums which made a timbling sound, their flag or Standard of the richest black silk & the devices upon it & gold lettering in gold Leaf.... When crossing the Delaware with the prisoners in flat bottom boats the ice Continually Stuck to the boats driving them down stream; the boatmen endevering to clear off the ice pounded the boat, & stamping with their feet beckoned to the prisoners to do the Same & they all set to jumping at once with their cues flying up and down soon shook off the ice from the boats.[68]

The Americans clearly expected to see a different species of being. Lieutenant Piel reported that as the prisoners waited on 9 January to cross the Susquehanna crowds of people arrived to look at the invaders from the old world – 'they had come to see Monsters (*Wundertiere*), and were vexed to find that we looked like human beings'.[69] It is not difficult to explain the blueish tinge of their complexions by the midwinter temperature and the tattered state of their uniforms. The boat in which Wiederholdt crossed was prevented by ice from reaching the Pennsylvania shore, and he and those with him had to jump into the freezing water up to their breasts and wade seventy paces to shore, breaking through the ice in some places.[70]

---

[65] John Shy, 'Charles Lee: The Soldier as Radical', in G. A. Billias, ed., *George Washington's Generals* (New York, 1964), pp. 22–53.

[66] Washington, *Writings*, VII, pp. 49 and 57; Commager and Morris, *Spirit of Seventy Six*, pp. 1162–4, Greene to Joseph Reed, 18 March 1781:

[67] Knyphausen's regiment. Lossberg's had red facings, Rall's blue with distinguishing red stocks.

[68] William S. Powell, ed., 'A Connecticut Soldier under Washington: Elisha Bostwick's Memoirs', *WMQ*, 3rd series, VI (1949), pp. 102–3.

[69] LB Kassel 4° Ms. hass. 188, Geschichte des ... Regiments von Lossberg, fol. 31.

[70] Wiederholdt 'Tagebuch', p. 31.

The Hessians

To Washington, however, the sight of those chilly Hessian prisoners with their cues flying up and down was a warming one. To display his triumph and the lost invincibility of the Hessians, he paraded his prisoners through Philadelphia. The old women in particular screamed at the mercenaries, who had come to deprive them of their freedom.[71] One old man reported they were a fine collection of hearty looking men, well clad and their looks satisfied.[72] His eyesight must have been defective, or his memory. Many were ill, their uniforms dirty, their footwear inadequate.[73] Americans pinched themselves and wondered how they had found the mercenaries so terrible – 'most people seemed very angry they should ever think of running away from such a set of vagabonds'.[74]

It was not the intention of Washington or Congress that the prisoners should be mistreated by the populace. The Pennsylvania Council of Safety instructed their committee at Lancaster, where the Hessians were to be quartered,

It will be very necessary to prevent our weak and over-zealous friends insulting them or putting them in mind of their past behaviour. It is our interest to improve the present opportunity to make them our friends, and sow the seeds of dissension between them and the British troops. The Germans [German-Americans], by treating them as brethren and friends, may do the most essential service to our cause.[75]

It was advised that they be well treated and 'kept from conversing with disaffected people as much as possible'.[76] Up till now there was no crime of which, according to American newspapers, the Hessians were not guilty; they were soldiery 'whose native ferocity, when heightened and whetted, by the influence and malice of the sceptered savage of Great-Britain, thirsting for the blood of his faithful American subjects, will exhibit such a scene of cruelty, death and devastation as will fill those of us who survive the carnage, with indignation and horror, attended with poverty and wretchedness'. They indulged in 'rapine and bloodshed', they delighted in torture.[77] Now the papers, for the moment no longer

---

[71] Reuber, fol. 92.
[72] John F. Watson, *Annals of Philadelphia* (3 vols. Philadelphia, 1844), II, p. 298.
[73] StaMarburg 4h.410. nr. 1, fol. 451, Dechow and Scheffer to Heister, 17 Dec. 1776; Nicholas B. Wainwright, 'A Diary of Trifling Occurrences, Philadelphia, 1776–1778', *PMHB*, LXXXII (1958), p. 419.
[74] Force, *American Archives* Fifth series, III, p. 1484.
[75] Ibid., p. 1511.
[76] Ibid., p. 1484.
[77] *The Norwich Packet*, 8 July 1776, quoted in Davidson, *Propaganda and the Revolution*, p. 371. As Kipping observes, these stories were recounted even before the Hessians had landed to give proof of their ferocity.

desirous of whipping up hatred and fear, encouraged kindness and sympathy for the captives. 'The wretched condition of these unhappy men, most of whom, if not all, were dragged from their wives and families by a despotic and avaricious prince, must sensibly affect every generous mind with the dreadful effects of arbitrary power.'[78] This admirable policy of kindness was carefully calculated to instill into the Hessian soldiers such principles 'that when they return to the British army, they may open the Eyes of their Countrymen, who have not the most cordial Affection for their English fellow Soldiers.'[79]

Upon receiving news of the defeat Donop fell back hastily from Bordentown, abandoning some of his seriously ill. Münchhausen excuses him on the grounds of lack of artillery ammunition,[80] but he acted with much less resolution than his second-in-command, Minnigerode, who immediately upon hearing of the defeat sent a grenadier company to reinforce the piquet covering the bridge over Crosswicks Creek, and a few minutes later led out his whole battalion.[81] Had Donop supported him and attacked, instead of ordering Minnigerode to withdraw, they might well have routed Washington, whose gallant force through a combination of exhaustion and intoxication was largely incapable of defence.[82]

Cornwallis, about to take ship for England, was recalled. With 8,000 men including the Hessian grenadiers and *Jäger* he nearly trapped Washington; but, by Clinton's account guilty of the most consummate ignorance of any officer above the rank of corporal,[83] permitted him to slip off on the night of 2/3 January and win further laurels at Princeton, shattering Mawhood's British brigade with a loss of 270 men, despite a gallant charge which Hugh Gaine, the Tory editor, managed to turn into a glorious British victory.[84] Amongst the casualties of Cornwallis's fruitless advance was a *Jäger* whose ghost reputedly haunted the blacks of the neighbourhood for some years.[85]

[78] *Pennsylvania Evening Post*, 31 Dec. 1776, quoted in Stryker, *Battles of Trenton and Princeton*, p. 369.
[79] Washington, *Writings*, VI, p. 232.
[80] Münchhausen, fasc. 3, fols. 78–9, note 11.
[81] Stryker, *Battles of Trenton and Princeton*, p. 190.
[82] 'There were great quantities of Spirituous Liquors at Trenton of which the Soldiers drank too freely to admit of Discipline or Defence in Case of Attack.' Letter of Joseph Reed quoted in Stryker, *Battles of Trenton and Princeton*, p. 206.
[83] Clinton, *Narrative*, p. 60.
[84] Moore, *Diary of the Revolution*, I, p. 372 n. 1.
[85] Stryker, *Battles of Trenton and Princeton*, p. 268.

The Hessians

The Hessian defeat was of great moral importance. Ambrose Serle reported in October that the rebels' dread of the Hessians was such that they almost ran away at the name.[86] This myth was now shattered and the rebel cause gained confidence. 'This reverse has given the Americans great spirits,' wrote Captain Harris of the 5th, 'which I am convinced they would never have had if the Hessians had not been surprised, but fought as I have seen them.'[87] So sudden was the defeat that various ingenious theories circulated as to its cause. One that held credence with some in England and Germany was that, in the midst of the battle, Charles Lee's division, dressed in British red coats, had come upon the Hessians from the rear and decided the issue.[88] For American patriots, however, there was no doubt but that the God-given genius of Washington had gained the victory. The English traveller Cresswell found his host Kirk at Leesburg, Virginia, who six weeks previous had been lamenting Washington's want of skill and experience in military matters, now extolling him to the clouds. 'Alexander, Pompey, and Hannibal were but pigmy Generals, in comparison with the magnanimous Washington.'[89] The effect on the common people was electric:

The minds of the people are much altered. A few days ago they had given up the cause for lost. Their late successes have turned the scale and now they are all liberty mad again. Their recruiting parties could not get a man ... last week, and now the men are coming in by companies. Confound the turncoat scoundrels and the cowardly Hessians together. This has given them new spirits, and got them fresh succours.... They have recovered their panic and it will not be an easy matter to throw them into that confusion again.[90]

And after his countrymen had been abused at Kirk's, Cresswell wrote in high dudgeon, 'It is the Damd Hessians that has caused this, curse the scoundrel that first thought of sending them here.'[91]

Ewald later wrote that this relatively trifling affair threw the British into such a panic that, although previously everywhere successful, they now thought to see Washington and his army in all

---

[86] Serle, *Journal*, p. 120.

[87] W. H. Wilkin, *Some British Soldiers in America* (London, 1914), p. 192.

[88] *The Diary of Thomas Hutchinson* (2 vols. New York, 1971), II, p. 136; Hans Droysen, 'Die Braunschweigischen Truppen in Nordamerikanischen Unabhängigkeitskrieg', *Jahrbuch des Geschichtsvereins für das Herzogtum Braunschweig*, XIII (1914), p. 173.

[89] Cresswell, *Journal* p. 181.

[90] Ibid., pp. 179–80.

[91] Ibid., p. 181. In certain quarters of the British army, earlier praise for the Hessians turned to scorn. A captain of the Royal Marines in a letter to his patron called them the worst troops he had ever seen. Marion Balderston and David Syrett, ed., *The Lost War: Letters from British Officers during the American Revolution* (New York, 1976), p. 125.

The Battle of Trenton

quarters. 'Such weak mortals are human beings, in good fortune over proud, and in bad times cast down.'[92] The Hessian officers were much concerned at the misfortune which had happened to their troops alone, although Grant did not escape just criticism. 'Various are the opinions (for you must know we are all Generals) in our army, of the propriety and Possibility of Supporting Rall' wrote Captain Francis Hutcheson to Frederick Haldimand. 'General Grant was at Brunswick and Commands in the Jerseys, could he have supported that post in time, it would have added to his Laurels, and prevented a deal of idle talk on the subject.'[93]

After Trenton, the great liberal historian G. O. Trevelyan assures us, the Americans, 'whether they were Continental regulars, or minute-men, or armed farmers in their shirt-sleeves', advanced to the attack disdainfully confident of victory whenever they found the mercenaries on their own.[94] The success which this assumption encountered may be easily illustrated. On 18 January Major General William Heath's three militia divisions appeared before Fort Independence near Spuyten Duyvil and summoned the garrison, composed of 400 Hessians and the Queen's Rangers, to surrender. To the mercenaries Heath particularly offered 'the same lenity which their brethren taken in the Jerseys now enjoyed'.[95] The commander, Captain Wilmowsky of Trumbach's regiment, refused and shortly thereafter emphasized his reply with cannonballs. The regiments Trumbach, Wissenbach, and Stein manned their alarm posts, and after an exchange of fire the enemy retired behind some high ground.[96] A week of ineffectual American effort followed. On 25 January the reinforced garrison attacked the besiegers, routed them near Delancey's Mills and cleared them from Valentine's House. Four days later Heath ended the fiasco by withdrawing. So much for the easy confidence of contempt.[97]

Indeed in the war of outposts which ensued that winter in New Jersey the Hessians gave a good account of themselves. On 1 February 1777 a large body of Americans fell upon the 42nd Highlanders as they were protecting a foraging party under Colonel Harcourt. Without waiting for orders Captain Philip von

---

[92] Ewald, *Belehrungen*, III, p. 131.
[93] Add. MS. 21680, fol. 163, 5 Jan. 1777.
[94] Trevelyan, *The American Revolution*, III, pp. 122–3.
[95] *The London Chronicle*, XLI (1777), p. 266, 'From the New York Gazette Jan. 23 and 30'; Kemble, *Journal*, p. 108.
[96] StaMarburg 12.11 I Ba 7 (Journal of the Regiment von Bose), fols. 29–30.
[97] Washington, *Writings*, VII, pp. 32 n. 57, 94, and 96 n. 76; Heath, *Memoirs*, pp. 117–23.

Wurmb, commanding Block's grenadiers in the colonel's absence, led his men against the attackers, threw them into confusion, and put them to flight. Wurmb lost only one grenadier shot through the throat and reckoned twenty enemy dead left on the field.[98] The Hessians' conduct contrasts favourably with that of the Waldeckers, a large party of whom were captured with trifling resistance.[99]

Was Trenton the turning point of the war? Certainly the British never again achieved quite the unbroken successes of the 1776 campaign, nor did Washington again blunder so close to total defeat. On 3 May 1779 Germain said in the Commons that the unlucky defeat at Trenton had blasted all their hopes.[100] But this was over two years later, after the bungling of 1777 and France's entering the war. The next year, 1780, Germain would be writing with assurance to Clinton, that the American war effort was exhausted; and an American army historian has called the summer of 1780, not the winter of 1776–7, the nadir of their fortunes: the currency worthless, the troops unpaid and mutinous, the French disillusioned, and Benedict Arnold about to betray his compatriots.[101]

Although the posts in the Jerseys had to be drawn in after Princeton, the King's forces still held the initiative: superior in numbers and training to Washington's, holding New York and Canada as springboards for attack with more reinforcements coming for 1777 including 1,300 Ansbachers and additional *Jäger*. Congress still had difficulty recruiting,[102] and Americans deserted in large numbers.[103] It was the consummate muddle of 1777, rather than Trenton, that threw away these advantages. Assured of victory, two British armies, Howe's and Burgoyne's, set off for objectives so separate that neither could assist the other. Both Donop and Henry Clinton thought it futile for Howe to sail for the Chesapeake in 1777. From Head of Elk Donop wrote to Prince

---

[98] StaMarburg 4h.409. nr. 3, fol. 191, Donop to Heister, 1 Feb. 1777; 12.11. 1 Ba 14 (Journal of Block's battalion), fol. 8. There is a British account in Lydenberg, ed., *Archibald Robertson's Diaries and Sketches*, pp. 123–4, an American in John Almon, ed., *The Remembrancer; or Impartial Repository of Public Events for the Year 1777* (London, 1778), p. 98, 'Extract of a letter from an Officer of Distinction ... Feb. 3, 1777.' By their own account they lost fifteen killed and as many wounded.
[99] *New Jersey Archives*, 2nd series, I, p. 270.
[100] *Parliamentary History*, XX, pp. 742–3.
[101] Maurice Matlock, ed., *American Military History* (Washington, DC, 1964), pp. 88–9.
[102] Washington, *Writings*, VII, pp. 318, 405, 413; VIII, pp. 148, 207.
[103] Ibid., VIII, p. 8; StaMarburg 4h.413. nr. 4, fol. 86, letter of Capt. Wagner, 29 May 1777.

Friedrich Wilhelm of Prussia that the expedition should have gone to New England to aid Burgoyne.[104]

Nevertheless the ultimate American victory was no more secured by Saratoga than by Trenton. The war dragged on through 1778 and 1779 as the French and Americans failed at Newport and Savannah and initiative passed once again to the British. Grasping the nettle with unsure hands, Clinton and Cornwallis succeeded in dividing British strength along the Eastern Seaboard without the requisite naval superiority, and gave Washington and De Grasse their opportunity at Yorktown.[105]

Thus it came about as Ewald wrote bitterly after Yorktown:

These are the fruits of conducting by absurd rules a war which we began, in which we followed no plan, merely tugged at the enemy on all sides, and in no quarter pressed him with all our strength. Because of this we have lost everything when we wanted to preserve it all. It is shocking to think, that the finest and most battle-worthy army, after six campaigns, was set back again to the place from which, six years before, they had marched forth ... with the most favourable prospects, and indeed against men who were scarcely soldiers and who could have been brought to their knees in the first year.... It would take a miracle to make up for this disastrous performance.[106]

HEISTER RELIEVED OF COMMAND

A search for the guilty party was inevitable after Trenton. For the Hessians it took the form of a prolonged court-martial to determine the conduct of the three beaten regiments. If the Landgraf was to remain a successful practitioner of the soldier trade, he had to determine why a brigade of his troops allowed itself to be captured after such feeble resistance, and to demonstrate to the military world that the faults had been rectified. For the British commander-in-chief, however, it was convenient to thrust the whole blame on to the mercenaries and conceal his own culpability and that of his friends like Grant and Cornwallis.

Howe's particular villain was old Leopold von Heister. The defeat of the Hessians was the climax to a long series of disappointments which Howe saw fit to attribute to this unimaginative

---

[104] Huth, 'Letters from a Mercenary', p. 499. For Clinton's view, see *Narrative*, pp. 61–2.

[105] There is not sufficient space here to discuss in length the causes of the British defeat, except insofar as the Hessians affected the result. The reader is referred to Professor Willcox's biography of Clinton, *Portrait of a General*, his introduction to *Narrative*, and his article, 'The British Road to Yorktown: A Study in Divided Command', *AHR*, LII (1946), pp. 1–35; and to Mackesy's *The War for America*.

[106] 'Tagebuch', IV, p. 284, quoted in Kipping, *Hessen-Kassel Truppen*, pp. 16–17.

soldier. From their first encounter Howe had found Heister's attitude at variance with his own intentions. The British had paid a vast sum to obtain trained regiments; they expected the mercenaries to fight vigorously for their pay, and Faucitt had offered Heister and Knyphausen a bribe to this end. Instead, Heister's first thought on landfall was for the rest and care of his men.[107] According to Germain, reading Howe's dispatches, Heister could be induced only by the most artful flattery to lead them into battle.[108]

Heister's reluctance to open the campaign immediately was due to his own exhaustion after the voyage (quite understandable in a man of his years, unused to the sea) and to his excessive concern for his sovereign's instructions to preserve the corps. Friedrich II was most solicitous for the health and preservation of his soldiers. He scanned the monthly muster returns with careful eye, and any battalion or company with more than its share of sick or dead was quickly brought to the attention of the Hessian corps commander, with a demand for an explanation and an improvement in the situation.[109] One need not put this down to altruism: with such a small country, Friedrich could not supply drafts in sufficient numbers to make good a Napoleonic wastage rate. If the officers and surgeons did not look after their men, the corps would soon be decimated and his business at an end. Thus Heister feared that, if his men began dying like flies on Staten Island, he would soon be looking for new employment or languishing in Spangenberg prison. Howe did not know this; nor, had he, would be have sympathized very much. Heister's judicious regard for the care of his men cut no ice when the British expected to finish the war in a single campaign.

Howe was equally dissatisfied with Heister at White Plains for moving too slowly and for his men failing to push home an attack on Chatterton Hill when ordered to advance. Major Nisbet Balfour, Howe's ADC sent home with dispatches, reported that the Hessians had behaved ill at White Plains, refusing to advance, upon which the British had passed them, insulting them and bidding them stand out of the way.[110] As we have seen, this is only

---

[107] Donop said that Heister asked for eight days rest. Donop's troops landed on 14 Aug.; they moved to Long Island on 22 August, eight days later. StaMarburg 4h.413. nr. 4, fol. 97.
[108] Bedford Record Office, Lucas Collection L29/213.
[109] For example, StaMarburg 4h.410. nr. 2, fol. 18, the Landgraf to Knyphausen, 3 Aug. 1777.
[110] Bedford Record Office, Lucas Collection L29/214.

part of the story, for the first British attack was repulsed, and the honour of the day belonged to the Regiment von Lossberg in particular. But Howe and those about him believed the version reported by Balfour. Howe also thought Heister failed to bring on his column quickly enough, and a compliment to Rall in his official dispatch was almost a back-handed slap at the Hessian commander for not being further forward.[111]

Münchhausen defended Heister in his commentary on Howe's *Narrative*. Münchhausen was not then Howe's ADC, but as captain-lieutenant of the Leib company of the Leib-Regiment, he happened to be marching at the very head of the Hessian column that day and had Heister constantly in his sight. He said that the Hessians were a good way behind, first, because they were marching in file as was the custom in America and the column was thus greatly extended; and second, because the British failed to keep closed up, a common failing of theirs, further extending the straggling column. When they were fired upon, everybody was caught by surprise, and the light dragoons and artillery deployed between the British brigades and the Hessians, further obscuring the latter's view. Thus it was some time before Heister knew what was happening.[112]

A further delay was occasioned by bad communications. Neither Howe nor Heister spoke the other's language, or even French particularly well. Heister's English adjutant who brought him Howe's orders, a man who stammered anyway, was on this occasion drunk as well, according to Münchhausen, which made him doubly incomprehensible. Probably the orders were mistakenly interpreted.[113] To the possibility of Heister being afraid in battle, Münchhausen wrote:

No one can believe that the man who distinguished himself in the previous war in Germany under the command of Duke Ferdinand of Braunschweig so often against the French that he received five wounds would not have wished to attack an enemy already beaten before. Especially since he himself had shortly before gone into the greatest danger, in that he rode from our Regiment to Lossberg's where the fire was fiercest, and where one of his ADCs, an Ordnance Dragoon, and also two horses from his suite were wounded.[114]

[111] CO5/236, fol. 3, Howe to Germain, 30 Nov. 1776. By courtesy alone foreign divisional commanders were usually mentioned in dispatches.
[112] Münchhausen, fasc. 3, fol. 69, note 6.
[113] Ibid., fol. 73. Of Heister's two British ADCs, Faucitt (the colonel's son) and Sheldon, this probably refers to the latter. He returned to Britain with Heister, Knyphausen retaining Faucitt.
[114] Ibid.

By this stage Heister could probably do nothing right in Howe's eyes. After White Plains he was employed less actively. Knyphausen led the assault on Fort Washington. The brigades of Donop and Rall were the only Hessians sent into New Jersey. Their activity and success made these two colonels much more favoured among the mercenaries by Howe than their elderly chief was.

Howe also believed that Heister encouraged his men to plunder with impunity. Balfour reported that 'the Hessian Officers were only desirous of making money, plundering &c', a belief commonly held at British headquarters, judging by Ambrose Serle's journal and Sir George Osborne's dispatches.[115] Even a subaltern of the 45th wrote that 'the infamous practice . . . was much encouraged by De Heister who shared in the profits of this lucrative occupation'.[116] It is not improbable that this story originated with his seniors. Howe and his brother hoped to conciliate the supposedly loyal populace. This was hardly likely to succeed if the Germans were robbing them of their goods.

Howe's estimate of Heister's military capacities is illustrated by his neglecting to consult him or even inform him of the plan of battle at Long Island. Instead, like a private on a barrack square, he was told to advance at the firing of signal guns. Heister, loyal to his sovereign's instructions for the preservation of the corps, delayed his attack rather longer than Howe expected. This saved casualties, but it can hardly have endeared him to Howe.[117] In contrast, when Knyphausen landed he led his men into action almost before they had time to draw breath.[118]

After Trenton Howe wrote Germain a letter denouncing nearly all the senior Hessian officers. Rall's misconduct was 'amazing', Donop's being lured off to Mount Holly was indefensible and his retiring from his post without orders denoted panic. The major generals were not fit to be entrusted with a command.

The two Lieut.-Generals Heister and Kniphausen are much too infirm for this war, tho' I believe the latter extremely zealous for his Majesty's service, but I tremble when I think the former may remain with us another campaign. He is

---

[115] Bedford Record Office, Lucas Collection L29/214; Serle, *Journal*, pp. 186–7; CO5/93, Part II, fol. 501, Osborne to Germain, 29 Oct. 1776.
[116] Wilkin, *Some British Soldiers*, p. 246. The whole question of Hessian plundering will be discussed below, pp. 171–83.
[117] StaMarburg 4h.410. nr. 1, fol. 360, Heister to the Landgraf, 3 Sept. 1776.
[118] Force, *American Archives*, fifth series, III, p. 1059, 'Extract of a letter from an English Officer dated New York, Dec. 3, 1776.'

exceedingly unsteady and so entirely averse to carry the Hessians into action, I must be very anxious for his removal.[119]

In a second letter he blamed his inability to catch Washington on the Hessian attachment to their heavy baggage. The Hessian major generals, totally unfit for the service, should be replaced as brigadiers by colonels. 'Four or five of them [the colonels] are officers of experience, and I may add are fully determined to render their utmost service in this war.'[120]

Howe's judgement of the major generals was accurate, but in fact they had been replaced throughout the campaign by colonels, one of whom was Rall. The reference to Knyphausen as too infirm was a slur on a man who had rendered at Fort Washington as valuable service as any in the King's army, and who, in Wiederholdt's words, tore down the abatis with his own hands and was exposed to the musketry and cannon fire like a common soldier.[121] As to quantities of baggage delaying them, the Hessians fought much of the campaign without their usual camp-equipage.[122] That of Rall's brigade, for example, caught up with them only just before they took up their post at Trenton.[123] Lieutenant Bardeleben was detached on 7 November to forward his regiment's baggage which had remained on board ship since the campaign had opened in August.[124] Returns of baggage and hospital wagons show that the Hessians had proportionately no more impedimenta than the British.[125] Howe himself, not Hessian slowness, had cost him his best chances to destroy Washington, at Long Island, New York, and on the Delaware.

Nor could Howe properly blame Heister for Trenton. It was entirely his own fault that Rall was posted there.[126]

Howe had already asked to be rid of Heister before Trenton. As early as 7 January 1777, long before news of the Hessian defeat

---

[119] HMC: *Report on the Manuscripts of Mrs. Stopford-Sackville* (London, 1904–10), II, pp. 53–4 (letter of 31 Dec. 1776).

[120] CO5/94, fols. 100–1, Howe to Germain, 17 Jan. 1777.

[121] Wiederholdt, 'Tagebuch', p. 23.

[122] StaMarburg 4h.410 nr. 1, fol. 507, Heister to the Landgraf, 21 March 1777.

[123] Ibid. 12. 11 I Ba 6 (Journal of the Regiment von Knyphausen), fol. 28.

[124] Bardeleben, p. 80.

[125] *Journals of the Commons*, XXXVII, pp. 1104–7.

[126] Both Howe and Burgoyne later put forward the defence that, since their mercenary detachments were on the left wing in the order of battle, it had been necessary for the sake of etiquette to detach these corps to Trenton and Bennington respectively. Thurlow, who led the ministry's attack on Burgoyne, remarked, 'So, because one damn'd blockhead did a foolish thing, the other blockhead must follow his example.' HMC: *Report on Manuscripts in Various Collections* (London, 1909), VI, pp. 271–2.

The Hessians

reached Europe, Suffolk wrote to Schlieffen saying that Howe in his last letters had represented it as impracticable to continue Heister in command of the Hessians and that the operations of the army ran the risk of several reverses if he stayed on. Suffolk asked Schlieffen to arrange the business of Heister's removal however he thought best, but to get Heister replaced by Knyphausen. To avoid repercussions, the King did not wish to declare in public his dissatisfaction with Heister, but to allege old age, his long service, and his infirmities as reason for recall.[127]

The Landgraf was in Italy on one of his cultural tours when the letter reached Schlieffen, who hesitated to act without consulting his sovereign. Normally the power of naming commanders and all officers and officials remained with the Landgraf who was, like the King, commander-in-chief in theory and practice. The Landgraf took decisions with the advice of ministers and councillors of state, but in his absence they would act only on questions of small importance in their own areas of responsibility.[128] Schlieffen sent the request on to Friedrich, but the latter's travels were so irregular that the letter would have difficulty reaching him. Friedrich's minister replied to Suffolk that only seniority of rank had induced the Landgraf to appoint Heister to the command and, distrusting his intelligence, he had given him Knyphausen as adviser. While keeping up appearances with Heister, Howe could in the meantime be served by Knyphausen as if he were actually in command:

> Heister will execute the job he has been charged with, with courage. But one must distrust his judgement and always keep him in combination. When Prince Ferdinand [of Braunschweig] commanded the army and he had to use an officer of this capacity, he made use of the means of placing by his side some officer in whom he had confidence, to guide him. On any occasion when Genl Howe cannot dispense with giving Heister a role, he should give him prompters of this kind. A vanity which is of the nature of a narrowness is his weakness. If one takes advantage of him by this means, instead of causing him offence, he will do everything one wishes. The Landgraf wished at first to give the command of the troops to Knyphausen, but there were 4 other Genls between him and Heister, and it presented him with great difficulties, which would also have caused him embarassment.[129]

This reply could give little satisfaction to Howe, who had been trying such expedients, and found they wore his patience thin.

---

[127] SP81/186, Suffolk to Schlieffen, 7 Jan. 1777.
[128] Kurt Dülfer, 'Fürst und Verwaltung: Grundzüge der hessischen Verwaltungsgeschichte in 16–19. Jahrhundert', *Hessisches Jahrbuch für Landesgeschichte*, III (1953), pp. 187 and 211.
[129] SP81/186, Schlieffen to Suffolk, 23 Jan. 1777.

Suffolk wrote again on 4 February, asking Schlieffen to act against Heister in a discreet manner, to avoid public disgrace for the old general. 'A formal and public representation against an officer in a situation like Genl de Heister's is would become a serious matter for the man against whom it is made. It is a measure which, in its consequences, might well plunge its object into total ruin and irreparable disgrace. We have too much sensibility here to expose the person concerned to such misfortune ... without first having recourse to softer measures.'[130] This, in spite of all the care taken, was what actually happened.

Suffolk's concern for Heister's sensibilities scarcely concealed the ministry's fear that Heister's public sacking would have a detrimental effect on the morale of his corps. He was in good favour with the troops, and of his senior subordinates Mirbach and Colonel Friedrich von Lossberg had expressed satisfaction at serving under him.[131]

The blow of Trenton sealed the business, giving the Landgraf a decisive pretext for recalling Heister. Suffolk wrote again on 25 February, the very day that news of Trenton reached London, greatly to the mortification of Kutzleben, Hessian ambassador to St James's.[132] 'The great displeasure which Genl Howe continues to hold against the conduct of this officer [Heister], and the manner in which he represents that the success of the coming campaign depends in fact upon the change which I have been instructed to obtain, leaves His Majesty no choice upon the subject and obliges me to demand with the greatest earnestness the recall of General Heister. ...' At the same time Suffolk added that the King wished this to be effected without unnecessary trouble, and that Heister's advanced age, the state of his health, or his personal affairs were to be alleged as reasons for his return. Since the Landgraf might not yet have returned from his travels, Suffolk added that he was persuaded that it would not be disagreeable to Friedrich if the conduct of 'this delicate and important business' were entrusted to Schlieffen's care.[133] Fearing that this was not enough, Suffolk sent a second letter under the same date which left no doubt: '*L'affair devient très serieuse. Il faut absolument qu'Heister soit rappelé. Le Roy en est déterminée. ...*'[134]

---

130 Ibid., Suffolk to Schlieffen, 4 Feb. 1777.
131 StaHannover 41 v Nr. 22, fol. 25, Estorff's report, 26 March 1776.
132 StaMarburg 4h.413. nr. 4, fol. 77, Kutzleben to (Schlieffen?), 25 Feb. 1777.
133 SP81/186, Suffolk to Schlieffen, 25 Feb. 1777.
134 Ibid. (the second of two letters). Italics original.

The business was only settled, however, when the Landgraf replied to Schlieffen's letter, as the latter pointed out to Suffolk.[135] This would probably have been done before Trenton had Friedrich been in Hessen, particularly since Schlieffen, in whom the Landgraf fully confided, was in favour of Heister's recall. Thus although Trenton is usually considered the reason for the old general's disgrace, it was rather an additional factor, albeit an important one, added to Howe's demands.

Friedrich returned to Kassel on 28 March. On 7 April he wrote to both Heister and Knyphausen, instructing the former to return 'temporarily' on account of his health and to consult with him about Trenton, while Knyphausen took command *ad interim*.[136] Schlieffen wrote the same day to inform Suffolk.[137]

Meanwhile Heister in his dispatches gave no indication of guessing what was being prepared for him. He continued to praise Howe for his continued kindness towards the Hessian troops and good relations with Heister himself.[138] Either Howe was a great dissembler, or Heister intentionally concealed their differences from his sovereign. It is true that the British spied on Hessian letters to check the morale and attitudes of their auxiliaries;[139] but the tenor of Heister's letters gives no hint that he was aware of this. Nor was Heister greatly concerned with explaining what happened at Trenton; his correspondence deals with routine matters, promotion, the corps administration, sickness, the quality of the recruits, and the Hessian order of battle.[140] On 21 January he wrote, 'The good harmony with the commanding general, Howe, and with the English generally still continues very strong', and on 9 February he asked to have Münchhausen back as his own ADC since he had done so well with Howe.[141] This was hardly the

[135] SP81/187, Schlieffen to Suffolk, 6 March 1777.
[136] StaMarburg 4h.410. nr. 1, fol. 493, to Heister, and ibid. nr. 2, fols. 1–3, to Knyphausen. Stryker, *Battles of Trenton and Princeton*, p. 227 mistakenly credits the second letter to Friedrich's son, the Erbprinz Wilhelm.
[137] SP81/187, Schlieffen to Suffolk, 7 April 1777.
[138] StaMarburg 4h. 410. nr. 1, fol. 564, Heister to the Landgraf, 5 June 1777.
[139] The *Kriegsrat* Lorenz complained that packets of Hessian letters had been opened, and a copy of a letter of Donop to the Prussian Crown Prince is found in the papers of George III. HMC: *American*, I, pp. 99–100, Lorenz to Capt. Mackenzie, 28 March 1777; *Correspondence of George III*, III, nr. 2054. Compare the latter with Huth, 'Letters from a Mercenary', p. 499. See also Add. MS. 23652, fol. 7, Sir Joseph Yorke to Col. Rainsford, 5 July 1776.
[140] The extracts of Heister's correspondence in Stryker give a very false impression. Parts of his letters dealing with Trenton were extracted from his despatches and placed with the Trenton documents in Marburg. In fact, after his initial report, Heister scarcely mentioned the action.
[141] StaMarburg 4h.410. nr. 1, fols. 475 and 486.

request of a man fearing that he would be relieved of his command at any moment.

When the troops in Jersey at last broke out of their dismal winter quarters and advanced toward the Highlands, Howe, for reasons of seniority, presumably, and good relations with the Hessians' gave Heister command of one of the two divisions of his army. Howe made three rather perfunctory attempts to ensnare Washington in June, 1777.[142] The Hessians were twice criticized for slowness in these operations. On 24 June Stirn's brigade 'by its delay in not passing alertly from Staten Island to the mainland in some measure prevented the success of the day'.[143] On 26 June Stephen Kemble was told that the march of Cornwallis's first division was retarded by the Hessians.[144] Yet it was on that day Howe gained his only success, largely through the action of Minnigerode's grenadiers at Short Hills. At 7.30 that morning they encountered several enemy battalions and three guns on the heights before Quibbletown, the enemy withdrawing before the fire of the amusettes and Ewald's *Jäger*, and from Cornwallis's superior numbers. After a pursuit march of three quarters of an hour in intense heat, the *Jäger* and light infantry encountered a detachment of a hundred men on a steep height and drove them off without any notable loss on either side. At that moment several cannon shots flew into the column from their right flank. Immediately Minnigerode's battalion supported by the English Guards was detached to strike the enemy's flank, and succeeded so well as to take sixty prisoners and three enemy guns, Minnigerode's claiming two and the Guards one. The attack had been pressed home at point of bayonet through grapeshot fire, but so wild was the enemy shooting that the battalion's loss was only eleven wounded and one missing.[145]

During these operations, in which Howe was repeatedly frustrated in his design of luring Washington into the open, Heister was clearly in disgrace. On 15 June Howe's suspicion that the Hessian cast a blind eye on plundering came into the open – 'Great symptoms of a disposition to plunder being perceived in the troops,

[142] Anderson, Howe's biographer, stated that he was already looking forward to his expedition to Philadelphia. *Command of the Howe Brothers*, p. 240.
[143] Egerton MS. 2135, fol. 25. This journal appears to be John Andre's.
[144] Kemble, *Journal*, p. 123.
[145] Amongst the newly arrived *Jäger*, however, four suffocated on the ground in the heat and five were missing, presumed taken while marauding. StaMarburg 4h. 409. nr. 3, fols. 251–2, Donop to Heister, 30 June 1777; 12. 11 1 Ba 16 (Journal of the Grenadier Battalion Platte), fol. 143; Münchhausen, fasc. 2, fol. 37. The last puts enemy losses at 400, an exaggeration presumably based on deserters' reports. Washington admitted sixty-four prisoners and claimed to have taken thirteen. Washington, *Writings*, VIII, p. 310.

the Commander in Chief sent a Message to Gen: Heister desiring him to warn the Hessians not to persist in such Outrages, as they would be most severely punished.'[146] On 22 June, as the army withdrew towards Amboy, Heister's division leading, Cornwallis's following, Heister halted without orders to cannonade the rebels who were annoying his rear. Münchhausen was sent with peremptory orders that he should continue his march without delay.[147] The Americans continued to harass the withdrawing columns, and at length Howe himself was obliged to take two regiments and several guns from Cornwallis's column to engage the attackers. Only after a fire-fight of two hours, a loss on the British side of thirty killed and wounded, and severe blasts of grapeshot from his guns, was Howe able successfully to disengage and continue the withdrawal. Immediately thereafter Münchhausen was detached again to order Heister 'not to permit himself to halt for anything, but, not only to continue his march, but also to lead the three Hessian and the several English regiments which he had with him to Staten Island on the boats which he would find ready waiting in the vicinity of Princess Bay....'[148] Once again Howe gave his third-in-command specific orders, but no idea of his plan or intentions.

On 23 June the order for Heister's recall arrived. According to Münchhausen it had been long expected at British headquarters.[149] Heister was embittered. He said not another word to Howe before his embarkation, except on 1 July when the British commander paid him a courtesy farewell visit, 'certainly for him [Howe] a very unpleasant visit', remarked Münchhausen.[150] And he penned an angry letter to the Landgraf explaining that it was not his fault that Rall had commanded the brigade at Trenton.[151]

Heister embarked on the frigate *Niger* with Colonel Block and other officers invalided home, sailed on 19 July, and reached Portsmouth roads on 22 August.[152] From there he wrote to Germain and Suffolk expressing his undying devotion to the King's

---

[146] Egerton MS. 2135, fol. 10.
[147] Münchhausen, fasc. 2, fol. 32.
[148] Ibid., fol. 35.
[149] Münchhausen, fasc. 2, fol. 36.
[150] Ibid., fol. 39.
[151] StaMarburg 4h.410. nr. 1, fols. 589–94, 14 July 1777.
[152] ADM51/637, Log of HMS *Niger* (Capt. George Talbot); StaMarburg 4h.413. nr. 4, fol. 80, Kutzleben to (the Erbprinz?), 30 Aug. 1777. He took with him an atlas of North America on which General von Jungkenn followed the subsequent campaigns. Jungkenn 2:47, Cochenhausen to Jungkenn, 8 Feb. 1779.

cause and his great regret at being recalled from the head of his troops. To Suffolk he remarked hopefully that, whatever the reasons were for his return, he was persuaded that they would not be disadvantageous to him in any respect, reminding the Secretary of State of Faucitt's promise of His Majesty's protection for his family.[153] Germain, however, wrote in the margin of Heister's letter to him, for his undersecretary Knox, 'The Throne will be so good as to answer this as civilly as possible without saying anything that may commit me or engage His Majesty to reward the differed [i.e. varied] services of this General.'[154]

The old soldier, greatly mortified by his recall, reached Kassel on 13 October. His active service ended in disgrace, his spirit languished; he fell suddenly ill and died on 19 November. Medically the cause of death may have been put down to inflammation of the lungs or 'un coup d'apoplexie'.[155] The real cause, as his widow wrote to Faucitt, was 'les Chagrins de son Rapelle au milieu de la Campagne, qui ne cessait point de ronger son âme sensible'.[156] From his very deathbed, Heister, formerly so shrewd at getting emoluments, penned a pathetic letter to his sovereign, begging that he be paid his field allowance for the months of July to October and the surplus for November, for the support of his family. 'Thus have I sought once again, even on my deathbed, for this as well as for the gracious provision of a yearly pension for my spouse, the favour of my benevolent Prince, from whom I have had the good fortune to receive so many marks of esteem during my life and in whom, likewise putting my trust of a merciful hearing, I die.'[157] This appeal, and those of Madame Heister to Suffolk and Faucitt, did not go unanswered. The Landgraf ordered a yearly pension of 600 thalers and an 'equitable settlement of the General's field allowance, in order to demonstrate the ever constant esteem that was held for the honourable deceased', to be paid to Madame Heister. From the King she received £200 annually.[158]

153 SP81/188, Heister to Suffolk, 22 Aug. 1777.
154 CO5/94, fols. 432–3, Heister to Germain, 22 Aug. 1777.
155 Moore, *Journal of the Revolution*, I, p. 519; SP81/165, Madame Heister to Suffolk, 27 Nov. 1777.
156 SP81/189, Mme Heister to Faucitt, 24 Nov. 1777. See also StaWolfenbüttel 237N86, fol. 22, Winzingerode to Riedesel, 10 Dec. 1777.
157 StaMarburg 4h.410. nr. 1, fol. 595, 19 Nov. 1777. Although Heister actually died on the day of the letter, the ending is not quite so pathetic as it seems: '*ich esterbe*' was a common form of submissive respect in concluding letters.
158 Ibid., fol. 597, the Landgraf to Mme Heister, 22 Nov. 1777; SP81/190, Suffolk to Mme Heister, 3 Feb 1778.

Heister's death, like Rall's, put him beyond the scope of any inquiry into the events at Trenton. For the surviving officers, however, the suspense lasted until 1782 when the *Kriegscollegium* approved the decision of the court-martial convened by Knyphausen in New York.[159] The lapse of time had two causes. The first inquiry failed ·to provide detailed evidence on the conduct of the regiments and in particular to explain why Lieutenant Colonel Scheffer of Lossberg's, who had taken command when Rall fell, had not withdrawn over the Assunpinck bridge. And the gathering of the surviving officers to testify proved difficult, since Lossberg's and Knyphausen's regiments were sent to Canada and Rall's to Savannah.

The court martial, headed by Major General von Kospoth[160] and composed of two colonels, four lieutenant colonels, three majors, three captains, three lieutenants, and three ensigns, finally rendered its verdict, the junior officers giving their findings first so as not to be influenced by the decisions of their seniors. As a conclusion Kospoth and *Stabsauditeur* Lotheisen appended their decision.[161] The findings were perhaps better evidence of professional solidarity amongst the officers than of the impartiality of the investigation. All ranks concurred in throwing the blame on Rall and Dechow, both conveniently dead, and acquitting all the living, recommending that the regiments be given new colours. Lieutenant Engelhardt of the artillery, who had misbehaved by abandoning his guns, was acquitted 'because he had distinguished himself on many occasions since'. The *Jäger* detachment was exonerated from failing to do their duty and running away at the start of the action because they had followed their commander, Lieutenant Grothausen; he too was dead, having been shot by Hand's Pennsylvanians on 2 January 1777.[162] Of two officers of Knyphausen's regiment who had tried to find an escape route across the Assunpinck, Captain Loewenstein, who had shot himself in Canada,[163] was held to have much to answer for; but Captain

[159] StaMarburg 4h.328. nr. 120, Actum Kriegs Collegium Cassel, 29 April and 2 May, 1782. The *Kriegscollegium* was the old *Generalkriegskommission* of 1714, formerly responsible for administering the Landgraf's military directives. Friedrich II renamed it, and stripped it of power save for the maintenance of military discipline and justice. Dülfer, 'Furst and Verwaltung', pp. 211–12.

[160] Former CO of Wutginau's regiment, he took over the grenadier brigade on Donop's death, serving at Charleston in 1780.

[161] StaMarburg 4h. 328. nrs. 118–19, reproduced in part in Stryker, *Battles of Trenton and Princeton*, pp. 411–19.

[162] Ewald, *Belehrungen*, II, p. 140.

[163] StaMarburg 12.11 I Ba 6 (Journal of the Regiment von Knyphausen), fol. 130.

Biesenrodt, who of course was still serving, was relieved of blame because he did not know of a shallow ford nearby.

And why not? All the living had their careers and families to think about. To condemn them would cut them off from the fount of promotion and honour, not to speak of probable confinement in Spangenberg prison. This was harsh on the memory of those who died, but the colonels in their verdict solvaged their consciences by noting that Rall 'having . . . died of the wounds he received at the attack on Trenton cannot be held to answer these charges, and a decision cannot justly be rendered against him'.[164]

Nor, although there was plenty of evidence for it, was the court martial foolish enough to put any blame on their allies and paymasters.

The historian Lowell called the Landgraf indiscriminate and unjust in his search for scapegoats and his treatment of the Trenton regiments.[165] This is untrue. A court martial was the logical consequence of the defeat of three of his front line regiments, under doubtful circumstances at best, and against an apparently untrained and demoralized foe. Soldiers were the Landgraf's stock in trade. His business would wither if his merchandise was not up to standard.

No modern army would allow such an incident to pass without an inquiry. By eighteenth-century standards the verdict was a merciful one. A British ministry had had Byng shot and Sackville disgraced for their failures. Charles Lee was condemned on insufficient evidence and never served again.[166] Lally, who lost France her Indian empire, was guillotined. Frederick the Great condemned Finck for his defeat at Maxen when the fault was his own. Wilhelm IX of Hessen's treatment of the officers who surrendered Rheinfels to the French in 1794 was far harsher than his father's to the Trenton regiments.[167] The Rall brigade had scarcely lived up to the device *Nescit Pericula* boasted on their standards. Yet in May 1778, when Major Matthaus of Rall's wrote asking for promotion for his son, a Freikorporal, the Landgraf, having threatened to cut off all the officers from promotion, granted the request.[168] The gallant Altenbockum, who had not disgraced him-

[164] Stryker, *Battles of Trenton and Princeton*, p. 413.
[165] Lowell, *The Hessians*, p. 97.
[166] Alden, *General Charles Lee*, pp. 238–40.
[167] Ditfurth, *Die Hessen in der Champagne*, pp. 397–429.
[168] StaMarburg 4h.410. nr. 2, fol. 269, Matthaus to the Landgraf, 6 May 1778. The son was promoted ensign in July 1778 and 2nd lieutenant in November, 1780.

self at Trenton, was promoted to major in 1781.[169] Andreas Wiederholdt found a secure post in 1785 as *Ober-kriegs- und Montirungs-Commissar.*[170] Lieutenant Colonel Franziskus Scheffer received his *Pour la vertu militaire* in 1783, and retired as a major general with pension, 16 November 1784.[171] This was no more than justice for men who campaigned bravely for their sovereign, but princes are not always so forgiving.

[169] Ibid. 4h.411. nr. 1, fol. 467, the Landgraf to Knyphausen, 12 March 1781.
[170] Ibid. 11. nr. 74, Ancienetäts-Liste.
[171] Ibid.; 4h.411. nr. 3, fol. 59, the Landgraf to Lossberg, 13 Feb. 1783.

5

The campaigns of 1777–81

THE ATTACK ON REDBANK

The reputation of the Hessian grenadiers is too well known to want an eulogium from my pen. In all times, in all places, in every situation, their conduct and valour have distinguished them.[1]

After his unsuccessful thrusts in New Jersey, Howe, intent upon the rebel capital Philadelphia, embarked the best of his troops at Staten Island in the first half of July 1777, and sailed on the 23rd, landing after a protracted voyage at the head of Chesapeake Bay a month later. The embarkation returns of the expedition show Howe's reduced dependence on the mercenaries: of 16,498 troops only 4,441 were Hessians.[2] Clinton was left to hold New York and its outposts with Provincials, the bulk of the Germans, and some British.

During Howe's campaign the *Jäger*, particularly Captains Ewald and Wreden, distinguished themselves on numerous occasions and defeated 'Scotch Willy' Maxwell's corps at Iron Hill.[3] Throughout the campaign a *Jäger* piquet of three officers and seventy men marched at the head of the army. But in the two major battles, Brandywine and Germantown, the British did the lion's share of the fighting. Hessian casualties were trifling in each: 6 killed and 24 wounded at Brandywine, 14 wounded at Germantown.[4] One British officer went so far as to write of Brandywine, that the Hessians 'had not the least share in this victory – having fired neither gun nor musket shot the whole day'.[5] In fact, the *Jäger* with

---

[1] George Hanger, Baron Coleraine, *The Life, Adventures, and Opinions of Colonel George Hanger* (2 vols. London, 1801), I, p. 41.

[2] Munchhausen, fasc. 2, fol. 21. This included about 170 Ansbach *Jäger*.

[3] Feilitzsch, fol, 19, 3 September 1777; StaMarburg 12.11 I Ba 17 (Journal of the *Feldjägercorps*), fols. 8–10.

[4] StaMarburg 4h.410. nr. 2, fols. 76–7. The return in CO5/94, fol. 328 includes Ansbach *Jäger* losses also.

[5] Robert Francis Seyboldt, ed., 'A Contemporary British Account of General Sir William Howe's Military Operations in 1777', *Proceedings of the American Antiquarian Society*, XL (1930), p. 79.

their rifles played a not inconsiderable part, as did Knyphausen as commander of one of Howe's two divisions.

The British took Philadelphia on 26 September, but American forts and a flotilla on the Delaware prevented supplies reaching the capital. British men and ships had to capture the American works and clear the *chevaux-de-frise* blocking the river. Early in October Howe began shifting forces from Germantown for this task, and erecting siege artillery on Province Island, a swampy feature at the mouth of the Schuylkill where it joined the Delaware. The task was not an easy one; the American defence was determined and resourceful.

On the morning of 11 October the Americans detected batteries under construction on Province Island and opened a heavy fire, under cover of which troops landed. The British behaved with unusual pusillanimity: Captain Blackmore of the 10th Regiment, commanding a partly completed battery with a twelve-pounder for defence, surrendered without firing a shot. A party of fugitives brought the news that the works and their occupants were taken and all was lost, to a detachment of Hessian grenadiers under Captain Philip von Wurmb and Lieutenant Friedrich von Berdot, who, having been in the forward positions all night, had been relieved at daybreak and posted on high ground commanding the Schuylkill ferry on the far side of the island. Wurmb, Lieutenant Groening, and Captain Moncrieff of the Royal Engineers decided to counterattack with ninety Hessian grenadiers. Groening led the way with a party of fifty. The Americans approached them with two white flags, hoping the newcomers would surrender as easily as Blackmore had, whereupon Groening's men opened fire and charged, recapturing most of the British prisoners. When some of the fugitives, having no desire to be rescued, ran off toward their captors' boats, Moncrieff fired on them in a rage with their own twelve-pounder. Groening secured the abandoned post, and Wurmb stationed himself to protect the flank. The enemy kept up a heavy cannonade from their ships and from Fort Mifflin on Mud Island, lasting into the night and setting the British powder store ablaze. Despite the danger of being blown to bits and having no gunners with them, Wurmb and Groening drove off two more attempted landings.[6]

Meanwhile Lieutenant Berdot also distinguished himself. On the orders of Major Vatas of the 10th, commanding all troops on the

[6] StaMarburg 4h.410. nr. 2, fols. 78–9, Wurmb to Donop, n.d.

island, Berdot was left with thirty grenadiers to hold the Schuylkill ferry as the only escape route. Half an hour after Wurmb's departure more English fugitives arrived, not merely to confirm the loss of the battery, but also claiming that the rebels had just captured Wurmb and fifty Hessian grenadiers, that the rest had retreated and would soon be taken, and that enemy detachments would cut off their own retreat. Vatas thereupon ordered Berdot and his men into the boats as quickly as possible. Berdot refused, pointing out that it was a matter of honour that they should not abandon the island, and unlikely that Wurmb's detachment had been captured without firing a single shot. When the enemy vessels discharged another salvo at them and yet more fugitives arrived crying out that the enemy were approaching, Vatas ordered Berdot to get to the boats. Berdot declined to obey, saying that the order to attack would be instantly carried out, but he would not do something which heaped disgrace upon him.

Thereupon he deserted me [wrote Berdot], crying out to the soldiers to follow him, and throwing himself into the nearest boat and crossing the river. The English fugitives and some grenadiers followed him and jumped into the other boats. As soon as I saw this confusion, I assembled the rest of my men into a body, ready to shoot into the boats, and cried out to those others that I would fire on them if they did not immediately turn back to the shore. – I cried out to two boats full of English grenadiers, already in the middle of the river, to think of the insult they were inflicting on a corps which had won so much glory in the last campaign and whose name alone was formidable to the enemy, inviting them to come back and join me, and with me to regain the fortunes of the day.

The British grenadiers, shamed to appear less valiant than the Hessians, rejoined Berdot, protesting that only on Vatas's express orders had they abandoned the post, but now they would obey Berdot's commands. He posted his men and obliged the English gunners, much against their will, to transport their twelve-pounder to a site he constructed out of fascines. In the distance they saw Wurmb's grenadiers on a small prominence, and it soon became clear that, far from allowing themselves to be taken prisoner, they had recaptured the battery and freed the British. Between one and two hours later Vatas returned to the island on Cornwallis's express order to take up his command again.[7] Both he and Blackmore were court-martialled, but rather than being disgraced were allowed to buy themselves out.[8]

[7] StaMarburg 4h.410. nr. 2, fols. 80–2, Berdot to Donop, 13 Oct. 1777.

[8] F. A. Whinyates, ed., *The Services of Lieut.-Colonel Francis Downman* (Woolwich, 1898), pp. 40 and 45. Charles Stedman gave the Hessians little credit in his history: 'From the

The fighting on Province Island was not yet over. Captain Friedrich von Stamford of Linsing's battalion relieved Wurmb with twenty-five of his own men and twenty-five British at 10 p.m. The next morning at break of day the enemy opened fire with floating batteries, continuing until ten o'clock when their galleys advanced toward the works. Landing craft disgorged attackers to left and right to strike Stamford's flanks, but he and his men opened on them 'a well directed and well sustained fire'. The flank parties halted to allow a frontal assault to go in, but this was repulsed, the attackers being 'shot down, killed or wounded, in large numbers, and fled precipitately to their boats, while the others followed their example'. Major Gardner of the British advanced to Stamford's support. His own casualties were two English and two Hessians killed, two English slightly wounded, and his own hat carried away by a shot which also damaged his hearing.[9]

Howe sent the grenadiers his thanks and twenty guineas. From their sovereign, Wurmb, Groening and Stamford all received the order *Pour la vertu militaire,* and Wurmb and Stamford their step to major.[10]

The work of clearing the Delaware was long and hard, against tenacious resistance. American defences comprised three strong points. The first, at Billingsport, abandoned and occupied by the 42nd Highlanders on 2 October, had two lines of *chevaux-de-frise,* long pointed timbers fixed in boxes weighted with stones and sunk to block the passage of vessels. Above them stood Fort Mifflin on Mud Island covering groups of *chevaux-de-frise* in the main channel. On the east or Jersey shore stood Fort Mercer on high ground known as Redbank,[11] because of the colour of the clay, protecting Mifflin's flank. An American flotilla including galleys, small well-

---

(Footnote continued)
    gallantry ... of a subaltern officer, the artillery was retaken, and the enemy compelled to retire.' *The History of the Origin, Progress, and Termination of the American War* (2 vols. London, 1794), I, p. 298.

[9] StaMarburg 4h.410. nr. 2, fol. 84, Stamford to Donop, 12 Oct. 1777; Karl W. Justi, 'Johann Ludwig Friedrich von Stamford', *Hessische, Denkwürdigkeiten,* IV (1805), nr. 2, pp. 77–9. An American account, the letter of an observer on the sloop *Speedwell,* agrees substantially with the Hessians' reports, although not specifically identifying their enemy as Hessians. *New Jersey Archives,* 2nd series, I, pp. 493–4.

[10] StaMarburg 4h.410. nr. 2, fols. 86 and 114.

[11] Perhaps because of its sanguinary associations, the Hessians referred to the post throughout as 'Redbank'; although, strictly, it was Fort Mercer that they attacked, I have followed the Hessian practice.

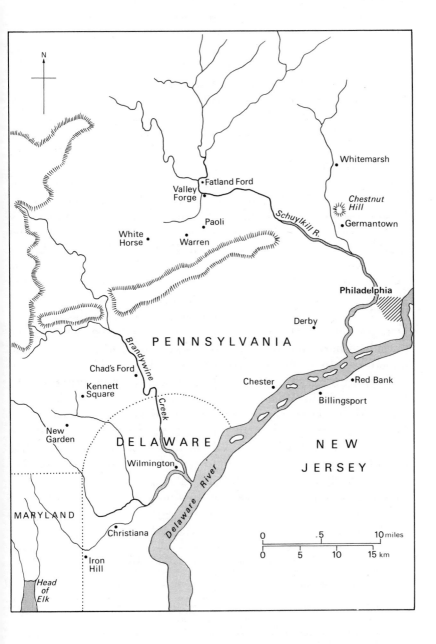

5   Operations round Philadelphia, 1777

armed craft powered by both oars and sail, assisted the forts.[12] Mud Island was the heart of the defence, but if Redbank were taken the former could not long be held. This was Howe's reasoning when he decided on 20 October to send an expedition against Fort Mercer. Donop, commander of the Hessian advanced troops, volunteered. His force was composed of three grenadier battalions, Linsing's, Lengerke's (formerly Block's) and Minnigerode's, the Regiment von Mirbach, and the *Jäger*, about 1,800 men in all.[13] Besides the battalion three-pounders, he took two eighteen-pound howitzers of the Royal Artillery; however, no siege guns or scaling ladders were provided.

Contemporary accounts agree that Donop volunteered for the expedition to signalize himself by some feat of arms, 'as the Hessians had done nothing of consequence this campaign'.[14] Captain O'Reilly of Lengerke's grenadiers attributed the disaster that followed to jealousy between Donop and Cornwallis. At Brandywine, Cornwallis having placed the Hessian grenadiers two hundred paces behind the British, Donop instructed O'Reilly if possible to manoeuvre Lengerke's battalion forward onto the left flank in line with the British. O'Reilly succeeded in this, much to Donop's delight. His love of glory was not satisfied with playing second fiddle to the British, and O'Reilly blamed his violent and impetuous ways for the trouble with Howe and Cornwallis.[15] Donop, without choosing his words carefully, often criticized the British leadership. When British guns and ships were vainly battering at Mud Island, Donop remarked ironically to Cornwallis that the attack reminded him of Frederick the Great's on Olmutz in Moravia, where Frederick stood encamped before one gate while the other four stood open.[16] Thus when Donop begged to be sent against Redbank with his brigade alone, Howe and Cornwallis were only too happy to give him the opportunity to find the open gate. They never meant that Donop's brigade should meet disaster, wrote O'Reilly, but thought he would have to return without

---

[12] Ebenezer David, *A Rhode Island Chaplain in the Revolution* (Port Washington, NY, 1972), pp. 46–8 describes the defences. See also the map on p. 121.

[13] All the battalions were understrength from sickness. At the end of September the grenadier battalions each had about 300 rank and file fit for duty. StaMarburg 4h.410. nr. 2, fols. 88–9.

[14] Wainwright, ed., 'A Diary of Trifling Occurrences', p. 453.

[15] Schweinsburg, 'Briefe eines hessischen Offiziers', pp. 308–9. O'Reilly's letter to his father-in-law, Baron Milchling of Schonstadt, is dated 22 Dec. 1777/18 Jan. 1778.

[16] Frederick's siege of Olmutz in 1758 failed because Austrian light troops remained in contact with the garrison and were able to destroy a Prussian supply train.

attempting anything or perhaps 'burn his fingers a little', and then have to eat his words.[17]

Howe intended that his orders should give Donop discretion to withdraw if he thought the defences too strong.[18] But Münchhausen tells us that Donop went convinced that he was to attack the fort at all hazards and that he repeated this conviction on his deathbed. For this mistake he holds responsible Cornwallis, who taunted Donop to take the fort, otherwise the British would do it.[19] Besides the mix-up in passing orders, the expedition was fated by bad intelligence. Howe's reports on Redbank, three weeks out of date, told him that the fort was still incomplete and not the insuperable obstacle it proved. Had Howe ordered Colonel Stirling of the 42nd to attack Redbank immediately after occupying Billingsport, when the information was still accurate, many lives would have been saved.[20] As Colonel William Harcourt wrote to his father, 'Unfortunately our intelligence was bad, and what was represented as a Battery, erected entirely against the ships and open behind, proved a very strong Fort with a deep ditch.'[21]

Early on 21 October Donop's fated brigade crossed the Delaware on fourteen flatboats. 'As I crossed the Delaware with Donop,' wrote O'Reilly, 'and saw the brigade alone at daybreak, without an Englishman, without guides, without heavy artillery, and without one English general, I shuddered for the consequences.'[22] The first wave started at six o'clock, but the artillery carts were not across until two in the afternoon. An hour later, the *Jäger* having scouted the route to Redbank down the Haddonfield road, Donop set off, Ewald and some sixty *Jäger* leading. Captain Lorey and another *Jäger* detachment were left behind to bring on the last ammunition wagons. The brigade leaguered for the night in Haddonfield, the troops lying on their arms in a square. The next morning they resumed their march at four o'clock, and after a delay at Newton's Creek, where the bridge had been broken, they

---

[17] Schweinsburg, 'Briefe eines hessischen Offiziers', p. 309.

[18] Howe, *Narrative*, p. 29.

[19] Münchhausen, fasc. 4, fol. 4. Max von Eelking appears to have enlarged on this story, putting an heroic speech in Donop's mouth: 'Go and tell your general that Germans are not afraid to face death.' *Die deutschen Hilfstruppen im nordamerikanischen Befreiungskriege 1776 bis 1783* (2 vols. Hannover, 1863) I, p. 219. Münchhausen's story contradicts Cornwallis's evidence given to the Commons during the inquiry into Howe's conduct.

[20] Münchhausen, fasc. 4, fol. 77 (unnumbered but between 76 and 78).

[21] Edward Harcourt, ed., *The Harcourt Papers* (14 vols. Oxford, 1880–1905), IX, p. 222.

[22] Schweinsburg, 'Briefe eines hessischen Offiziers', p. 309. O'Reilly was not strictly accurate: the expedition was accompanied by Major Charles Stuart and two British howitzers.

reached a point within two miles of Redbank at one o'clock in the afternoon. A captured rebel officer informed them that the garrison numbered 800, roughly 200 more than its actual strength.

Both Adam Ludwig Ochs and Quartermaster Ungar of Minnigerode's battalion later wrote that Donop, having neared the fort unseen by the garrison, should have stormed it promptly rather than alerting them to his presence by a summons. A letter of Major Sam. Ward to Washington shows that the Americans were, in fact, aware of Donop's approach, a point which they tried to conceal by leaving their washing hanging out.[23]

Donop had three hours for his reconnaissance. Every indication is that it was inadequate. He did not appreciate that an outlying work to the east of the fort had been abandoned. According to his ADC, Lieutenant Carl von Heister, he did not even observe the enemy rowing galleys in the Delaware, their powerful armament able to enfilade an attacker's flanks.[24] He did however realize that the works were complete and Howe's instructions based on out-dated information. Why did he not retire, or at least send for heavy artillery? Münchhausen does not hesitate to point out that Donop thought his orders were peremptory. Major Charles Stuart accom-panied Donop on his reconnaissance, and both agreed on the impropriety of attacking without heavy guns. Donop said that if Stuart would advise him he would delay the attack, to which Stuart replied that he was too young (i.e. junior) and had not sufficient authority to have delay of the commander-in-chief's orders rest on him.[25]

Stuart can hardly be blamed for this. Donop, an officer of experience and high reputation, should have been able to take the decision himself. Probably he wanted an Englishman to agree to the delay. Concepts of honour were then very strong, Donop commanded the élite of the Hessians, and was thirsting to achieve something for the honour of his corps. By O'Reilly's account, he had also talked himself into a position where withdrawal would be personally humiliating. These reasons do not excuse his fatal

---

[23] Ochs, *Betrachtungen über die neuere Kriegskunst* (Kassel, 1817), p. 38; StaMarburg 12.11 1 Ba 15 (Journal of Minnigerode's battalion), fols. 101–2; Washington, *Writings*, IX, p. 422 n. 27.

[24] Heister, 'Tagebuch eines vormaligen kurhessischen Offiziers', p. 262; see also Ewald, *Belehrungen*, II, p. 16.

[25] Stuart-Wortley, *Prime Minister and Son*, p. 117. A somewhat different account of this is given by Samuel S. Smith, *Fight for the Delaware 1777* (Monmouth Beach, NJ, 1970), pp.20–1, based on Ewald's journal. He mistakenly refers to Stuart as 'Stewart'.

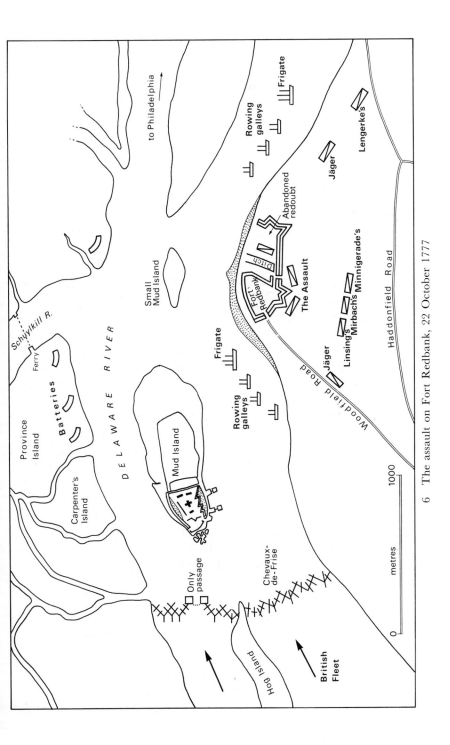

6 The assault on Fort Redbank, 22 October 1777

125

decision to attack. Nor is Howe blameless for failing to provide artillery because of bad intelligence.

The fort, a simple pentagonal redoubt with a sound earthen rampart, ditch, and abatis, was held by good Rhode Island troops under Colonel Christopher Greene. The too-extensive works had been converted by the French engineer Mauduit du Plessis into an ingenious trap: he abandoned the outlying defences, causing only one part, a salient angle, to be occupied by American sharpshooters, giving the impression that it was still held in its entirety.[26]

The traditional summons to surrender, accompanied by a threat of no mercy to the survivors, possibly a bluff by Donop, was returned unflinchingly by Greene. The interval had been employed in making fascines, to be borne by one hundred men at the head of each battalion. Donop deployed his regiments in line, Minnigerode's on the right, Mirbach's in the middle, Linsing's on the left. Lengerke's battalion secured the line of retreat; the *Jäger* protected the artillery and the flanks. Immediately upon the messenger returning to the corps with Greene's reply to the summons, a brisk fire was begun upon the fort from the battalion guns and howitzers. Ewald and sixteen *Jäger* marksmen peppered the top of the parapet making gravel and dust fly up with their good shooting; Donop and his officers placed themselves at the head of their men, and brought them on at a quick step. Minnigerode on the right entered and secured the detached work, Mauduit's riflemen taking refuge in the main fort.[27] All three battalions were in the ditch when struck by a tremendous fire from the fort and in particular from the row-galleys on their flanks. These made particularly good execution, communicating to the garrison with 'speaking tubes'. Hessian observers and participants described the galleys' fire as decisive.[28] Within the fort, officers went about striking with rifle butts and hangers anyone who flinched from his post.[29]

All accounts agree that the attack was pressed with remarkable courage. Some of the grenadiers were actually killed in the em-

---

[26] The Marquis de Chastellux, *Travels in North America in the Year 1780, 1781 and 1782* (2 vols. London, 1837), I, p. 261.

[27] Hence American accounts all speak of an attack made in two columns.

[28] Smith, *Fight for the Delaware*, p. 22; Feilitzsch, fol. 27; Heister, 'Tagebuch eines vormaligen kurhessischen Offiziers', p. 263; StaMarburg 12.11 I Ba 15, fol. 103; ibid, 4h.412. nr. 4, fol. 87; and Johann Carl Buettner, *Buettner der Amerikaner: eine Selbstbiographie* (Camenz, 1828), p. 52.

[29] Smith, *Fight for the Delaware*, p. 23.

brasures. Others, realizing how hopeless the assault was, took refuge on the parapet below the walls, where they were captured. The loss in officers was heavy. Captain von Stamford, gallant as always, was the first to reach the embrasures before he fell, thrice wounded.[30] Donop himself had his hip shattered, and Lieutenant von Toll of Mirbach's was shot down with several grenadiers trying to drag him off. Toll was only grazed, but his best friend Carl von Wurmb was killed, never having found his wealthy American heiress.[31] Colonel von Schieck of that regiment was also killed and Minnigerode wounded. After nearly forty minutes' slaughter, the shattered remnants fled, leaving nearly 400 comrades killed, wounded, or captured.[32]

Donop was found beneath a pile of dead and dying, and taken to a Quaker's house where he died after three days. Chastellux reported his last words as, 'I die the victim of my ambition and of the avarice of my sovereign.' This contrasts oddly with the enthusiasm Donop had previously shown for the America expedition, but is supported by the testimony of von Kalb.[33] Certainly he died unhappy, a sadly tragic figure, his unrealized ambitions the cause of his fate. Colonel von Loos reported him as saying, 'I have done my duty as a soldier, but as a brigadier I have conducted affairs like a novice (*wie ein Fähnrich gehandelt*). What will the Landgraf say when he hears that I have lost so many men? For that I am greatly afraid.'[34]

The following day the Royal Navy also suffered heavy losses. The 64-gun *Augusta* and the sloop *Merlin*, which had run aground on the 22nd trying to get upstream to aid the Hessian attack, engaged the batteries at Fort Mifflin. Both ran aground again, and were set ablaze, the former by burning wads from her own guns.[35]

---

[30] Ditfurth, *Das Leibgarde-Regiment*, p. 42.

[31] Hammer, *Friederike von Wurmb*, pp. 150–2.

[32] The official return in StaMarburg 4h.410. nr. 2, fol. 107 gives 371 as the total loss, but both O'Reilly and Lt Rueffer of Mirbach's give a higher figure. Col George Osborne gave 127 as the number killed. Eelking, *Hilfstruppen*, I, pp. 222–3; CO5/95, fol. 438, Osborne to Germain, 26 Oct. 1777. Besides sources in previous footnotes, my account of the battle is based on StaMarburg 4h.410. nr. 5, fols. 109–10, Lt Werner's account, 25 Oct.; 4h.412. nr. 5, fol. 64, Baurmeister to the Erbprinz; and Evelyn M. Acomb, *The Revolutionary Journal of Baron Ludwig von Closen 1780–1781* (Chapel Hill, 1958), pp. 121–2.

[33] Chastellux, *Travels in America*, I, p. 266 (also quoted in Kapp, *Soldatenhandel*, pp. 222–3); Huth, 'Letters from a Mercenary' p. 489; Stevens, *Facsimiles*, VIII, nr. 757, de Kalb to the Comte de Broglie, 2 Nov. 1777.

[34] Jungkenn 1:55, Loos to Jungkenn, 30 Nov. 1777. Dr Fischer of Stadtarchiv Frankfurt kindly gave me this last information.

[35] *The London Chronicle*, XLII (1777), p. 543, Admiral Lord Howe to Philip Stephens, 25 Oct. 1777; J. K. Laughton, ed., 'The Journal of Henry Duncan', *The Naval Miscellany*, I (Publication of the Naval Records Society, 1902), p. 154.

The amphibious coordination of the Delaware operations reflects
little credit on those famous brothers, the Howes. Not until 15
November was sufficient firepower brought to bear on Fort Mifflin
to oblige the garrison's survivors to withdraw after a most gallant
and tenacious defence.[36] Once Mifflin was gone there was little
point in holding Redbank. On 17 November Cornwallis led a corps
including Lengerke's battalion 'to burn our moustaches a second
time against Redbank', as O'Reilly put it. On 19 November heavy
artillery, of which there was adequate provision on this occasion,
was disembarked on the Jersey shore, and on the 20th they made
directly for the fort only to find it abandoned and the guns spiked.
When O'Reilly asked the local inhabitants why the fort had been
given up without a struggle, they told him it was due to the rebels'
fear that the Hessians with Cornwallis would give no quarter to
avenge their comrades. According to O'Reilly, the British, after
seeing the strength of the works at Redbank, were struck with awe
and could not comprehend the Hessians' daring in attacking the
place. A countryman whose house was close by the fort told
O'Reilly he had often heard it said among the rebel officers who
dined at his home, that they had never seen such courage as was
displayed in the attack, particularly by the officers.[37]

Redbank marks a turning point for the Hessian corps in
America. If Trenton destroyed the myth of Hessian invincibility,
Redbank shattered the physical reality. Their best troops had
suffered devastating losses, which, added to those dead of sickness
in the winter before, made great gaps in those fine regiments which
had sailed from Bremerlehe in April 1776.[38] In the Hessian army,
where nearly all the officers knew each other, if they were not
actually related, the loss of twenty-two of their number seemed all
the greater. O'Reilly wrote, 'Since this fatal episode, one hears only
of tragic occurrences, such as the unlucky Schotte[n] of the Regiment von Mirbach having his arm amputated, after which Captain
Groening the elder was buried here; next it was poor Wagner,
Donop's Aide-de-Camp, who passed away; and three days ago it
was the excellent Gotschall who was likewise buried. My God;
what will a disconsolate mother say? I grieve the loss with all my
heart.'[39] Baurmeister struck the same note, lamenting the loss of an

[36] Jungkenn 1:52, Cochenhausen to Jungkenn, 28 Nov. 1777.
[37] Münchhausen, fasc. 1, fol. 76, O'Reilly to (Trumbach?), 28 Nov. 1777.
[38] Col Osborne reported that the Hessian grenadiers lost over 300 men in two months of a
putrid fever. CO5/94, fol. 426, Osborne to Germain, 15 May 1777.
[39] Münchhausen, fasc. 1, fol. 78, 28 Nov. 1977.

arm by Lieutenant Schotten, his sister's son: 'Especially regrettable is the loss of so many worthy officers. . . It is truly to be desired that this miserable war will end soon.'[40]

One cannot help observing, however, that these men were mercenaries. They were paid to fight, and violent death was a hazard of the occupation. It is more noteworthy for the historian that Redbank, not Trenton, killed Hessian enthusiasm for the American war. 'For some time we have lost our desire to serve the English' wrote O'Reilly in January 1778. The spy James Lowry reported from London on 5 December 1777 that a Hessian officer arrived from America was en route to Hessen to make strong representations against General Howe for sending Donop's brigade against Redbank, of which the British general was ignorant, without heavy battering cannon.[41] This officer was Major Karl von Eschwege, O'Reilly's comrade at Kip's Bay, recalled in fact to rejoin the Landgraf's Guards, so that part of the story is incorrect. But there must have been something to Lowry's report, for Sir Joseph Yorke wrote to Lord Howe on 13 January 1778 to assure him that the Hessians were not thinking of pulling their troops out of the war: 'There is not a word of truth about the states of Hesse those countries are only afraid you should send back their troops.'[42]

The correspondence of the Hessian corps turned more and more to officers' requests to return to Hessen for reasons of health or to be granted their discharge, until under Knyphausen's successor Lossberg it reached such proportions as to include everyone from Lossberg's second-in-command Lieutenant General Carl von Bose to seventy-year-old regimental surgeon Gechter, whose sight was failing and who could no longer carry out his duties.[43] Doubtless many requests for recall were for legitimate health reasons, for the officers as a whole tended to be elderly; but increasing war-

---

[40] Baurmeister, *Journals*, pp. 127–8. Like most invalided officers, Schotten was provided for, the Landgraf making him *Rentmeister* at Melsungen.

[41] Stevens, *Facsimiles*, XIX, nr. 1756, Lowry to Mr St Pierre (Dr Bancroft), 5 Dec. 1777. Beaumarchais in Paris exaggerated this report to Vergennes: 'a Hessian officer has arrived in London, commissioned to make the most bitter complaints of the manner in which the Hessians are sacrificed on every occasion, and to threaten their leaving the English service in a body . . .' A good index on the reliability of second- and third-hand information on the Hessians. Ibid, XX, nr. 1778, 15 Dec. 1777. There is also a report in the opposition *London Chronicle* of 13–16 Dec. 1777, 'By a German officer now in town, we are assured, that the Germans in general discover the utmost aversion to serve in the American war.' But an opposition newspaper is a very unreliable source.

[42] HMC: *Dartmouth MSS.*, II, p. 453.

[43] StaMarburg rh.415 nr. 5, fol. 130, Capt. Klingender to LtGen v. Ditfurth, 5 Oct. 1782; 4h.411. nr. 3, fol. 48, Lossberg to the Landgraf, 13 Sept. 1782. See also 4h.411. nr. 2, fols. 46–7, Knyphausen to the Landgraf, 20 Feb. 1781.

weariness and homesickness made them more eager to lay down the burden of conducting a difficult and unsuccessful war. Lieutenant Colonel Ludwig von Wurmb wrote in January, 1779, 'I wish we were out of this miserable country with honour', and the adjutant general, Major Baurmeister, informed Jungkenn in June, 1781, 'Everyone wishes as much as a soldier has a right to wish, that he may soon return home.'[44] The letters of the soldiers show an anxiety that loved ones had forgotten them or thought them dead, and the irregularity of the mails increased their worries.[45] A British doctor who first reached New York in 1780 thought that the mercenaries' heart was no longer in the business.[46]

In the campaign of 1776 the Hessians played a role that exceeded their relative strength in the King's forces. At Kip's Bay, White Plains, and Fort Washington they had been in the forefront of the attack. Trenton had cast a cloud over the successful campaign, but judging from their correspondence the Hessians regarded the defeat as something of a random shot, a once-only affair due to Rall's exceptional negligence. In 1777 they still played a considerable part. After that disastrous year, however, the British conduct of the war changed from an attempt to knock out the rebellion by conventional means to a war of raids and of utilizing supposed Loyalist strength, mainly in the south.[47] Inevitably the Hessians as conventional European soldiers played a secondary role in this phase. From 1778 onwards the Landgraf's battalions increasingly did little more than garrison duties, varied only by raids and expeditions. The *Jäger* and the Regiment von Bose with Cornwallis are the exceptions to this rule.

THE JÄGER AND THE LITTLE WAR

The whole war in this country is an orderly hunting drive; we are the beaters and often at the same time the prey, and the rebels are the marksmen. For as soon as we come to the forest, they fire on us, turn about, loading as they run, lay their guns on their shoulders and fire back at us ... here there is nothing but thick forest, thus when we come into these woods, we cannot neglect any suspicious tree, for on these the rascals sit and shoot our men dead.[48]

[44] Both quoted in Kipping, *The Hessian View of America*, p. 34.
[45] Kipping, *The Hessian View of America*, p. 8.
[46] Jackson, *Formation, Discipline, and Economy of Armies*, p. 103. Jackson actually wrote, 'the heart is rarely in the act of the hand'.
[47] John Shy, 'The American Revolution: The Military Conflict considered as a Revolutionary War', in Stephen G. Kurtz and James H. Hutson, ed., *Essays on the American Revolution* (Chapel Hill and New York, 1973), pp. 139–40.
[48] StaBamberg C 18, 1 Coll. Spiess Nr. 26, fol. 89, a letter from New York, 19 Sept. 1777.

The campaigns of 1777–81

Throughout the campaigns the European soldiers spoke of the *kleine Krieg* or *petite Guerre*.[49] One is tempted to call this guerrilla war, and remarks like those of Major Robert Donkin give credence to this interpretation:

The rebellion now in America seems to come under this head [of little war], from the nature of the country, and the cowardliness of the rebels, who delight more in murdering from woods, walls, and houses, than in shewing any genius or science in the art military.[50]

Donkin added that a partisan commander ought to have carte blanche to operate as the opportunity arose. But it is clear from his work that Donkin, like his contemporaries, regarded this warfare as secondary and subordinate to the pitched battles, the manoeuvring of the main armies, and the sieges. The main task of the partisan ranger was to keep the enemy from his own main force, so that they should not have to be standing to arms constantly.[51] Most of Donkin's examples came from classical Greece and Rome, his contemporary ones from the war in Germany, like Laudon's cutting off Frederick the Great's supply convoy, thus raising the siege of Olmutz, and the work of Austrian irregulars driving the Prussians from Bohemia in 1744.[52]

On the American side Washington too saw this war of outposts, as it was also called, as complementary to the operations of the continental army, and it was only with reluctance that he depended upon the militia.[53] Only in the fighting between Loyalist and Patriot in the southern colonies was there a full-scale guerrilla type war with its concomitants: hit and run tactics, a struggle for the control of the civilian population carried on at local level, and atrocities to 'punish' or intimidate political opponents.

In Europe the war of outposts was the province of the light troops: *Jäger* in most German armies, and most notably the Croats and Pandours of the Austrian Empire. Hussars became a standard form of light cavalry. During Ferdinand of Brunswick's campaigns in Germany there was a constant outpost war, and by 1762 his army included 8,000 light troops, the French 11,000.[54]

---

49 The English 'little war' was seldom used. The *Encyclopaedia Britannica* (2nd edn, Edinburgh, 1780), X, p. 8840 spoke of 'the petite Guerre' as 'the manoeuvres of the Partisan in secret marches, occupying, defending or attacking posts, reconnoitring countries or the enemy, planning of ambuscades &c'.
50 Robert Donkin, *Military Collections and Remarks* (New York, 1777), p. 222.
51 Ibid, pp. 243–4.
52 Ibid, pp. 239 and 244.
53 Marcus Cunliffe, *George Washington: Man and Monument* (New York, 1958), pp. 110–11.
54 David Dundas, *The Principles of Military Movement* (London, 1788), p. 265.

The Hessians

The need to coordinate the activity of the light troops with the formal linear tactics of the main armies, and the difficulty of reconciling the initiative which such troops required with methods of discipline then prevalent, provoked a considerable literature in the late eighteenth century, of which Johann Ewald's *Abhandlung über den kleinen Krieg* is only one of many examples.[55] In practical terms the contribution of states like Hessen-Kassel was to make full use of its trained woodsmen and hunters, *Jäger*, as an adjunct to the field regiments. Unlike the British light infantry, the *Jäger* were without bayonets, and thus, like American riflemen, in danger of being spitted by a bayonet charge. Colonel Simcoe of the Queen's Rangers, for example, always taught his men to rush upon riflemen: 'there was little danger ... from troops who were without bayonets and whose object it was to fire a single shot with effect'.[56] Ewald recommended combining riflemen and fusiliers in one corps, so that the latter's bayonets could protect the former.[57] In America the *Jäger*, if not working with light infantry, were combined with bodies of Hessian grenadiers who, according to Ewald, did service as light troops in the 1776 campaign.[58] An example was the crossing of the Schuylkill on 22 September 1777 by a mixed detachment of *Jäger* under Captains Wreden and Lorey and grenadiers under Captain Westernhagen, a feint that enabled Howe to gain other fords and subsequently take Philadelphia. Covered by the fire of four guns and seventy *Jäger*, both mounted and on foot, thirty grenadiers with fixed bayonets led by four *Jäger* on foot and six mounted crossed the stream. Immediately the far bank was secure, the remainder of the *Jäger* and seventy more grenadiers under Westernhagen crossed. Twenty grenadiers secured the crossing by occupying an island in midstream, the rest of the force held the bridgehead and sent out patrols in a two hundred metre radius. Another hundred grenadiers were posted on the original bank.[59]

Unlike soldiers of the field and garrison regiments, the *Jäger* had to be men of sufficient reliance and intelligence to work in small

---

[55] Published in Kassel in 1785, its aim was to teach officers of lower rank how to lead detachments. A subsequent enlarged edition was *Abhandlung vom Dienst der leichten Truppen* (Flensburg, 1790), translated into English as *A Treatise upon the Duties of Light Troops* (London, 1803).

[56] John Graves Simcoe, *A History of the Operations of a Partisan Corps called the Queen's Rangers* (London, 1844), p. 229. See also John W. Wright, 'The Rifle in the American Revolution', *AHR*, XXIX (1924), pp. 293–9.

[57] Ewald, *Abhandlung über den kleinen Krieg*, pp. 19–20.

[58] Ibid, pp. 157–8.

[59] StaMarburg 4h.410. nr. 2, fol. 59, Knyphausen to the Landgraf, 17 Oct. 1777.

parties. 'They possessed the essential virtues of light troops – they were good shots, agile, intelligent, and self-reliant.'[60] On the field of battle itself, at Flatbush, Heister and Donop proposed to Howe increasing the original two companies of *Jäger* by four more on foot and one mounted, to a total strength of over a thousand. The proposal was approved.[61] Foresters capable of handling rifled weapons were recruited from all over Germany by offering higher bounties and high pay, including ration douceurs: thus a Hessian *Jäger* captain received £8 6s 4d monthly and four ration douceurs each worth 15s.[62] The *Jäger* were volunteers and specialists. As Schlieffen informed Suffolk when the latter complained about the slow recruiting of the additional Jäger companies, 'This corps . . . is by no means composed like the infantry of the lowest class of people. It is drawn from those employed in hunting and in the forests, in Germany a well esteemed class, and forms by consequence what one calls a corps of distinction.'[63] It is notable as witness to the *Jäger* effectiveness that American newspapers referred to these German woodsmen as 'banditti', just as British soldiers and politicians spoke of the American militia.

The later companies, however, were not as good as the first two. Lieutenant Colonel Andreas Emmerich reported that those who arrived in summer, 1777 were 'good for nothing'.[64] Ewald wrote of the reaction to the new arrivals thus:

The Prussian-style unit is composed of deserters and an ill-bred rabble, at which all of us from the old stock, having hitherto received into the ranks uprighteous and sought-after people, felt our blood turn to water and our spirits sink. Colonel Donop himself, whose plan it was to provide for the strengthening of the Jager corps, was horrified by the rabble. . . The discontent of our men was so great that they refused to do duty with this mob. In the meantime, however, their anger calmed down little by little, because these people had brought over 60 'Amazons' with them, and the men soon made their acquaintance.[65]

Such unreliable types were bound to cause trouble when the *Jäger* were always manning the outposts. In November, 1777 a *Jäger* piquet was surprised and beaten up by Americans under Lafayette, despite aid from Captain Wreden's company. Wreden put down the losses, thirty-one in all, to inexperience at manoeuvring and not

[60] Fuller, *British Light Infantry in the Eighteenth Century*, p. 69.
[61] StaMarburg 4h.410. nr. 1, fol. 372, Heister to Howe, 2 Sept. 1776; CO5/140, fol. 29.
[62] Eelking, *Hilfstruppen*, I, pp. 170–1; SP81/187, Faucitt to Suffolk, 4 March 1777; HMC: *American* MSS., I, p. 114.
[63] SP81/185, Schlieffen to Suffolk, 10 October 1777.
[64] Add. MS. 34,414, fol. 263, 26 October 1777.
[65] Ewald, 'Tagebuch', I, fol. 167, quoted in Kipping, *Hessen-Kassel Truppen*, p. 42.

loading quickly enough in action. The loss would have been greater had not fifty *Jäger* of the old stock quickly rallied to the newcomers.[66] On 12 October 1778, the Bayreuth *Jäger* lieutenant, Carl von Feilitzsch, serving with the combined *Jägercorps* of both Hessian and Ansbach-Bayreuth *Jäger*, noted that an American patrol surprised and routed a piquet because the NCO in charge was drunk.[67]

Although the quality of the men declined, the *Jäger* officers were nearly all good, one notable exception being Lieutenant Grothausen, commanding the *Jäger* detachment at Trenton, whose slack patrolling Ewald blamed for the Hessian defeat.[68] Ewald wrote that an officer in charge of light troops had to be capable of looking after, on a small scale, those things which a general saw to on a large scale.[69] Some rose from the ranks, like Ochs who began as an NCO and became a general, and Bickel who, as a sergeant, distinguished himself at Brandywine, falling on the enemy's flank with a party of twenty men.[70] Of twenty-five Hessian officers decorated with the order *Pour la vertu militaire* in the war, five belonged to the *Jäger*: Ludwig and Philip von Wurmb, Ewald, Wreden, and Lieutenant Colonel von Prueschenk. Ewald became noted for his writings after the war, but his active service was also quite remarkable. In the first part of the war, under Donop, he served in the corps of Cornwallis, whom he respected as a soldier, calling him 'one whom we can rightly term England's support'.[71] Donop reported Ewald's company as having been almost constantly engaged throughout the winter of 1776–7 with distinction, for which Cornwallis awarded them fifty Spanish dollars. On 9 January 1777, when Cornwallis visited Ewald's advanced post and found the *Jäger*, clad in tattered uniforms and worn out with arduous duty, but still cheerful, he promised that he would reclothe them at his own expense.[72] In the Philadelphia campaign Ewald's and Wreden's companies played a leading part in the rout of American light troops at Iron Hill, and were in the forefront of the

---

[66] StaMarburg 4h.410. nr. 2, fols. 128–9, Knyphausen to the Landgraf, 30 Nov. 1777.
[67] Feilitzsch, fol. 66.
[68] Ewald, *Belehrungen*, II, p. 132.
[69] Ewald, *Abhandlung über den kleinen Krieg*, p. 12.
[70] Leopold, Freiherr von Hohenhausen, *Biographie des Generals von Ochs* (Kassel, 1827), passim; StaMarburg 4h.410. nr. 2, fols. 70 and 116.
[71] Ewald, *Belehrungen*, II, p. 391.
[72] Kipping, *Hessen-Kassel Truppen*, p. 46.

attack of Cornwallis's column at Brandywine. On 16 September 1777 the *Jäger* again 'routed and dispersed the advance Troops of the Enemy', for which they were complimented on orders.[73] When Cornwallis left the army to return to England in December, 1777, he wrote to Ewald:

I cannot leave this country without desiring you to accept my best thanks for your good services during the last two campaigns, in which I have had the honour to command the Hessian Chasseurs. If the war should continue I hope we shall serve together. If we should be separated, I shall ever remember the distinguished merit and ability's [sic] of Cap. Ewald.[74]

And Howe on his departure wrote a similar note to both Ewald and Wreden:

La conduite des deux premières compagnies des Chasseurs hessois incitées par le zèle et brave exemple de leurs chefs – vous Messieurs – a été remarquée de toute l'armée et a fait par jamais une telle impression sur moi.[75]

When the British withdrew from Philadelphia, Ewald frustrated an enemy attempt to break down a bridge, which might have delayed the march of Clinton's whole army.[76] His company and that of Captain Hinrichs distinguished themselves by their sniping of the defenders at Charleston in 1780, and once again earned the British commander-in-chief's compliment on orders.[77] In Benedict Arnold's raid on Portsmouth, Virginia, Ewald was given an important post to defend. When Arnold questioned whether his company was up to the task, Ewald replied, 'So long as one *Jäger* lives, no damned American can come over these walls.'[78] On 19 March 1781, he and his small party defended the post for four hours against a superior force under General Muhlenberg. The enemy withdrew leaving thirty dead.[79] In the final Virginia campaign he served with Colonel John Graves Simcoe, commander of the Queen's Rangers, one of the few truly successful Loyalist units. The two were good friends and their corps worked admirably together. Simcoe, writing to Knyphausen to commend Ewald's service in a

---

[73] Kemble, *Journal*, p. 497.

[74] Zwenger, 'Johann Ewald in hessischen Dienst', p. 197.

[75] Ibid.

[76] Ibid, p. 207; Add. MS. 21807, fol. 5, Clinton to Germain, 5 July 1778.

[77] Bernhard A. Uhlendorf, ed., *The Siege of Charleston* (Ann Arbor, Michigan, 1938), passim; 'The Siege of Charleston: Journal of Captain Peter Russell, December 25, 1779 to May 2, 1780', *AHR*, IV (1898), p. 497.

[78] *Tagebuch*, IV, fol. 110, quoted in Kipping, *Hessen-Kassel Truppen*, p. 21.

[79] StaMarburg 4h.412. nr. 5, fol. 81, Baurmeister to the Erbprinz, 26 April 1781.

skirmish against Lafayette, called him 'that most excellent officer'.[80] Both men were trapped with Cornwallis at Yorktown. Ewald's company was down to a sixth of its original strength when Cornwallis surrendered. Ewald himself was dangerously ill for several weeks.[81]

Ewald was a strict disciplinarian, recommending that marauding always be punished. He advocated gaining the friendship of local inhabitants by protecting their property, for they repaid such kindness by bringing information. He asserts that before the battle of Germantown a local inhabitant, who was certainly no friend of the King, but whose property the *Jäger* had protected, brought word of Washington's coming attack.[82] The German-American historian Rosengarten tell us, 'it is significant of the man [Ewald] that, after carrying off from the Hopkinson house at Bordentown, New Jersey, the volume edited by Provost Smith of the College of Philadelphia, containing young Hopkinson's prize essay, he returned it with thanks, and the book is still in the possession of the Hopkinson family as one of their rare treasures'.[83] Generally the *Jäger* officers practised what Ewald preached.

Ewald was also no believer in mincing words with his men. While declaring that an officer must show his men the love and concern he feels for them, he said that it was most important that unnecessary complaints should not go unpunished, for war is not all that hard. For officers commanding mounted piquets, he recommended that any man who complained loudly should be threatened with a pistol shot through the head.[84]

Captain Carl August von Wreden, who commanded the other *Jäger* company in 1776, was probably as good a leader, although he left no voluminous writings. Hinrichs, who served under him, wrote that he could scarce describe the emotion he felt when Wreden 'bade solemn farewell to his company' on returning to

---

[80] Ibid 4h.411. nr. 2, fol. 92, 4 April 1781. See also ibid, fol. 86, Knyphausen to the Landgraf, 30 April 1781.

[81] Eelking, *Hilfstruppen*, II, pp. 122–3.

[82] Ewald, *Abhandlung über den kleinen Krieg*, pp. 16–17 and 28; *Belehrungen*, II, pp. 32–3.

[83] J. G. Rosengarten, 'American History from German Archives' *Proceedings of the American Philosophical Society*, XXXIX (1900), pp. 138–9.

[84] Ewald, *Abhandlung über den kleinen Krieg*, pp. 17 and 143. Ewald enlivened his writings with numerous examples, knowing that the taste of young officers did not usually extend to learned works. It must be admitted, however, that nothing he wrote was particularly new. Scharnhorst in a review of *Abhandlung vom Dienst der leichten Truppen*, wrote, 'It contains quite useful rules for the service of light troops. However, those who know Jenny and Grandmaison will not find anything exactly new in it.' Paret, *Yorck and Prussian Reform*, p. 42 n. 109.

Europe. 'It is now the sixth year since I have known him, and for three years we have been sharing joy and sorrow, and gone through innumerable dangers, fatigues, and earning honours and laurels.'[85] Wreden was obviously a man who won the loyalties of those set under him. Morale and esprit de corps were high in the first two *Jäger* companies. They had only one deserter in the first campaign, although opportunities were much greater than in the regiments;[86] and when Lieutenant Rau of Ewald's company had his foot shattered in a fight with Hand's Pennsylvanians, four of his men carried him to safety under fire.[87]

The *Jäger* corps, incorporating those of Ansbach-Bayreuth under Captain von Cramon after spring, 1777, reached a total strength of over a thousand in 1781.[88] Usually fighting in detachments, they were involved in all the raids and expeditions of the latter part of the war, and held an important post at Kingsbridge which involved them in frequent skirmishing.[89] The *Jäger* commander, Lieutenant Colonel Ludwig von Wurmb, was both a leader and a trainer of light troops. After Wurmb's successful action at Kingsbridge on 3 July 1781, Clinton wrote to Knyphausen, 'Tho'' there wanted nothing to convince me of Colonel Wurmb's Military Talents, I can not resist the desire I have to express to that Officer, the high sense I entertain of his very judicious and spirited arrangement on that occasion'.[90] Ochs, who served for a time as his adjutant, said, 'He was a man who combined bravery and activity with military science, and under him several outstanding officers were educated, who are still today [1819], partly in foreign service, men of high standing.'[91]

Intelligence gathering was a vital task of the light troops, and in this Wurmb's penetration surpassed that of Clinton's own staff. In July and August, 1781, as Washington's and Rochambeau's armies

---

[85] Captain [Johann] Hinrichs, 'Extracts from Hinrichs' Letterbook', *PMHB*, XXII (1898), p. 161.

[86] StaMarburg 13 Acc: 1930/5 Nr. 232, fol. 3.

[87] Ewald, *Belehrungen*, III, pp. 30–1.

[88] A *Jäger* return for 5 Sept. 1781 shows 624 present and fit for duty at New York, 274 serving in the south, 184 sick (still termed 'effective', although unfit for duty), and 16 prisoners. The corps' total strength in America, not including Ansbachers, for whom there is a separate return, was 18 officers, 17 servants, 13 staff, and 1,047 NCOs and privates. CO5/184, fol. 240.

[89] StaMarburg 12.11 I Ba 17 (Journal of the *Feldjägercorps*), fols. 143–53, 156, 177–8, 181, 187–92, 200, passim.

[90] For the action see ibid, fols. 189–92 and the *London Chronicle*, XLIX (1781), pp. 229–30, 'From the New York Gazette'; for Clinton's letter StaMarburg 4h.411. nr. 2, fol. 152, 7 July, 1781.

[91] Strieder, *Hessischen Gelehrten Geschichte*, XVIII, p. 421.

137

skirmished with the posts about New York on their way to Virginia to besiege Cornwallis, Wurmb surmised their true direction to lie southward from two pieces of information: the enemy had sent their forage and commissary to Trenton, lying on their route; and an American woman, the mistress of a French officer of distinction, was also awaiting the army there. Clinton, however, persisted in believing that Washington's objective was New York, not Cornwallis's army.[92] The importance of Wurmb's intelligence, had it been acted upon, need hardly be emphasized.

THE REGIMENT VON BOSE WITH CORNWALLIS

Of the field regiments, only Bose's[93] had an opportunity to uphold the tradition of Hessian arms in battle in the war's later years. This regiment had remained on Staten Island throughout the 1776 campaign. In 1777 it played a minor role in Clinton's expedition up the Hudson. Occupying lines around Fort Knyphausen, it provided detachments for various raids. In April, 1780, Major Johann Christian du Buy of Bose's led a raiding party of the Queen's Rangers, Diemar's Hussars, Loyalists, 150 men of his own regiment, and 100 of Mirbach's into New Jersey to attack a rebel force under Major Thomas Byles believed to be cantonned at Paramus. Du Buy, born in Dresden, had been a soldier for thirty of his forty-four years, and participated in thirteen battles during the Seven Years War. He rejoined his regiment from Knyphausen's staff in August, 1779.[94] He was undoubtedly one of the ablest Hessian officers, Knyphausen recommending him 'as most capable, gallant, and meritorious man'.[95] Colonel Simcoe noted the care du Buy took in briefing his officers before the expedition and acquainting himself with the local terrain: 'the Major was particularly attentive to a minute description of the situation;' 'The plan of this expedition was well laid and well executed: Major DuBuy seemed to be a master of the country through which he had to pass, and was well seconded by Captain Diemar.'[96]

[92] StaMarburg 12.11 I Ba 17, fol. 199; Ochs, *Betrachtungen ueber die neuere Kriegskunst*, pp. 65–7. Ochs gives a Frenchwoman as Wurmb's informant.
[93] Formerly Trumbach's. Major Gen. Carl Levin von Trumbach became chief of Rall's old regiment in 1778; Carl von Bose, formerly colonel of Ditfurth's, received Trumbach's regiment. Strieder, *Hessischen Militär-Geschichte*, pp. 285 and 334.
[94] StaMarburg 11, Conduitenlisten 1788; 12. nr. 483, Rangier-Rollen (1784); 12.11 I Ba 7 (Journal of Bose's regiment), fol. 66.
[95] Ibid 4h.411. nr. 1, fol. 348, 2 July 1780.
[96] Simcoe, *History of the Queen's Rangers*, pp. 140 and 142. Diemar was Hannoverian by birth and held a commission in the 60th Regiment. He recruited a Loyalist Freikorps, largely out of escapees from German troops in Burgoyne's convention army.

The campaigns of 1777–81

On the evening of 14 April the infantry passed over the Hudson near Fort Lee on flatboats, the cavalry crossed from Staten Island to Bergen Neck. The two parties rendezvoused and marched overnight through Hackensack to Paramus, where Byle's force was found to have withdrawn to Hopperstown. The march was continued, and a rebel detachment on the bridge over Sable Creek overpowered by the cavalry. The horsemen were then ordered forward so as not to give the enemy time to escape, and began to attack them in their cantonments. The infantry coming up in support, the enemy fled, but several houses in which they were hidden were surrounded and the occupants taken. Major Byles himself was shot by one of Diemar's hussars.

Various parties of militia harassed the return march, and a constant fire was kept up on both sides until the infantry reached Fort Lee, below which they re-embarked. The cavalry made their own way to Staten Island. A number of soldiers had exhausted their cartridges in the fire-fight, and it might have been a tricky situation; but du Buy kept his men well in hand, and the militia as usual did not venture too close.[97]

On 8 October 1780 the regiment with 17 officers and 519 men present and fit for duty, embarked as part of a corps under Major General Alexander Leslie to raid the Virginia coast as a diversion in support of Cornwallis further south.[98] On the 23rd du Buy landed at Newport News with the advance party of 400, including 165 men from his own regiment. A local American detachment retired before superior numbers as the raiders marched to Hampton, where forty militia were taken. A schooner, sloop, and twenty smaller vessels were burnt, and tobacco, flour, rum, and other goods in the storehouses taken. The fleet then sailed on to Portsmouth where the troops landed again and threw up earthworks. There was no disorder or plundering, and Leslie commended the behaviour of the Hessians.[99]

Receiving orders from Cornwallis, Leslie re-embarked his force and sailed to Charleston, arriving on 16 December after an uncomfortable voyage of almost four weeks. From there they joined Cornwallis at Camden.

The ensuing campaign was the harshest that any Hessian regi-

[97] The attackers lost 7 killed and 31 wounded, mainly in the withdrawal. The regimental journal of Bose's claimed 40 rebels dead, 53 captives, and 51 wounded, some of the latter also being brought off but others too serious to move. Simcoe however claimed nearly 200 prisoners. StaMarburg 12.11 1 Ba 7, fols. 69–76.
[98] Colonel von Bischhausen fell ill, and du Buy commanded the regiment throughout.
[99] StaMarburg 12.11 1 Ba 7, fols. 98–105; CO5/101, fol. 46, Leslie to Clinton, 19 Nov. 1780.

ment underwent during the American war. The Hessians disliked the southern colonies with their burning heat and general unhealthiness.[100] The regimental journal records much sickness from drinking bad water, from long marches in intense heat, and from having to forage for provisions.[101] Bose's regiment like the rest of Cornwallis's troops was obliged to make the campaign without the usual impedimenta of European armies: at Ramseur's Mill, Cornwallis ordered them to burn their tents, destroy rum and extra rations save what could be carried in haversacks, and all the wagons except those necessary to carry ammunition, salt, medical supplies, and the sick and wounded.[102] They then set off on a march of nearly 1,500 miles.[103]

On 15 March with his little army of 1,875 men, Cornwallis attacked Nathaniel Greene's 4,400 at Guilford Court House, in broken wooded country where every advantage of terrain and local knowledge favoured the enemy. Despite these difficulties, Cornwallis's regulars triumphed. With justice Clinton called those battalions, including Bose's, 'as good troops as any general officer need wish to take with him into the field'.[104] As the battle opened, Bose's regiment on the right, with the 71st Highlanders on their immediate left, threw off their knapsacks and other hindrances, advanced through a water-filled ravine, and pressed the enemy back through a mixture of wheatfield and woods. But as the 71st pushed after the enemy towards their left, a gap opened between the two battalions. Colonel William Campbell's Virginia riflemen and those of Henry Lee's Legion were able to pass through this gap, encircle the Hessians' left flank, and come upon them from the rear.

I was obliged [wrote du Buy] to cause the two companies of the left wing to turn right about, in order to defend our flank and rear. The 1st Battalion of the Guards, whose right wing was similarly outflanked, lost many men and a little ground. In this extremity I advanced with the three companies of the right wing, giving the Guards time to form and advance. Hereupon the enemy, except for a few sharpshooters, abandoned the place and withdrew deeper into the thick woods. LtCol Tarleton, who had been sent by Lord Cornwallis to discover our

---

[100] See below, pp. 168–9.
[101] StaMarburg 12.11 1 Ba 7, fols. 121–2.
[102] Ward, *War of the Revolution*, II, p. 765, says that after this, 'scores' of Hessian soldiers deserted. Total desertion from Bose's in 1781 was 45. StaMarburg 13 Acc: 1930/5 Nr. 232, fol. 9.
[103] The regimental journal claimed the mileage covered to be 1486 at Portsmouth, Virginia on 23 July 1781.
[104] Clinton, *Narrative*, p. 231.

situation, approached for the purpose (*à propos*) of putting the flying enemy fully to rout.[105]

In the broken countryside the advantage was with the American riflemen, who inflicted heavy losses on the Hessians. Yet only the latter's action prevented Lee and Campbell getting around Cornwallis's flank and falling upon his rear. Cornwallis gave them full credit in his dispatch: 'the Hessian regiment of Bose deserves my warmest praises for its discipline, alacrity, and courage, and does honour to Major DuBuy, who commands it, and who is an officer of superior merit'.[106] The Germans in British pay thought Bose's regiment had played a vital part in the victory. Ludwig von Wurmb wrote to Riedesel, 'sur l'aile droit il n'y avait que le Sangfroid et la bonne Discipline du Regiment de Bose qui assurait la victoire'.[107] The regiment lost 11 killed and 66 wounded of British totals of 109 and 389 respectively. Du Buy's contribution was vital, but the British regiments in the centre of Cornwallis's attack, the 23rd, 33rd, and the Guards, suffered even more heavily, the Guards losing 50 per cent of their strength.[108]

Cornwallis reached Wilmington on 14 April, and rested there for ten days, having failed to catch Greene or secure the Carolinas. However heroic his march and battle had been, strategically they were useless. He had exhausted his corps, while the Americans were as strong as ever. The re-equipping of the Hessians at Wilmington shows the state to which they were reduced. Their worn out muskets were exchanged for new British ones, and each soldier was issued with two pairs of shoes, one free, the other to be reckoned against future pay deductions, because 'the whole corps had had to go barefoot during the long marches, and the majority had made themselves slippers from cowhide'. 'Also, since every soldier was destitute of clothing to cover his legs, linen was provided so they could make long hose for marching in.' Three days were required to send the wounded down the Cape Fear River by boat.[109] The achievement of Bose's regiment was much admired at Kassel when the reports arrived, somewhat exaggerated. The historian Müller wrote in September, 1781, 'a few

[105] StaMarburg 4h.411. nr. 2, fol. 117, du Buy to Knyphausen, 9 June, 1781. Henry Lee also paid tribute to du Buy and Bose's regiment. Henry Lee, *Memoirs of the War in the Southern Department of the United States* (New York, 1869), p. 281.
[106] CO5/184, fol. 110, Cornwallis to Clinton, 17 Mar. 1781.
[107] StaWolfenbüttel 237N86, fol. 165, 9 Oct. 1781.
[108] StaMarburg 12.11 I Ba 7 (Journal of Bose's regiment), fols. 129–30.
[109] Ibid., fols. 138–9, 142–3.

weeks ago a single regiment, surrounded in a wood, attacked by 8,000 Americans,[110] after a march of 500 English miles, without bread, without wine, without rum, almost barefoot, in burning heat, after they had waded up to the neck through seven rivers, fought so well, that Cornwallis praised these troops before all others, and from this privilege of distinction the good Hessian entirely forgot the misery which he had had to suffer'.[111]

In August Cornwallis received reinforcements including the Regiment Erbprinz. Bose's was augmented by recruits and a hundred men under Major O'Reilly, recuperated from fever. O'Reilly now took command of the regiment, du Buy, promoted to lieutenant colonel, returning to New York in the frigate *Richmond* to take over as Quartermaster General from Cochenhausen.[112]

The courage and discipline of Cornwallis's battalions were of no avail when the army was too weak to hold dispersed posts along the eastern seaboard without naval supremacy. As early as March, Riedesel had written to Major General William Phillips, 'je désapprouve tout à fait les mouvements trop amples et trop extensives de Lord Cornwallis, notre Armée est trop faible pour maintenir un si grande terrain, nous sommes de nous despérser trop'.[113] By early October the regiments of Bose and the Erbprinz and Ewald's *Jäger* company, with the rest of Cornwallis's corps, were trapped in Yorktown. Germans fought under three flags during the siege: the troops of Steuben and Muhlenberg in the American army, the Zweibrucken (Deuxponts) Regiment in Rochambeau's French corps, the Hessians and Ansbach-Bayreuth soldiers with Cornwallis. The French and American guns battered the lines day and night. The journal of Bose's regiment recorded on 9 October that fifty-eight mortar bombs and 104 shells fell on the works every hour. By the 13th the besiegers' trenches were within thirty paces of the defences. By that date, Bose's regiment, suffering severely from sickness, had seventy-two ill and thirteen more lying wounded.[114] The battalion's surgeons had been sent back to Charleston when Cornwallis marched into North Carolina, so the sick and wounded did not enjoy expert care.[115] The -Regiment Erbprinz lost their

[110] This is fairly steep. Even the regimental journal recorded only 7,000!
[111] Müller, *Sämmtliche Werke*, XIV, p. 232.
[112] StaMarburg 12.11 1 Ba 7, fols. 168–9 and 171.
[113] StaWolfenbüttel 237N76, fol. 246, 26 Mar. 1781.
[114] StaMarburg 12.11 1 Ba 7, fols. 185–7.
[115] Ibid, 4h.412. nr. 5, fol. 107, Baurmeister to the Erbprinz, 6 Nov. 1781.

chief surgeon, Bauer, killed in the siege.[116] On 14 October Captain Roll of Bose's had his left arm torn off by a bomb, and died in moments. The regimental journal claimed, with understandable exaggeration, that one third of Cornwallis's army was killed and wounded and that not a house remained standing in the town.[117]

On the night of 14 October two vital redoubts fell. The Americans took the smaller, held by forty-five men including sixteen of Bose's, five of the Hessians being killed and eleven captured.[118] The larger redoubt with 150 men in it including a detachment of the Erbprinz's gave the French a much harder task. Resistance was very fierce, and Lieutenant Andresohn of the Erbprinz's, who distinguished himself on the parapet, was awarded *Pour la vertu militaire*.[119] Ninety-six of the French attackers were killed and wounded, the prisoners numbered seventy-three.[120]

On 17 October Cornwallis asked for terms, and two days later his troops, British, Loyalist, and German, marched into captivity. It must have been mortifying for Major O'Reilly, who had routed the raw Americans at New York five years before, to surrender his regiment. Baron von Closen, a Palatine serving in the German Zweibrucken Regiment in Rochambeau's corps, described the captured Germans: '[The Ansbach Regiments] were very handsome and very neatly dressed, better even than the Hessians. The Hessian Regiment of Bose was not comparable in appearance to the last two, but it served throughout this war with the greatest distinction, and during the entire siege not a man deserted from it, whereas we received many Ansbach deserters and two English nationals.'[121]

There were 365 prisoners from Bose's regiment including 11 taken on 14 October, 41 wounded and 89 sick. Seventeen men had been killed during the siege. The Regiment Erbprinz suffered even more severely, losing 22 killed, 62 wounded, and 482 prisoners.[122]

[116] Baurmeister, *Journals*, p. 475.
[117] StaMarburg 12.11 1 Ba 7, fols. 185 and 193.
[118] Ibid., fol. 189.
[119] Ibid, 4h.412. nr. 4, fol. 166, Col. Hachenberg's report, n.d.; 4h.411. nr. 2, fol. 224, Cornwallis to Knyphausen, 8 Dec. 1781.
[120] Samuel Abbott Greene, *My Campaigns in America: a Journal kept by Count William de Deux-Ponts 1780–81* (Boston, 1868), pp. 147 and 148 n. 76.
[121] Acomb, *Baron von Closen's Journal*, pp. 153–4. In her introduction the editor estimates the Germans and Swiss in the French corps as one third of total strength.
[122] StaMarburg 12.11 1 Ba 7, fols. 219–220; 4h.411. nr. 2, fols. 206–8.

6
Anglo-Hessian relations

‾‾‾‾‾‾‾‾‾‾

The British already had experience of quarrelling and disagreement in an army composed of their own troops and various
mercenary contingents. Only with the greatest difficulty had
Ferdinand of Braunschweig welded the whole together in the Seven
Years War. Despite the success of Ferdinand's army, the various
parts did not always pull smoothly in harness together. In
November 1758 it was reported that Lord George Sackville, commander of the British corps, had so offended Britain's paid German
allies that none of them could bear him and a fracas between the
different contingents would soon break out.[1] Relations between
Ferdinand and Sackville were so strained that the latter declined to
support his commander at an important moment during the battle
of Minden.[2] No Hessian general let down the British so badly in
America.[3]

Of the various mercenary contingents serving in the middle
colonies, only the Hessians had general officers. Riedesel commanded a brigade on Long Island during the first six months of
1781, but most of his service was in Canada or with the
Convention Army. The senior Ansbachers, Waldeckers, and
Hanauers were battalion commanders, and an extract from
Münchhausen's letters sums up the British attitude to them: 'For
the occupation of Amboy [12 June 1777] there are left behind two
Ansbach regiments, one Waldeck, and one English, under the
command of Colonel von Eyb of the Ansbachers.[4] But I have to tell

---

[1] Lewis B. Namier and John Brooke, *House of Commons, 1754–1790* (3 vols. Oxford, 1964), III,
p. 391.
[2] The tangled conflicts of British politics were also involved here. Alan Saxon Brown, *The
American Secretary* (Ann Arbor, Michigan, 1963), pp. 3–15.
[3] It is notable that the Hessians preferred Clinton, who had served in Germany, to Howe, a
veteran of American campaigns, although on the latter's departure Knyphausen paid him
a generous tribute. Hinrichs, 'Extract from Letterbook', p. 144; Mackesy, *War for America*,
p. 213 n. 2; StaMarburg 4h.410. nr. 2, fol. 255, Knyphausen to the Landgraf, 15 April
1778.
[4] Eyb commanded the Ansbach regiment, Colonel von Voit that of Bayreuth. Eyb as senior
was brigadier. Eelking, *Hilfstruppen*, I, p. 173.

the colonel to do nothing without the advice of an English captain left with him.'[5]

Despite the article of alliance in the subsidy treaty, the Hessians too were in a position of strict subordination; they were not really junior partners of an alliance. Heister, and after him Knyphausen and Knyphausen's successor Lossberg,[6] had no part in making war strategy. The Hessian corps commander was simply one of a number of subordinate generals summoned to councils of war by the British commander-in-chief. Faucitt was instructed to make it clear to the Hessians, when they embarked for America, that they should never hold supreme command.[7] The British second-in-command, first Clinton and then Cornwallis, was furnished with a 'dormant commission' which guaranteed his succession to the command on the death or disability of his superior, irrespective of Hessian seniority.[8] Besides this, no Hessian, with the notable exception Knyphausen, commanded a major post during the war. When the command of the Halifax garrison fell upon Colonel Seitz on the death of Brigadier General Maclean, Clinton was quick to appoint Lieutenant Colonel Bruce, Seitz's junior, acting brigadier, pointing out to Seitz that it was always necessary that a British officer command the Halifax garrison.[9] Major General Augustine Prevost specially appointed Lieutenant Colonels Mark Prevost and John Maitland to succeed him in Georgia, rather than Lieutenant Colonel Friedrich von Porbeck, nominally senior, should something befall him.[10] Senior British officers were often given antedated seniority over their Hessian opposite numbers, a measure which aroused some resentment. Thus in February, 1779 the promotion of Lossberg, Bose, Huyn and Kospoth to major general caused Clinton to advance seven British brigadiers to equal rank, dating their commissions before those of the Hessians.[11] In July 1781, because Lossberg and Bose received their step up to lieutenant general, Clinton gave Alexander Leslie and John Campbell similar acting rank.[12] Riedesel felt the same irritation at finding a junior major general placed above him in Canada.[13]

[5] Münchhausen, fasc. 2, fol. 29.
[6] For Lossberg, see p. 150.
[7] SP81/181, Suffolk to Faucitt (Private and Secret), 6 March 1776.
[8] Clinton, *Narrative*, p. 61; CO5/96, fol. 225, Germain to Cornwallis, 12 April 1778.
[9] HMC: *American*, II, pp. 276, 288–9, 295.
[10] Ibid., I, p. 448.
[11] StaMarburg 4h.411. nr. 1, fol. 12, Knyphausen to the Landgraf, 14 Feb. 1779.
[12] CO5/102, fol. 230, Clinton to Germain, 4 July 1781.
[13] Add. MS. 21811, fol. 278, Riedesel to Germain, October 1781.

The Hessians

The British commander-in-chief, then, had no need to thrash out mutual strategy with his Hessian subordinate, but merely to give orders as to a divisional commander. Münchhausen, who had to interpret between the two, said that Heister was called for consultation only after Howe had already decided on a course of action.[14] However, for the good of the service, it was in the British interest to keep their mercenary chiefs happy and their men well fed. Thus although Howe secretly despised Heister, he seems to have convinced him right up to June 1777 that they were on the best terms. Indeed, Royal Instructions given to Colonel Clavering when he was sent to spy on the Landgraf in 1760 might have been the blueprint for the British commanders' behaviour to the Hessians: 'you may repeat such Assurances as of Our Constant Desire to confirm & improve the good Understanding, Harmony & Alliance, that subsists between Us & Our said Good Cousin, as may appear to You to be necessary for the good of Our Service, as Circumstances may arise.'[15] Or, as Suffolk put it, there was no point in allowing His Majesty's service to be impeded by the idle jealousies or punctilious attention to those innumerable little points of etiquette which always arise.[16] Other British generals beside the commander-in-chief behaved in this sensible manner, for when Alexander Leslie, commanding at Charleston in 1782, was writing privately to Clinton in critical terms of the Hessian colonels, Westerhagen and Benning, he praised Benning publicly on orders.[17] The only failure of the system was the jealousy between Corn wallis and Donop, which contributed to the Hessian disaster at Redbank.

There seems a strong element of hypocrisy in this, but it would have been very foolish for the British to jeopardize military success by alienating a large corps of their army. Allied jealousies and mistrust were to play a major role in the failure of their campaign against the French in Flanders in 1793–4, a campaign which ended in disastrous retreat with the soldiers of the various contingents openly fighting one another.[18]

Within his limitations Heister did his best, but he angered Howe by his apparent dawdling and a seeming willingness to counten-

---

[14] Münchhausen, fasc. 2, fol. 4, 25 Nov. 1776.
[15] SP87/39, fols. 1–2, n.d.
[16] SP81/182, Suffolk to Faucitt (Private and Secret), 12 Feb. 1776.
[17] HMC: *American*, II, p. 434; StaMarburg 12.11 I Ba 13 (Journal of the Regiment von Huyn), fol. 138.
[18] Sir John Fortescue, *A History of the British Army*, IV (London, 1906), part i, p. 320.

ance plundering by his own troops.[19] Knyphausen restored the good relations, and during the Philadelphia command held several commands of British as well as his own troops, with both of whom he was in great credit and esteem.[20] A British subaltern wrote, 'Gen. Knyphausen who is said to be one of the best Generals in Germany . . . has by the severity of his discipline in a great measure put a stop to the infamous practice of plundering, which was much encouraged by De Heister who shared in the profits of this lucrative occupation.'[21] His command of the column which occupied Washington's attention at Chad's Ford on the Brandywine, enabling Howe and Cornwallis to get round the enemy flank, shows he was better consulted than Heister regarding battle plans. Howe reported, 'Lieutenant General Knyphausen, *as had been previously concerted*, kept the Enemy amused in the Course of the Day with Cannon, and the Appearance of Forcing the Ford, without intending to pass it, until the Attack upon the Enemy's Right, should take Place.'[22] He also had the trust of Howe's successor, who gave him half the army and a twelve-mile-long baggage train to protect in the retreat from Philadelphia,[23] and the command at New York when the Charleston expedition sailed. A young Englishman wrote to his parents in March 1780, from New York, 'General Knyphausen is Com'r in Chief and very much loved.'[24] He also had a tolerant sense of humour, but no excessive leniency, regarding the conduct and education of young officers, as his letter of 15 April 1778 to the Landgraf shows: 'The conduct of Ensign von Lützow with my own regiment has continued up to now just as bad as ever. Ah, well! he is only a young fellow, and I hope that the arrest now imposed on him for an undetermined time, whereby he is compelled to do his duty, will contribute to his improvement.'[25] His expedition into New Jersey in June 1780 showed, however, that his military talents were those of a divisional commander rather than an independent general.

The undertaking was prompted by reports from deserters and

[19] John André, *Major André's Journal*, Henry Cabot Lodge, ed. (2 vols. Boston, 1903), 1, p. 42. Hessian plundering is more fully discussed below.
[20] CO5/94, fol. 436, Osborne to Germain, 13 Oct. 1777.
[21] Wilkin, *Some British Soldiers*, p. 246.
[22] CO5/94, fol. 320, Howe to Germain, 10 Oct. 1777. My italics.
[23] Just before the retreat he received news of his wife's death in Hessen. Jungkenn 2:2, Cochenhausen to Jungkenn, 2 June 1778.
[24] Violet Biddulph, 'Letters of Robert Biddulph', *AHR*, XXIX (1923), p. 93.
[25] StaMarburg 4h.410. nr. 2, fol. 254. Lützow's conduct did improve after six months under open arrest.

Loyalists of discontent in Washington's army. Knyphausen's information was that Washington had only 4,000 men left after the dispatch of Sullivan's corps against the Iroquois of upper New York. With the concurrence of British generals under him, and quite probably on the advice of Major General James Robertson, an American, he crossed with 6,000 men from Staten Island to New Jersey, landing near Elizabethtown on 7 June.[26] He expected to take up a position on Short Hills between Springfield and Chatham after the first day's march, and by a subsequent move from that 'commanding position' to oblige Washington to abandon Morristown, leaving part of his stores and artillery behind for want of horses.[27] This first step foundered on the militia's active resistance, and it might have been just as well to cut losses and abandon the attempt at that point.

In the first day's constant skirmishing, the *Jäger* expended all their ammunition in twelve hours' fighting. Two bridges over marshy creeks needing repair caused further delay, and on the night of 8/9 June Knyphausen, appreciating that his information was incorrect, withdrew to Elizabethtown. Washington, mystified by the uncertain manoeuvres, believed the expedition was some sort of decoy to draw him away from the Hudson so that Clinton, returning from Charleston, could advance up the river and seize American posts on it.[28] No such plan had been concerted. Instead, skirmishing continued around Elizabethtown. The Americans remained active and alert. An attempt by the mounted *Jäger* to surprise an American cavalry piquet on 13 June failed. 'It is almost impossible to surprise the enemy on any occasion,' reported the *Jägercorps* journal, 'because every house that one passes is a warning piquet, so to speak; for the farmer, or his son, or his servant, or even his wife or daughter fires off a gun, or runs by the foot-path to warn the enemy'.[29]

Clinton considered the expedition ill-advised. Nevertheless, on his return he ordered Knyphausen's corps to make a new thrust to prevent a possible movement by Washington up the Hudson against New York.[30] A pontoon bridge was constructed between Elizabethtown and Staten Island to facilitate communications.

[26] Hinrichs, 'Extracts from Letterbook', p. 69; Jungkenn 3:34, Cochenhausen to Jungkenn, 30 June 1780.
[27] CO5/183, fol. 13, Knyphausen to Germain, 3 July 1780.
[28] Washington, *Writings*, xviii, p. 444.
[29] StaMarburg 12.11 1 Ba 17, fol. 49.
[30] Clinton, *Narrative*, p. 193.

Early on the morning of 23 June Knyphausen advanced again, the *Jäger* leading. Again skirmishing delayed the movement, and although he got possession of Springfield, an attempt to turn the enemy's left failed, and the corps withdrew across the pontoons. The cost of the two week failure was 25 killed, 234 wounded, and 48 missing.[31] 'A very pretty expedition,' wrote Ensign Thomas Hughes, 'six thousand men having penetrated 12 miles into the country – burnt a village and returned.'[32]

The whole expedition served merely to stoke the fires of American propaganda. Newspapers reported it as if the only aim were to burn American farms and kill helpless civilians.[33] Springfield had been burnt, contrary to Knyphausen's orders, because the soldiers were angered by rebels firing at them from its houses.[34] Lieutenant Colonel Ludwig von Wurmb, commanding the *Jägercorps*, was saddened at the embarrassment of his chief and the misconduct of his corps. By 15 June he had written to Riedesel that Knyphausen must lose much of his reputation by this manoeuvre. Wurmb himself had already seen the Loyalists plunder the house of a certain Smith in Elizabethtown, in which his own *Jäger* joined, to his anger. Consequently he forbade them entering the town.[35] By 22 June he reported that the town was almost ruined and all the inhabitants save the women had fled.[36] The greatest atrocity attributed to the British, the shooting of the defenceless Mrs James Caldwell at Connecticut Farms, may however have been incorrectly laid at their door. A British officer writing in the *Royal Gazette* stated, 'it appears beyond a doubt that the shot was fired by the rebels themselves, as it entered the side of the house from their direction and lodged in the wall nearest to the British troops, then advancing'.[37]

Despite this failure Friedrich II regarded Knyphausen's presence as essential for the maintenance of his troops. With monotonous

---

[31] StaMarburg 4h.411. nr. 1, fol. 360. Of this total 85, including 8 officers, were amongst the *Jäger*.

[32] Thomas Hughes, *A Journal by Thomas Hughes 1778–1789*, E. A. Benians, ed. (Cambridge, 1947), p. 90.

[33] Moore, *Diary of the Revolution*, II, pp. 285–9; Davidson, *Propaganda and the Revolution*, pp. 367–8. These accounts reached the Landgraf, who was very sorry to hear accounts of depredations by his troops. The British assured him that Loyalist troops committed the excesses, which seems correct from Wurmb's account below. SP81/193, Stormont to Faucitt, 30 Sept. 1780.

[34] T. Balch, ed., 'Mathew's Narrative', *Historical Magazine of America*, I (1857), p. 105.

[35] StaWolfenbüttel 237N86, fol. 65, 15 June 1780.

[36] Ibid., fol. 66, Wurmb to Riedesel, 22 June.

[37] Moore, *Diary of the Revolution*, II, p. 290.

regularity Knyphausen wrote each year asking to return to Hessen for reasons of age and health. The Landgraf's reply of February 1778 is typical of his answers: 'As I recommend to the honourable Lieutenant-General the well-being and preservation of my corps once again in the best manner possible, so the full trust which he has on all occasions gives me the most reassuring affirmation, that the Lieutenant-General will employ every means possible in this regard and that I could not have chosen better than to entrust to him the fate of so many of my gallant Hessians in that part of the world.'[38] Not until he was nearly blind in one eye from cataract was Knyphausen permitted to return, in May 1782. Even in the letter granting permission, Friedrich wrote that he would be delighted to hear of an improvement in his health so that he could stay on in command.[39]

His successor was Friedrich Wilhelm von Lossberg, formerly commanding officer of the Leib-Regiment and later chief of the Regiment jung-Lossberg (previously Mirbach's, not to be confused with that Regiment von Lossberg from Rinteln). He came of an old soldier family which had migrated from Thuringia in the seventeenth century to escape religious persecution. He commanded a brigade at the capture of Newport in 1776 and likewise at its defence in 1778. In his sixty-second year, he continued the Hessian tradition of elderly corps commanders.[40] By then operations had ceased, but he successfully brought the Hessians back from America, receiving from Sir Guy Carleton a generous tribute to 'the exemplary behaviour of the Hessian troops under his orders' and to Lossberg's own 'zeal and attention on all occasions to forward the King's Service'.[41]

Other Hessians earned British admiration. Colonel Friedrich von Minnigerode won esteem as both an amiable gentleman and a gallant soldier.[42] Clinton spoke of his distinguished character and eminent services as commander of a grenadier battalion.[43] When he was buried in the Lutheran graveyard at New York on 19 October 1779, after dying of sickness, the cortège was followed by

---

[38] StaMarburg 4h.410. nr. 2, fol. 150, 16 Feb. 1778.
[39] Ibid., 4h.411. nr. 2, fol. 181, 12 Nov. 1781.
[40] Robert Friderici, 'Karl von Lossberg 1804–1885', in *Lebensbilder aus Kurhessen und Waldeck*, Ingeborg Schnack, ed., III (Marburg, 1942), p. 267.
[41] StaMarburg 4h.411. nr. 3, fols. 206–7, Carleton to Lossberg, 15 Nov. 1783.
[42] Ibid., 12.11 I Ba 13 (Journal of Huyn's Regiment), fol. 113, quoting from the obituary in Gaine's *Gazette*.
[43] CO5/98, fol. 230, Clinton to Germain, 26 Oct. 1779.

all the British generals of the garrison, by whom he was loved as much as by the Hessians.[44]

Major General Alexander Leslie reported from Charleston in 1781–2 that Carl von Bose was an excellent man who did everything in his power to forward the King's service.[45] Simcoe wrote of his 'reliance on the acknowledged military talents of his friend Ewald, and the cool and tried courage of his Yagers'.[46] When the Regiment von Lossberg was sent to reinforce the garrison in Canada, British generals in New York recommended its commanding officer Colonel Johann von Loos as a man of merit and distinguished character, whose good services and agreeable acquaintance would be a welcome acquisition to Haldimand's forces.[47]

A number of officers struck up friendships: Münchhausen with another ADC, Captain Knight; Lieutenant von Heister, the general's son, with Lord Rawdon; Bardeleben exchanged hospitality with both English and Scots officers; Ensign Langenscharz and his father were on close terms with several officers at Halifax, including some the elder man had known in the previous war; and Malsburg made friends with almost everybody. He tells a charming story of a dinner party which he attended on Rhode Island, given by the Hessian brigade major, Captain Waldenberger, for a number of Hessian and British officers, including Lords Percy and Rawdon. Music was provided by the hautbois of two Hessian regiments. After the meal Rawdon went into the next room and invited a Miss Barton of that house and a number of her young lady friends to join them in dancing: 'they required no further invitation [wrote Malsburg], and we had an opportunity to see models of excellent dancers, who, by their fine dress and manners too, enhanced even more the very favourable impression which we had formed of the daughters of this continent'.[48]

Colonel Block of the grenadiers earned favour by his efforts to learn English before landfall at Sandy Hook in 1776,[49] and Dinklage tried to teach himself on the voyage by reading the *Adventures of Roderick Random* with the aid of a dictionary. He seems to have been successful, for while in Philadelphia he visited the

[44] Dinklage, fols. 233–4.
[45] HMC: *American*, III, p. 434, CO5/107, fol. 219, 27 Dec. 1781.
[46] Simcoe, *History of the Queen's Rangers*, p. 232.
[47] Add. MS. 21807, fols. 70 and 74, Jas. Pattison and Clinton to Haldimand, 8 and 9 Sept. 1779.
[48] Malsburg, fol. 79 (19 Dec. 1776).
[49] Add. MS. 21680, fol. 133, Hutcheson to Haldimand, 8 Aug 1776.

Academy there, where a professor showed him a collection of fauna.[50] But there were language difficulties, particularly at the outset. Malsburg describes using a mixture of French and English to communicate on Staten Island in August, 1776: 'How many sentries *avez-vous ici, Monsieur?*'[51] As late as October, 1778 Ensign Thomas Hughes of the 53rd encountered a German officer on Rhode Island who spoke to him in 'a language neither German nor English'.[52] Only in the course of time, noted Quartermaster Kleinschmidt of Huyn's, was the Hessians' broken English understood; and Conrad Doehla, a Bayreuth soldier, wrote at the beginning of 1778 that language difficulties prevented relations between English and German being closer.[53]

In fact, cases of friendship are the exception rather than the rule in Anglo-Hessian relations. Language was not the only divisive factor. Doehla wrote that the English officers looked on the Germans as hired mercenaries to be censured for fighting for pay.[54] An English officer wrote that 'differing as we do in language, manners, and ideas, English and Hessian did not coalesce into one corps', and visits exchanged between the two were 'rather national civilities than personal kindnesses'.[55] Typical is the letter of Robert Biddulph, a young man working for a civilian contractor supplying the army, in December 1779; 'The ensuing Winter will be a very dull one, as we are garrison'd by Hessians, who, tho' they all speak English, do not make their Way among the Inhabitants who are sociable talkers.' Sailing for Charleston in November 1780, he felt he was in for another dull winter for 'the Hessians do not mix at all'.[56] This is borne out by Friedrich von der Lith, who saw the Hessians as far stuffier and more etiquette-ridden than the British:

The English officers avoided going off parade with the German officers, the inhabitants received them unwillingly into their society; the children born of German parents were ashamed' to speak German, and sought to conceal their German origin. I ascribe the cause of this mainly to the character of the Germans

[50] Dinklage, fols. 25 and 179–80.
[51] Malsburg, fol. 45.
[52] Hughes, *Journal*, p. 45.
[53] StaMarburg 12.11 I Ba 13 (Journal of the Regiment von Huyn), fol. 47; Johann Conrad Doehla, 'Tagebuch eines Bayreuther Soldaten aus dem Nordamerikanischen Freiheitskrieg 1777–1783', *Archiv für Geschichte und Altertumskunde von Oberfranken*, XXV (1912), pp. 144–5.
[54] Ibid., p. 144.
[55] Almon ed., *The Remembrancer for the year 1777*, pp. 82–3. The whole of the published letter bears out what Doehla thought.
[56] Biddulph, 'Letters', pp. 92 and 96.

and their lack of freedom amongst the common people. The pedantic, obsequious character of the Germans, empty of compliments, contrasts too greatly with the open, unaffected, noble ways of the English, for it to please them, and of individual freedom the Germans had scarcely any idea. Even many of the German officers felt this lack and sought to make up for it in their outward behaviour, but usually fell into a swaggering tone that made them laughable. They wished to speak and behave freely and openly, and through this only betrayed all the more their slavish sentiments in which they had been brought up and the servile fear in which they were kept. If the youngest English officer laid bare all his thoughts without shyness at the table of the commanding general with the greatest frankness and assurance, our German generals sat like schoolboys stiff and silent, and full of anxious modesty scarcely dared to speak and move. – The wonder is, that this pedantic character of the German people blossomed even in that clime. The German is distinguished by untiring energy and hard work even in America, but otherwise he plays a subordinate role and has little part in public affairs.[57]

Those amongst the British most hostile to the Hessians were Americans serving their King. Stephen Kemble wrote of the Hessians 'outrageously cruel and licentious to a degree',[58] Major General James Robertson testified to the Commons that Washington returned twenty-one wagon loads of plunder from the Hessians taken at Trenton,[59] and Galloway said that at that battle 'they were more attentive to the safety of their plunder than their duty' and could not be formed.[60] These men, not unnaturally, did not like to see hired foreigners coming to America to restore Royal government, but in fact more German auxiliaries than American Loyalists fought for the British: over 30,000 of the former came to America, not including Scheither's recruits, while about 19,000 Loyalists took up arms.[61]

Officers on active service like Simcoe and Ewald, who had to fight their way out of tricky situations together, were likely to sink national differences and find qualities of mutual admiration. The idleness of garrison duty and winter quarters, however, bred disagreement between British and Hessian, particularly as the war

[57] Strieder, *Hessischen Gelehrten Geschichte*, XVIII, p. 353. An American put the contrast between the two nations more simply: 'The British officers gay in spirit and action, and the German officers stiff in motion and embroidery.' Watson, *Annals of Philadelphia*, II, p. 57.

[58] Kemble, *Journal*, p. 98.

[59] Commager and Morris, *Spirit of 'Seventy Six*, p. 528.

[60] Galloway, *Letters to a Nobleman*, p. 44. The story of Hessian plunder was widely reported by the British, receiving credence at headquarters. See Add. MS 21680, fol. 173, 10 Feb. 1777; and 34, 413, fol. 153, letter from New York, 3 Jan. 1777; also Stuart-Wortley, *Prime Minister and Son*, p. 99. Not a single eye-witness, Hessian or American, reports it. Carrington rightly characterized such tales as 'fables'.

[61] Paul Smith, 'The American Loyalists: Notes on their Organisation and Numerical Strength', *WMQ*, 3rd series, XXV (1968), pp. 259–67.

began to go wrong. After Trenton, it was reported, the British taunted the Hessians with their defeat.[62] The Hessians for their part found fault with the carelessness and arrogance of the British. George Forster wrote in 1779 that scarcely a letter was received in Kassel from Hessian officers in America, that was not full of praise for the Americans and showed a contempt for the English scarce to be believed. The only requisite of a soldier which the latter possessed was courage. The writer of one letter, fed up with British dandies, was expecting to hear next the order for them to make their toilette in the entrenchments and to perfume the gunpowder.[63] Hinrichs charged the British with carelessness at the siege of Savannah; whether from conceit or neglect, they omitted to repair their works or prepare gabions and fascines, although the defences were half crumbled.[64] Of Tarleton's defeat at Cowpens, Ludwig von Wurmb wrote that it was due to the young commander's reckless and disorderly pursuit of advanced troops thrown forward as a decoy: 'il n'a aucune Expérience et prévaience [sic] ... il treatte l'affaire comme une partie de chasse.'[65] Münchhausen believed that Howe entrusted the most exposed posts to the Hessians in December 1776 'because the English always believe themselves to be too secure and are certainly by a long way not so careful as the Hessians. Perhaps it is a consequence of the great bravery which is natural to them, that in their outposts, patrols, and other like matters pertaining to security, they are terribly negligent.'[66] After Yorktown even Dinklage wrote that 'this outcome was seen by nearly everyone, but the English pride, the disagreements of the English generals, and most of all the English ministry, which constructed the operations plans on false reports, and in that way bound the hands of the commanding general, are the causes of this misfortune'.[67] Those criticisms, however, were not unique to the Hessians, and although quite accurate they had all been heard before. In the Seven Years War Ferdinand of Braunschweig found that British officers 'do not trouble their heads about the service; and understand of it, very few excepted, absolutely nothing whatever, and this goes from the ensign on up to the general'.[68]

[62] Martin Christian Friedrich Daniel Schubart, *Deutsche Chronik aus das Jahr 1774–1777* (Augsburg and Ulm, 1774–7). Kipping, *Hessen-Kassel Truppen*, p. 22 n. 88.
[63] Forster, *Briefwechsel*, I, p. 244.
[64] Uhlendorf, *Siege of Charleston*, pp. 161–3.
[65] StaWolfenbüttel 237N86, fols, 94 and 99, Wurmb to Riedesel, 19 and 28 Feb. 1781.
[66] Münchhausen, fasc. 4, fol. 14, note 11.
[67] Dinklage, fol. 298.
[68] Quoted in Barnett, *Britain and her Army*, p. 185.

From the common man in both contingents, Hessian and British, there was a more open display of hostility. Accounts of scuffles and fisticuffs begin with Major General Stirn applying the birch to a British seaman who hurled a burning coal at a Hessian sentry on the last leg of the voyage to America,[69] and end with an affray at the *Hill House* public house, Chatham, in January 1784.[70] In the majority of cases British or Loyalist soldiers were the offenders. Sergeant von Krafft and a Freikorporal of Donop's regiment rescued a Hessian private being beaten up by members of a Provincial light horse unit. On another occasion English soldiers attacked a Hessian grenadier sergeant with their bayonets, wounded him in many places, robbed him, and left him lying on the spot, where he soon after died.[71] Krafft identified members of Lord Rawdon's Volunteers of Ireland as the worst culprits. Major General Robertson was obliged to remonstrate on public orders, 9 February 1778, against a number of soldiers who with knives had wounded and defaced three Hessian soldiers and perpetrated several other similar acts of discord.[72] A Sergeant Thomas of the Georgia Loyalists was broken to private for assaulting a Hessian sentry at Savannah.[73]

Trouble also occurred over the little vegetable gardens which each regiment cultivated in its cantonments. Normally when one regiment succeeded another in a post, it inherited the vegetables as well as the duties. But in August 1781 the 54th Regiment relieved at Paulus Hook by German troops rooted up all their cabbages, and only the prudence of the officers present prevented brawling.[74]

Although these occurrences were frequent enough to warrant notice and, on some occasions, disciplinary action, they were nothing more than what was to be expected between men of various nations, ignorant of one another's customs and language, particularly when the armies were composed of the lowest or most pugnacious elements of the populace. After their joint failure at Rhode Island in 1778, Americans rioted against D'Estaing's seamen in Boston, killing a noble French officer.[75] It hardly seems that

[69] StaMarburg 4h.410. nr. 1, fol. 352, Heister to Hotham, 5 Aug. 1776.
[70] *The London Chronicle*, LIV (1784), p. 98; *The Gentleman's Magazine*, LIV (1784), p. 69.
[71] John Charles Philip von Krafft, *The Journal of Lieutenant John Charles Philip von Krafft 1776–1783*, Thomas H. Edsall, ed. (New York, 1883), pp. 82 and 90.
[72] *New Jersey Archives*, 2nd series, II, p. 115.
[73] StaMarburg 12.11 I Ba 12 (Journal of the Regiment von Wissenbach), fol. 420.
[74] Mackenzie, *Diary*, II, p. 594. The German soldiers involved were from Braunschweig and Zerbst.
[75] Heath, *Memoirs*, p. 178.

any of these national animosities had any effect upon the conduct of the war. American newspapers constantly published accounts of Hessians refusing to march to the aid of the British or do their duty; vowing to go straight back to Hessen; and being at daggers drawn with their allies at Charleston.[76] So far as they affected the conduct of the war, these stories were entirely false. British officers probably felt, like Clinton, that 'the overproportion of foreigners . . . tho' they may be faithful cannot be supposed equally zealous',[77] but they did not accuse them of refusing to do their duty. Lith rightly observes that discord between British and Hessian never came to an outburst of any significance.[78]

British warmth of feeling for the Hessians generally increased with familiarity. Nicholas Cresswell, who saw them only once, on parade, called them 'a set of cruel unfeeling people'; but Captain George Beckwith, who served several campaigns as Knyphausen's ADC, declared, 'I would be highly ungrateful were I not to express on all occasions how much I owe to my good friends, the Hessians, for their kindness to me during several Campaigns that I resided with them, and I shall never forget the real kindnesses and many good Offices done me by General Knyphausen.'[79] And George Hanger, who commanded a *Jäger* company, spoke 'with pleasure' of 'my old companions in war, the Hessian troops, than whom there are no braver or better disciplined forces in the world'.[80] Colonel William Harcourt is a case in point. Although he had not seen them, he wrote of the Brunswickers when they arrived at Portsmouth in 1776, 'no intermediate age between grandfathers and grand-children, with Coaches and every other impedimenta for their officers, and without a necessary for their men. The generals marched, or rather reeled off the Parade. . . .' One could scarcely be more critical than this. Yet Harcourt served amicably

---

[76] *New Jersey Archives*, 2nd series, I, p. 336; Force, *American Archives*, Fifth series, II, pp. 948 and 996; Rodney, *Letters*, p. 152; Moore, *Diary of the Revolution*, II, pp. 419–20.

[77] CO5/96, fol. 161, Clinton to Germain, 8 Oct. 1778.

[78] Lith, 'Feldzug der Hessen', pp. 48–9.

[79] Cresswell, *Journal*, p. 221; StaWolfenbüttel 237N55, fol. 55, Beckwith to Riedesel, 25 Aug. 1782.

[80] Hanger, *Life, Adventures, and Opinions*, I, pp. 39–40. Two British officers served in the Hessian corps during the war: Hanger, and Capt. Bennett Wallop of the Guards, captured by a privateer en route to America and never actually taking up his post as a captain in Knyphausen's regiment. StaMarburg 12.11 I Ba 6 (Journal of the Regiment von Knyphausen), fol. 139. A number of Hessian officers transferred into British and Provincial regiments, among them a Captain Wolff, formerly of Ditfurth's, killed leading the grenadiers of the 16th in an attack on an American vessel, the *Rattlesnake*, near Stono Ferry in June 1779. Ibid, nr. 12 (Journal of the Regiment von Wissenbach), fols. 298–9; HMC: *American*, I, p. 447.

throughout the winter of 1776–7 with Donop, and after the latter's death at Redbank, he wrote with regret of the Hessian colonel, 'very justly the pride of the Hessians, and undoubtedly an excellent officer'.[81]

Thus although most British and Hessians were not good friends, or even amicably disposed to one another, British commanders were not foolish enough to jeopardize their opportunity of getting good services from the Germans. It would have been impossible for Britain to carry on the war without a corps of 20,000 foreigners, of whom roughly two-thirds came from Hessen-Kassel.[82] By flattery on public orders, by exchanging national civilities, by Knyphausen's good will and leadership, but also by keeping them in strict subordination, the British got good service from their Hessian auxiliaries, although increasingly as the war progressed this was in garrison duties and fairly static tasks. However much or little zeal they showed for the service, it was not the Germans who lost the British the war, but their own strategic mistakes in 1777 and 1781.

[81] Harcourt, *Papers*, IX, pp. 168 and 222.
[82] The constant strength of the German contingents (as opposed to total numbers sent, which exceeded 30,000) was roughly Hessen-Kassel 13,000; Braunschweig-Wolfenbüttel 4,300; Waldeck 650; Hessen-Hanau 800; Ansbach-Bayreuth 1,300; and Anhalt-Zerbst 650.

7

The Hessian view of the American
Revolution

This land is now a stage for the cruellest scenes. Here there is one neighbour against the other, children against their father. Whoever thinks or speaks differently from the Congress in those provinces in which it is obeyed soon becomes looked on as an enemy, is given over to the hangman, or must take flight, either into our lines or back into the wilderness. But for the tyranny of the Congress party, no people in the world could have lived better than these.[1]

As early as the engagement at Flatbush, where Americans fell an easy prey to Hessian bayonets, there were signs that the rebels were not a typical enemy. Bardeleben reported that when the prisoners were gathered at the rear of the Hessian lines General Heister went amongst them and gave them wine to drink the King's health. One captured officer, a schoolmaster, not refusing the wine, declined to drink to George III. This defiance was unacceptable to the victors, come to America to restore the people to their proper obedience. The man was taken out from the others and threatened with shooting, to no avail. He answered with all possible calmness, that since he had been a schoolmaster he had taken it as his duty, and employed all his efforts, to educate his pupils in the belief that they should never declare themselves for the King of England. Therefore, he would gladly offer up his life before he would change his opinion.[2]

[1] Dinklage, fols. 213–4. The subject of this chapter is dealt with in Kipping, *Hessian View of America*, pp. 13–20 and 22–34.

[2] Bardeleben, pp. 62–3. Another story is told of Heister, after the battle of White Plains, in a Loyalist newspaper at New York: 'It happened one day that a party of rebel prisoners dined with General de Heister, the Hessian General, who, as soon as the cloth was taken away, drank "The King". Some of the provincials drank the toast, others drank their wine and said nothing. At last, one who had more plain dealing about him than the rest refused drinking it, giving it as a reason, with many apologies, "that if it had been a favourite toast with him, he would not then be in the situation he was at present". This occasioned some confusion, and in particular brought on an altercation between him and the General, which in the end terminated in the latter so far forgetting himself as to strike the former with his cane. This is no doubt nothing more than what is common in German discipline, yet, though it may be thought advisable for us to want their assistance as soldiers, it is to be hoped that British generals will reprobate such feelings and manners.' Moore, *Diary of the Revolution*, I, p. 351. With its obvious Prussianism held up as a moral

158

The Hessian view of the American Revolution

Not merely education, but religion too in America ran contrary to the way of things accepted by the Hessians. Chaplain Kümmel of Huyn's regiment discovered that, far from being a prop for the existing order, sustaining loyalty to one's rightful sovereign, it was a weapon of subversion. Kümmel was quartered on Manhattan Island near New Rochelle with Colonel Kurz and the regimental staff in the house of a preacher. The preacher had gone off with the rebels. At the pulpit of the church behind the house, Kümmel discovered large folios of the Books of the Martyrs, stories in Greek and Latin of the Apostles and the early Christians. From the annotations and the reports of neighbours, Kümmel concluded that the preacher used the martyrs' stories to incite his flock against the Royal establishment.[3] And Lieutenant Henckelmann of Stein's regiment wrote, 'The clergymen ... have taken the gun and cartridge-box with them into the pulpit, explained to their hearers how they ought to fight and from the church directly they have gone to the war.'[4]

However much they came to admire American courage, the Hessian officers never looked on the Americans as men with a just cause for rebelling. The colonists were the ungracious subjects of a too gracious monarch; they had grown incorrigible through kind treatment and an excess of luxury. The opposition to taxes was just a trumped-up excuse for seizing power. They ignored the sums of money spent by the mother country on their defence.[5]

The Hessians' background had given them no awareness of the Rights of Man as expressed in the Anglo-American political tradition. Their knowledge of the issues came solely from what British officers and Loyalists told them, and it did not run very deep. When the local pastor at Newtown, Pennsylvania, denounced ad nauseam those officers captured at Trenton for coming to America, the officers, finally weary of the harangue, bade the old man shut up, saying they had not come to decide who was right of the two parties, but to fight for the King of England.[6] Their letters showed them scarcely capable of political analysis. Hinrichs, who attemp-

(*Footnote continued*)
    lesson, the story is suspect. At least Lord Stirling testified that Heister treated his officer prisoners with consideration (schoolmasters excepted!). LB Kassel 4° Ms. hass. 188, Geschichte des Fusilier-Regiments von Lossberg, fol. 29.
[3] Kümmel, fol. 7.
[4] Wiederholdt, 'Tagebuch' introduction, p. xv. The man referred to was Peter Muhlenberg, Lutheran clergyman who became a continental general.
[5] Pettengill, *Letters from America*, p. 229; Huth, 'Letters from a Mercenary', p. 498.
[6] LB Kassel, 8° Ms. hass. 188, Geschichte des Fusilier-Regiments von Lossberg, fols. 28–9.

ted to sum up the causes of the revolution for Schlözer, said there had been two rebellions. The first, fifty years before, had been by the Quakers, 'hypocrites practising malice, envy, and ambition under the guise of religion'; they had deceived the German settlers in the colonies. The second, the present one, by the élites who had previously established themselves as leaders in the colonies, was 'an Irish-Scotch Presbyterian Rebellion' to throw off Royal government and establish their own tyranny.[7] The whole story is so completely ludicrous as to lead one to conclude that Hinrichs' difficulties with English prevented him from understanding what he had been told.

Dinklage was scarcely closer to the mark when he put the rebellion down to a conspiracy of merchants, lawyers, and priests. His informant was a Dutch farmer on Staten Island in August 1780. According to the Dutchman, the colonial farmers had had nothing to complain of Royal government, paying only a trifling quitrent of eighteen coppers before the revolution. The cause of the trouble was 'the people in the cities . . . who had not enough to do and wanted to be great lords and get rich quickly, especially the merchants, lawyers, and even the priesthood'. The merchants had lost business to men and goods from England, so they roused the rabble to throw English wares into the sea. The lawyers, 'who enjoyed fishing in troubled waters, agreed with the merchants, indeed, even more so, because they were the people who expected to take the most distinguished and profitable part in the new state. . . The priesthood also hoped to have great advantage from it, for if the English government were abolished then the Episcopal Church should no longer impose its parish system on the local community churches. . .' Unbearable taxes, thought Dinklage, would be the least evil consequence of a rebel victory.[8]

A common view was that the wealth of the country, where commoners lived better than Hessian nobles, caused the inhabitants' insolence, pride, and greed. Hinrichs thought everyone in Germany who took the rebels' part ought to spend some time in America and learn how things really were, for the meanest man here, if only he busied himself, could live like the richest in Germany. Thus America's German partisans would learn that idleness and pleasure, not necessity, were the causes of the revolt.[9]

[7] Hinrichs, 'Extracts from Letterbook', pp. 137–8.
[8] Dinklage, fols. 271–4.
[9] Pettengill, *Letters from America*, pp. 165–6.

The Hessian view of the American Revolution

Henckelmann waxed indignant about the sybaritic waste: 'The amount of wood which is consumed here within 24 hours in such a fire-place would last us a week at home. The fat which here drips into the fire would in our country be made into good soup. – What do you think now of the inhabitants here?'[10] There is not a little of embittered envy in this, perhaps, but the common soldiers wrote the same. Sergeant Major Martin Appell of Rall's told his parents, 'the inhabitants each have their houses and estates and most of all their black slaves who do the work for them, and have had a lordly manner of living, but without order, each one does what he likes, and in a heathenish manner carries on his life.'[11] Valentin Asteroth, a soldier in Huyn's, reported on Rhode Island, 'No man here gives anyone anything. He only looks after himself and his appetite... However poor a man may be, so will he first of all provide tea twice a day for himself, for otherwise they think they cannot exist.'[12]

For the political debates and the free press, whose accounts in that age were often highly inaccurate or partisan, the Hessians had a true military man's contempt, particularly since American news-papers carried exaggerated stories of Hessian brutality. Colonel Heringen wrote to his chief Lossberg from Long Island, that the papers were just like the pathetic Parliamentary debates in England, one side inveighing against the other for the sake of faction.[13] In March 1777 Heister told his sovereign that the newspapers were nine-tenths lies.[14] The officers' contempt for democratic process was strengthened by knowledge of apparently low social origins of some of the leaders. Henckelmann wrote, 'Another member of Congress ... bears the name of von Sellwitz. Prior to the rebellion he was a chimney-sweep in New York, left his post, went to Philadelphia where he recommended himself to the favour of Mr. Penn by piano playing and singing, so that the latter suggested his name as a member of Congress into which he was received and where he is still playing a role. Are not these distinguished members? I should like to see the entire body.'[15]

Yet many of the officers had common origins, and in no way did

---

[10] Wiederholdt, 'Tagebuch', introduction, p. xv. Henckelmann was writing to his brother, a clergyman.
[11] LB Kassel, 4° Ms. hass. 293/3, Brief vom Soldat Martin Appell (2 July 1777).
[12] Ibid, 8° Ms. hass. 127, Erinnerungen aus dem amerikanischen Krieg, fols. 45–6.
[13] Heringen, 'Einige Briefe aus dem amerikanischen Krieg', p. 4858.
[14] StaMarburg 4h.410. nr. 1, fol. 508, 21 March 1777.
[15] Wiederholdt, 'Tagebuch', introduction, p. xiv. There was in fact no Congressman named von Sellwitz.

they form a class with great wealth and estates like the British aristocracy. Their embittered hostility to the rebellion and their contempt and dislike for its leaders stemmed, like their inability to understand its motives and issues, from their background. It was not only that, as soldiers and subjects of an absolutist prince, they knew nothing of democratic and liberal ideals. Their whole outlook corresponded to a different pattern of behaviour. They were motivated primarily by a concept of 'honour' which involved both doing their duty on the battlefield and fulfilling the trust granted them by their sovereign when he commissioned them.[16] It seemed to the Hessians, however, that American society was moved by the bourgeois principle of individual self interest, and that Americans invoked the Rights of Man against tyrannic government merely to protect this self interest. The states of German princes were based on a very different rationale.

Germans argued that the people enjoyed the protection of a prince who maintained order through religion, laws, and a standing army; that the variety of religious practice in the small states made for toleration throughout; and that the multiplicity of these states, creating a multiplicity of armies, protected Germany from foreign conquest or corruption:[17]

The more warlike a state is, the less it has to fear being conquered by foreign customs, prejudices and vices, whilst the martial spirit embodies the character of a nation; that is, it contains its strength and manliness; and only the military can bring to our people a national character. At least the German soldier by his association with other peoples has come to perceive this most convincingly. Unfounded is the suggestion that the martial spirit hinders the advance of culture both in morals and science. Just as the warlike profession is the first to which the Muses granted a domain, so is it the last to succumb to the effects which one encounters in the wake of corruption.[18]

This was the complete antithesis to the American view that a standing army was destructive of morals as well as a threat to political freedom.[19]

Although the Hessians sought to realize 'honour' by their conduct, their expectation was that honour would bring them promotion to company and regimental chief, thus becoming financially profitable. Like the Americans whom they criticized, they

[16] Redlich, 'The German Military Enterpriser', II, pp. 144–7. Redlich treats this theme only in the Prussian context.
[17] Riesbeck, *Travels through Germany*, II, p. 184; Ochs, 'Das hessische Militär', p. 195.
[18] Wiederholdt, 'Über den kriegerischen Charakter der Deutschen', pp. 67–9.
[19] Cunliffe, *Soldiers and Civilians*, p. 29; Higginbotham, *War of American Independence*, p. 45.

were far from free of materialistic interest. In this respect small states like Hessen were at a disadvantage compared to Prussia, where the state itself was to be exalted to a mystical entity for which the officer would sacrifice life and limb. The Hessian army had to depend upon esprit de corps (identification with one's regiment) and loyalty to the prince himself. To secure this loyalty, the Landgraf had to be sure that his officers knew the fount of honour (promotion) remained open to them all. On the whole he appears to have succeeded. Münchhausen, for example, weighed up purchasing from his American pay a small estate in Hannoverian or Brunswick lands against his probable advancement to full captain and thus company chief, in which case his career was assured. Otherwise, he told his mother, there was little point in remaining in Hessian service. The Landgraf did give him a company and the patent of *Flugeladjutant* (Honorary ADC), and Münchhausen turned down an offer to enter British service, asserting to his brother that being a Hessian company commander was equal to being a British major.[20]

Lieutenant Colonel von Cochenhausen, feeling his promotion to be overdue, dropped numerous hints in letters to Jungkenn who, as the Landgraf's favourite, was a route to the fount of honour. Disappointed, Cochenhausen wrote in May 1778, 'Is it really possible or can it be, that they should forget a man in his 33rd year of service? I believe *No*! I know my good prince aright and beg that I may lay myself at his feet.' By June he was sending his delighted thanks to his good patron, Jungkenn, for his promotion to colonel. By February the following year, he was in an agony of decision as to whether he would do better to take the patent of a regimental chief or remain on as Quartermaster General (Chief of Staff), for from his pay and forage money he would soon have paid off all his old debts. Cochenhausen finished the war as colonel of the Regiment Erbprinz and a knight of the order *Pour la vertu militaire*. He had his sovereign and Jungkenn's patronage to thank also for placing his sons in the cadet corps, following their father's footsteps on the road to honour and profit.[21]

---

[20] Münchhausen, fasc. 1, fols. 74–5, to his mother, 9 Aug. 1777; ibid, fols. 38–9. He seemed to have secured his future in Kassel further when in 1779 he married the daughter of LtGen. von Bardeleben, military governor of the town. However he moved to Braunschweig as a Chamberlain (*Kammerherr*). He died in 1795, aged only 41. A. F. von Münchhausen, *Geschlechts-Historie des Hauses von Münchhausen von 1740 bis auf die neueste Zeit* (Hannover, 1872), p. 36.

[21] Jungkenn 1:73, 2:2, 2:47, 3:45 and 4:40, Cochenhausen to Jungkenn, 23 May and 2 June 1778; 8 Feb. 1779; 7 Sept. 1780; and 4 July 1781.

The Hessian officers saw their careers as inextricably dependent upon the favours of the Landgraf, whose views on honour and conduct they shared. The military was a favoured class in Hessen, as in most German states, and they identified themselves with their sovereign.[22] At the end of a successful campaign Heister assured his prince,

> The rest of my days shall be only unceasing effort to make myself worthy of your service, and the last breath of my body shall be an encouragement to my children to remain loyal to their Prince and Fatherland with their last drops of blood, and to conduct themselves as duty and honour demand, thus to make themselves worthy of such great favours.[23]

One may suspect that, as he was a sacrificial victim to the Landgraf's particular business, Heister said other things in his last breath. Nevertheless, his son Carl Levin remained in the service and became the Landgraf's *Flugel-adjutant*.[24] Knyphausen was rather more fortunate, and could write to Riedesel in May 1784 that he had commanded his regiment with pride for twenty years and was now made governor of Kassel.[25] Knyphausen had been successful, not merely in that he had proved a brave and skilful soldier, but he had risen by his conduct to the favoured circle around the prince.

The new society in America was not merely antithetical to the Hessian officers' ideas of life, it was completely beyond their range of experience. Perhaps European ideas of honour had crossed the Atlantic to a degree sufficient that American officers felt they had to defend theirs by duelling, but there was no professional officer class set apart by particular ideals and activity. The Hessians were both shocked and amused to find that horse doctors, salesmen, innkeepers, barbers, merchants, and smiths were officers in their enemy's army. Not merely was there no hierarchical and ordered society, but there was no prince dispersing honours, and the game of success and failure was played under totally different rules. Birth, education, breeding, even honour and courage counted for much less than industry and entrepreneurial skill.[26] It is hardly surprising that when the Hessians saw the enormous material richness of the

---

[22] That many Hessian officers came from other services does not invalidate this statement. They merely transferred their preconceived loyalties form one prince to another.

[23] StaMarburg 4h.410. nr. 1, fol. 463, 22 Dec. 1776.

[24] *Hochfürstlich Hessen-Casselischer Staats- und Adress-Calendar* (1792).

[25] StaWolfenbüttel 237N70, fols. 72–3, Knyphausen to Riedesel, 20 May 1784.

[26] Of course there were élites and nepotism in colonial America, and Blacks and Indians were excluded from the road to success; but it was still a very different society from any the Hessians knew.

land and the pursuit for gain in all classes – which would not have been possible in Hessen, where trade was very largely in the hands of the Jews – that they put the rebellion down to purely selfish motives, the slogans of the Rights of Man as a cover for materialistic designs. No wonder Hinrichs wrote from Philadelphia, 'the city is beautiful, the country pleasant, and the people very stouthearted – for money'. And even someone as favourable to America as Lith observed that the spirit of commerce animated the inhabitants of New York in the highest degree.[27]

Thus the Hessians' political comments on America were quite wrong-headed. As an American historian writes, 'One may search in vain, in the voluminous correspondence and diaries of the Hessian officers, for any faintest indication that they knew what the Americans were fighting for, or realized that the Whigs had any case at all, however fantastic.'[28] I have, for example, discovered only one reference anywhere to Tom Paine's *Common Sense*, and even this did not mention the import of its contents, but classified it with the offers of land made by Congress on 17 August 1776 as a means of causing Hessian soldiers to desert.[29] This is not because the Hessians were stupid or uneducated men; they simply operated within a completely different frame of reference. Languages, mathematics, geography, mapmaking, and field fortification they were acquainted with, but the language of Tom Paine and Thomas Jefferson was completely foreign to them.

Outside the sphere of political theory, however, they were keen and accurate observers. Their comments on slavery strike an almost modern note. American treatment of black slaves, in contrast to their protestations of the equality of man, convinced the Hessians of the rebels' hypocrisy. In February 1780, as Clinton closed in on Charleston, the Hessian generals occupied a plantation, where Captain-Lieutenant Dörnberg of Loewenstein's grenadier battalion was shocked at the signs of the plantation owner's treatment of his human chattels:

we found numerous marks of the barbarous treatment which the owners had inflicted on their negroes. The master of this place, on the day of our arrival, having done all the damage possible himself and having taken away the best of his negroes and those of his animals which he could gather together in haste, left nothing in his home save a dozen slaves, men as well as women, who are all

---

[27] Pettengill, *Letters from America*, p. 191; Strieder, *Hessischen Gelehrten Geschichte*, XVIII, p. 353.
[28] Lundin, *Cockpit of the Revolution*, p. 179.
[29] StaMarburg 12.11 I Ba 13 (Journal of the Regiment von Huyn), fol. 40 (8 Nov. 1776). Congress had Paine's work printed in both English and German.

misshapen or disfigured by a series of ill treatments which they had received, or the rigour of the work to which they were subjected in all seasons almost without clothing. Their food is nothing but rice, and their dwellings miserable cabins dispersed around the house of the master, which are in no way comparable to the stables.[30]

Dinklage, who saved a Negro from being flogged to death by whites in Charleston, was appalled at the neglect of Christian education for the black slaves, who were suffered to live like animals 'to the shame of the so-called Christians'. 'It is a sad sight when one views these people, who in their capacities and the quality of their intelligence yield nothing to the whites, sold like cattle in the market to the highest bidder.'[31]

Andreas Wiederholdt discovered that the whites used religion to hold the blacks in a position of inferiority. His comrade in captivity at Dumfries, Lieutenant Sobbe, brought great happiness to a Negress called Kitty simply by assuring her that there was one God for both white and black and that He would accept her into his keeping if she lived as a Christian, just as He would a white. Wiederholdt thought the whites' treatment of their slaves a disgrace; animals were treated better in Hessen than black slaves by Americans. 'If the blacks were educated,' he wrote,

they would excel in many ways, for they are not only eager to learn, but also have native genius. A black in my quarters here put a few brass chords across a piece of wood full of holes, whereby he was able not only to make all kinds of tones, but also truly to play a sort of music, or at least keep rhythm.

The children of the black danced to the father's rhythm, much to Wiederholdt's delight.[32]

The Hessians also sympathized with the Loyalists, and were sorry to see their homes burnt by the rebels and the people themselves compelled at the end of the war to take ship for Nova Scotia. Dinklage noted the sad faces of the Loyalists in Philadelphia in June 1778 as the British prepared to depart: 'most faces are sorrowful and await their fate with impatience, between fear and hope'.[33] Unlike the British, however, they put little hope in the numbers of Loyalists and mistrusted the Americans for the most part. In this they were proved realistic. Münchhausen declared that the Americans who took an oath of loyalty and received protection papers from Howe's army in December 1776 were

[30] Dörnberg, *Tagebuchblätter eines hessischen Offiziers*, II, p. 2.
[31] Dinklage, fol. 202.
[32] Wiederholdt, 'Tagebuch', pp. 51–2.
[33] Dinklage, fol. 185.

mostly rebels and spies, for these papers were found on the bodies of enemies killed in battle: 'one can see from this how little basis General Howe's information concerning the enemy had, when it was said that the majority of inhabitants of America were [favourably] disposed to the King, and this application of the inhabitants for protection was pointed to, as a proof of it'.[34] Feilitzsch was even blunter, for he was in the front lines:

These are the worst people one can imagine, their malice and hatred towards us is written on their faces. We are not permitted to take the smallest thing from them, or to obstruct them in any way, but this only adds to their malice all the more, and we must therefore beware the farmers in their homes even more than the enemy in the open.[35]

The Americans' civil strife did not endear them to the Hessians. In 1781 Dinklage, seeing a Loyalist party and their rebel 'brethren' shooting at each other from opposite banks of the East River, asked himself why brother shot at brother, and answered, 'from party spirit, personal hatred, and eagerness to raise oneself and oppress the others'. Had it not been for the spirit of faction, thought Dinklage, no people in the world could have lived more happily than the Americans.[36]

On the other hand they were full of praise for the natural beauty and abundance of the new world. There is something endearing in their observations of the landscape, the plants, and new animals. Dinklage and his comrades made a special trip to visit a waterfall on the Pasaic River after the fighting had stopped.[37] Cochenhausen could not write to Jungkenn in the spring without observing, 'The tulip trees, the wild laurel, and the magnolia, now in bloom, make this vicinity and its gardens beautiful.'[38] The feature most worthy of note in the Leib-Regiment's cantons at Kingsbridge in the winter of 1778–9, wrote Quartermaster Lotheisen, 'is a magnolia which stood in the middle of our cantonment, and carried a small flow.er, which looks very similar to the tulips in colour and form, but had no scent. This tree was so large, that the whole regiment held church services under it the following summer, as it protected us against the summer heat.'[39] The men of the Regiment von

---

[34] Münchhausen, fasc. 3, fol. 74, note 8.
[35] Feilitzsch, fols. 28–9, 30 Oct. 1777.
[36] Dinklage, fols. 213 and 288–9.
[37] Ibid, fol. 317, 16–18 Oct. 1783.
[38] Jungkenn 2:64, 14 June 1779. Jungkenn had a particular interest in botany, for Cochenhausen sent him ten species of trees from Philadelphia.
[39] StaMarburg 12.11 1 Ba 10 (Journal of the Leib-Regiment), fol. 32.

Huyn, making the march from John's Island to Charleston Neck in February 1780 found their attention held by everything there new to them: the cabbage tree, rice, indigo, cotton plants, alligators, opposums, the cardinal (*der ganz rote Vogel*), and many kinds of snakes.[40]

But in many ways the colonies did not suit them. Much of the landscape seemed monotonous and uninviting. A Hessian officer captured at Trenton soon grew tired of seeing nothing but pine woods around Dumfries:

> Virginia is not my land. Numerous pine woods, here and there a few wooden huts, not a single fine view – in a word – I see, hear, and smell nothing here which I cannot hear, see and smell much finer in Germany... There are no nightingales here and, I believe, not even roses, at least I have not seen one. Oh, my beloved German homeland![41]

There was also the extreme climate. To read Hessian journals kept in America, one would think there had never been snow or burning heat in Europe, nor that soldiers ever died of sickness or sunstroke campaigning in Germany. Lightning was fiercer, the heat more striking, and downpours of rain heavier in America.[42] Extremes of climate were held to be the cause of much sickness, particularly when the battalions went without their baggage and camp comforts necessary to make life in the field endurable.

Climate certainly inflicted losses in the south. Dörnberg who landed on Tybee Island with the Charleston expedition thought it a savage place unfit for habitation: 'The soil offers only a thirsty and burning sand which is unfit for the cultivation of any sort of grain ... and the little vegetation which one finds here and there is completely burnt and withered by the excessive heat of the sun.'[43] Ewald's *Jäger* company were attacked on the march by crowds of sandflies and stinging insects which stung the soldiers so badly they were unable to sleep peacefully for a week afterward. And so stricken were they with sickness that only 12 of 129 men were able to keep up.[44] Colonel von Porbeck reported that the extreme heat, the humidity, the unwholesome water which came through boggy

---

[40] StaMarburg 12.11 1 Ba 13 (Journal of the Regiment von Huyn), fol. 121.

[41] Kröger, *Geburt der USA*, pp. 208–9. The writer is almost certainly Lt. Piel of Lossberg's. Compare LB Kassel, 4° Ms. hass. 188, Geschichte des Fusilier-Regiments von Lossberg, fol. 31.

[42] StaMarburg 4h.412. nr. 1 (Journal of the Regiment von Ditfurth), fols. 9–10, 15, and 18; Feilitzsch, fols. 10–11; Dinklage, fol. 150; Bardeleben, p. 70; Heringen, 'Einige Briefe aus dem amerikanischen Krieg', p. 4858.

[43] Dörnberg, *Tagebuchblätter eines hessischen Offiziers*, I, p. 27.

[44] Ewald, 'Tagebuch', IV, pp. 203 and 261, cited in Kipping, *Hessen-Kassel Truppen*, p. 55.

rice and indigo fields made Georgia so unhealthy that few of the locals lived to be more than forty.[45] Losses from malignant fevers in the regiments at Charleston and Savannah were so severe that the Landgraf refused repeated British attempts to persuade him to permit his corps to serve in the West Indies. Faucitt reported, 'the Landgrave's prejudices against the West-India Islands in particular, from the ideas which His Highness has imbib'd, of the great Sickness & Danger peculiar to that Climate, are so strong & so firmly rooted, that it will be utterly in vain to solicit his consent'.[46]

Even in those parts of America where the Hessians might be expected to have felt at home, where German settlers predominated, the mercenaries were not exactly pleased with people of their own kind. Wiederholdt termed the German settlers of Dumfries the meanest sort and the dregs of their nation. Despite attempts to imitate the freedom and open-heartedness of the English inhabitants, they remained ignorant and uncouth German peasants. They had attempted to enter into the spirit of American liberty, but to them it was only a slogan. They had no concept of its true significance. Yet out of foolish enthusiasm for liberty, they were worse than all the other inhabitants, virtually insufferable.[47]

In Rhode Island and Philadelphia in particular the mercenaries were astonished at the variety of religious sects to be found together in a single place. To the devout Calvinist Hessians, the toleration of such a variety of religious practice was proof, not of faith, but of religious indifference. Dinklage said of New York that the French and Dutch each had their own churches, the Germans two Reformed and three Lutheran, and besides there were Anglican, Presbyterian, Methodist, Baptist, and Anabaptist churches or meeting houses, yet there was little of true belief. 'Was it to be wondered, that with all these varieties of religious observance one heard little or scarcely anything of religion spoken.'[48] At Winchester, Virginia, the Trenton captives found religion asleep: the Lutherans had not completed their stone church, while the Reformed church was built but had no pastor.[49] Of the Quakers of Philadelphia, Hinrichs went further, calling them hypocrites, prac-

[45] StaMarburg 4h.328. nr. 153, fols. 71–2, Porbeck to the Landgraf, 1 Jan. 1781.
[46] SP81/193, Faucitt to Stormont, 14 Jan. 1780. The Landgraf took a particular interest in the battalions stationed in the southern colonies: there are two separate volumes of correspondence with them in Marburg.
[47] Wiederholdt, 'Tagebuch', p. 37.
[48] Dinklage, fol. 202.
[49] LB Kassel, 8° Ms. hass. 188, fol. 35, 7 Sept. 1778.

ticing malice, envy, and ambition under the guise of religion.[50]

The unfavourable attitude of the Hessian officers toward many aspects of America and its revolution is in direct contrast with the views of German intellectuals. The latter looked upon the new Republic as the realization of the ideal of freedom.[51] Indeed, America became a symbol of all that these men wished to see in their society and a handy whip to beat abuses, as the publicist Schubart admitted with comic frankness:

> Oh, you beloved America, you are still the hobbyhorse upon which we journalists can canter at ease. My heart jumps for joy when I hear your name. How nicely you have often helped me out of trouble! If one does not know anything, one always knows something about you! One cannot worry about trifles, whether the reports of you are always true. Just so there is something to report! So, happily forward to America![52]

The Hessians saw the matter very differently. The revolution had been based on spurious issues originating from selfish and materialistic motives. Hinrichs' gauge of judging an American's political allegiance was a simple one:

> The safe rule, according to which one can always ascertain whether a man is a loyalist or rebel, is to find whether he profits more in his private interests, his mode of life, his way of doing things, etc., when he is on our side or on that of the enemy. There are only very few exceptions to this rule: on the side of the enemy are a few enthusiasts and some pseudophilosophical-political dreamers who have read, but do not understand, Hugo Grotius' *Law of Nations*, while on our side there may be a small number of which one can say with conviction that love and faithfulness to God and their lawful King has brought them under the colors of their sovereign.[53]

---

[50] Hinrichs, 'Extracts from Letterbook', p. 138. Other Hessians commented more favourably on the kindness shown to their wounded by the Quakers.

[51] Dippel, 'Deutschland und die amerikanische Revolution', p. 323.

[52] *Deutsche Chronik*, 27 Feb. 1777, quoted in Kipping, *Hessian View of America*, p. 21.

[53] Hinrichs, 'Extracts from Letterbook', p. 138.

8

Hessian plundering

The Hessians have long been regarded as villainous plunderers in the American War of Independence. Reared in traditions of pillage and rapine going back to the Thirty Years War, they came to America, it was asserted, expecting to find a land of immense wealth where they could make their fortunes at the expense of the inhabitants. Ignorant and brutal, not speaking the language, they could not distinguish between friend and foe, and plundered indiscriminately. John Almon's *Remembrancer* spoke of 'the infamous habit of plundering, begun first by the Hessians . . . mentioned in every letter from America';[1] American newspapers published accounts, not merely of Hessian plundering, but of the rape of farmers' daughters and the desolation of their homes.[2] Fear and detestation of the mercenaries was increased by the newspapers printing affidavits attesting to every misdeed, assiduously collected by rebel committees.[3] Letters described the inability of the British to restrain their auxiliaries and of a German greed for plunder so strong that it brought them to blows with their allies.[4] Thus, when Hessian grenadiers entered Philadelphia with Cornwallis's vanguard in October 1777, one observer shrank with horror:

The Hessians composed a part of the van-guard, and followed in the rear of the British grenadiers – their looks to me were terrific – their brass caps – their mustaches – their countenances, by nature morose, and their music, that sounded better English that they themselves could speak – plunder – plunder – plunder – plunder – gave a desponding, heart-breaking effect, as I thought to all; to me it was dreadful beyond expression.[5]

Here was the impression of German soldiery on an American used only to seeing militia in homespuns; already prepared by propaganda for the worst, he expected nothing else. In fact, whatever

[1] Almon, ed., *The Remembrancer for the Year 1777*, p. 154.
[2] Force, *American Archives*, Fifth series, III, p. 1188.
[3] Galloway, *Letters to a Nobleman*, p. 43.
[4] Force, *American Archives*, Fifth series, II, pp. 524, 948 and 996.
[5] Watson, *Annals of Philadelphia*, II, p. 283.

171

else the British and Hessians may have done in Pennsylvania, they observed good discipline in Philadelphia itself.[6]

General Howe and his compatriots shared this view of the Germans. Sir George Osborne wrote to Germain,

The circumstance of Plunder is the only Thing, I believe, gives Trouble or Uneasiness to General Howe with respect to the foreign Troops, it is that which I fear no publick Orders can ever reclaim, as the Hessian Troops even in their own Country could never be restrained from the Crime of Marauding more or less, and they were unfortunately led to believe before they left the Province of Hesse Cassel, that they were to come to America to establish their private Fortunes, and hitherto they have certainly acted with that Principle.[7]

Admiral Lord Howe appears to have agreed with his brother; at least his secretary described the Hessians as 'more infamous and cruel than any'.[8] Major John Andre accused the Hessians of virtually demolishing a flock of sheep brought in as forage for the army, and of arresting British marauders but allowing their own to go unpublished.[9] Major General James Robertson and Major Stephen Kemble, both Loyalists serving in the British army, recounted with indignation incidents of Hessian plundering.[10]

The American war was very much one of the *ancien régime* with regard to plundering, although being a civil war it was embittered with fratricidal strife. Far more than in the religious wars of the seventeenth century or those of the twentieth, eighteenth-century civilians were protected from the ravages of the armies; and the art of war itself was precise, mechanical, and rational. Yet the battles themselves were remarkably sanguinary, as at Zorndorf where Russian casualties were fifty per cent of total strength; and a city captured by *coup de main* could be put to the sack with all its attendant horrors. The armies subsisted mainly on supplies gathered in magazines, yet widespread foraging was necessary to feed both men and horses. And levies of manpower, money, and foodstuffs were made in occupied territory,[11] as the French did in Hessen and the Prussians in Saxony and Moravia. Even supposedly

[6] Ibid., pp. 50 and 284; Baurmeister, *Journals*, pp. 150 and 153; StaMarburg 12.11 1 Ba 15 (Journal of Minnigerode's battalion), fol. 108.
[7] CO5/93, Part II, fol. 501, Osborne to Germain, 29 Oct. 1776.
[8] Serle, *Journal*, p. 246.
[9] *Major Andre's Journal*, pp. 39 and 42.
[10] Commager and Morris, *Spirit of 'Seventy-Six*, p. 528; Kemble, *Journal*, pp. 91, 96, 98. All these journalists were with Howe at headquarters, not leading detachments at the front.
[11] International jurists accepted the right of troops both to moveable property as booty and the levying of contributions from the subjects of the enemy. Vattel, *Law of Nations*, pp. 291–5; Wolff, *Jus Gentium*, pp. 437–9; Samuel Pufendorf, *Of the Law of Nature and Nations* (Oxford, 1703), p. 235.

friendly country could be abused, as when the British artillery train inflicted damage on the Hessian village of Rauschenberg in September 1762, after the peasants refused to provide forage. The commander of the train, the then Colonel William Phillips, defended his men on the grounds that the forage collected in the barns of the peasants was the chief provision which the army had, and 'it may be supposed that when Troops go to seek for it, they will take it by force, in case the Peasants refuse to make a voluntary delivery'.[12]

Contrary to the impression one might obtain from Sir George Osborne's letter, it was the British and not the German auxiliaries who had to be restrained in Germany. By the admission of Lieutenant Colonel the Earl of Pembroke, German discipline was better in this respect.[13]

Although the Americans were convinced – or managed to convince themselves through their newspapers – that no people in history had been subjected to such a licentious soldiery, there was in fact no widespread destruction and atrocities were relatively few, limited only to the heat of action. Even by comparison with contemporary war in Europe the country was relatively unharmed by military action. The burning of Fairfield and the plunder of New Haven were small beer compared to Marlborough's devastation of Bavaria in 1704, or Frederick the Great's wanton bombardment of Dresden, destroying churches, fine buildings, and whole streets of dwellings after all hope of forcing the place to surrender had gone.[14] Major General Robertson was mistaken when he testified to the Commons that there was more plundering in America than in Europe; being an American, he was singularly uninformed on Germany.[15]

Major Kemble wrote that the Hessian officers paid no attention to protests made against the pillaging and actually directed the depredations.[16] Yet as professional soldiers, they were opposed to indiscriminate plundering as detrimental to discipline.[17] It is also

---

[12] SP87/48, fols. 167–8; ibid., fols. 133–48 deals with the claims of Rauschenberg inhabitants for damages of over £5,000. The claim was rejected, but it was clear that the British gunners had taken grain from the villagers by force.

[13] HMC: *The Manuscripts and Correspondence of James First Earl of Charlemont*, I, (London, 1891), pp. 259–60.

[14] Moore, *Society and Manners*, II, p. 285.

[15] For Robertson's career, see Lewis Butler, *Annals of the King's Royal Rifle Corps*, I (London, 1913), p. 327.

[16] Kemble, *Journal*, p. 91.

[17] Ewald, *Abhandlung über den kleinen Krieg*, p. 16.

highly improbable that they were unaware that Howe reprobated excesses, particularly since his orders were repeated on Hessian General Orders; and even more improbable that they would intentionally antagonize a commander who also held the purse strings. Nor would they wish to displease their prince. Friedrich II was unalterably opposed to marauding as destructive of discipline and bad for the reputation of his troops. He wrote to both Heister and Knyphausen to ensure that examples were made to check excesses.[18]

Nevertheless, a certain amount of plundering did go on, and it may be set down to three reasons. First, the soldiers regarded booty taken from captured troops as the customary spoils of war. Kemble thought it shameful when the Hessians tried to strip the captured garrison of Fort Washington of their clothing.[19] But for the Hessians this was not only customary booty, but also revenge for the Americans' stripping thirteen of their number killed in a skirmish the week before.[20] Under common usage a town or fortress not surrendered before it had become untenable was given over to looting and no quarter permitted.[21] The American commandant Magaw had rejected the British summons, and thus the post fell into that character.

Second, although they knew it was bad for the morale and discipline of the troops, junior officers tolerated pillaging because of the excessive brutality of the punishments: death by hanging or running the guantlet. These penalties undoubtedly seemed disproportionate to the crime to officers who, serving with the men, sympathized with them more than with the victimized Americans.[22] As Maurice de Saxe wrote, 'A Soldier caught pillaging is hanged. The result is that no one arrests him because they do not want to cause the death of a poor fellow who is only trying to

---

[18] StaMarburg 4h.410. nr. 1, fol. 495, the Landgraf to Heister, 7 April 1777; ibid., nr. 2, fols. 27 and 148, to Knyphausen, 22 Sept. 1777 and 16 Feb. 1778.

[19] Kemble, *Journal*, p. 100.

[20] Force, *American Archives*, Fifth series, III, p. 360; LB Kassel, 8° Ms. hass. 123, Heft 1, Langenscharz, Meine militär Laufbahn, fol. 21 (giving the date incorrectly as 30 Oct. when there was also a skirmish). An American sergeant boasted his victory by wearing on parade the uniform he had stripped from the slain Lt. von Schwein of Stein's regiment. Alexander Graydon, *Memoirs of his own Times with Reminiscences of the Men and Events of the Revolution* (Philadelphia, 1846), p. 188.

[21] John W. Wright, 'Sieges and Customs of War at the Opening of the Eighteenth Century', *AHR*, XXXIX (1934), p. 631.

[22] By modern standards the relationship of officers and men was not very close, but the journals of Wiederholdt and Bardeleben and the writings of Ewald show the concern of junior officers for the welfare and morale of their men.

live. If instead [he were punished less severely] the officers of the patrols would arrest them by the hundred.'[23] Sergeant von Krafft recorded that in September 1778, soldiers who had been admonished not to take anything from the people in their homes were not punished even when discovered in the act.[24] The intentions of the generals were often more severe, but they were not always in a position to observe what was going on; and they fully appreciated the value of trained soldiers, difficult to replace whether killed by the enemy or executed by courts-martial.

A third and most important reason is the blurring of the distinction between foraging and pillaging. What the soldiers regarded as gathering forage for their own subsistence appeared to be plundering to those civilians whose farms were 'foraged'. Soldiers requisitioning cattle, horses, and grain were none too careful whether the locals were treated fairly, particularly when hunger was the army's alternative as at Philadelphia in November 1777 when American defences blocked supplies coming up the Delaware. As the native Hessians were progressively replaced in the ranks by recruits drawn from the undesirables of the German Empire, behaviour got worse on such food gathering expeditions. Knyphausen blamed new recruits in particular for the disorders.[25]

Nevertheless, the majority of apparent pillaging was never wanton, but always related to material needs. Even Dr Robert Jackson, who had little good to say of the German soldier, observed that 'unlike the troops of some other nations, he rarely destroys wantonly, or carries away mischievously, that for which he has no occasion.'[26] Two contemporary accounts of British and Hessian plundering in America are concerned almost exclusively with what were plainly foraging expeditions.[27] The 84-year-old inhabitant of Princeton who lived through the 'twenty-six days tyranny' of British occupation in December 1776 and January 1777 and set down his experiences (including everything he was told, not merely what he saw), was horrified that the King's soldiers in the middle

---

[23] Quoted in Redlich, 'The German Military Enterpriser', II, p. 221.
[24] Krafft, *Journal*, p. 61.
[25] StaMarburg 4h.410. nr. 2, fol. 129, Knyphausen to the Landgraf, 30 Nov. 1777. This deterioration in the standard of the soldier is not a major factor, however, as most accusations of Hessian pillaging were levelled in 1776-7, before large numbers of replacements had arrived.
[26] Jackson, *Formation, Discipline, and Economy of Armies*, p. 104.
[27] Varnum Lansing Collins, ed., *A Brief Narrative of the Ravages of the British and Hessians at Princeton* (Princeton, NJ, 1906); Robert Morton, 'The Diary of . . . kept in Philadelphia while that city was occupied by the British Army in 1777', *PMHB*, I (1877), pp. 1–39.

of winter should tear down fences and take all the loose boards and firewood for themselves. They also robbed the tanners of leather, both tanned and untanned. 'What use the latter may be to them I know not, unless it be to make leather Scarce in the Country and impoverish the owners.' The need for leather in an army with horse-drawn transport should have been evident, not to mention the requirement for slings for muskets and shoulder straps for canteens, cartouche pouches and knapsacks. The worst atrocity the Hessians committed in Princeton was to pull some men's hats from their heads and laugh. This was tame stuff compared to coating colonial officials with hot tar.[28]

The diary of Robert Morton, a Quaker in Philadelphia, showed that the soldiers' behaviour was unlikely to win the King's cause many friends among that sect. But the Quakers would probably have been shocked by eighteenth century soldiery whatever the latter did. The British and Hessians rooted up vegetables from people's gardens because they were unable to bring supplies up the Delaware, and they burnt isolated houses near Philadelphia to prevent them being used as sniping posts by the militia.[29] These reasons were little enough solace for those who lost homes and crops, but they show that the destruction was less wanton than American historians have usually been willing to admit.

The destruction of houses and mills was, like foraging, a vexed question. Mills were a legitimate military target, their destruction denied supplies to the enemy, and Washington's policy in this respect was no different to Howe's.[30] Many other buildings were burnt in New Jersey because the enemy turned every available structure into a vantage point to shoot at the British, who were not lenient with either owners or marksmen if they caught them. Ewald wrote that America, with its parish halls and meeting houses, offered the best and most numerous strongpoints in war.[31] However, Münchhausen said that the common soldier had good reason to be angry with the local people, for not only did they employ every means to inflict losses on the British and Hessians, but as soon as it was no longer possible to fight them either openly

---

[28] Collins *Ravages of British and Hessians*, pp. 4, 8 and 9.
[29] Morton, 'Diary', pp. 20, 28 and 30; Watson, *Annals of Philadelphia*, II, p. 39.
[30] Washington, *Writings*, IX, p. 315. When Washington's army burnt mills, it was of course 'a procedure authorized by the common practice of armies', but Howe's men did it for the purpose of 'distressing the inhabitants and increasing the common calamities incident to a state of war'. Naturally Howe made the same accusations.
[31] StaBamberg C 18, 1 Coll. Spies nr. 26, fol. 89, letters from two officers in Capt. Seitz's grenadier company, 21 Sept. 1777; Münchhausen, fasc. 1, fol. 77, O'Reilly to (Trumbach?), 28 Nov. 1777. Ewald, *Belehrungen*, III, p. 42.

or secretly, they took the oath of allegiance and secured their protection.[32] The little war in New Jersey in the winter of 1776–7 was perhaps the bitterest part of the struggle contested by the two major armies.[33] Ambrose Serle wrote on 20 March 1777, 'The militia firing from behind walls and hedges had so much exasperated the Soldiers that when they came up with such people they gave them no quarter', while on the other side Washington warned Cornwallis, 'I cannot answer to the militia who are resorting to Arms in most parts of this state [New Jersey], and exceedingly exasperated at the Treatment they have met with, from both Hessian and British troops.'[34]

Robert Morton wrote that the King's army was much less discriminating than Washington's, plundering friends as well as enemies.[35] Probably the Hessians with their language difficulties, particularly in the first campaign, were guilty, despite the protection papers issued to Loyalists being written in German as well as English.[36] The Americans with their local knowledge were able to select the King's friends for their own particular depredations. Johann Buettner, a young Saxon who served in both armies, described how the German corps of Major von Ottendorf detached parties of half a dozen men to the homes of suspected Loyalists each night, pretending to be Hessians and asking for information of Washington's army. If the people seemed pleased to see them and told them what they asked, the entire corps soon arrived, stripped the house and drove away the cattle. Buettner was in the corps six months, and said this went on nearly every night.[37] A detailed study of New Jersey community during this period shows that the inhabitants who wished to be neutral had as much to fear from Americans as British.[38]

Washington, like Howe, published repeated warnings and

---

[32] Münchhausen, fasc. 3, fol. 3, note 13.

[33] The fighting was less bitter however than that between Iroquois and whites in Upper New York, and between Whigs and Tories in the south. Here all the horrors of modern war, although on a small scale, were to be found: the 'execution' of captives, the mutilation of bodies, and wholesale destruction of entire communities (Iroquois villages).

[34] Stevens, *Facsimiles*, XXIV, nr. 2052; Washington, *Writings*, VI, p. 480.

[35] Morton, 'Diary', p. 30.

[36] Münchhausen, fasc. 3, fol. 74, note 8.

[37] Buettner, *Buettner der Amerikaner*, pp. 80–2. Buettner calls his commander 'Ortendorff', but Francis B. Heitman, *Historical Register of Officers of the Continental Army during the War of the Revolution* (2nd edn, Washington, DC, 1914), p. 422 has Nicholas Dietrich, Baron von Ottendorf. Most of his Pennsylvania battalion was captured by the British, the remnants being incorporated into Armand's corps in October, 1780. Buettner deserted to the Hessians.

[38] Adrian C. Leiby, *The Revolutionary War in the Hackensack Valley: The Jersey Dutch and the Neutral Ground* (New Brunswick, NJ, 1962), pp. 104–5.

threats on General Orders to prevent plundering by his own troops.[39] In both cases repeated prohibitions indicated the generals' failure to stamp out misbehaviour. Governor Livingston of New Jersey was obliged to issue a proclamation on 5 February 1777 ordering militiamen to stop plundering and carrying away goods on the pretence that the victims were enemies.[40] Even attempts by Americans to pillage only 'the disaffected' [Loyalists] led to indiscriminate robbery of the type the British army was generally accused of. On 25 October 1777 Washington delivered a stern reprimand to his dragoon commanders:

I am sorry to find, that the liberty I granted to the light dragoons of impressing horses near the enemy's lines has been most horribly abused and perverted into a mere plundering scheme. I intended nothing more than that the horses belonging to the disaffected, in the neighbourhood of the British army, should be taken for the use of the dismounted dragoons, and expected, that they would be regularly reported to the Quarter Master General, that an account might be kept of the number and the persons from whom they were taken, in order to have a future settlement. Instead of this, I am informed that under the pretence of the authority derived from me, they go about the country, plundering whomsoever they are pleased to denominate Tories, and converting what they get to their own private profit and emolument.[41]

It is sufficiently clear that all three – British, Hessians, and Americans – were guilty of plundering. The local militia could be more selective in their depredations and even get credit for paying off old scores, while the King's troops ruined the Howes' policy of conciliation by carrying on similar activities but with less discrimination. The question remains whether the Hessians, supposedly bringing their own particular Teutonic brutality to the war, did more than the redcoats in bringing disrepute to their cause. The British diarists are unequivocal on this point, believing, as Ambrose Serle wrote, that it would have been better 'if the Rebellion could have been reduced without any Foreign Troops at all, for I fear our Employment of these upon this service will tend to irritate and inflame the Americans...' 'It is a misfortune we ever had such a dirty, cowardly set of contemptible miscreants [as the Hessians].[42]

A perusal of Hessian accounts throughout the war hardly bears this out. It is not merely as one would expect, that they defend their own people from the charges; but rather, that the whole

[39] Washington, *Writings*, VI, pp. 8–9, 13, 234, 237; IX, pp. 243, 268; XIII, p. 119; XX, pp. 33, 96, 303; XXII, pp. 327–8; XXIII, pp. 199, 294.
[40] *New Jersey Archives*, 2nd series, I, pp. 283–4.
[41] Washington, *Writings*, IX, p. 432.
[42] Serle, *Journal*, pp. 77 and 246.

weight of testimony throws the guilt back on the accusers. Major Baurmeister in particular felt that the conduct of the King's troops fed the flames of rebellion and made the country people all the more embittered rebels.[43]

Mercenary depredations were supposed to have begun at the first engagement at Flatbush, and Serle, who visited the battlefield after the fighting, described the devastations wrought by the Hessians on homes, demolishing furniture, glass, windows, and hangings, and depositing filth.[44] Yet Bardeleben, who was actually there before the battle, found that the damage had been done before he arrived; and Captain Wagner, Donop's adjutant, in the forefront of the Hessians, wrote, 'Other than horses, we can boast of no booty. The English troops have plundered terribly, in spite of the strongest orders against it.'[45] But much of the damage which Hessians and British blamed on one another was the work of the Americans. Certainly General John Sullivan's men set part of Flatbush village alight to flush the *Jäger* out of it, but they were not merely content to burn, as a directive from Washington to Putnam shows:

> The Officers also are to exert themselves, to the utmost to prevent every kind of abuse to private property or, to bring every Offender to the punishment he deserves: shameful it is to find that these men, who have come hither in the defence of the rights of mankind, should turn invaders of it, by destroying the substance of their friends.
>
> The burning of Houses, where the apparent good of the Service is not prompted by it, and the pillaging of them, at all times, and upon all Occasions, is to be discountenanced and punished with the utmost severity.[46]

As Hinrichs told Schlözer, Flatbush was a fine village before rebel incendiaries burnt most of it.[47]

After the subsequent landing on Manhatten Island, Hinrichs had an opportunity to demonstrate his humanity by forbidding his men plundering abandoned houses full of rich goods. When the families returned they were duly grateful, and Hinrichs, wounded at Harlem Heights by a musket ball through the left breast some four fingers' breadth from the heart, was nursed by the widow of the Reverend John Ogilvie who lived in one of the houses.[48]

[43] *Baurmeister, Journals*, pp. 139 and 185.
[44] Serle, *Journal*, pp. 186–7.
[45] Bardeleben, p. 60 (26 Aug. 1776); StaMarburg 4h.413. nr. 4, fol. 20, letter of 3 Sept. 1776.
[46] Washington, *Writings*, v, p. 488 (25 August 1776).
[47] Pettengill, *Letters from America*, p. 178.
[48] Ibid., pp. 172–3.

The *Jäger* as detached troops had the greatest opportunities for ravaging, yet *Jäger* officers were among the best disciplinarians. In 1777 both Donop and Ludwig von Wurmb were commended on orders for their endeavours to prevent plundering, and Ewald advised that it paid to treat local inhabitants well and that trying to win the affection of one's men by permitting them to plunder only caused the breakdown of discipline, the hatred of local people, and the loss of honour.[49]

Captain Kutzleben reported from London on 24 December 1776, having read various American dispatches, that the Waldeck regiment had conducted itself badly and indulged in pillaging, refusing to advance unless its booty were safeguarded. Kutzleben shuddered to think of such a thing happening in a Hessian battalion. If it did, he would lay the blame firmly on the shoulders of the commanding officer.[50]

On taking up quarters on Rhode Island in December 1776, Captain von der Malsburg resolved that he would maintain the strongest discipline against plundering and thus win the trust of the inhabitants. It was probably due to the efforts of Malsburg and others that Major General von Huyn received a testimonial from the inhabitants thanking him for maintaining good discipline. Huyn replied that he was 'happy to understand that the Troops under his Comand has behaved in such a Soldier like manner, as to do Honor to their King, the Generals & the Officers that commands them'.[51]

The Hessian corps commanders strove to maintain good order. On 16 August 1776, the day after all the troops were ashore, Heister published an order that the Hessians should look on the inhabitants as loyal subjects of the Crown. Howe's warnings on General Orders were repeated on Hessian orders; on 21 June 1777 they were cautioned that anyone setting houses alight would be executed.[52] Heister did not watch plundering go unpunished. On the evening of 20 June 1777, light infantry pillaged an occupied house, and set fire to two others not a pistol shot's distance from Hessian headquarters. As soon as this was reported, Heister turned

---

[49] Kemble, *Journal*, p. 479 (After Orders, Elk Ferry, 27 Aug. 1777); Ewald, *Abhandlung über den kleinen Krieg*, p. 16.

[50] StaMarburg 4h.413. nr. 4, fol. 54, copy of a letter from Kutzleben, 24 Dec. 1776.

[51] Malsburg, fol. 77; StaMarburg 12.11 1 Ba 13 (Journal of the Regiment von Huyn), fols. 110–11.

[52] StaMarburg 4h.410. nr. 1, fol. 364, Heister to the Landgraf, 3 Sept., 1776; 4h.409. nr. 3, fol. 248, 21 June 1777. See also ibid., 12.11 1 Ba 12 (Journal of the Regiment von Wissenbach), fols. 45–6.

out the guard and had nine of the plunderers arrested.[53] Knyphausen had ten men of Stirn's brigade run the gauntlet for excesses committed in August 1777.[54] Outside Philadelphia, Hessians protected Loyalist homes from rebel militia. In April 1778 Captain Münchhausen led Lieutenant Mertz with mounted *Jäger* and a grenadier company in pursuit of a party burning houses near the Schuylkill; overtaking them, they cut down nine and made ten prisoner.[55]

By the accounts of Baurmeister and others, it was not the Hessians who plundered on the withdrawal through New Jersey in 1778. As Kipping points out, 236 Hessians could hardly have deserted during the march in a hostile land in which they had earned the mortal enmity of the inhabitants. Sergeant Krafft wrote of the pillaging of Freehold on 26 June that not a Hessian was to be seen amongst the culprits. Three days before, he and another sergeant, sent to bring in two deserters, had come upon English soldiers with stolen goods. They told Kraft that he could find other Hessians plundering further on, and he did indeed discover houses pillaged, beds torn apart, feathers strewn about, and boxes and chests broken open. But two frightened women and several children who appeared from hiding said that the English, not the Hessians, had done it. They begged Krafft and his companion to spare them, saying they were good Loyalists. When he assured them that he would, one woman said that there was plainly no truth in the stories she had been told to Hessian cruelty. Only the English were to blame for the plundering.[56]

When the British and Hessians captured Savannah in December 1778 the journalist of Wissenbach's regiment proudly recorded, 'The inhabitants of the city praised the Hessians, because they had not given themselves up to plundering like the other troops, and this may have been the reason why the two Hessian Regiments were quartered in the fine barracks.' The Hessians of the Regiment Landgraf in Tryon's Connecticut Coast raid were sorry to see the town of Fairfield set alight by the raiders: 'A sad example was it, to witness how one of the best laid out little towns became a mass of flames. General Sullivan himself had a very fine home, which his wife and children had only left the morning before. General Tryon

---

[53] StaMarburg 4h.409. nr. 3, fol. 246.
[54] Baurmeister, *Journals*, p. 100.
[55] StaMarburg 4h.410. nr. 2, fol. 254, Knyphausen to the Landgraf, 15 April 1778.
[56] Baurmeister, *Journals*, p. 185; Kipping, *Hessen-Kassel Truppen*, p. 73 n. 242; Krafft, *Journal* pp. 43–6.

slept in it during the night, and as soon as he left it, it was set alight.'[57] The Hessians were posted on high ground beyond the town to protect it, and had no part in the depredations.

Thus Hessians accused British and Loyalists of excesses, just as the British and Loyalists accused them. Who is one to believe? Americans blamed both, but there is evidence that the Hessians were less cruel. Concerning the treatment of civilians, Deputy Quarter-master General Nicholas Biddle wrote to the Committee of Safety on 28 December 1776, 'I am not alone in assuring you that the Inhabitants of Jersey of whom we had an opportunity of enquiring of the Behaviour of the Hessian Troops declare that their Officers & Soldiers treated them in general with more Lenity, than those of the British Troops, w[hi]ch Justice to our Prisoners [taken at Trenton], calls for an acknowledgement of, as false reports had been spread to the contrary.'[58] Washington informed Samuel Chase in February, 1777, One thing I must remark in favour of the Hessians, and that is, that our people who have been prisoners generally agree that they received much kinder treatment from them, than from British officers and Soldiers.'[59] This is substantiated by the account of Lieutenant Robert Troup, captured on Long Island. Troup said he and his fellows were threatened with hanging by the British, and kept a week on short rations of biscuit and salt pork, but the Hessian soldiers took pity on them and gave them apples and on one occasion fresh beef.[60]

Lith wrote that the Americans at first blamed all cruelties and plundering on the Hessians, and that perhaps this idea was strengthened by the English; but soon they could see by the separate quartering of British and Hessian in the country which one conducted the war in 'the merciless, cruel and inhuman fashion (as they called it)'. The increasingly friendly relations of Hessians with

[57] StaMarburg 12.11 1 Ba 12 (Journal of Wissenbach's), fol. 269; ibid., nr. 4 (Journal of the Regiment Landgraf, later the Leib-Infanterie-Regiment), fol. 10. It appears in both cases that Loyalist regiments were the culprits: at Savannah the majority of Lt. Col. Archibald Campbell's troops were Loyalists, and at Fairfield the Hessian journalist states specifically that 'refugees' set the town alight. In their official reports, Campbell denied that there was any disorder, and Tryon said the town was burnt because the inhabitants refused to return to their proper allegiance. Doubtless burning their homes was a way of recovering their loyalty. CO5/98, fol. 119, Tryon to Clinton, 20 July 1779; CO5/182, fol. 33, Campbell to Germain, 16 Jan. 1779

[58] Quoted in Stryker, *Battles of Trenton and Princeton*, p. 370.

[59] Washington, *Writings*, XII, 108.

[60] Henry Onderdonk, *Revolutionary Incidents of Suffolk and Kings Counties; with an Account of the Battle of Long Island, and the British Prisons and Prison-Ships at New York* (New York, 1849), p. 211.

the people with whom they were garrisoned is further evidence against the charges of brutality.[61] The Americans gradually learned what Aaron Burr had guessed early on about newspaper stories of Hessian atrocities: that most reports were 'incredible and false'.[62]

As to stories that Hessian officers and soldiers expected to make their fortunes in America, and that their eyes bulged when they saw the wealth awaiting them, I have discovered only one reference in their letters and journals: an expression of disappointment by Captain Wagner: 'What can one take from people who are equipped like mendicant Jews [*Betteljuden*], and receive nothing but paper instead of specie money? To plunder the houses of wealthy inhabitants disposed to the rebels is not a thing for everyone; and even these have taken their hard cash into safety; and to carry off with one the fine furniture is not worth the trouble. . .'[63] Simcoe's account of the Hessian reaction to charges of plundering supports the impression given by Wagner:

A very respectable officer of the Hessians observed, and it was not contradicted by any of those present who had served in Germany, 'that even the allied army, when it drove the French marauders from Hesse, pillaged the country more than the Hessians or British did America;' and added he, with great indignation, 'no American town has been laid under contribution, and what is there to destroy? wooden houses deserted of their inhabitants, pigs and poultry?'

Simcoe noted that Boston, Philadelphia, Newport, Charleston, and Savannah were occupied by the British and evacuated unharmed, while New York they actually saved from fire.[64]

Ochs, who served later in the Napoleonic campaigns in Spain and Russia in command of Westphalian troops, wrote afterward of the so-called depredations in America:

Everything that the writers of history say about brutality which is supposed to have happened in that war is mostly fiction, or at least greatly exaggerated.

Everything which the author has subsequently seen in this regard greatly exceeds what one should term cruelty in America, which, in comparison with more recent times, can be regarded as nothing more than a harmless puppet show.[65]

---

[61] Lith, 'Feldzug der Hessen', pp. 17–18. See also Lynn Montross, *Rag, Tag and Bobtail: The Story of the Continental Army 1775–1783* (New York, 1952), p. 458: 'after the first few years, judging by diaries, the Hessians were not hated as much as the loyalists and redcoats'.

[62] Matthew L. Davis, *Memoirs of Aaron Burr with miscellaneous selections from his correspondence* (2 vols. New York, 1971, reprint of 1836–7 edn), I, p. 107.

[63] StaMarburg 4h.413. nr. 4, fol. 87, copy of a letter for 29 May 1777.

[64] John Graves Simcoe, *Remarks on the Travels of the Marquis de Chastellux in North America* (London, 1787), pp. 14 and 55–6.

[65] Ochs, *Betrachtungen über die Kriegskunst*, pp. 60–1.

9
Hessian desertion

Whenever a Prince undertakes to sell his Subjects to a Foreign Power for infamous and wicked purposes, without their knowledge or consent, we are of the opinion, such subjects have a right to vacate the contract as soon as opportunity offers. This doctrine we conceive to be authorized by the law of nations, by reason and by common sense.[1]

The view of society which they brought with them to America disposed most Hessian officers to look unfavourably on the new Republic. But some did find the American way of life attractive. Captain Friedrich von der Malsburg of Ditfurth's and Ensign Friedrich von der Lith of the Leib-Regiment admired the political and social freedom of America. Malsburg was a very gallant officer, winning the order *Pour la vertu militaire* for leading one of the attacking columns with a party of *Jäger* against Sullivan's troops on Rhode Island in August 1778. His battalion commander wrote on his confidential report in 1788, 'The good qualities and conduct [of this officer] are unsurpassed . . . he performs his duties with alacrity and exactness.'[2] Unfortunately he was involved in the disgraceful abandonment of Rheinfels to the French in 1794, and stripped of his Order by Wilhelm IX.[3] During the war in America he married the daughter of Sir Egerton Leigh, the King's Attorney General of South Carolina;[4] after it he corresponded with those Hessian officers who had taken their discharge to settle in America, and he became an honorary member of the German Society of New York, which had Steuben as its president. The letters sent to Malsburg show how quickly Hessian officers who settled in America adapted to and imbibed the principles of liberty which most of their former comrades reprobated.[5]

---

[1] StaMarburg 4h.411. nr. 1, fol. 23, Copy of an advertisement in the *Pennsylvania Packet*, Thursday, 24 December 1778.

[2] StaMarburg 11 Conduitenlisten 1788.

[3] Ditfurth, *Die Hessen in der Champagne*, pp. 397–429.

[4] H. Hale Bellot, 'The Leighs in South Carolina', *Royal Historical Society Transactions*, 5th series, VI (1958), p. 187.

[5] StaMarburg, 340 von der Malsburg, Escheburg, Briefe an Friedrich v.d. Malsburg

Hessian desertion

Lith, an Ansbacher, like many adventurous youths of his generation, wished to go to America to fight for the colonists. This proving impossible, after a great personal struggle Lith satisfied part of his wish by joining the Hessian recruit transport of 1778 as an ensign in the Leib-Regiment.[6] He wrote of America with enthusiasm, bathed in the Hudson at sunrise and sunset, delighted with the play of porpoises coming into New York harbour with the tide, and after the fighting had stopped enjoyed the easy conviviality of leading Americans gathered at Princeton for the sitting of Congress. Here is a typical extract from his journal when he joined these men for dinner:

Full of the prejudices then still holding sway in a European mind, I entered the room and found – no lords decorated with knighthood's orders and stars, no one inflated with excessive political wisdom, no aristocrats proud of their spiritually oppressive jurisprudence, but plain, upright men, simply dressed, some of whom wore their hair tied up unpowdered, some with wigs cut short. They sat happily round the table, laughed and jested, set down gay verses, and spoke of political topics without reservation. Lucky! I thought to myself, lucky must be the country and state, which are ruled by persons whose greatest distinction is to be men and citizens, who do not hold this position from elevation of birth, upbringing, and rank, do not give themselves airs and fancy themselves great because they conduct public affairs, and do not believe themselves exalted above their fellow men, because they hold prosperity and suffering in their hands.[7]

There was a strong element of Rousseau's 'natural man' in Lith's writings on America.[8] His views are a powerful contrast to those of most of his comrades. But Lith returned to Hessen at the war's end, defended the mercenaries in his 'Feldzug der Hessen', and served with the corps until his tragic death by his own hand in 1806, after the Hessians had surrendered their arms to the French without resistance, on the order of their prince, a disgrace keenly felt among the officers.

The attraction of America to the private soldiers lay in the prosperity of the common folk and the excellent wages paid to craftsmen and labourers. German soldiers were accustomed to supplement their incomes at home as artisans or farm workers; in America, as prisoners 'farmed-out' to work in agriculture or iron-

(*Footnote continued*)

1784–1823, Ludwig Murarius to Malsburg, 31 Mar. 1788, and J. H. Scheuber to Malsburg, 12 Feb. 1796.

[6] Strieder, *Hessischen Gelehrten Geschichte*, XVIII, pp. 347–8. The sympathetic sketch of Lith's character here is by Karl Justi, who met him as a young student and became his life-long friend. He mistakenly gives Lith's regiment as the Landgraf's.

[7] Ibid, pp. 354–5.

[8] See Lith's 'Amerikanische Anekdoten', *Journal von und für Deutschland* (1788), pp. 563–6.

works, they were to find they could make better wages than they had ever known.[9]

While the treaties for hiring troops were before Parliament in 1776, the opposition predicted a speedy German defection from British ranks. Pointing to the vast German emigration to America, James Luttrell said that the mercenaries' former countrymen, settled in Pennsylvania, New Jersey, and along the Mohawk river, would invite them to desert, offering lands and protection. The transports of mercenaries would people America with Germans just as surely as the Palatine ships had done.[10] Throughout 1776 opponents of the Ministry expected the German soldiers 'whose pay was wretched and service hard and hopeless' to join their countrymen in America. Their military successes at Long Island and Fort Washington were the reverse of the expected.[11]

The Americans were quick to direct their arts of seduction at the German auxiliaries.[12] As early as May 1776, when they obtained copies of the treaties with Kassel, Braunschweig, and Hanau, Congress had decided to offer lands and protection to German deserters; and in August, when the Hessians actually appeared on Staten Island, Congress resolved to accept any foreigners leaving the King's army and choosing to become citizens of the United States, and to grant them fifty acres of land each. Copies of a proclamation, printed in German with Hancock's famous signature, were dispatched to Washington for distribution by suitable means. Franklin suggested that the documents be placed in canoes with tobacco as a lure for the Hessian soldiers, and that these canoes then be floated across to Staten Island. One story has it that Christopher Ludwick, baker-general of Washington's army and a

[9] Lucie Leigh Bowie, 'The German Prisoners in the American Revolution', *Maryland Historical Magazine*, XL (1945), pp. 186–7; Kipping, *Hessian View of America*, pp. 10, 24, and 43–6.

[10] *Parliamentary History*, XVIII, pp. 1178–9. The Palatine emigrants escaping the ravages of Louis XIV's armies moved into England beginning in 1709, and thence to the colonies, settling in the Schoharie and Mohawk valleys. Oscar Kuhns, *The German and Swiss Settlements of Colonial Pennsylvania: a Study of the So-called Pennsylvania Dutch* (Privately printed, Harrisburg, Pa., 1945), p. 48.

[11] Horace Walpole, *Journal of the Reign of George III from the Year 1771 to 1783* (2 vols. London, 1865), II, pp. 72 and 89. It is also clear from the letters of Capt. Evelyn and Henry Clinton that the British officers expected offers to be made to the German troops. See above, p. 24.

[12] My account of the American plan is based on Lyman H. Butterfield, 'Psychological Warfare in 1776: The Jefferson-Franklin Plan to Cause Hessian Desertions', *Proceedings of the American Philosophical Society*, XCIV, nr. 2 (June, 1950), pp. 233–41; and Carl Berger, *Broadsides and Bayonets: the Propaganda War of the American Revolution* (Philadelphia, 1962), pp. 102–24.

native of Hessen-Darmstadt, went to Staten Island and moved among the auxiliaries there urging them to desert.[13] Another supposed agent was Haym Saloman, a German-speaking Polish Jew arrested by the British after the fire at New York and then used to translate letters to the Hessians. In later years, seeking a pension from the American government for services rendered, he claimed to have encouraged Hessians to desert with considerable success.[14]

Offers from Congress, dated 27 August 1776, began to appear quite early in the Hessian brigade of Colonel Friedrich von Lossberg on Staten Island. On 15 September a Negro belonging to one of the locals found them scattered along a road.[15] Ten days later Heister wrote to his sovereign of the typical treachery and 'upside-down thinking' of the rebels.[16] Quartermaster Lotheisen of the Leib-Regiment recorded that in October the rebels stole across at night in boats to Staten Island to leave bits of paper with promises for deserters, 'but since our soldiers were well provided with provisions and rum, and knew well enough that the rebels were lacking in both of these as well as proper clothing, it had not the least effect'.[17] When the second division arrived in mid-October, there were sufficient copies for someone to show Quartermaster Kleinschmidt of Huyn's one of them straight away.[18]

At first the offers had little effect. The Hessians themselves took precautions: General Orders of 15 August instructed all ranks not to go outside camp without special permission because of rebel attempts to get them to desert;[19] all apparent deserters from the

---

[13] 'Christopher Ludwick, Baker-General in the Army of the United States during the Revolutionary War', *PMHB*, xvi (1892), pp. 343–8. The story was told by Dr Benjamin Rush after Ludwick's death and seems improbable. One possibility is that he was a German calling himself Mosengeil who landed at Malsburg's piquet on 27 September, saying he originated from Hessen-Darmstadt and was deserting. He showed Malsburg a pass from Congress appointing him to discover sulphur deposits for making gunpowder, but having failed in this he was obliged to take up arms. The coincidence is interesting, yet the man was sent to headquarters on Staten Island, and it is unlikely if he really were Ludwick he could have escaped detection. Malsburg, fol. 54.

[14] Charles E. Russel, *Haym Saloman and the Revolution* (New York, 1930), pp. 78–82.

[15] Malsburg, fol. 51.

[16] StaMarburg 4h.410. nr. 1, fol. 93, 25 Sept. 1776. He does not specifically speak of the offers, but I assume this is what he means by 'die masen Kuhne'. Fol. 370 of the same volume is one of the leaflets.

[17] Ibid 12.11 i Ba 10 (Journal of the Leib-Regiment), fols. 11–12.

[18] StaMarburg 12.11 i Ba 13 (Journal of Huyn's regiment), fols. 40–2.

[19] Ibid, 4h.409. nr. 3, fol. 72.

enemy were to be sent to headquarters for prompt interrogation.[20] Heister told Colonel Sir George Osborne that whenever a Hessian soldier brought him an instance of a rebel temptation, he rewarded the soldier equal to that temptation, a rather improbable story; since the latest handbills were offering NCOs a hundred acres, private soldiers fifty, and officers more proportionate to their rank,[21] it would have obliged Heister to grant his soldiers large tracts of American farmland. But it indicates Heister's wish to relieve British anxieties.[22]

The Hessians soon had evidence other than handbills of the American policy. Two captured *Jäger* whom the Americans returned in late October could not praise enough the good treatment they had received. They had been given German-speaking companions who promised them great rewards if they would enter rebel service and urge their countrymen to do likewise.[23] A grenadier of Captain O'Reilly's company, taken marauding on 25 October, was brought before Washington and given food and drink. When he declined to take service with the Americans, Washington gave him a guinea, assuring him that the Americans treated Hessians kindly, and sent him back.[24] Other captives were put under the care of Christopher Ludwick, who showed them the wealth of Philadelphia and the surrounding countryside where German settlers had prospered.[25] John Hancock was at this time urging the early exchange of these prisoners so they could carry the good word to their comrades.[26]

Despite these enticements, there was no Hessian desertion until 14 November, when a soldier went over near Fort Washington. Considering the large numbers of British and Americans who had already passed from one army to another by this time, this was a

[20] Kemble, *Journal*, pp. 386–7 (General Orders, 11 Oct. 1776).
[21] Colonels were offered 1000 acres, lieutenant colonels 800, majors 600, captains 400, ensigns 200. These offers were made on the advice of Colonel James Wilson of the so-called 'Flying Camp', who had been informed of a Hessian colonel intimating that he would listen to overtures. Of this I can find no Hessian evidence; it may have been a British trick to learn of the American plan. Force, *American Archives*, Fifth series, I, p. 1065.
[22] CO5/93, Part III, fol. 495, Osborne to Germain, 23 Sept. 1776. Osborne reported the graduated offers of land as being copied precisely from the King's proclamation of 1763 to British troops who had served in America. Ibid, fol. 501, 29 Oct. 1776.
[23] Baurmeister, *Journals*, pp. 62–3.
[24] Malsburg, fol. 63; StaMarburg 12.11 I Ba 15 (Journal of Minnigerode's battalion), fol. 36.
[25] Watson, *Annals of Philadelphia*, II, p. 44; Baurmeister, *Journals*, pp. 58–9.
[26] Burnett, *Letters of Continental Congress*, II, p. 153.

remarkable fact.[27] This man reported to the Americans that he and his comrades had been told that the rebels would hang them. It seems certain the British, probably as individuals rather than a systematic policy, had told the Hessians of cruelties inflicted by Americans on their prisoners and that no mercy could be expected from them, a measure that could be only temporarily effective against American blandishments.[28] Dr James Thacher, a surgeon in the American army, wrote in November:

> A number of Hessians and Waldeckers have fallen into our hands. The German officers and soldiers, by a finesse of the British, to increase their ferocity, had been led to believe that Americans are savages and barbarians, and if taken, their men would have their bodies stuck full of pieces of dry wood, and in that manner burnt to death. But they were very agreeably disappointed, and much pleased, on meeting civil and kind treatment.[29]

The story, probably exaggerated, must have its origin in truth. Animosity against the Americans was not difficult to arouse, for the Hessians knew nothing of the country before they arrived, and the story that the colonists had rebelled against their lawful sovereign was probably sufficient political explanation for the war. Two Hessian officers who later deserted to the Americans said in their manifesto that as Hessians they had been taught from early infancy the highest reverence and respect for a sovereign.[30] The colonists' revolt thus contravened the laws of God and man; and the burning of New York, blamed on the rebels, was recorded in Hessian journals and letters as the act of uncivilized men.

The remarkable lack of American military success was also a deterrent to desertion. Article 13 of the subsidy treaty forbade Hessians settling in America without their prince's approval. In 1776 it appeared that the rebellion would be crushed, and any Hessian foolhardy enough to take lands from the Americans would soon lose them and be returned to Hessen to the Landgraf's tender mercies.

[27] Mackenzie, *Diary*, I, p. 102; *New Jersey Archives*, 2nd series, I, p. 232.
[28] See above, p. 60.
[29] James Thacher, *A Military Journal during the American Revolutionary War from 1775 to 1783* (2nd edn, Boston, 1827), p. 67. It is worth remembering that before the modern age of nationalism when a soldier's duty was to oppose and frustrate his enemies in every way possible, both deserters and captors were likely to pass on whatever information they thought might gain them a favourable reception. No doubt the Germans were quite pleased to lay any infamy at the door of the British to excuse their own participation in the war. (One consequence of deserters' information is vastly exaggerated casualty reports given by both sides of their foe's losses.)
[30] StaMarburg 4h.411. nr. 1, fols. 23–4, Copy of an Advertisement in the *Pennsylvania Packet*, Thursday, 24 Dec. 1778.

A third deterrent was confiscation of a deserter's goods after a period of two years.[31] Soldiers with families still in Hessen would think carefully before deserting. Yet this prohibition had decreasing effect: the majority of Hessian soldiers were young men without property, and the majority of recruits arriving after 1776 were non-Hessian.

Before Trenton the Americans had no military success and few prisoners. After Trenton and Princeton 1,046 Hessians in American hands were exposed to the attractions of the new Republic.[32] Officers and men were segregated, so that the privates could have the proper principles instilled into them and on their return 'open the eyes of their countrymen'. Even then there was no wholesale desertion as expected in English opposition circles. By mid May it was reported that the captives had resisted every temptation to enlist in rebel service.[33] The German publicist Schubart reported in his *Deutsche Chronik* of that year,

It is not true, that the Hessians captured at Trenton have willingly entered American service. Indeed, the Congress has offered them lands to cultivate, but they declared themselves steadfast and German: they had sworn the oath of loyalty as subjects of their Landgraf and would hold to it even as prisoners; They would thus rather be treated as captives, than become faithless.[34]

Two NCOs of Knyphausen's regiment demonstrated their aversion to captivity by escaping and, with the help of local inhabitants who supplied them with food and showed them paths, travelled one hundred and twenty miles through the wilderness to return to their corps.[35] Grenadier Reuber of Rall's wrote when exchanged in 1778, 'Finally we came to our Hessian brothers again. What joy and pleasure there was now, because we were freed once and for all from our slavery.'[36] After Trenton American outposts began to call across to Hessian piquets near them, urging them to desert and make common cause against the English, or live in peace in America. 'The Hessians constantly answered them with derision, and desertion was generally rather rare amongst them.'[37]

---

[31] This was made law by an ordnance of 1760, but not until 4 Nov. 1784 was an order published in Hessen declaring that soldiers captured who had not returned after two years would lose their property. The majority of deserters' goods, paid to the Karlshafen Military Hospital, were of amounts of less than 10 talers.
[32] The 1,046 included a number of sick and wounded taken at Princeton. StaMarburg 4h.410. nr. 1, fol. 533.
[33] CO5/94, fol. 426, Osborne to Germain, 15 May 1777.
[34] Quoted in Losch, *Soldatenhandel*, p. 35.
[35] StaMarburg 4h.410. nr. 2, fol. 386, Knyphausen to the Landgraf, 23 March 1778.
[36] Reuber, fol. 103.
[37] Lith, 'Feldzug der Hessen', p. 17.

Hessian desertion

With time, however, American efforts succeeded. Loyal NCOs and soldiers like Reuber might spurn the offers, but others were more susceptible. Knyphausen reported, after the first prisoners were exchanged, that some had not returned, deciding to settle down amongst the farmers of Pennsylvania and New Jersey. When Americans delayed the exchange, purportedly because dragoons sent to bring in the prisoners from the farmers with whom they were quartered had difficulty collecting them, the Hessians thought the delay intentional to give more time for persuasion to work. When 460 prisoners were exchanged on 17 September 1778, a number showed great aversion to rejoining their regiments. They had been promised the best treatment if they deserted by American officers, and sixteen did so on the march from Lancaster, where they had been in captivity, to Philadelphia. After a further 279 prisoners returned on 7 November, Knyphausen reported that the remaining 132 probably wished to stay with the Americans.[38] Many of those who returned were also instrumental in causing further desertion among their comrades.[39] Of those who stayed behind, some eventually changed their minds: two men returned to Rall's regiment in 1783, and Sergeant Major Karl Wolff rejoined Lossberg's in Canada on 23 June of that year.[40]

Printed appeals to the Hessians to desert continued. A proclamation of Israel Putnam's dated at White Plains, 16 November 1777, appealed to the mercenaries to abandon the British cause and lead useful and peaceful lives among the free men of America. This was answered by Lieutenant Colonel Andreas Emmerich, a partisan born near Hanau who led a loyalist *Freikorps* in America. In *An die Deutschen in Amerika*, printed at Germantown, Emmerich appealed to the Hessians to stand by England's cause.[41] In September the same year, Brigadier General James Varnum sent a letter to Colonel Friedrich von Lossberg at Rhode Island under a flag of truce, appealing to the Hessian in terms of brotherhood: 'the man who fights for gain (a sordid mercenary) – what is he? Why do Hessians contend with Americans? By nature they are brethren,

---

[38] StaMarburg 4h.410. nr. 2, fols. 386, 398–9, and 474, Knyphausen to the Landgraf, 6 and 19 July and 7 November 1778; Jungkenn 1:73, Cochenhausen to Jungkenn, 23 May 1778.

[39] See below, p. 194.

[40] StaMarburg 12.11 I Ba 3 (Journal of the Grenadier Regiment von Bischhausen, formerly Rall's), fol. 16; ibid, nr. 2 (Journal of the Regiment von Lossberg), fol. 147.

[41] Eelking, *Hilfstruppen*, I, pp. 229–32; Oswald Seidensticker, *The First Century of German Printing in America 1728–1830* (Philadelphia, 1893), p. 97.

the offspring of one universal parent, bound by universal laws of God to mutual benevolence. The glittering coin of Britain, or her dark intrigues, has interposed.[42]

Such appeals had little attraction for veteran soldiers like Lossberg, but Hessian leaders were unable to prevent desertion indefinitely. Only rapid victory and return to Europe could have done that. The absence of national or religious enthusiasms, the brutal and unremitting discipline, the class of people from which recruits were drawn – all these made desertion endemic in mercenary armies, who by definition were composed of men who had no interest in the cause. Methodical manoeuvres were as much a function of preventive measures against desertion as they were a consequence of the generals' caution. In eighteenth-century armies losses were almost as heavy in peace as in war. The Prussians lost 30,216 men from 1713 to 1740.[43] The average annual desertion from the Irish establishment of the British army as 1,200, one sixth of total strength.[44] In the Seven Years War the Prussians lost 80,000 men by desertion, the French about 70,000, and the Austrians over 62,000.[45]

The American war was no different from others of the century in that respect. There was almost constant movement from one army to another. 'The troops desert from each army almost every night,' wrote Colonel George Weedon, 'four left their posts two nights ago and went over to the Enemy . . . four from the Enemy came over to us Yesterday.'[46] By the end of the campaigns in the southern colonies, the armies included so many of the enemy's deserters that General Nathaniel Greene remarked, 'we fought the enemy with British soldiers and they fought us with those of America.'[47]

Hessian commanders employed the usual preventive measures. On 7 August 1778, after a particularly heavy period of Hessian desertion, Musketeer Benedictus Schumann of the Regiment Erbprinz was hanged for leaving an outpost. On Rhode Island a soldier of the Regiment Landgraf was executed, as a deterrent to others, on 14 October that year for trying to desert from Newport. But trained soldiers were scarce and valuable items, and other punishments were usually substituted for death. Lieutenant von

---

[42] *The London Magazine or Gentleman's Monthly Intelligencer*, XLVI (1777), p. 484.
[43] Losch, *Soldatenhandel*, p. 37.
[44] Fortescue, *History of the British Army*, III, p. 518.
[45] M. S. Anderson, *Europe in the Eighteenth Century 1713–83* (London, 191), p. 138.
[46] Clark, *Naval Records of the Revolution*, VI, p. 1199, letter dated 10 October 1776.
[47] George F. Scheer and Hugh Rankin, *Rebels and Redcoats*, New York, 1957, p. 532.

Hessian desertion

Feilitzsch noted on 15 March 1778 that a Hessian *Jäger* named Pfremel, condemned to hanging for attempted desertion, was pardoned and instead ran the gauntlet two days in succession. In June 1779 two fusiliers of Knyphausen's regiment caught attempting to desert were condemned to death, and led to the gallows, but at the eleventh hour the sentence was commuted to two days' running the gauntlet. This had the desired effect for a time, Knyphausen reporting on 4 July that desertion had ceased.[48]

In Canada a practice was made of sending out Indians after would-be deserters, with orders to bring back their scalps within twenty-four hours.[49] In the southern garrisons, Charleston and Savannah, Loyalist and black dragoons served the same purpose. Colonel von Porbeck warned his men of Knoblauch's Garrison Regiment in February 1782 that deserters caught beyond the lines would be cut down or shot dead, and three privates who deserted on the night of 9 March met just that fate. The remainder were told to take an example from this.[50]

When the fighting ended and regiments waiting in New York found time heavy on their hands, they were exercised four times daily, not to train recruits, who were subsequently released in Europe, but to keep them occupied.[51] When news of peace was confirmed and embarkation imminent, the Hessian troops were encamped at Newtown's Creek on Long Island, partly in readiness to embark but also against desertion.[52]

The increase in Hessian desertion was due in part to Britain's declining fortunes in war. The first major British retreat, from Philadelphia in 1778, was also the first period of heavy Hessian desertion, some 236 leaving the colours during the march.[53] These

[48] StaMarburg 4h.410. nr. 2, fols. 416 and 492, Knyphausen to the Landgraf, 23 August and 17 December 1778; ibid, 4h.411. nr. 1, fols. 108 and 123, Knyphausen to the Landgraf, 15 June and 4 July 1779; Feilitzsch, fol. 48. For an example similar to the last, see Krafft *Journal*, p. 186 (14 July 1783).
[49] StaWolfenbüttel 237N67, fol. 319, Haldimand to Riedesel, 19 Dec. 1782.
[50] StaMarburg 12.11 I Ba 12 (Journal of the Regiment von Knoblauch, formerly Wissenbach's), fols. 459 and 462–4.
[51] Ibid, nr. 3 (Journal of the Grenadier Regiment von Bischhausen), fol. 76.
[52] Ibid, fols. 76–7.
[53] StaMarburg 4h.410. nr. 2, fol. 389. In CO5/96, fol. 249, William Porter, Osborne's successor as muster master to the foreign troops, gives 219 deserters for the period 25 Dec. 1777 to 24 June 1778, and 118 from 25 June to 11 Aug. 1778. The first figure is the one in Mackesy, *War for America*, p. 215 n. 2. As the retreat beginning on 18 June overlapped the two periods, Porter's figures tend to support those in Marburg. Washington's figure of 440 is probably based on reports of various detachments in his army, some of whom counted the same deserters twice, or, relying on deserters' statements, gave exaggerated numbers. It was not in the British interest to allow the Hessians to conceal their losses, as they would have to pay for extra men.

236 deserters are also a testimony to the gathering success of the American plan to cause desertions at a time when the war seemed to be running against the British. Knyphausen reported:

The cause of this [heavy desertion], so far as I can guess, is that printed leaflets were spread about amongst the men in a secret manner, in which each man who would desert and settle here in the country was promised a quantity of land, two horses, one cow, and similar encouragements; Also those who were exchanged from captivity have made such glowing descriptions of the regions there, and how well they had been received; Which we can also presume, because the desertion in the three captive regiments, especially mine, of which the most men have been returned from captivity, was proportionately the greatest.[54]

When the war in the north stabilized, a period of garrison duties and small raids followed, and Hessian losses dwindled to a trickle once again. In six months from 25 June to 24 December 1779, there were only twenty-seven deserters in ten battalions stationed at New York. Amongst the *Jäger*, however, where chances of escape were much greater and the proportion of non-Hessians higher, there were fifty-three deserters in the same period.[55] Some of these did return. Three *Jäger* of Ewald's company who deserted in May and June 1778 turned up in Trumbach's regiment at Savannah the following summer.[56]

After Yorktown Hessian desertion reached its highest figures, particularly in the two battalions captured with Cornwallis: Bose's lost 103 men, the Erbprinz's 145, two thirds of its total desertion for the war.[57] It is nevertheless worth noting that while 248 captives elected to remain in America, 408 rank and file returned to the Hessians.

Regiments not in captivity suffered increasing desertion from late 1781 onwards, when the British had lost and it was clear that those who took land could not be returned to Hessen. After the Treaty of Versailles was made public on 7 April 1783, desertion became particularly bad.[58] Of 2,949 deserters officially reported, 1,666 made off in the years 1781–3.[59] Large numbers of non-Hessians, many of whom had enlisted only for the duration of the war, clamoured for discharge when they saw the other German con-

[54] StaMarburg 4h.410. nr. 2, fol. 386, Knyphausen to the Landgraf, 6 July 1778.
[55] CO5/183, fol. 39.
[56] CO5/182, fol. 172.
[57] StaMarburg 4h.411. nr. 3, fols. 125–6, 129, 133–5; ibid, 12.11 1 Ba 11 (Journal of the Regiment Prinz Friedrich, formerly Erbprinz), fols. 119 and 227ff.
[58] StaMarburg 12.11 1 Ba 15 (Journal of Minnigerode's battalion), fol. 164.
[59] Ibid, 13 Acc: 1930/5 Nr. 232, fol. 2.

tingents releasing their 'foreigners'.[60] The *Jäger* had the heaviest desertion, the outposts which they manned giving greater opportunities. In 1776 there had been only one deserter from the two companies under Wreden and Ewald.[61] Lossberg's regiment lost seventeen men in Canada in the five days prior to embarkation.[62]

The desire for land and a new life was undoubtedly a powerful motive in Hessian desertion, but even more important were the attachments which Hessian soldiers formed with local girls and their families wherever they were in garrison or captivity. On closer examination the colonists found the bloodthirsty Hessians not so fierce after all. The Hessians for their part thought American women very attractive. References to their good looks, fine hairstyles and clean clothes, as well as to the predominant role they played in American life, are legion in Hessian journals.[63] Captain Münchhausen complained of a young man sent out to be his groom, that he spent his whole time in America chasing skirts.[64] There is evidence of temptation held out to officers as well as men. In Fredericksburg, Virginia, Lieutenant Andreas Wiederholdt, quartered on the inhabitants like other Trenton prisoners, received a very poignant invitation:

said a fair one who was much inclined to me, and whom I shall always revere with esteem: Would to God you could stay here, and that I should never be so unhappy as to be torn from you, as will happen tomorrow and perhaps for ever! But you go! To where duty and honour call you and may you always be fortunate! This was magnanimity which does not exist in all rebels: (for she was a well-disposed American, beautiful and rich). I had to stop mentioning her, so as to ward off the grief which ran so strongly through me.[65]

Officers like Wiederholdt were more likely to resist such attractions than private soldiers who had few prospects in Germany to look

[60] Ibid, 4h.411. nr. 3, fols. 161 and 171–2, Lossberg to the Landgraf, 12 and 24 July 1782.
[61] Ibid, 13 Acc: 1930/5 Nr. 232, fol. 3.
[62] Ibid, 12.11 I Ba 2 (Journal of the Regiment von Lossberg), fol. 149.
[63] For such compliments, and references to friendships with American girls, see Dinklage, fol. 131; Malsburg, fols. 45, 49, 59, 79; StaMarburg 12.11 I Ba 10 (Journal of the Leib-Regiment), fol. 16; ibid, nr. 4 (Journal of the Regiment Landgraf), fols. 35–6; ibid, nr. 13 (Journal of the Regiment von Huyn), fol. 78; Krafft, *Journal*, p. 188; John R. Sellers *et al.*, *Manuscript Sources in the Library of Congress* (Washington, DC, 1975), p. 74, mentioning letters exchanged by Captains Ewald and Stamford and the Misses van Horne (presumably those of Boundbrooke, NJ); and F.v. Gilsa, 'Aus dem Stammbuche des landgräflich hessischen Kapitäns im Leibregiment Christian Friedrich von Urff 1774–1792', *Hessenland*, XIII (1899), p. 108. In his autograph book Urff wrote, 'The first forty pages are devoted to the ladies', and on one of those forty sides Miss Peggy Grim of New York wrote a romantic poem suitably entitled 'The Friendship'.
[64] Münchhausen, fasc. 1, fol. 73, Münchhausen to his mother, 16 July 1777.
[65] Wiederholdt, 'Tagebuch', p. 57.

forward to. Those without families to care for at home were not slow to begin a new life, and the inhibitions of some may have been overcome by the custom of 'bundling' as described by Friedrich von der Lith:

> A young stranger when he first comes into a house is invited to dinner in a friendly manner. If the master of the house has one or more daughters, after the table has been cleared he offers that the stranger should also stay at his place and pass the night in bed with his daughter. This offer is, quite naturally, seldom refused, if the young lady is good looking as well. The father himself brings the two to bed without further formalities, where the stranger is granted the complete fulfilment of his wishes. This wonderful practice is called in English *bundle*.... The only inconvenience of it is that the stranger, as soon as he has lain together with the daughter of the house and if such a night has consequences, must either marry the young lady or at least support her together with the child.[66]

Lith does not specifically say so, but very probably these weddings of circumstance furthered Hessian desertion. Pastor Cöster, chaplain to the Regiments of Lossberg and Donop, married a number of men to American girls whom they got with child. Being men of religious conscience, Hessians were likely, feeling responsibility for mother and child, to marry a girl in such circumstances.[67]

American offers to Hessian deserters included land, cows, oxen, and other livestock – all the accoutrements of a farm except the *Hausfrau*.[68] American girls soon made up this discrepancy, beginning in winter quarters in Philadelphia in 1777–8. An investigation of the desertion of three grenadiers in Linsing's battalion in March 1778 showed they had been suborned by women in the town. By the end of that month a number of NCOs and privates were seeking permission to marry Americans.[69] By the end of the war the attractions of American women took effect in a more striking manner: Quartermaster Broeske of Linsing's absconded from New York on 23 May 1783 with the battalion's subsistence

[66] Lith, 'Feldzug der Hessen', pp. 20–1. The actual 'bundling' was intended to prevent sexual intercourse, but doubtless in the passion of the moment what Lith describes often occurred.

[67] August Woringer, 'Protocoll der Amtshandlungen, die der Feldprediger G. C. Cöster bei den beiden löblichen Regimentern von Donop und von Lossberg und andern verrichtet', *DAGeschBl*, XX–XXI (1920–1), pp. 281, 286–7, 289 and 292.

[68] Congress's offer of January 1778 put aside 20,000–30,000 acres for deserters. A captain who came over before 1 Sept. 1778 received 800 acres of good woodland, 4 oxen, 1 bull, 3 cows, and 4 hogs; a sergeant received 400 acres, 2 oxen, 2 cows, 4 hogs. Carl Berger, *Broadsides and Bayonets* (Philadelphia, 1962), p. 115.

[69] StaMarburg 4h.410. nr. 2, fols. 203 and 207, Knyphausen to the Landgraf, 23 March 1778.

allowance of £340, to join a certain Sally Bunn who had already made her way to Amboy.[70]

Both local connections and American overtures caused desertion in the troops garrisoning Charleston and Savannah.[71] Major General Alexander Leslie reported to Clinton that Hessian troops at Charleston, forming various connections in the town, had become so untrustworthy that they allowed prisoners to escape.[72] Brigadier General Alured Clarke considered the men of Knoblauch's Garrison Regiment at Savannah too untrustworthy to man the outposts in 1782. A proclamation enticing Hessians to desert had succeeded in drawing off five from a piquet. Clarke sent a party of dragoons in pursuit, and they killed all five.[73] Colonel von Porbeck of Knoblauch's reported that the rebel proclamations were spread amongst the garrison by the females in the town. The rebels had also disseminated the rumour that the Hessians were to go to the West Indies, and not back home, when they left Savannah.[74] The inhabitants hid deserters in their homes, three of whom were recaptured just before embarkation.[75]

Similar incidents occurred at Charleston. On 1 November 1782 a patrol of black dragoons shot two of three deserters from Benning's regiment, and to make an example of them the two corpses were laid beneath a gallows on which, that very morning, the British had hanged a soldier taken in the act of deserting.[76] But once orders for the town's evacuation became known, all efforts against desertion seemed in vain: deserters in large numbers concealed themselves in houses, of whom only one seems to have been found and one other reappeared to claim a general pardon for

---

[70] HMC: *American*, IV, pp. 142–3.
[71] Woellwarth's (formerly Rall's) and Wissenbach's regiments reached Savannah with LtCol Archibald Campbell in December 1778, remaining there, except for MajGen. Augustine Prevost's expedition against Charleston, until July 1780, when the former, now d'Angelleli's, joined Ditfurth's and Huyn's at Charleston. MajGen v. Huyn died in August 1780, and his regiment was given to Col. v. Benning, who arrived in the 1781 recruit transport. Savannah was evacuated in July 1782, Charleston in December the same year.
[72] PRO30/55/37, nr. 4315, 27 March 1782.
[73] PRO30/55/36, nrs. 4221–2, Leslie to Clinton, 12 March 1782 (two letters of the same date, the second marked 'Private'); StaMarburg 12.11 1 Ba 12 (Journal of the Regiment von Wissenbach), fol. 464.
[74] StaMarburg 4h.328. nr. 153, fols. 151 and 110–1, Porbeck to the Landgraf, 1 March and 19 April 1782.
[75] Ibid, fol. 114, 31 July 1782.
[76] Ibid, 12.11 1 Ba 13 (Journal of the Regiment von Huyn), fol. 140.

deserters.[77] For the embarkation, all townspeople were instructed to keep their doors and windows shut and to stay indoors, and the troops were ordered out under arms at first light and kept together until embarkation.[78]

The evacuation of New York was undertaken with similar reluctance by many soldiers and precautions by commanders. On 20 November the night before embarkation,[79] Lieutenant Krafft went several times through the men of his company because of the apprehended desertion. Yet Krafft, who had carried on a love affair while at New York, felt the same regret as the fleet anchored at Staten Island in preparation for the voyage: 'My whole heart is full of sadness when I see fading from my view the receding landmarks and house-tops, in whose midst I leave my whole happiness behind me.'[80] Krafft obtained his discharge and returned to marry and settle in America. Lossberg, granting his discharge, told his sovereign that Colonel von Lengerke considered Krafft an officer whose loss would easily be made good.

Beside the positive temptations, Hessian prisoners also 'deserted' because of poor treatment: although American policy was to show kindness to the auxiliaries, often local hostility, inefficient supplying, or simply official indifference left the prisoners in dire straits, compelling them to become labourers or enlist in America *Freikorps*. The Board of War reported to Washington on 3 January 1780 that they had to let out as many prisoners as possible, chiefly Germans, to local farmers in order 'to save public Provisions and because we had not Guards to keep them safely.'[81] Quartermaster Müller of Knyphausen's regiment, taking pay and clothes to the Trenton

[77] Ibid, 4h.411. nr. 3, fol. 76, Bose to Lossberg, 18 Nov. 1782; LB Kassel, 8° Ms. hass. 127, Asteroth, Erinnerungen, fol. 121. Asteroth, a private soldier in Huyn's, mis-dates some of these occurrences, which can be checked in regimental journals.

[78] StaMarburg 12.11 1 Ba 3 (Journal of the Regiment von Bischhausen), fols. 71–4; Reuber, fol. 134. Reuber, like Asteroth, gives some incorrect dates. That of the Charleston embarkation he states as 21 September instead of 13 December.

[79] There were in fact two final Hessian embarkations. The regiments Erbprinz, Knyphausen, Bose, Ditfurth, d'Angelleli, Knoblauch, Benning and Bunau left New York on 15 Aug. 1783; the grenadier battalions and the regiments of jung-Lossberg (formerly Mirbach's), Prinz Karl, the Landgraf, Donop, and the Leib-Regiment remained until the last embarkation in November. 'I think it will be right to keep the strongest and best Regiments untill the last', Carleton told Lossberg. StaMarburg 4h.411. nr. 3, fol. 187, 7 Aug. 1783. These latter regiments wintered in Chatham, Portsmouth, and Dover Castle, plagued by English colds, and did not reach Kassel until late May 1784.

[80] Krafft, *Journal*, p. 199.

[81] Burnett, *Letters of Continental Congress*, V, p. 2. Bowie, 'German Prisoners in the Revolution', *Maryland Historical Magazine*, XL (1945), pp. 185–6 describes prisoner-of-war administration. In practice it does not appear to have worked altogether successfully.

prisoners at Lancaster in May 1777 found few in the town. They had been threatened with half-rations if they did not go out and work with local farmers.[82] Quartermaster Kitz of Rall's on the same errand in the following January found that, while those who were working for the farmers were making good money, about thirty *Jäger* and grenadiers who had refused to take such employment were in the gaol in the saddest state, one dying while Kitz was there, partly from hunger and partly from cold. When Kitz protested the Commissary of Prisoners blandly assured him that the Hessians were treated best of all the captives. The Hessian prisoners all told Kitz that they wanted to return to their regiments.[83] Surgeon George of Linsing's grenadiers, sent to inquire after wounded prisoners taken at Redbank, found them in the country about Bethlehem, badly cared for and lacking clothing and money to pay for provisions.[84]

A small number of Hessian soldiers were found with Brunswickers and Hanauers on a captured American frigate, the *South Carolina*. They testified that they had been compelled to take service on the ship by being kept on a starvation diet in the cramped gaol at Reading, and being compelled to pay their gaolers for both water and fuel. After six months they took service on the frigate, on the advice of Loyalists that the vessel might soon be taken by the King's ships. This story no doubt lost nothing in its telling, but its essentials must be true: unless compelled, the Germans, who were all landsmen, would more probably have become American soldiers or farmers than seamen.[85]

Thirty prisoners of Knyphausen's regiment, captured from a transport en route to Canada, had their lot made so miserable in gaol at Philadelphia that they agreed to work for the ironmaster, Jakob Faesch, whose works were at Mount Hope, New Jersey.[86] The prisoners had been repeatedly told that they must go without provisions in return for the cruel treatment meted out by the British to American captives.[87] When the war ended and an exchange of prisoners agreed upon, these thirty petitioned to be freed, but were refused. They had been indentured to Faesch in

---

[82] StaMarburg 4h.410. nr. 2, fol. 97, QM Müller's report, 18 Aug. 1777.
[83] Ibid, fols. 185–8, QM Kitz's report.
[84] Ibid, fol. 178, Knyphausen to the Landgraf, 7 March 1778.
[85] HMC: *American*, III, pp. 314–5.
[86] HMC: *American*, II, p. 407; George G. Lewis and John Mewha, *History of Prisoner of War Utilization by the United States* (Washington, DC, 1955), p. 17.
[87] Baurmeister certainly thought the motive was revenge. Baurmeister, *Journals*, pp. 434–5.

return for £30 per head. Faesch regarded them as his property until he was reimbursed.[88]

These men were in a very different situation from former Hessian soldiers who, pleased to be earning good American wages or living with American girls, wished to stay in the new Republic. In vain did Brigadier General Alured Clarke, last muster master of the Hessian troops, write at Lossberg's request to Benjamin Lincoln asking him to take the necessary steps to procure the liberation of Hessian prisoners still in American hands but desirous of returning.[89] Lincoln replied that there were numbers of Hessian prisoners who had taken oaths of allegiance and become American citizens and that if they were now indentured servants it was a civil matter.[90] The prisoners concerned were not American citizens, having been compelled by harsh treatment to leave the gaol and take work. Lossberg persisted, for Clarke wrote again referring specifically to Faesch's ironworks. Brigadier General Moses Hazen investigated and reported to Lincoln that the prisoners had been given three alternatives: enlisting in American service, purchasing their own redemption at £30 per man, or returning to the Philadelphia gaol where, in their own words, they had been miserably treated and threatened by American officers.[91] This was contrary to the seventh article of the peace treaty which stipulated, 'All prisoners on both sides shall be set at liberty.'[92] Lincoln, however, declined to free the prisoners.

Some of them attempted to escape. Corporals Roeder and Kistner of Knyphausen's got away to New York, reporting that four others who tried the same were captured by a farmer to whom they were indentured and 'cruelly whipped'.[93] The prisoners at Mount Hope wrote to Lossberg, begging not to be abandoned, requesting him to make available from army funds the £30 per man to free them. Lossberg dispatched Baurmeister, the adjutant general, to investigate. Congress refused Baurmeister's plea that they honour the free return of prisoners, saying it was a private matter, the soldiers' release depending upon their owners who must be reimbursed. President Boudinot did not omit to imply that the

---

[88] HMC: *American*, II, pp. 407–8.

[89] Ibid, III, p. 101.

[90] Ibid, p. 103.

[91] Ibid, pp. 131–2 and 407–8, 'Extract of a letter from 35 Hessian prisoners of war to his Excellency Lieut. General de Lossberg.'

[92] Henry Steele Commager, ed., *Documents of American History* (New York, 1958), p. 119.

[93] HMC: *American*, IV, p. 153, 'Memorandum ... extracted from the German, New York, 14 June 1783. H. R. Motz, secretary.'

treatment of the Hessians was in retaliation for the British allowing Americans to suffer in prisons and for British admirals cruelly impressing seamen.[94]

Baurmeister then visited various bodies of Hessian, Brunswick, and Hanau prisoners, with mixed results: some wished to settle in America, others who had been initially persuaded to desert desired to return to Germany. Lieutenant Ungar of Knyphausen's regiment was then sent with the cash 'owed' to Faesch to redeem the Hessians at Mount Hope. Twenty-one of twenty-seven left with Ungar, six choosing to remain in New Jersey. Previously two others had paid to free themselves and come back to their regiment, eight others had escaped and made their way to New York.[95]

Beside the rank and file, a small but significant number of officers deserted. The two best known, Ensigns Kleinschmidt and Führer, had been captured at Trenton and exposed to offers of land and citizenship; but they had an additional motive for deserting – fear of punishment for debts contracted while in captivity. The Americans made things difficult for Hessian officer prisoners by obliging them to pay for foodstuffs in hard specie but charging them at the inflated prices of the continental paper money, local merchants thus enriching themselves at the expense of their 'captive market'.[96] On 20 April 1778 Knyphausen named Kleinschmidt and Führer as two of three officers with the heaviest debts of those returned from captivity.[97] The two must have been aware that the rebels would regard them as a prize catch when they crossed to the enemy on 7 August at White Plains, using hired horses.[98] They had the presence of mind to give their rank as first lieutenant, and were given a step up to captain. They published a public advertisement in the *Pennsylvania Packet*, setting out their motives and claiming that, as men of honour, they had not deserted while prisoners but had returned to resign their commissions.[99] This they certainly had not done. Knyphausen, hoping they might repent and return, allowed a very considerable time

[94] Baurmeister, *Journals*, pp. 572–5; HMC: *American*, IV, p. 230; StaMarburg 4h.411. nr. 3, fol. 171, Lossberg to the Landgraf, 24 July 1783.

[95] Baurmeister, *Journals* pp. 579–80; StaMarburg 12.11 I Ba 6 (Journal of the Regiment von Knyphausen), fols. 147 and 150.

[96] StaMarburg 4h.410. nr. 2, fols. 186–7, QM Kitz's report. Kitz said that at this time (Jan. 1778) 1 Guinea was worth 32 Continental dollars.

[97] Ibid, fol. 260, Knyphausen to the Landgraf, 20 April 1778. Krafft, *Journal*, p. 59, also gives debts as the cause of their defection.

[98] Ibid, fol. 410, Knyphausen to the Landgraf, 23 August 1778.

[99] See above p. 184.

before having them cited by beat of drum at New York on 16 August 1779, to return within six weeks or be considered deserters.[100] But he again delayed, and not until 1 October 1781 was a gallows raised with their pictures affixed to it.[101]

In the intervening period Kleinschmidt came to regret his decision. In June 1780 he wrote to Knyphausen from Virginia begging forgiveness, claiming that he had been duped by his friend Führer, who had deceived him and cheated him of his money. Knyphausen declined to reply, for in his view Kleinschmidt had given insufficient satisfaction.[102] Kleinschmidt attempted to put his resolution to return into action, but chose a most unfortunate time. At the siege of Yorktown, he was captured on 6 October 1781, on the glacis of the works trying to get to the Regiment von Bose. He was imprisoned on a ship, but presumably freed by the victorious French and Americans, as Hessian sources do not mention his further fate.[103] Führer settled down in Virginia where he died a prosperous farmer in 1794. His goods in Hessen were confiscated; in 1789 his sister applied, apparently unsuccessfully, for their return.[104]

Washington had regarded all German deserters as unreliable recruits, who caused his own men to desert.[105] The defection of two Hessian officers caused him to alter his opinion. He recommended that a corps of German deserters, prisoners of war, and inhabitants be formed.[106] But the two new captains had no success in recruiting this corps. Führer tried to enroll exchanged Trenton prisoners as they passed through Philadelphia, promising officer rank to the NCOs, but in vain. He claimed that other Hessian officers, and first of all Lieutenant Andreas Wiederholdt, would follow their example. Wiederholdt was so indignant that he wrote to the rebel command demanding that Führer be punished for this libel, but not surprisingly obtained no satisfaction.[107]

Lieutenant Montluisant, a Frenchman in the *Jägercorps*, jour-

[100] StaMarburg 12.11 I Ba 6 (Journal of the Regiment von Knyphausen), fol. 98.
[101] Krafft, *Journal*, p. 151.
[102] StaMarburg 4h.411. nr. 1, fols. 402–3, Kleinschmidt to Knyphausen, 28 June 1780, marked on the outside 'Par faveur de Monsieur Rocheblaue et Lieutenant Schlieffen' (?); ibid, fol. 297, Knyphausen to the Landgraf, 12 August 1780.
[103] StaMarburg 12.11 I Ba 7 (Journal of the Regiment von Bose), fol. 184; ibid, 4h.412. nr. 5, fol. 105, Baurmeister to the Erbprinz, 6 Nov. 1781.
[104] J. Führer, 'Ein zeitgenossisches Urteil über den "Soldatenhandel" Landgraf Friedrichs II und seine Würdigung', *Hessenland*, XIV (1900), p. 37.
[105] Washington, *Writings*, XI, pp. 81 and 98–9.
[106] Ibid, XII, pp. 304–5.
[107] StaMarburg 4h.411. nr. 1, fol. 132, Knyphausen to the Landgraf, 19 July 1779.

neyed to America with the recruit transport of 1778, apparently for the express purpose of leaving Hessian service once there and obtaining a commission or lands in America.[108] After submitting his second request for discharge, Knyphausen reported that he was completely unreliable because of his French inclinations.[109] The discharge obtained, Montluisant attempted to cross to the enemy, but was taken at the last outpost and placed under arrest. Returned to Europe, he was back in America in 1781, but Congress did not employ him.[110]

Lieutenant Carl Juliad, serving with the Regiment Landgraf on Rhode Island, was reported as having deserted to the enemy in August 1778. But in October he and five other soldiers from Pulaski's Legion stole out of Little Egg Harbour and brought Captain Patrick Ferguson information of enemy dispositions that enabled him to surprise Pulaski's infantry on 5 October.[111] Brought to New York and investigated, Juliad gave his own story of his desertion: he was seized by Americans near Providence River on Rhode Island the day before Sullivan's corps landed; an American captain put a pistol to his breast and threatened to shoot him if he did not come with them. Taken to Providence, he there got a pass to Philadelphia. In Philadelphia he refused Führer's request to join his corps, but in order to find a way of rejoining his regiment, he took a post as a captain of infantry in Pulaski's Legion. When the Legion moved from Germantown to Little Egg Harbour, Juliad and five others made their way in a fishing boat to an English frigate anchored outside the harbour.[112]

Ensign von Micklaskewiecz, a Polish officer serving with the Regiment Landgraf, deserted in December 1779. Dr Thacher wrote in his journal, 'During the present month [December 1779], one Hessian lieutenant and seven Hessian soldiers, and four British, deserted from the enemy at New York. The lieutenant pretended a desire to enter our service as a volunteer, but deserters are

---

[108] Woringer, 'Ausländer als Offiziere', *Hessenland*, XXVI (1912), p. 265.
[109] StaMarburg 4h.410. nr. 2, fol. 367, Knyphausen to the Landgraf, 14 June 1778.
[110] StaMarburg 4h.411. nr. 1, fol. 47, Knyphausen to the Landgraf, 26 Feb. 1779; Feilitzsch, fol. 76; Baurmeister, *Journals*, p. 259 and n. 27.
[111] StaMarburg 4h.410. nr. 2, fol. 433, Knyphausen to the Landgraf, 13 Sept. 1778; ibid, fol. 484, Capt. Ferguson to Capt. Beckwith, 25 Oct. 1778.
[112] Ibid, fols. 479–81, 'Actum Morris Haus 27 Octobris 1778', Juliad's testimony to Capt. v. Dinklage and Lt. v. Ende of Linsing's. MajGen. Carl v. Bose's subsequent investigation revealed that Juliad was seriously in debt and guilty of misbehaviour, such as threatening local people on Rhode Island. Juliad was put on half pay until his debts were made good. Ibid, fols. 500–2, Bose to Knyphausen, 13 Nov. 1778; fol. 493, Knyphausen to the Landgraf, 17 Dec. 1778; fol. 511, the Landgraf to Knyphausen, 22 Feb. 1779.

generally suspicious, or worthless characters, underserving of attention.'[113] Micklaskewiecz published his own resignation in Rivington's *Gazette* under the title 'Copy of Dismission'. In reply Knyphausen caused to be published in the same paper a demand that Micklascewiecz reappear in a fortnight's time and justify himself, or be prosecuted as a deserter. He did not appear.[114]

A sixth officer, Ensign Spangenberg of Bose's, deserted from the Yorktown prisoners at Fredericksburg, Virginia, settled down in that state with an American wife, and gave Latin lessons.[115]

Was the Franklin–Jefferson plan to cause Hessian desertion a success? One historian writes, 'The American psychological warfare campaign against the mercenaries was the most successful one of the revolution.'[116] Certainly judged by absolute numbers it fared well against the Hessen-Kassel contingent: of nearly 19,000 who came to America, over 3,000 remained behind more or less willingly.[117] In addition, a number of officers, including Bardeleben's brother, took their discharge during or after the war, to settle in America. However, claims for the plan's success ignore the enormous degree of desertion endemic in contemporary armies. Even in the year of heaviest Hessian desertion in America, a smaller proportion deserted than in 1762 in Hessen: in 1762 roughly ten per cent of the corps of 22,000 deserted. In 1783 the Hessians lost 734 men out of nearly 13,000, less than six per cent.[118] Much desertion was simply a consequence of the nature of recruiting in Germany. Many drafts were Austrian and Prussian deserters, men (as Washington wrote of deserters enrolled in his own ranks) 'who have given glaring proof of a treacherous disposition, and who are bound to us by no motives of attachment'.[119] Having deserted once, they were likely to do so again. Others enlisted in Germany solely to get free passage to America, and often stipulated when they engaged that they be released there at the end of hostilities. Knyphausen reported to his sovereign with concern in

[113] Thacher, *Military Journal*, p. 180. Gen. Heath put the date as Nov. 1, 1779. Heath, *Memoirs*, p. 223.
[114] StaMarburg 4h.411. nr. 1, fol. 261, Knyphausen to the Landgraf, 13 Dec. 1779; ibid, fol. 272 gives Micklaskewiecz's printed resignation.
[115] Ibid, 4h.411. nr. 3, fol. 19, Major Scheer to Lossberg, 11 May 1782; ibid, fol. 20, Lossberg to the Landgraf, 18 June 1782.
[116] Berger, *Broadsides and Bayonets*, p. 123.
[117] For my figures, see Appendix C.
[118] StaMarburg 13 Acc: 1930/5 Nr. 232, fol. 2.
[119] Washington, *Writings*, XI, pp. 98–9.

November 1777 on the decline in quality of his regiments:

The recruits, consisting of foreigners, for the most part conduct themselves badly and desert at the first opportunity, from which they may not be employed in the outposts. The intention of most of them has been to profit from the opportunity to get over here in some manner, and never to see Europe again, doing it differently from others who establish themselves here, who have to work four years to pay their travel costs in some manner. It is to be feared that the Regiments, which have already suffered a large wastage of our gallant Hessians, and are still suffering, may fall at length, if this situation persists, into a very evil state from this recruiting.[120]

Lossberg reported in April 1783 that many foreigners were deserting, having come to America only to settle there.[121] Many of those signed on only for the duration clamoured to be released, and this clamour increased notably after the Waldeckers, Ansbachers, and Brunswickers discharged their foreigners in America.[122] These men would have deserted even if there had been no propaganda campaign; they had been convinced before they sailed for America. The American plan probably did convince waverers that they would get a friendly reception, and its particular success was the desertion of 236 soldiers, the majority native Hessians, during Clinton's retreat in 1778.[123]

Moreover, a contemporary German army, recruited in the same manner as the Hessian and with the same discipline, but not exposed to any 'psychological warfare campaign', suffered a higher proportion of loss from desertion in a single campaign. This was Frederick the Great's Prussian army, which lost 16,052 deserters out of 154,000 men during the so-called Potato War in Bavaria in 1778, in which the soldiers were by no means exposed to such hardships of campaigning as were the Hessians in America.[124]

A second index to judge the failure of the American plan was its lack of impact on the outcome of the war. The Americans aimed, not solely to provide new homes for poor German farmboys, but to cripple the Hessian auxiliary corps as a fighting force. In 1776, the

---

[120] StaMarburg 4h.410. nr. 2, fols. 129–30, Knyphausen to the Landgraf, 30 Nov. 1777.
[121] Ibid, 4h.411. nr. 3, fol. 123, Lossberg to the Landgraf, 29 April 1783. Slagle in his work on Lossberg's regiment proved, by comparison of muster lists for 1775, 1778 and 1783, that the majority of Hessian soldiers who worked with American farmers and others, and who subsequently declined to return to their regiments, were new recruits (i.e. probably non-Hessian). His figures are given in Kipping, *Hessian View of America*, p. 46.
[122] StaMarburg 4h.411. nr. 3, fol. 172, Lossberg to the Landgraf, 24 July 1782.
[123] Of the deserters, 162 were Hessians, 74 'foreigners'. Ibid, 4h. 410. nr. 2, fol. 388.
[124] The figures on desertion are from Gaston Bodart, *Losses of Life in Modern Wars* (Oxford, 1916), p. 38; those on total strength from Curt Jany, *Geschichte der Preussischen Armee vom 15. Jahrhundert bis 1914* (2nd edn, Osnabruck, 1967), III, p. 111.

only campaign in which the Hessians played a major attacking role, desertion had no effect. Subsequently the mercenaries were used mainly for garrison duty and occasional raids. Defeats at Redbank and Trenton, not desertion, were the cause of their new mode of employment. And after the summer of 1778 the British turned from a conventional war against the main American army, to one of raids and attrition and a reliance on supposed Loyalist strength. If desertion had been a convincing factor, the *Jäger*, who lost most heavily from this cause, would not have been employed. Instead, they were the most active Hessian unit in this period of the war. There is no evidence I have found of a British post being taken, a detachment beaten, or a campaign ill-planned because of the probability or occurrence of Hessian desertion.

10
Recruiting in Germany

The Landgraf had contracted to keep his corps up to strength by providing recruits annually to fill the gaps of battle, disease, and desertion. Twice yearly the British muster master assembled and mustered the Hessian regiments and, according to returns which he submitted, Suffolk sent to Schlieffen an estimate of the number of recruits needed for the following campaign. Recruits were collected by the Landgraf's recruiting officers at the depot, first at Rheinfels, and after 1777 at Ziegenhain, and disciplined and drilled as much as time permitted. When the German roads and the river Weser became passable in spring, the British sent instructions to Kassel to put the recruits in motion towards Bremerlehe. The Admiralty Board, notified of probable numbers, provided shipping at two tons per head for the Atlantic crossing. Faucitt was dispatched to the embarkation to inspect the recruits, reject the unserviceable, and swear the remainder into British service. Only then would they receive British pay and emoluments, and the Landgraf his thirty crowns per head.

The usual route for the recruits from Ziegenhain was as follows: to Kassel, where they were paraded on the *Rennbahn* before the Landgraf, who went through the ranks taking complaints and noting the quality of the recruits;[1] thence to Karlshafen on the Weser, where they were embarked upon barges called *Bremerböcke*; to Bremen by water, except for those recruits of Prussian origin, who were disembarked to make a roundabout march to avoid Prussian customs at Minden; at Bremen onto lighters, which brought them to the transports.

The majority of these recruits were non-Hessians. Already his subjects had born a heavy burden in filling out the first two divisions, and the Landgraf could not have been unaware that

---

[1] Günderode, *Briefe eines Reisenden*, p. 168. The *Rennbahn* was located above the Aue Gardens by the Fulda. 'The Bowling Green' on the Aue was another traditional parading place of Hessian troops.

drawing off more able-bodied men would throw an intolerable burden on those remaining behind, probably ruining agriculture.[2] Numbers of the young men had already fled into Hannover and neighbouring states to escape service.[3] Hessen had cartels with Cologne, Mainz and Darmstadt for the return of deserters,[4] but wholesale flight of the rural populace was something different.

On 19 November 1776, Friedrich issued a notice to be circulated by all his local officials informing the people that he, 'with a sovereign's regard for the indispensable and necessary cultivation of our farms and agriculture in the state', intended to replace Hessian losses in America with non-Hessians.[5] This was not a new departure. The Hessian infantry manual and the recruiting regulations of 1762 first apportioning cantons recommended the recruitment of foreigners. In 1761 Hessian regiments had been brought up to strength by recruiters in the Hanse towns.[6] For the American war such recruiting had to be undertaken on a large scale. Wastage was high, the British reckoning it as one in ten after the first campaign.[7] Three days after his circular, the Landgraf sent formal requests for permission to recruit to various princes and free cities of Germany. The Kriegskabinett also tried to arrange other recruitment areas. Of those asked, the Prince of Solms-Braunfels, the Counts of Wied-Neuwied, Wied-Runkel, Neu-Isenberg, Wittgenstein, and Lippe-Detmold, and the cities of Heilbronn, Wimpfen, Mulhausen, Frankfurt-am-Main, Worms, and Speyer gave permission for recruiting to take place. The Count of Erbach, the Margrave of Ansbach-Bayreuth, and the Hanse ports of Bremen, Lübeck, and Hamburg refused. Even in areas where recruiting was not openly allowed, it went on surreptitiously: in Offenbach, where it was carried on from Lippe-Detmold, in Württemberg, and even in Switzerland.[8]

Governments probably allowed recruiting for three reasons. First, recruiters aimed not at prosperous citizens or master craftsmen, but at the unemployed, vagrants, and deserters from other armies, and those who were potential troublemakers. Thus an

---

[2] See below, pp. 222–4.
[3] SP81/185, Faucitt to Suffolk, 26 Aug. 1776; SP81/186, Faucitt to Suffolk, 27 Jan. 1777.
[4] StaMarburg, *Hessen und die amerikanische Revolution: Ausstellung der hessischen Staatsarchive zum Hessentag 1976* (Marburg, 1976), pp. 20–1.
[5] StaMarburg 12. nr. 8529.
[6] SP81/165, Clavering to Bute, 13 Oct. 1761.
[7] SP81/185, Suffolk to Schlieffen, 15 Nov. 1776.
[8] Kipping, *Hessen-Kassel Truppen*, pp. 40–1; Dippel, 'Deutschland und die amerikanische Revolution', p. 98.

Recruiting in Germany

observer at Hamburg noted in February 1777 that there were nightly disturbances, blows, and bloodshed between the recruiters of various states, but added:

I have long wondered [why] the magistracy have not put a stop to recruiting here, but I am told it is a political stroke of theirs, for as Hamburgh is a free city, it is the reservoir of all the rogues, rascals and runaways in Germany, and as the army and the gallows refuse none, they by that means get rid of them.[9]

The Hamburg magistrates declared that recruiting carried off all the vagabonds who would otherwise become thieves and murderers.[10]

Second, except for the Margrave of Ansbach, these governments were not competitors in the soldier trade. Third, they may have suspected, rightly, that if recruiting were not allowed openly, it would go on secretly, and if open it could at least be kept within bounds. Thus instructions to Hessian *Jäger* sent to recruit in Lemgo and Detmold, in Lippe-Detmold, required them to report to the government Chancellor there, show him their recruiting passes, and await further instructions from him, and 'to abstain from each and every act of violence, and solely to conform to instructions given by him [the Chancellor]'. His instructions to the Hessian Kriegscollegium were that only foreign volunteers, and no local subjects, were to be recruited, and each recruit was to attest before the town government that he had been recruited voluntarily.[11]

The main centres of Hessian recruiting proved to be Frankfurt-am-Main, Wetzlar, and Offenbach, the county of Lippe-Detmold, and the Schaumberg enclave of Hessen around Rinteln, garrison town of Lossberg's regiment, where young men could be recruited from the neighbouring territories.[12] Recruits were first taken to Rheinfels. However in 1777 the authorities of Mainz and Treves removed some of their subjects from Colonel Benning's transport en route down the Rhine, and the depot was then removed to Ziegenhain, which possessed a strong and ancient fortress.[13]

Recruiters, usually from the Guards and dragoon regiments

---

[9] *The Morning Chronicle and London Advertiser*, 11 March 1777, 'Extract of a letter from Hamburgh, Feb. 27'.

[10] *Adams Weekly Courant*, 30 Dec. 1777, 'Extract of a letter from Hamburgh, 12 Dec.'

[11] StaMarburg 4h.328. nr. 158/I, fols. 11–12, the Landgraf to MajGen v. Bulow, 10 Jan. 1782; copy of instructions of *Kanzler* and *Rath* Hoffman at Detmold to the Kriegscollegium, 13 Dec. 1781.

[12] Kipping, *Hessen-Kassel Truppen*, p. 40; StaMarburg 13 Acc: 1930/5 Nr. 234, fols. 46–7.

[13] SP81/155, Cressener to Suffolk, 24 Mar. and 21 April 1777; Kapp, *Soldatenhandel*, pp. 120–1.

remaining in Hessen, established recruiting posts at strategic points. Although violence was strictly forbidden by their sovereign, he also judged these men by how many recruits they enlisted, and they were not always careful how they did it. Landrat Baumbach at Sontra complained of *Jäger* recruiters getting young men drunk, and then persuading them to enlist in the *Jägercorps* for America.[14] Lieutenant Willichs recruiting at Frankfurt was able to claim success because Imperial and Danish NCOs brought him numbers of men. An imperial officer who had been indiscreet in this business had been expelled from his regiment.[15] The government of Eisenach complained in November 1778 that two of its subjects were recruited by force by the Hessians.[16]

The recruiters' most common offence was failing to pay promised bounty money. The majority of recruits were men who, in the German phrase, 'took their skin into the market' and enlisted for the bounty. Increasing competition from Prussian, Austrian, Dutch, and Danish recruiters, from those of other subsidiary princes, and even from recruiters for the 60th Foot, forced the Hessians to increase their bounties; for, as Faucitt reported to Stormont from Hanau in early 1781, 'the number of Austrian, Prussian, Hessian & Dutch Recruiting Officers, is so uncommonly great in this part of the Country at present, Who stick at no price, & take every Thing, tall or short, young or old, who offer. . . .'[17] The Hessian recruiters promised considerable sums to their recruits, which the latter were to receive when they reached the recruit depot. Often these amounts exceeded what they were authorized to grant. On other occasions recruits were promised travelling expenses for presenting themselves at the depot. Colonel Leopold of the Prinz Friedrich Dragoons stationed at Ziegenhain reported disorders amongst the recruits there in June 1777, because they had not received the sums promised. A 'ten-inch recruit' had presented himself and demanded thirty talers. Leopold gave him only half that. None of the others who had arrived had received any bounty. The following month four more recruits arrived who had been promised three ducats each, which he had no authority to pay out.[18]

[14] StaMarburg 12. nr. 8529, Baumbach to the Landgraf, 10 Feb. 1779
[15] Ibid., 4h.328. nr. 158/II, fols. 8–11, Willichs to the Landgraf, 23 Aug. 1782.
[16] StaMarburg, *Hessen und die amerikanische Revolution: Austellung der Staatsarchive*, p. 20.
[17] SP81/194, 1 February 1781. See also SP82/95, Mathias to Suffolk, 30 April 1776; SP82/98, Mathias to Weymouth, 4 Oct. 1779; Thomas Nugent, *Travels through Germany* (2 vols. London, 1768), I, p. 136 describes such recruiting even in peacetime.
[18] StaMarburg 4h.328. nr. 157, Leopold to the Landgraff, 2 June and 13 July 1777.

Recruiting in Germany

Soldiers often arrived in America without having received the bounty promised them when they first enlisted. Knyphausen sent his sovereign a list of 126 men of various regiments who had not been paid their full bounty. No less than sixty-one of these men were *Jäger* who, as trained marksmen, could demand the most on the open market.[19]

Recruiting was a *cause célèbre* in the eighteenth century, and the recruiting officer a notorious figure, pilloried in literature and on the stage. However it would be wrong to conclude from this that the replacements for the Hessian corps sent to America in the years 1777 to 1782 were innocents pressed into service against their will. The transports were a very mixed bag, and included adventurers, misfits, and failures of all sorts. Not surprisingly, considering the hardship of life at that time, recruitment amongst poor people increased in winter when they simply sought refuge against cold and hunger.[20] Some had failed in their usual occupation or got into amorous difficulties. Captain Dörnberg derived particular amusement from a recruit in the transport of 1779, who had played the role of Harlequin with several touring companies but found his talents insufficient to support body and soul. He was performing for his comrades on their Bremer barge when another recruit, a Prussian deserter from the Minden garrison taking his wife with him to America, was suddenly confronted by a previous wife whom he had abandoned at Minden and who boarded the barge. Colonel Keudell commanding the transport promptly annulled the second marriage, and awarded the first wife her man.[21]

Prussian deserters formed a considerable part of each transport, there being149 in the 900-odd rank and file in1782.[22] The number of his men deserting to take service in America may have caused Frederick the Great to make difficulties over the passage of recruits through his territory.[23] Others arriving in July 1777 were a good half composed of Saxons, Hannoverians, and Württembergers.[24] The Duke of Württemberg, whose finances were so disordered that he was obliged to offer his military to the English, for otherwise he would be unable to maintain what troops he had, subsequently lost a good number of his *Jäger* to Hessian and Hanau recruiters after Faucitt had rejected the

---

[19] Ibid., 4h.410. nr. 2, fols. 210–19, Knyphausen to the Landgraf, 23 March 1778.
[20] StaMarburg 4h.328. nr. 158/1, fol. 170, MajGen. von Bulow to the Landgraf, 8 July 1782.
[21] Doernberg, *Tagebuchblätter eines hessischen Offiziers*, I, p. 11.
[22] StaMarburg 4h.328. nr. 158/1, fol. 120, Bulow to the Landgraf, 22 April 1782.
[23] SP81/189, Faucitt to Suffolk, 17 Nov. 1777; SP81/155, Cressener to Suffolk, 17 Nov. 1777.
[24] CO5/94, fol. 428, Osborne to Germain, 4 July 1777.

Württembergers.[25] Ewald described the first body of additional *Jäger* thus: 'The NCOs and *Jäger* were composed partly of deserters of all nations, partly of failed officers and aristocrats who had had misfortune, students of all faculties, bankrupts, merchants, and all sorts of adventurous people.'[26] Ewald spoke of the other Hessian recruits as the 'refuse of mankind'.[27] Sergeant von Krafft noted in their number 'some unfortunate persons of high social rank', including a former lieutenant of a Prussian Freikorps and an erstwhile Prussian councillor of war.[28] Some were adventurous young men urged on by the traditional German *Wanderlust*, others were seeking a free passage to America simply to make a new start there regardless of who won the war.[29] The quality on the whole was not good. Deserters, bankrupts, ne'er-do-wells – such reinforcements must have caused anxiety even to hardened veterans like Knyphausen and Lossberg. The traveller Günderode, seeing a transport leaving Kassel for America in 1780, wrote, 'And I saw many amongst them, of whom I believe that it would be a good thing if Germany could be purged of all such people who are like them.'[30] An observer of the Hessian transport embarked at Dordrecht in April 1777 commented,

> I never saw worse made men. My host where I put up told me they were not Hessians, nor did the Empire give birth to them, for they were of all countries, and many of them might as well be called any thing as soldiers, for what they knew of arms, but that they wore uniforms . . . they are of all ages, sizes, countries and complexions . . . If these are the men who are to fight the battles of the English in America, little, I think, can be expected from them.[31]

Newly arrived recruits were responsible for an increase in violence and theft within the corps in November 1777, which could scarcely be checked.[32] In March 1778 they were already deserting faster than anyone else in the corps, and could not be trusted on piquet duty.[33] Those in the 1778 transport behaved in a shocking manner

[25] SP81/187, Faucitt to Suffolk, 4 Mar. 1777. Faucitt's reports to Suffolk on the Duke of Württemberg's military establishment demonstrate that other German princes would have liked to do what the Hessian Landgrafs achieved, but were unable to maintain troops in a state of sufficient training and readiness. SP81/186, 7 and 17 Feb. 1777. Paraphrased somewhat by Kapp, *Soldatenhandel*, pp. 128–30.

[26] Tagebuch, II, p. 42, quoted in Kipping, *Hessen-Kassel Truppen*, p. 43.

[27] Ibid.

[28] Krafft, *Journal*, p. 122, 18 Oct. 1780.

[29] StaMarburg 4h.410. nr. 2, fols. 129—30, Knyphausen to the Landgraf, 30 Nov. 1777.

[30] Günderode, *Briefe eines Reisenden*, p. 172.

[31] *The Morning Chronicle and London Advertiser*, 23 April 1777, 'Extract of a letter from Amsterdam, April 12'.

[32] StaMarburg 4h.410 nr. 2, fol. 129, Knyphausen to the Landgraf, 30 Nov. 1777.

to their officers and revolted en route.[34] These men had no particular loyalty to the Landgraf, no interest in the traditions of Hessian arms, and none in the English cause. The deterioration of standards of discipline and training in the Hessian corps is one reason why the majority of regiments spent the latter part of the war on simple garrison duty fighting desertion and disorder within their own ranks.

Nor was the physical quality of many recruits high. Colonel Keudell reported to his sovereign that Faucitt had rejected twenty-one recruits from the transport of 1779: one, a certain Helwig Zulauff, had no teeth and had already been recruited and rejected three times; another was lame, two had epilepsy, eleven were 'broken', and Friedrich Richebitter was sixty years old when recruits were not to exceed forty. Faucitt had also missed another twenty whom Keudell reckoned as unfit for duty.[35] Colonel Rainsford who mustered the transport of March 1777 in S'Gravendael found five or six Quixotic figures with one eye; others were very old, a still larger number only boys, and on the whole the recruits very indifferent.[36] Inspecting the transport of 1782 on the *Rennbahn*, Friedrich II himself found recruit Heinrich Brinkmeyer 'completely lame, limping badly, and one of his legs several inches shorter than the other'.[37]

Much trouble arose on the recruit transports from a failure to satisfy the high expectations which the recruits had of bounty money and English pay and provisions. The worst occurrence was a minor revolt amongst those of 1777. Colonel Hatzfeld of Rall's second battalion commanded this transport as far as Cork, where he was to see it on its way to America. The trouble was caused by a delay at Cork, which meant that the officers consumed all their provisions. Hatzfeld having paid the officers their wages for that month (February) only, the *Jäger* and recruits who had run out of tobacco and clean linen demanded to be paid all the wages owed

---

[33] Ibid., fol. 203, Knyphausen to the Landgraf, 23 Mar. 1778.
[34] Ibid., fol. 264, Knyphausen to the Landgraf, 9 May 1778.
[35] StaMarburg 13 Acc: 1930/5 Nr. 197, fols. 17 and 19, Keudell to the Landgraf, 11 June 1779.
[36] SP81/187, Rainsford to Suffolk, 28 Mar. 1777.
[37] StaMarburg 4h.328. nr. 158/I, fol. 102, the Landgraf to LtGen v. Gohr, MajGens v. Biesenrodt and v. Bulow, 13 April 1782. Bulow replied that Brinkmeyer, a deserter from the Prussian regiment at Bielefeld, had been inspected by the garrison surgeon at Ziegenhain – possibly a comment upon Hessian surgeons of the day. Ibid., fol. 114, 22 April 1782.

them, without the usual deductions for ship's provisions. When Hatzfeld offered them each two shillings, sufficient for tobacco and linen, refusing to pay them more until they reached America, trouble broke out on one of the ships:

the *Jäger* took hold of their rifles, the recruits grasped the marlin-spikes and several large bits of coal, and said they would not leave the ship until they had their full pay. I threatened them that a ship of war would come, and put them down by force, whereupon they all shrieked that that was good, they would all sell their lives dearly enough, they would all die together, but the officers would die first. I wanted to take the rifle from a *Jäger* named Leinhos, who did the most disputing, but he refused to give it to me; quite the contrary, he reached into his pouch, took out a cartridge and gave it to the *Jäger* Mülhan, who was obliged to load his rifle before my very eyes. I was ringed round by others, Leinhos cocked the hammer and pushed the weapon against me.

One of Hatzfeld's subalterns then knocked the rifle away and called to Hatzfeld, should he shoot the offender? Prudently, Hatzfeld did not give the order to fire. The greatest confusion reigned, everyone in a state of rebellion. When Hatzfeld tried to quiet them, saying that they should have what was owed them, that it was truly a disgrace that Hessian troops should so conduct themselves, they all cried out 'that they were no Hessians, they served the King of England, and wished to be paid like Englishmen'. Hatzfeld then went to the English colonel in command of all troops in the harbour at Cork, asking for a ship of war to compel the men by force; the colonel refused, saying that if the *Jäger* and recruits did not wish to behave, they would have to be sent back to Portsmouth. Fearing to go aboard the troublesome vessel again, Hatzfeld sent a *Jäger* NCO 'to acquaint them regarding pay that the recruits could not receive so much as the *Jäger*'. In gratitude the mutineers rushed at the NCO as he was climbing the ship's ladder and tried to push him into the sea. Sailors rescued him. Finally the English Colonel pacified the troublemakers with a promise to pay them extra should any English soldier receive higher wages than they did. Hatzfeld then paid them to the end of February, and the troublemakers were immediately put on other ships.[38] Such occurrences were repeated, to a lesser degree, on other recruit transports.[39]

---

[38] StaMarburg 13 Acc: 1930/5 Nr. 187, fols. 30–2, Hatzfeld to the Landgraf, 13 Feb. 1778.
[39] StaHannover 41 V Nr. 34, fol. 50, Capt. Niemeyer's report, 29 March 1778; ibid., nr. 37, fol. 11, Niemeyer's report, 21 May 1777; ibid., fol. 30, Niemeyer's report, 18 Dec. 1777; ibid., nr. 35, fol. 264, Niemeyer's report, 29 March 1780; StaMarburg 13 Acc: 1930/5 Nr. 197, fol. 17, Col. Keudell to the Landgraf, 11 June 1779; Dörnberg, *Tagebuchblätter eines hessischen Offiziers*, I, pp. 10–11.

Recruiting in Germany

The Hessians prided themselves particularly that their regiments were composed mostly of loyal *Landeskinder* and not the international rabble of the Prussian and Austrian armies.[40] Ewald wrote, 'The Prussian-style unit is composed of deserters and an ill-bred rabble', and when his *Jäger* made shoes from cowhide to replace those that had worn out he gave it as 'further proof that German soldiers, by a strict discipline which is unique to the Hessians, never complain and make do under all conditions.'[41] By May 1778 Hessian recruiting had spread over the whole Empire,[42] and Hessian battalion commanders in charge of very heterogeneous rank and file were plagued by the problems of desertion and indiscipline common to armies of the *ancien régime*.

[40] Hanger, *Life, Adventures, and Opinions*, I, p. 40.
[41] Tagebuch, I, pp. 155 and 189, quoted in Kipping, *Hessen-Kassel Truppen*, pp. 42 and 75 n. 253.
[42] StaMarburg 4h.410. nr. 2, fol. 247, the Landgraf to Knyphausen, 18 June 1778.

11

The impact of the war on Hessen

Hessen-Kassel had barely recovered from the effects of the Seven
Years War and the French occupation when the treaty with
England was signed in early 1776. Bad harvests from 1769 onwards
had delayed her recovery, and were harmful to the populace.[1] The
young traveller from Höchst near Frankfurt, writing in the guise
of a Frenchman just after the American war, described the impact
of the treaty on Hessen as unfavourable:

> The sending the Hessian troops to North American cannot be considered as
> hardship in itself, considering the intimate connection of this country with Great
> Britain; but the connection itself is a very unprofitable one for this country. The
> English subsidies can never make amends for the loss which the treaty has hitherto
> brought on the prince and the people. The country was stripped of all its young
> men, after the last Silesian war [the Seven Years War] and scarcely had it begun
> to bloom again, when they were sent to America. At least twenty thousand Hessians,
> of whom one half will never come home, are gone to that part of the world. The
> country has therefore lost a sixth of its most useful inhabitants, by the tea-burning
> business at Boston... Though the Landgrave has remitted his subjects a part of
> the taxes for as long a time as the war shall last, they desert in great numbers, and
> go into Hungary, Poland, and Turkey.[2]

Riesbeck's estimate of the numbers sent to America and the
casualty rate are too high, and those young men who ran off
tended to go to Hannover and Holland rather than Hungary,
Poland, and Turkey.[3] Nevertheless, Riesbeck was right. A population of 350,000 could not send off over 13,000 of its young men
without causing suffering amongst their families.

Certain elements in the country, however, did well from the war.

---

[1] Demandt, *Geschichte des Landes Hessen*, p. 281.

[2] Riesbeck, *Travels through Germany*, III, pp. 147–8. Maty, the English translator of this
edition, wrote mistakenly that Riesbeck was from Württemberg. For his life and work, see
Rudolf Schäfer, *Johann Caspar Riesbeck 'der reisende Franzose' aus Höchst* (Höchster
Geschichste Heft 1a. Frankfurt-am-Main, 1971). A new edition of his travels was
published at Stuttgart in 1967.

[3] SP81/185, Faucitt to Suffolk, 26 Aug. 1776. For an imaginative description of the suffering
in Hessen by a famous American historian see George Bancroft, *History of the United States
of America* (London, 1876), V, p. 180.

The impact of the war

The Karlshafen Trading Company had a monopoly on the supply of goods to the troops, sending quantities of wine and other wares with each contingent to America.[4] Refusing a request that they use British textiles, the Landgraf ordered his soldiers to wear shirts, stockings, and other items of clothing manufactured in Hessen, and ordered them to repair their own muskets rather than use foreign ones.[5] By 14 January 1780 the corps had been supplied with 6,000 new shirts and 3,400 new pairs of shoes at a total cost of about 8,700 talers.[6] This was good for the prosperity of Hessian textile masters, centred in Hersfeld, but had a disastrous effect upon the appearance of the Hessian soldiers. The quality of the uniforms was so poor that they were ruined after the first season's campaigning, and in the new year, 1777, Heister and Donop requested new ones, irrespective of colour.[7] Captain-Lieutenant Dörnberg wrote that the grenadier battalions after the siege of Charleston in 1780 looked more like a troop of Bohemians than a body of soldiers.[8]

Hessian muskets and bayonets were produced near the iron mines in Schmalkalden. Some of the weapons were sold in the Frankfurt market to American colonists before the war, and may have been used to shoot Hessians.[9] Adam Ochs said that the quality of the Schmalkaldic iron and steel was perhaps second to none in Europe,[10] but judging by the damage suffered in transit the weapons were not sufficiently robust.[11] After the battle of Guilford Court House in 1781, Cornwallis issued new muskets to Bose's regiment, giving the Hessian ones to the Loyalists to use as best they could.[12]

Fitting out the Hessian field hospital in 1776 cost 6,282 talers. That this sum was spread amongst a wide variety of suppliers and contractors is shown by such miscellaneous payments as 9 talers 21 albus and 4 heller to the widow Sangerin for fifty-four hogshead of lard,

---

[4] Jungkenn 1:5, Cochenhausen to Jungkenn, 10 April 1776; SP81/188, Faucitt to Suffolk, 31 May 1777.

[5] Both and Vogel, *Landgraf Friedrich II*, p. 48; StaMarburg 4h.411. nr. 2, fols. 197–8, the Landgraf to Knyphausen, 13 Dec. 1781.

[6] StaMarburg 12.11 I Ba 9 (Ordre Buch vom Regiment Mirbach), fols. 158–70.

[7] Ibid, 4h.409. nr. 3, fol. 179, Donop to Heister, 6 Jan. 1777; 4h.410. nr. 1, fol. 490, Heister to the Landgraf, 15 Feb. 1777.

[8] Dörnberg, *Tagebuchblätter eines hessischen Offiziers*, II, p. 24.

[9] Both and Vogel, *Landgraf Friedrich II*, p. 49.

[10] Ochs, 'Das hessische Militär', p. 214.

[11] The Hessians claimed repair costs of £363 17s 11d for damage of arms and equipment on the voyage. Of 165 new muskets delivered to Lossberg's regiment by Col. Hatzfeld in July 1783, nearly all needed repair. A03/55/2 Nr. 7.

[12] StaMarburg 12.11 I Ba 7 (Journal of the Regiment von Bose), fol. 142.

21 albus and 4 heller to the widow Kuntzin for surgery utensils, and 3 talers 22 albus to the basketmaker Fischer for surgery hampers.[13]

Architects and builders at Kassel involved in the Landgraf's various building projects, new libraries, a new museum, a garrison hospital, new guardhouses on the *Friedrichstor*, did well out of the profits of the soldier trade. The accounts show that 7,000 talers were paid out for work on the new library and 12,826 talers for reconstruction work on the city wall and the new town.[14]

At the same time one might feel, as did a correspondent of *The London Chronicle*, that there was a certain irony in all this splendid building for a country said to be depopulated:

> The Landgrave of Hesse Cassel hath given orders for building not only 27 villages, but also a new town, which is to be named Friedrichstadt, said to extend from Cassel to the Castle of Weissenstein. It is even said at Cassel, that this Prince has entered into contracts with Builders and Workers for a still greater number of new villages, and that all the Subsidies which his Serene Highness receives from Great Britain for his troops will be employed on these establishments. But, at the same time, it may be asked, how the loss they are likely to sustain of their men, which go to America, will contribute to people their new villages?[15]

By 1776 the whole population of Hessen had been organized to a remarkable degree towards providing a mercenary corps. All the young men between sixteen and thirty were listed on rolls held by the local bailiffs, and each man was liable for service with the regiment in whose canton he lived. In practice those country people holding less than 250 talers in property were regarded as liable for service in America,[16] those with more paid taxes to support the military apparatus. Like any mercantilist government, the Landgraf's sought to protect those in vital industries, craftsmen, and people whose presence was essential to the prosperity of their farms or families. Thus metal workers, miners, foresters, servants of a lord, sons of widows, young men with land of their own to work, and students were amongst those exempted.[17] As Quartermaster Carl Bauer of Koehler's grenadiers noted, the efforts to save all these people and exchange them for those more

[13] A03/55/2 Nr. 16, Accounts of the Hessian Field Hospital.
[14] StaMarburg 6b, 254, 'Acta die zugestandene Einsicht der Landstände in die Kriegs- und Oberrathkammercasse-Rechnungen' (1815).
[15] *The London Chronicle*, XLI (1777), p. 530, 'Foreign intelligence. Frankfort on the Main, March 15.' On Friedrich's new towns, see below, p. 251.
[16] StaMarburg, *Hessische Truppen im amerikanischen Unabhaengigkeitskrieg (HETRINA)*. Indix nach Familiennamen, Eckhardt G. Franz et al., eds. (4 vols. Marburg, 1972–6), II, p. 19.
[17] StaMarburg 12. nr. 8539, Die Einrichtung der Werbe Cantons.

able to go to America hindered mobilization and training of the second division.[18] The workers of a silk factory in Kassel were excused from serving in America, and when two of them enrolled themselves among the new *Jäger* companies in early 1777 an investigation ensued to make sure they actually wanted to go.[19] A wigmaker in one small town was not sent to America partly because he was the only one in town and therefore an essential worker.[20]

The Landgraf also sought to protect his subjects, both as potential soldiers and as manpower for trade and manufactures, by measures against foreign recruiting. No pensioner from the army was to let his son go into foreign service under threat of losing his stipend.[21] Government orders prescribed the strictest vigilance against foreign recruiters by all subjects, not just officials. Anyone helping them was to be punished with 'irons – first class', branding, perpetual banishment, or even hanging.[22] In September 1776 these warnings were repeated. The papers of foreign recruiters passing through the country were to be scrutinized with the greatest attention by local officials in the villages in which they stopped, and the greatest vigilance was to be employed to prevent them recruiting. If they tried to get any of the locals drunk, a sure method of pressing their prince's shilling on them unawares, they were to be arrested promptly.[23]

Parents were held responsible for sons who emigrated. Five young men from the bailiwick of Trendelburg left the country in 1780 to go to the spinning mills in Elberfeld. Landrat von Stockhausen was instructed to arrest the parents of all five and hold them in prison until the return of their sons.[24]

By an order of 15 May 1778, native Hessians who enlisted in

[18] Ibid, 12.11 i Ba 16 (Journal of the Grenadier Battalion Platte), fol. 3.
[19] Ibid, 12. nr. 8529, report of the *Kriegs- und Domänenkammer*, 23 Jan. 1777.
[20] Ibid, 11 F 1 d, Capt. Fritzen to the Landgraf, 20 March 1781: In this odd case, Caterina Maria Hosbach petitioned the government that her husband, the wigmaker, an idle drunkard who neglected his family, be sent to America and part of his wages assigned to her to maintain her family. The petition was rejected, partly for the reason given above and partly because local church elders could not establish that Hosbach was indeed as immoral as claimed.
[21] Ibid, 4h.328. nr. 100, 16 Dec. 1773.
[22] StaMarburg 4h.328. nr. 100, 19 March 1773.
[23] Ibid, 19 Sept. 1776.
[24] Ibid, 11 F 1 d, Landrat v. Stockhausen to the Landgraf, 9 Nov. 1780. The Landgraf's directives are usually scribbled onto the first page of such documents with the words 'ist besorgt' (has been taken care of).

foreign service and then returned on leave to their homeland were to be arrested.[25]

The burden of producing recruits for the Hessian army fell far more heavily on the countryside than the towns, not merely because the vast majority of Hessians lived on the land,[26] but also because skilled craftsmen exempt from military service were more likely to be found in the towns. The parish records of Kassel, Marburg, and even a small place like Spangenberg (population 1,250) show no drop in the number of baptisms during the years of the Hessians' absence in America.[27] The story in the villages must have been very different. Thirty men including twelve heads of families went to America from Niedervellmar outside Kassel, Johannes Reuber's home.[28] Ironically it was the towns, particularly Kassel, which derived the greatest benefits from the sacrifice of the country people. General Langenscharz (as he became) wrote in later years:

In those days under the reign of Landgraf Friedrich II there was a lively and merry life in Kassel, although much simpler then than now. Only at the court and among the upper classes was there luxury, this had not yet reached the lower classes: hence there was even more satisfaction and content among the latter. Each restricted himself in his spendings to what he earned, and was satisfied with what his pursuits or trade brought him. The court by contrast was brilliant in appearance. The Landgraf, a great patron of arts and science, favoured these in every way possible. He maintained an excellent orchestra, Italian opera, French theatre with ballet, each in its way of the greatest perfection. The court personnel were numerous, *Oberhofchargen, Kammerherren, Kammerjunker, Hofjunker*, &c. &c.[29]

Although, as Langenscharz indicates, the common people fairly readily accepted hard and simple lives, despite the contrast of their own situation with the court's splendour, the demands of the soldier trade wrought many small tragedies among them. The case

---

[25] Ibid, Landrat von Baumbach to the Landgraf, 29 May 1780.

[26] 'Hessen has no towns, but merely villages', wrote one Hessian official. 'All Hessen is a village. The towns are villages ringed with walls.' LB Kassel, 8° Ms. hass. 16a, Fehler, Missbräuche, und Verbesserungen in Hessen (Memorandum of the *Kammerdirektor* Bopp), fol. 44.

[27] StaMarburg, Kirchenbücher: Reformirte Gemeinde Marburg, Reformirte Gemeinde Kassel, Oberneustadt Kassel, and Spangenberg. See also *Hessische Beiträge zur Gelehrsamkeit und Kunst* (2 vols. Frankfurt-am-Main, 1785–7), II, p. 679 for a list of baptisms, burials, and marriages in Kassel, 1765–85. I had hoped to gauge the impact of the American war on Hessen by the drop in numbers of marriages and births in local communities, but unfortunately StaMarburg holds few parish records for these years, and these show no significant variation for the years 1776–83.

[28] Reuber, fol. 3.

[29] LB Kassel, 8° Ms. hass. 123, Heft 1, fols. 68–9.

of Grenadier Johannes Horch of Knyphausen's regiment provides a pathetic example.

Horch, a veteran of seven and a half years' service, had just obtained his discharge in 1776 when, being an able-bodied man, he was taken for service in America. Although married, he had no farm of his own or widowed mother to care for. His second wife accompanied him to America to provide whatever comforts she could in the ardours of the campaign. A child by his first marriage he left behind with relations. In America Horch's wife left him 'in an excess of passion' for Corporal Cartheuser of Donop's regiment in the same grenadier battalion. Horch, taunted by his comrades, took solace in drink; and discovering his spouse and Cartheuser lying together during the retreat from Philadelphia, deserted from shame and sorrow, determined to make his way home to his child. He went to Philadelphia and from there to North Carolina where he engaged himself as a smith, earning sufficient money to get a ship to the West Indies at Easter, 1779. He worked for nine weeks for a merchant at St Eustatius, making four dollars a week, and took a Dutch ship to Amsterdam, whence he made his way at last to Hessen. He was not home six days when he was arrested as a deserter and taken to the recruit depot at Ziegenhain, whence he was sent to America with the recruit transport of 1781. Rejoining his old company, he found that his wife had died and his comrades forgotten his former disgrace, making life there endurable. On his return to Hessen, however, he found that his goods were to be confiscated because he had deserted. He pleaded against this decision on two grounds: first, that his desertion was due to the passions of his wife; and second, that he subsequently returned to service. The Kriegscollegium judged the reasons insufficient and confiscated his property.[30]

Rather more commonplace were appeals made for the return of Conrad Gerland and Jacob Haussman. Gerland was a soldier in Bose's regiment. His house, on which he paid *Kontribution* of 7 albus and 2 heller, was falling into disrepair in his absence. His father, who also paid tax, was too old to cope with looking after his own land. His wife's father, aged sixty-three, a farmer also paying *Kontribution* of 9 albus 2 heller, was unable to keep his house in repair or cultivate his farm. His daughter living with him found it too much to do the work and also look after her young child, so

---

[30] StaMarburg 4h.328. nr. 100, fol. 561, copy of the evidence taken at Ziegenhain, 21 Dec. 1784. The details of the story were told by Horch himself.

both parents asked *Landrat* von Stockhausen for the return of the young man for the good of the family as well as the conservation of their property.

Jakob Haussman was serving in America in Major Bode's company of d'Angelleli's.[31] His aged parents had no proper farm, but a house, farmyard, and nine acres of land. Their only son was in America, their only daughter married at Niedervellmar. The father was a wagon maker, but too weakened by age to carry on his trade. Their plot of land was going to waste because they were unable to work it, and they asked for the return of their son from America and the granting of his discharge. But both their request and that of Gerland's parents were refused.[32]

Such cases were not always as clear as they seemed, and sometimes the officials had perfectly sound reasons, from their point of view, for denying an apparently reasonable petition. Caspar Möller applied to the *Commisarius loci* at Melsungen, Captain Schotten,[33] for the discharge of his second son enrolled in the army. Möller was sixty-eight years old with various bodily ailments and lame. He paid a monthly *Kontribution* of 27 albus and 5 dinarius. His first son was with the Leib-Dragoons, and only with the help of his second boy could Möller maintain his own lands and his trade. Now he was threatened with ruin.

Upon investigation, however, Schotten found that Möller had two other sons who had gone to Holland, probably with the father's approval, to escape the mustering of young men. Möller had already sought his first son's discharge several times, and it had been refused since another son had been on his travelling apprenticeship (*Wanderschaft*) for nearly five years in Holland, instead of looking after his father's lands and household.[34] Möller's example, and the flight of other young men abroad, demonstrates that a part of the populace did not accept uncomplainingly the military system imposed upon them.

The best evidence for the hardship of the rural populace is the report of the Landrat Schenk zu Schweinsburg to his prince shortly after the corps' departure for America, that a number of families had been placed in the greatest distress.

So, for example, in Niederwald, in Fronhausen, in Niederwalgern, in Lohr, in

[31] Formerly Rall's.
[32] StaMarburg 11 F 1 d, Stockhausen to the Landgraf, 27 Jan. 1780.
[33] Baurmeister's nephew, wounded at Redbank and invalided home.
[34] StaMarburg 11 F 1 d, Schotten to the Landgraf, 10 March 1781.

Langenstein and several villages, there are wives left behind of the soldiers who have marched off, who in part indeed have their land and houses, but with them outstanding debts, and at the same time many children; of them it is reported to me the eldest are not above 8 or 9 years, the youngest only a few months old, and some are even so frail that they cannot do for an instant without the attention and care of their mothers, some of whom are pregnant.

Without the help of relations, Schenk reported, these poor wives were incapable of procuring bread to sustain life, paying the money for the schooling of their elder children, rendering all the necessary dues, and paying the *Kontribution.* While their husbands were in the country, even doing military service, they were able to support their families by working during furlough and making arrangements for cash to be paid to them while on duty. Now none of this could take place, and distress among this class of people had reached the highest level. There was an extreme shortage of money in the country, worsened by fathers giving whatever savings they could collect to sons who had gone to America, and demonstrated by the low level of consumption in the country; thus even those whose property put them among the well-to-do were unable to aid the poorer and lower classes.[35]

The Landgraf called for a detailed report of those in distress. Schenk responded with a list of forty-five soldiers from his district, thirty-one of whom had wives and a total of fifty-five children in varying states of distress, the other fourteen having elderly parents who had been dependent on them. Schenk asserted that he could have added other names of men transferred from the dragoon regiments to the artillery for the American expedition, but his knowledge of them was uncertain. He reiterated that farmers could not aid the poorer people, affirming that they possessed more talers in the last war than at present.[36]

It may have been this report which decided the Landgraf to conduct his recruiting throughout the war largely outside Hessen. In January 1777 Faucitt reported difficulty in getting drafts because 'the foreign recruits, upon whom the Landgrave's ministers had placed their dependence, do not come in so fast as they expected. And the country has been so severely drained by the

[35] StaMarburg 11 F 1 d, Schenk to the Landgraf, 23 March 1776. Schenk's report is a good indication of how much the Hessians relied on seasonal employment in agriculture to keep their regiments up to establishment strength.

[36] StaMarburg 11 F 1 d, Schenk to the Landgraf, 5 April 1776. Of the 45 soldiers, 25 were in Wutginau's regiment, 11 in Ditfurth's 3 in the artillery, and 1 each in Trumbach's, the Erbprinz's, Knyphausen's, Donop's, Mirbach's and Huyn's. As only one was in a garrison regiment, the majority were probably long term servicemen.

departure of the 12,000 men now in America, the greatest part of whom were natives of Hesse, that they are exceedingly unwilling to force any more of them into the service.'[37] In 1779, when recruiting was going particularly badly, they consented only with reluctance to posting notices in Hessen to encourage voluntary recruiting.[38] Nevertheless, distress continued throughout the war, and in February, 1782, Landrat Baumbach reported from Sontra near Eschwege that many wives, parents, and other relations of soldiers in America were in direst need, their lands falling into ruin unless the soldiers returned. Baumbach suggested that, if relations could bring a recruit to the depot at their own cost to replace the man in America, the latter might be recalled. The suggestion was refused, presumably because it meant replacing trained and loyal men with foreigners of doubtful quality.[39]

Schenk also reported a shortage of labourers to work on the farms and the farmers having to pay exceptionally high wages to men and young lads who came from Hessen-Darmstadt, a further drain on their finances.[40] Labour shortage in agriculture remained a serious problem throughout the war, and foreign labourers from Paderborn and elsewhere had to be hired in the place of young native Hessians.[41] On the other hand, the Landgraf's officials who had to fill out the second battalions of Hessian Garrison Regiments remaining in the country found certain sources of manpower untapped.[42] Landrat von Stockhausen at Immenhausen proposed that all kinds of good young men, serving as shepherds, labourers, or servants with their lords should not remain exempt from military service, but report to local officials for the regular mustering. He also proposed that he take fully grown young men without property, registered with the Garrison Regiments, and transfer them to the Field Regiments. The exemption of both these groups threw an unfair burden onto the rest of the populace.[43]

Stockhausen also offered a solution to another problem: the

---

[37] SP81/186, Faucitt to Suffolk, 27 Jan. 1777.
[38] SP81/192, Faucitt to Suffolk, 12 Feb. 1779.
[39] StaMarburg 11 F 1 d, Baumbach to the Landgraf, 20 Feb. 1782.
[40] StaMarburg 11 F 1 d, Schenk to the Landgraf, 5 April 1776.
[41] Ibid, Landrat von Biedenfeld to the Landgraf, 30 June 1781; 12. nr. 8529, Landrat von Münchhausen to the Landgraf, 2 Jan. 1777.
[42] On the troops' departure a second battalion was formed of the *unabkömmlich* of each garrison regiment. In 1778 these were amalgamated, either into Rall's second battalion or the Garrison Regiment Balecke, nominally part of the Upper Rhine Circle troops of the army of the Holy Roman Empire. Strieder, *Grundlage zur Militär-Geschichte*, pp. 31, 97, 104, 109, 146, and 171–2.
[43] StaMarburg 11 F 1 d, Stockhausen to the Landgraf, 6 Aug. 1778, and 20 Aug. 1781.

temporary emigration of the young men during the time of mustering recruits and second battalions of garrison regiments for annual training. According to Stockhausen Hessian subjects were in the habit of crossing the border to escape being put on the lists as potential soldiers. Because once they were on the lists they no longer thought of emigration and seldom deserted, not wishing to break the oath they had taken upon being sworn in, Stockhausen proposed in July 1780 that an official be appointed to actually swear in as 'Disposition Recruits' all the young men in the villages entrusted to him. The company chiefs of garrison regiments would form them in ranks for training once annually, thus having them at their 'disposition' for exercises, but they would be at home to help on their parents' farms. This would prevent them leaving the country, yet enable them to do agricultural work.[44]

The Kriegscollegium, however, reported that such a change in the regulations would further hinder the young natives in their trades and other pursuits and cause even greater emigration and desertion. They recommended keeping in force the ordinance of 8 October 1773, whereby young men were not sworn in as recruits until they were regarded as capable of service and able to be spared from the farms (*abkömmlich*).[45] The Landgraf accepted the Kriegscollegium's findings, but ordered that at the end of September, when it was most likely certain young men would leave the country at the next mustering, they were to be promptly sworn into service by local magistrates.[46]

Efforts to fill the ranks of these second garrison battalions and to provide recruits for America and for the Guards and dragoon regiments remaining in Hessen were hindered by the shortage of young men. Captain Spangenberg, *Commisarius loci* at Wolfhagen, reported difficulty getting men to complete Rall's second battalion in October, 1776.[47] Landrat von Eschwege found that so many young men had gone from Schmalkalden that he was in no position to complete the second battalion of Stein's garrison regiment, much less provide men for the Prinz Friedrich Dragoons. When Eschwege went through local villages to do a survey of those available, not only did the young men make off, but the parents shut up their houses and would not let him come in.[48] Baumbach

[44] StaMarburg 12. nr. 8826, Stockhausen to the Landgraf, 17 July 1780.
[45] Ibid, report of the *Kriegscollegium* to the Landgraf, 4 Sept. 1780.
[46] Ibid, 29 Sept. 1780.
[47] Ibid, 11 F 1 d, Spangenberg to the Landgraf, 26 Oct. 1776.
[48] Ibid, Eschwege to the Landgraf, 19 Nov. 1776.

reported that young men on furlough from the field regiments and those listed as 'effectives' with the garrison regiments, who thought they might be sent to America, made themselves scarce each year at the time for raising recruits for America; then, after the transport had departed for Bremerlehe, they took advantage of the subsequent general pardon, in force for a year, to write from Holland, Hannover, or wherever they had gone, receive pardon and return. In Baumbach's own village there lived four dragoons who had disappeared in the spring at the levying of the recruits, three of whom were already back with their pardons. Presumably they would do the same the next year. Baumbach said this was unfair on the rest of the populace, as he was obliged to take instead men who were genuinely *unabkömmlich,* often with wives and children.[49]

Harsh measures were prescribed against families of those on the muster lists who did not turn up at the annual levy. Captain Fritzen, *Commisarius loci* at Treysa, arrested the fathers of two young men whom he had cited to appear at the muster and who had not turned up. A third young man, Sebastian May, who had gone to work in a Dutch noble's household in 1780 and returned to Hessen to be married, Fritzen also arrested, giving as the reason the probable outbreak of war between Holland and England, in which case they would lose all possibility of having May's service in Hessen.[50]

Every expedient was used to get suitable men who were not of direct support to their families. The gardener Schellhausen at Kassel had reportedly given himself up to drink for several years, and led such a dissolute life that his wife twice left him and sought protection from his mistreatment with her father. He was fined several times for brutal treatment of servants. When his father-in-law reported that the wife and two children were in danger, Schellhausen was arrested by order of the *Policey Commission* and put in the recruit depot for America. However, on his wife's representations that she could not cope with his land and orangery by herself, Schellhausen was released on payment of costs, with a warning that if any more complaints were heard he would be back in the depot.[51]

---

[49] StaMarburg 11 F 1 d, Baumbach to the Landgraf, 10 Oct. 1781.
[50] Ibid, Fritzen to the Landgraf, 18 Jan. 1781.
[51] StaMarburg 11 F 1 d, report of the *Policey Commission*, 26 Sept. 1781, and Frau Schellhausen to the Landgraf, 21 Sept. 1781 (the Landgraf's resolution of 5 Oct. is written on the outside.)

The impact of the war

Some of the distress was mitigated by sums of money which the soldiers sent back from America. In the fourth year of the war the Landgraf had the option of terminating the treaty and bringing his troops home, or continuing to lease them to the British. Schlieffen believed the treaty was beneficial to Hessen on the whole, and wrote his sovereign that by that date, December 1779, the soldiers had sent home 591,721 talers via the *Kriegskasse*.[52] Schlieffen's argument convinced his sovereign, for Friedrich wrote to the King on 15 December, a week after Schlieffen's letter, informing him that although the term of four years had nearly expired and more reasons than one impelled him to bring the troops home, his attachment to the King's cause obliged him to keep them on.[53]

Others were not so easily convinced. The subsidy treaties of the six princes (Hessen-Kassel, Hessen-Hanau, Braunschweig-Wolfenbüttel, Waldeck, Ansbach-Bayreuth, and Anhalt-Zerbst) with Great Britain caused an unprecedented furore. 'Formerly customary, they now caused repugnance,' wrote the Swiss historian Müller, 'because of the distance of the theatre of war and the natural love of freedom which interested the best men in all countries in the cause of America.'[54] Certain intellectual circles were united in deploring the hiring of troops.[55] A letter of 7 April 1777, from Braunschweig, speaks for public opinion of the time:

I have constantly wanted to ask, my dear friend, on which side in the English war are you. I hope, on the American. Washington has now retaken everything which he previously lost. I am only sorry for the poor Hessians and our poor people. Recently we received letters from a Hessian officer in New York. He is a friend of my father, and thus complains candidly that [the war] does not suit him, and that the Americans have more spirit and are cleverer than they had wished. The poor devil had received a wound at Trenton and lost 3 horses and his servant with all his equipment.... You can imagine that everyone here is eager for news from America, as so many have friends and relations there.... For the rest, Braunschweig is just like England divided into two parties. All those who belong to the court are on the English side. But all others are for the Americans.[56]

---

[52] Kapp, 'Friedrich II und die neuere Geschichtsschreibung', *Historische Zeitschrift*, XLII (1879, nr. 2), p. 327.

[53] SP81/192, Friedrich of Hesse to George III, 15 Dec. 1779.

[54] Müller, *Sämmtliche Werke*, III, pp. 447–8.

[55] G. P. Gooch, 'Germany and the French Revolution', *Royal Historical Society Transactions*, 3rd series, X (1916), p. 53, quoting the remarks of Henriette Herz, a Jewish bluestocking of Berlin.

[56] Paul Zimmerman, 'Beiträge zum Verstandnis des zwischen Braunschweig und England am 9. January 1776 Geschlossenen Subsidienvertrages', *Jahrbuch des Geschichtsverein für das Herzogtum Braunschweig*, XIII (1914), p. 173. The letter was from Friedrich Gärtner, son of a professor there.

If fact, the bulk of the populace was largely indifferent, but soldiers, courtiers, and middle-class intellectuals were deeply divided. The campaigns were followed in the gazettes with keen interest. 'With eagerness I have read everything [in your journals]' wrote Colonel von Winzingerode from Kassel to his friend Riedesel. 'My prayers and imagination accompany you by means of all the maps of America which ornament my room.'[57] At the outset of the war, numerous German publicists favoured the British, but the German adherents of the American cause gradually got the upper hand. George Cressener, British ambassador to Cologne, reported with chagrin that the account of Trenton was exaggerated throughout the German Empire 'where the generality are all good Americans'.[58]

The American revolutionary period marks a watershed in German public opinion. As Müller pointed out, subsidy treaties, once an accepted thing, had now become odious. The change is marked by Friedrich Karl von Moser. Writing of subsidy treaties in the 1760s, he did not oppose them in general, but judged them as to whether their effect was favourable to the Empire as a whole, or to a prince's particular interest. But after the American war, his essay *Über den Diensthandel deutscher Fürsten*[59] breathes a new spirit and speaks a new language: it is an indictment of absolute princes, who have become merchants of their people, disregarding 'Laws and Justice, the Rights of Man, the life and limb of their own subjects'. The treaties he terms *Menschenhandel*.[60]

One must be careful, nevertheless, not to mistake opinions belonging to the era preceding and during the French Revolution for those held by contemporaries of the American war. Moser's work did not appear until 1786. The Swiss educational reformer Pestalozzi condemned the trade in soldiers, but in 1793.[61] Johann Gottfried Seume's attack on the 'seller of souls', the Landgraf of Hessen, was published, not when he received his discharge from the Hessian corps, but in 1802.[62] George Forster, a radical at the time of the French Revolution, is supposed to have been overwhelmed

---

[57] StaWolfenbüttel 237N86, fol. 86, Winzingerode to Riedesel, 10 Dec. 1777.
[58] HMC: *Report on MSS in Various Collections*, VI, p. 129, Cressener to Knox, March 1777.
[59] Leipzig and Frankfurt, 1786.
[60] Brauer, *Die hannoversch-englischen Subsidienverträge*, pp. 93–5.
[61] Dippel, 'Deutschland und die amerikanische Revolution', p. 105.
[62] Compare his letter from Halifax in 1782, in Oskar Planer and Camilla Reissman, *Johann Gottfried Seume* (Leipzig, 1898), pp. 26–34, with an extract of his later work translated by Margaret Woelfel, 'Memoirs of a Hessian Conscript: J. G. Seume's Reluctant Voyage to America', *WMQ*, 3rd series, V (1948), pp. 553–670.

with repugnance while in Kassel in the years 1778–82.[63] Yet his correspondence at this time is concerned only with seeking academic posts and expressed admiration for Schlieffen, whom he termed 'Maecenas'.[64]

Some of the attacks on the soldier trade were French propaganda, appearing particularly in French and Dutch newspapers, and in the writings of Mirabeau and the Abbé Raynal. In January 1777 the *Leiden Gazette* accused the Waldeck regiment of plundering and then refusing to advance. The *Mercure de France* in September 1780 recounted tales of Hessian brutality in New Jersey. Both princes proved sensitive to such criticism, indicative of a change in the climate of opinion since their grandfathers' time.[65] It was against the Abbé Raynal's 'Declamateur' that Schlieffen penned the Hessian apologia, 'Les Hessois en Amerique'.[66] Two of the best read contemporary German publicists, Schlözer and Wekhrlin, favoured the British cause in the war. Wekhrlin defended the hiring out of troops, tracing it back to the Greeks and pointing out the family ties of German princes with the British Royal Family.[67] Schiller depicted the cruelty of sending young men to America in his play *Kabale und Liebe* (1782), but in *Nachrichten zum Nüzen und Vergnügen*, which he edited, the brave conduct of the Hessians is recorded with approval.[68] Much of the Hessians' odious reputation stems from Liberal attacks of the nineteenth century, when Ben Franklin's *Uriasbrief* was read aloud in the Hessian Parliament, when the Liberal journalist Friedrich Oetker attacked the Hessian Electors in his *Hessische Morgenzeitung*, and books appeared like Kapp's and the anonymous *Kurhessen und seine Dynastie. Ein politischer Ehescheidungs-prozess. Von einem Enkel der nach Amerika Verkauften*, the latter published in Berlin in 1866, the year that Prussia seized Hannover, Braunschweig, and Hessen.[69]

Frederick the Great is supposed to have condemned the soldier

---

[63] Gordon A. Craig, 'Engagement and Neutrality in Germany: the case of George Forster, 1754–1794', *Journal of Modern History*, XLI (1969), pp. 1–16.

[64] Forster, *Briefwechsel*, I, pp. 186–7 and 321.

[65] SP81/186, Faucitt to Suffolk, 11 Jan. 1777; SP81/193, Extract of the Mercury of France, nr. 40, 30 Sept. 1780.

[66] Kapp, *Soldatenhandel*, pp. 192–5.

[67] John A. Walz, 'Three Swabian Journalists and the American Revolution', *Americana Germanica*, IV (1902), pp. 287–8.

[68] Ibid, p. 127.

[69] The impact of the war on German political awareness is fully described in Dippel, 'Deutschland und die amerikanische Revolution'. Kapp discusses the literature briefly in *Soldatenhandel*, pp. 185–201; Losch reviews it from the Hessian point of view in his counterblast *Soldatenhandel*, pp. 42–55.

trade, and his letter to Voltaire disclaiming any connections with the Landgraf of Hessen is well known:

> If he [the Landgraf] had come out of my school, he would not have turned Catholic, he would not have sold his subjects to the English, as one sells cattle to have their throats cut. This last act is in no way compatible with the character of a prince who poses as the preceptor of monarchs. The pursuit of a sordid interest is the sole cause of this unworthy proceeding. I pity those poor Hessians who will terminate their careers unhappily and uselessly in America.[70]

Frederick nonetheless approved the Braunschweig treaty with Britain for the reason that the state was bankrupt and the measure necessary to save the Duchy.[71] This reason could have applied equally to five of the six mercenary states, Hessen-Kassel being the only one whose finances were not disordered. That the Erbprinz of Braunschweig, Karl Wilhelm Ferdinand, was one of Frederick's protégés and chief of a Prussian regiment may also have influenced him. Less well known is that Frederick attempted to get troops from Hessen-Kassel to garrison Wesel for him during the War of the Bavarian Succession, and was refused.[72] Two of Friedrich of Hessen's sons, the Erbprinz Wilhelm and his brother Karl, served as volunteers with the Prussians in the 1778 campaign.[73] Frederick's moral indignation at the commerce in soldiers cannot have been very strong when he counted two of the merchants in his ranks, namely the Erbprinzen of Braunschweig and Hessen. Indeed, Frederick felt no particular concern for the fate of America. On hearing news of the rebels' defeat at Long Island he wrote to his brother Prince Henry, 'The English have defeated their colonists on Long Island, near New York. . . . If it continues thus, they may perhaps subjugate the Americans in a couple of years. All that concerns us very little; meanwhile, the price of tobacco rises enormously, which is disagreeable to me.'[74] And at the end of the American war, on 26 May 1783, he informed his minister at the Hague, 'I am very much persuaded that this so-

---

[70] Theodore Bestermann, ed., *Voltaire's Correspondence*, XCIV (Geneva, 1964), p. 155. The letter is usually quoted without the reference to Friedrich's Catholic conversion. See Kapp, *Soldatenhandel*, p. 155, and Lowell, *The Hessians*, p. 24. Friedrich had written and sent to Voltaire an essay entitled *Pensées diverses sur les Princes*, thus he posed as a 'preceptor of monarchs'.

[71] *Politische Correspondenz Friedrich's*, XXXIX, pp. 193–4; Hans Droysen, 'Die Braunschweigischen Truppen in Nordamerikanischen Unabhangigkeitskrieg: aus den Briefen der Herzogin Philippine Charlotte von Braunschweig', *Jahrbuch des Geschichtsvereins für das Herzogtum Braunschweig*, XIII (1914), p. 148. The Duchess was Frederick's sister.

[72] *Politische Correspondenz Friedrich's*, XLI, pp. 57, 82, 84, 92, 166 and 166n.

[73] Ibid, XL, p. 404.

[74] Ibid, XXXVII, pp. 384–5.

called independence of the American colonies will not amount to much ... and that little by little, colony by colony, province by province will rejoin England on their former footing, with perhaps certain advantages which they will stipulate regarding commerce, or other similar matters.'[75]

For a critique of the soldier trade in Hessen, one need not turn to the opinion of the intellectuals or the doubtful testimony of Frederick of Prussia, but to a Hessian official, the Kammerdirektor Bopp. Bopp, educated at the universities of Gotha and Eisenach, had served in Prussia for twenty years before coming to Kassel in 1773 as Kriegs- und Domänen-Rath, being appointed Kammerdirektor in the same year. He was much relied upon in implementing the Landgraf's Prussian-style reforms, appointing local town officials in 1774 and changing the management of the domain lands to a system of leases. He was working on a financial plan at the beginning of November 1776, when he somehow incurred the Landgraf's enmity, lost all his posts, and spent the rest of his life in isolated poverty, with only the small consolation of a pension from Friedrich's successor Wilhelm IX. He died in 1791.[76]

Bopp's critique of the effects of the soldier trade is contained within a memorandum criticizing the administration of Hessen as a whole.[77] 'There is no firm plan, no basic thought-out system,' wrote Bopp; nor, he added, were there tables of records or statistics available on Hessen by which one could judge what government revenues should be. And the economy of town and country (i.e. trade and manufactures on the one hand, agriculture on the other) were muddled up, the two neither clearly defined nor complementary to one another. The government had allowed the country to become dependent upon foreign merchants for trade goods, draining money from the land. The Jews had been allowed to dominate commerce: in various lists of mistakes which Bopp set down, Jews and soldiers alternate as the main cause of trouble.[78]

[75] Marvin L. Brown, *American Independence through Prussian Eyes* (Durham, NC, 1959), p. 201. Frederick's attitude to Britain and America is discussed in P. L. Haworth, 'Frederick the Great and the American Revolution', *AHR*, IX (1904), pp. 460–78, and Horst Dippel, 'Prussia's English Policy after the Seven Years War', *Central European History* IV (1971) pp. 195–214.

[76] Strieder, *Hessischen Gelehrten Geschichte*, I, p. 503, and IX, p. 353.

[77] LB Kassel, 8° Ms. hass. 16a, Fehler, Missbräuche und Verbesserungen in Hessen. The library lists the work *c.* 1776, Dippel gives it as about 1778. It appears to have been written, in part at least, after Bopp's fall from grace, which must have affected its tone. Even hostile nineteenth-century historians like Kapp and Treitschke had called Hessen one of the best administered German states.

[78] Ibid, fols. 2, 13, 18 and 79.

His basic criticism of the soldier trade was that it cost Hessen labour, consumers, and heads of families, and forced the country to support an outsize army. 'The young men: they take them all for soldiers, [so] who will carry on the farming and properly cultivate the fields?' he wrote. 'They take the apprentice lads away and send them to America.' A soldier's pay was not sufficient to enable him to support his parents, Bopp felt.[79] The people of the country were taken to be soldiers, out of all proportion to their numbers. Hessen, by sending its young men to America as soldiers, weakened the populace, lessened their consumption and their ability to produce food. Both manufactures and agriculture were hindered. Under the heading 'Cantons: Recruiting', Bopp noted, 'In Prussia they take 1 man from every 14 houses. Here in Hessen they take 1 man from 4 houses.'[80]

These criticisms are those of a practical man of government, who observed what he described first hand. They demonstrate clearly that the people and the economy were burdened with taxes and levies of men to maintain an inordinately large military establishment in a state even more militaristic than Prussia. Yet his recommendations for improvement – rationalizing state administration, providing aid for farmers, establishing factories, promoting trade, and managing the domain lands more efficiently[81] – were measures which Friedrich of Hessen undertook. The walls of Kassel were demolished to open the town for new building and trade (also having a salutary effect upon the city's health), sixteen new colonies were founded in Hessen, there was a fund to help farmers, an annual market begun at Kassel to which merchants were obliged to come, and a government porcelain factory. Friedrich declared the need for a close consolidation of the state's financial strength in his *Pensées diverses sur les Princes*, and had attempted to achieve this by combining all financial bodies under the Kriegs und Domänen-Kammer in 1760.[82] Prices were fixed to protect the consumer. The profits of the British subsidies were partly spent on Hessian textiles and metal goods for the army, a very modern way of boosting the economy. These measures were all part of the

---

[79] Referring to Hessian pay, not what they received in British service.
[80] LB Kassel, 8° Ms. hass. 16a, fols. 25, 38, 44, and 87.
[81] Ibid, fol. 96.
[82] Kurt Dülfer, 'Fürst und Verwaltung', *Hessisches Jahrbuch für Landesgeschichte*, III (1953), p. 205. The aim of bringing all finances under one body failed, however; due to conditions of war, the boards of finance in the military administration were not combined with civilian ones.

programme of an enlightened despot.[83] Bopp doubtless intended that Hessen should develop by planning as Prussia had, but the state was too small for either Bopp or the Landgraf to practice mercantilism successfully.[84] Tough soldiers were the Landgraf's best export.

Of the soldiers who went to America nearly 5,000 died or were killed in battle and over 3,000 deserted.[85] The majority of the former at least were native Hessians. This loss, and the absence of young men in America did slow Hessen's population growth, which remained considerable nevertheless. In the years 1773–81 the number of inhabitants rose from 342,000 to 383,000, an increase of roughly 12 per cent.[86] In the state of Lippe, with a similar Calvinist population, the increase in the slightly longer period 1776–88 was 24 per cent, or double Hessen's.[87]

The country did not suffer as severely as Bancroft and other historians imagined. Most of the young men who fled across the borders during recruiting time returned, as we have seen, to obtain pardons, much to the frustration of recruiting officials. Agriculture improved steadily with government aid and the introduction of the potato, while in the towns the number of bakers, shoemakers, tanners, potters, and textile workers rose steadily.[88] The economic life of the country may not have satisfied Bopp, but it was not unimpressive for a minor state. Most profitable were wool and textiles. The number of sheep in Hessen rose from 258,000 to 472,000 in the years 1773–81. In the textile centre of Bad Hersfeld trade was booming to such an extent the young weavers were able to eat roast meat and drink wine every day on their earnings.[89]

Hessen was undoubtedly better off than it had been in the Seven Years War, when not only did the army draw off young men from a land 'which is so drain'd that one sees only old people and children in the villages',[90] but the French levied tribute. During the American war more money flowed into Hessen than out of it.

[83] For the various reforms, see Both and Vogel, *Landgraf Friedrich II*, pp. 40–54.
[84] Sauer, *Finanzgeschäfte der Landgräfen*, p. 13; W. H. Bruford, *Germany in the Eighteenth Century* (Cambridge, 1935), p. 38.
[85] Appendix C.
[86] Both and Vogel, *Landgraf Friedrich II*, p. 46. StaMarburg informed me that these figures are as reliable as one can obtain for the time, no firm statistics being kept before 1793.
[87] G. Benecke, *Society and Politics in Germany 1500–1750* (London and Toronto, 1974), p. 13. More reliable figures than those for Hessen, based on census.
[88] Both and Vogel, *Landgraf Friedrich II*, p. 46. For the number of sheep, see ibid, p. 43.
[89] StaMarburg 40b, Rubr. 36, Gen. 59, Vom Wohlstand der Tuchmacher.
[90] SP87/28, fol. 134, Boyd to Holderness, 3 June 1760.

12

Conclusion

The majority of Hessian battalions passed the war in dull garrison duty punctuated by moments of intense action or marches in the burning sun. Thus the Regiment von Mirbach during seven years was in action for only forty disastrous minutes at Redbank, losing its colonel and ninety-five others killed and wounded.[1] Until the Regiment Erbprinz was besieged at Yorktown, it had sustained six wounded during the whole war. The Regiment Prinz Karl, doing little more than guard duties, had one man wounded in seven years. The Garrison Regiment von Stein (later von Seitz) passed most of the war in Halifax. The Regiments von Lossberg and von Knyphausen suffered all their battle losses in 1776. Even a regiment that served fairly actively had long periods of quiet: the Leib-Regiment was at White Plains, the capture of Rhode Island, Brandywine and Germantown, the retreat from Philadelphia, and the Elizabethtown expedition, yet one of its company commanders, Dinklage, managed to spend most of the war searching for fossils and the remains of America's Stone Age inhabitants. He noted that the long periods of boredom made his comrades long for action, but he was quite content with a good book to read.[2] Most officers, remarking on the abundance of game, used their firelocks more for hunting than battle.

Rall's old regiment was an exception.[3] Aside from its role both glorious and shameful in the 1776 campaign, its men as part of the Combined Battalion took part in the expedition against Philadelphia and the withdrawal from it.[4] After the regiment had

---

[1] LB Kassel, 4° Ms. hass. 28 (Journal of the Regiment jung-Lossberg, formerly Mirbach's), fol. 30. Other casualty figures in this section taken from T38/814, nr. 3, fol. 19, unless otherwise stated.

[2] Dinklage, fols. 120–1, 179–80, 188, and 192.

[3] With three changes of chief, it was successively called von Woellwarth, von Trumbach, and d'Angelleli.

[4] The remnants of Rall's brigade were formed into one battalion, which served in 1777 under Col. Johann August von Loos.

Conclusion

been reformed in autumn 1778, it helped Colonel Archibald Campbell capture Savannah, marched against Charleston under Major General Augustine Prevost, and defended Savannah against d'Estaing. At Stono Ferry (20 June 1779) the officers and men fought so well against Benjamin Lincoln's attacking force that they were restored to the Landgraf's 'gracious favour' and on their return to Kassel their sovereign himself presented them with new colours on the Bowling Green.[5] Attrition was severe among the battalion's senior officers: Rall died of his wounds, his successor Colonel Wolfgang Friedrich von Woellwarth succumbed to sickness on a hospital ship near Philadelphia, Lieutenant Colonel Bretthauer died in captivity and Major Matthaus of fever at Savannah. The rank and file fared no better, 136 dying of sickness and wounds in 1779 alone, of a total strength of less than 500.[6]

The *Jäger* and grenadier battalions also saw fairly constant service. Nevertheless, the trifling casualties in battle – 535 killed and 1,309 wounded – bear out Ochs' remark: 'Nowadays we would call all the battles fought in America only serious skirmishing, for we fought battles there in the same manner as we skirmished in Germany.'[7]

Morale probably suffered more during periods of inactivity, when the soldiers had time to consider their situation, than in active campaigning when survival was uppermost in their minds. The order book of Mirbach's regiment indicates that outbreaks of indiscipline – thefts, violence, destruction of property – occurred more frequently in winter-quarters, or at least that head-quarters then had more time to spare for these matters.[8] For some the strain, the harsh discipline, the boredom of a soldier's life were too much, impelling a number of poor wretches to take their own lives, including one man who led his wife and children out of New York in 1781 and shot them before killing himself.[9] Many of the unpleasant aspects of nineteenth-century industrial life – unre-

---

[5] StaMarburg 4h.411. nr. 1, fols. 144–5, Major Endemann to Knyphausen, 7 July 1779; 4h. 328. nr. 152, fol. 30, the Landgraf to Endemann, 19 Nov. 1779; CO5/182, fol. 123, Prevost to Germain, 4 Aug. 1779. There are American accounts of the battle in William Moultrie, *Memoirs of the American Revolution* (2 vols. New York, 1802), I, pp. 495–9, and Moore, *Diary of the Revolution*, II, pp. 170–2.

[6] StaMarburg 13 Acc: 1930/5 Nr. 232, fol. 7. Strength at embarkation for Georgia in November, 1778 was 471 effectives. CO5/96, fol. 211.

[7] Ochs, *Betrachtungen über die neuere Kriegskunst*, p. 23.

[8] On Orders of 19 Dec. 1778, for example, the soldiers were reprimanded for stealing cattle within the regimental canton itself. StaMarburg 12.11 I Ba 9, fol. 65.

[9] Conrod Doehla, 'The Journal of Conrad Doehla', Robert Tilden, ed., *WMQ*, 2nd series, XXII (1942), p. 232.

mitting discipline, unspeakably boring labour, shift work (guard duties), and monotonous surroundings – were already present in eighteenth-century armies. The majority of soldiers, however, adapted to their situation, building shelters against the weather, sometimes only 'caves dug in the ground',[10] planting out little gardens to supply greens,[11] keeping hens for fresh eggs, and in the better units remaining on fairly good terms with their officers. Münchhausen, visiting Trumbach's (later Bose's) regiment in quarters at Fort Knyphausen in May 1777, found that the men had built a sort of summer house on high ground with a most beautiful view for their popular major, Hilmar Borries von Münchhausen.[12] Regimental cantons often looked like villages. The officers 'ate the best oysters in North America' at New York, and maintained menageries to supply their needs. Dinklage's included two dogs, two horses, and ten hens; others had cows and sheep in their retinue, and there is no doubt that many had women.[13] Both officers and men solaced themselves with female companionship, and although recorded instances of intimate relations with American women are not numerous, many others were concealed; for the Hessians could marry only with their prince's permission, and Lossberg reported in 1783 that many had married secretly.[14] A case emerged in May, 1784, when Colonel Georg Emanuel von Lengerke asked for permission to marry the widow Elisabeth Johnson, formerly of New York, with whom he had lived for seven years and by whom he had had four children, of which two sons were still alive, whose education Lengerke asserted he would see to himself. Permission was granted.[15] The careful detail with which Friedrich von der Lith described 'bundling' indicates he enjoyed the experience on at least one occasion.[16] When the Regiment Landgraf was quartered at Bloomingdale on the Hudson in 1782, Quartermaster Bockewitz made the acquaintance of a country gentleman who sold the regiment hay, and the gentleman's house became a favourite visiting point for Bockewitz and other officers of

[10] Buettner, *Buettner der Amerikaner*, p. 86. See also LB Kassel, 8° Ms. hass. 227, Asteroth, Erinnerungen, fol. 80 (October, 1779).

[11] Krafft, *Journal*, p. 138.

[12] Münchhausen, fasc. 2, fol. 23.

[13] Dinklage, fol. 197.

[14] StaMarburg 4h.411. nr. 3, fols. 33–4, Lossberg to the Landgraf, 6 Aug 1783.

[15] Ibid, 11 Militärkabinett T 2 III Pak. 3, Lengerke to the Landgraf, 27 May 1784. The note of permission is written at the bottom of the letter.

[16] Lith, 'Feldzug der Hessen', pp. 20–1.

Conclusion

the battalion, 'partly because he had such good Madeira wine, partly but more especially because he had such lovely ladies as daughters.'[17]

One may suspect that the hospitality was not limited strictly to Madeira wine. An indication perhaps is the testimony of Barbara Rheider, the daughter of an Anabaptist of Rhode Island, who told Chaplain Cöster that an illegitimate child she bore on 17 April 1780 was the son of Lieutenant Christian Henrich Dietzel of the Hessian artillery, and that she had also had another child by Dietzel. The Hessian lieutenant had died in August 1780, but Barbara Rheider insisted on calling herself Frau Dietzel, asserting that their marriage had been celebrated before God.[18]

Lith left the best description of battalion life in a hut encampment around New York:

> I lived here in a hut built half under and half above the earth. The roof was of straw, and so dilapidated that I was often covered with snow in my bed. One single opening in the wall gave me light. I warmed my frozen limbs before a miserable fireplace, and my household goods consisted of one mean bed, a camp stool, and flask. Often we went without even bread when supplies failed. In short, this sojourn was a true school of abstinence. And in spite of this we were happy, and here I perceived that the greatest complaint is much more easily borne in fellowship than alone. The soldiers jested and laughed when they had nothing to eat; and when the rain forced itself in through their roofs and they were almost swimming in their beds, they began to steer themselves about as if they had become pilots on ships.[19]

Young George Julius von Langenscharz later wrote that he could count the years he spent at Halifax as among the happiest of his life, having enjoyed the favour of many good men, both young and old.[20] The ordinary soldiers were perhaps not so contented as this, yet their simple piety made them stoic in adversity and danger. 'My life has already been in danger many times', wrote Sergeant Major Martin Appell of Rall's to his parents in early 1777, 'and I have stood alone under fire, and have only God's Grace to thank, that I am still alive: Should my life come to its end here in America, and we should expect that I should fall before there is peace, it must not cause you grief, I am prepared to lose it in the

---

[17] StaMarburg 12.11 1 Ba 4 (Journal of the Regiment Landgraf), fol. 35.
[18] Woringer, 'Verlust im Hessen-Kasselschen Offizierkorps', *NGFKW*, v (1930), p. 147. The church records of Chaplain Cöster show that many more illegitimate children were born to soldiers than to officers. Woringer, 'Protocoll der Amtshandlungen der Feldprediger Cöster', *DAGeschBl*, xx–xxi (1920–1), pp. 280–304.
[19] Strieder, *Hessischen Gelehrten Geschichte*, xviii, p. 351.
[20] LB Kassel, 8° Ms. hass. 123, Heft 1, fol. 43.

237

hope of a better one, in which some day we shall happily see one another.'[21]

The death rate in the corps was high. Fully one quarter of those who crossed to America failed to survive, and of these only one tenth were killed in battle.[22] Colonel Osborne described the Hessian hospital as 'the Branch of their Service the worst conducted',[23] and there seems evidence of dishonesty by Lorentz, the hospital commissary, who laid out great sums on tobacco, tea, coffee, butter, claret, porter, and strong beer under the heading of medical expenses.[24] The British doctor, Robert Jackson, criticized the Hessian surgeons for failing to use 'the bark' (quinine) during fever epidemics in Georgia.[25] In actual efficiency in saving lives, however, the Hessian hospital was at least equal to the British and far better than the American.[26] Its chief doctor, August Wilhelm Eskuche, educated at Rinteln and Gottingen, was an able man whose death at Philadelphia in May 1778 was severely felt.[27] His successor, Michaelis, was also university educated, at Gottingen.[28]

It is impossible to write of the Hessian corps without mentioning the women and children who accompanied them. Friedrich II gave permission for six wives to go with each company.[29] The recruit transports took more, and a serious effort had to be made to limit the numbers.[30] They were a hardy lot, certainly not backward when it came to marauding,[31] and one at least gave birth on the Atlantic crossing in very unpleasant surroundings.[32] Nevertheless,

---

[21] Ibid, 4° Ms. hass. 293/3. Martin Appell was killed at Stono Ferry, 20 June 1779.

[22] StaMarburg 13 Acc: 1930/5 Nr. 232, fol. 2 gives 4983 total deaths of about 19,000 who crossed to America. See Appendix B. Ochs, however, who served in Spain in 1809 and Russia in 1812 wrote that, since German troops in America never lost as many as two thirds of their number, arrangements for care and victualling were proved good. *Betrachtungen über die Kriegskunst*, pp. 59–60.

[23] CO5/95, fol. 414, Osborne to Germain, 15 March 1777. The original reads 'the worse conducted'.

[24] CO5/97, fols. 54–5, Drs Mallet and Nooth to Rawdon, 19 Nov. 1778. After a close investigation, Dr Mervin Nooth ordered the Hessian hospital to be put on the same footing as the British, but with rigid controls on the purchase of medicines. Ibid, fols. 50–5 and StaMarburg 4h.411. nr. 1, fols. 218–9 and 304–8.

[25] Dr Robert Jackson, *A Treatise on the Fevers of Jamaica with some observations on the intermitting Fever of America* (London, 1791), pp. 329–30. See also Mackenzie, *Diary*, I, p. 239.

[26] The British had 118 deaths per thousand from sickness, the Germans 81.25, and the Americans 200. Louis C. Duncan, *Medical Men in the American Revolution, 1775–1783* (2nd edn, New York, 1970), p. 375.

[27] StaMarburg 4h.410. nr. 2, fol. 279, Knyphausen to the Landgraf, 23 May 1778; Strieder, *Hessischen Gelehrten Geschichte*, III, p. 482.

[28] Jungkenn 2:68, Cochenhausen to Jungkenn, 23 Aug. 1779.

[29] StaMarburg 13 Acc: 1930/5 Nr. 195, fol. 52, order to the regiments, 20 Jan. 1776.

[30] Ibid; nr. 234, fol. 4, the Landgraf to LtGen. v. Gohr, 9 Jan. 1781.

[31] *The Remembrancer for the Year 1777*, p. 154.

[32] Kipping, *The Hessian View of America*, p. 8.

Conclusion

the children were all baptised, received religious instruction, and were confirmed.[33] Educated soldiers and field chaplains did their best for their education. Valentin Asteroth of Treysa, a soldier in the Garrison Regiment von Huyn, held a school at Charleston for the children of soldiers in his regiment:

> On Rhode Island I had a boy from the regiment whom I taught: Jakob Voelcker, now a drummer in the Regiment von Benning [formerly Huyn's]. As it happened that I was in the garrison at Charleston, four young lads had grown big enough to be ready for school. I had a pleasant little room there. The Pastor said to me that I should hold a school for the children. And it began successfully on August 1, 1780. Every day in the morning from 8 until 10 or 11 o'clock. In the meantime we occupied another quarter, where a low Quaker church was right beside us, in which the benches themselves could serve as a school. I went to the man in charge of it, asked permission to hold a school there. With the greatest respect and good will, he took me straight away to the church, where I was to collect the key every Monday. My pupils were: Friedrich Voegt, George Reiss, Johann Doers, Conrad Schnack, and 2 from the town of Charleston. On September 23 I had pupils from Benning's regiment. Charlie Prensell, Martin Mann, Johannes Neumann, Henrietta Schnackin, Conrad Dinges.[34]

No doubt most of the soldiers' lads ended up like Asteroth's first pupil, as drummer boys or musketeers, and the girls often married soldiers. The wife of gunmaker Gottlieb Leopold of Rall's, for example, had come to America in 1776 as the nine-year-old daughter of a sergeant in Wutginau's regiment.[35] But not all were cut off from further education. Philipp Hunold went to America at the age of eleven with his father, a soldier in the Regiment Prinz Karl. Chaplain Schrecker continued the lad's Christian education, and he was confirmed at Newport in the winter-quarters of 1777. In 1778 Chief Surgeon Johannes Amelung took him under instruction into the Hessian hospital at New York. He showed a great inclination for medicine, but his parents were too poor to support his studies after his return to Hessen. However, 'several worthy men whose favour he had won in America, enabled him to continue his studies at the Collegium Carolinum, and after a period as a company surgeon in the former Regiment von Mirbach, he studied to be a doctor of medicine at the University of Marburg 1788–90, receiving the degree on 8 May 1790.[36]

When the Hessians crossed the Atlantic to bring the rebellious

---

[33] Max Reinhardt, 'Aus dem Tagebuch eines hess. Feldpredigers im amerikanischen Freiheitskrieg 1776–1783', *NGFKW*, XVI (1941), pp. 1–16.

[34] LB Kassel, 8° Ms. hass. 127, fols. 114–5.

[35] StaMarburg 12. nr. 8084, 'Akten betreffend Amerikaner Pensionen 1831–1833'.

[36] Strieder, *Hessischen Gelehrten Geschichte*, XVIII, pp. 242–5.

colonists back to their proper obedience,[37] the two most warlike peoples of the western world confronted each other.[38] But whereas the Americans were a fighting people because they lived in a frontier society where most of the male population was accustomed to use firearms, the Hessians were soldiers because their princes had made a lucrative business of hiring them out. Except for the *Jäger*, they did not fight as individuals. They marched and wheeled in straight lines at the orders of their officers, just as at home their lives were ordered and regulated to a high degree by an established state church, the Landgraf's civil servants, and tradition. Some have written that they were useless against the colonists, quoting in support Haldimand's reference to the Germans as 'by Nature and Education totally unfit for an American War'. But Haldimand was writing of the worst of the Brunswickers, 'only the refuse of those who accompanied General Burgoyne', and of the Anhalt-Zerbst regiment.[39] His opinion of the Hessian troops who served under him was different; when he had to return the Regiment von Knyphausen from Canada to New York he wrote to Clinton how inconvenient it was 'to part with Troops of their Merit'.[40] If German methods were so unsuited to America, Washington would scarcely have had Steuben, a Prussian, to train his continentals.

Liberals at the time in Europe believed that the enthusiasm of the Natural Man, fighting in America for his liberty, would bowl over the armies of European slaves. 'An Old Soldier' wrote in the *London Chronicle* of 1778:

In the mercenary armies of Europe, it is absolutely necessary to train up the soldiers (by the constant observance of a thousand trifling forms) to such an habit of obedience, that they may at last conceive nothing to be so difficult, or dangerous, as to disobey their officers. Without this they could never be led to action, having no attachment to the cause in which they fight; but the Americans, who fight for everything that is dear to freemen, stand in no need of so rigid a subordination; all that is requisite for them, is such confidence in their officers as may induce them to follow their directions: enthusiasm does more than supply the rest.[41]

This enthusiasm as the supposed substitute for training and discipline was little in evidence at Camden and Guilford, where the

---

[37] As Friedrich II wrote to Voltaire. Bestermann, *Voltaire's Correspondence*, XCIV, p. 121.
[38] Walter Millis, *Armies and Men* (London, 1958), p. 18 calls the colonists the greatest arms-bearing people of their time. On the Hessians, see Müller, *Sämmtliche Werke*, XIV, p. 232, and Riesbeck, *Travels through Germany*, III, p. 147.
[39] CO5/98, fols. 188 and 284, Haldimand to Clinton, 26 May and 29 August 1779.
[40] CO5/104, fol. 59, 28 September 1781.
[41] *The London Chronicle*, XLIII (1778), p. 60.

militia fired one round or none at all, before hastily decamping.[42] The militia's resolution was indeed sufficient to enable it to defend a dug-in position like Breed's Hill against the foremost of European regiments, but it did not extend to standing firm in the open against a bayonet attack. Compared to the American militia, the Hessian garrison regiments – composed of peasant boys not brought up to the constant use of firearms, but disciplined in a more formal manner, with regular officers and NCOs – were certainly inferior in fieldcraft and shooting; but no militia force, however gallant in defence or at harrying regular columns, could have pressed home the assault the Hessians did at Fort Washington. 'The courage of our troops I cannot sufficiently describe to you', wrote Captain Ries of Lossberg's of this occasion, 'and never had I thought that our young lads had so much pluck and determination.'[43]

Another military observer, contrasting the two types of soldier, wrote,

The subjects of a despotic prince being from their birth taught obedience and subordination, two essential qualities to form a good soldier, if not entirely alienated and weakened by oppression and poverty, are preferable to those of republics, unless they are animated by the enthusiastic fire of liberty; of which they are very susceptible, if conducted by an able hand, and become invincible: but if destitute of this principle, they make but indifferent soldiers, because their pretensions to liberty clash continually with that blind subordination, which constitutes the very foundation of a good army.[44]

The performance of the Americans improved in the course of the war from their deplorable beginning at Long Island, where the Hessians recorded it as no honour to defeat such men, to a battle steadiness that drew constant admiration from the mercenaries, who candidly acknowledged 'That no troops could possibly behave better than the Americans have done ... manoeuvred and engaged with a skill, steadiness and Ardor that would have done Honor to the best Veterans.'[45] Colonel Johann von Loos marked the change; in September 1776 he thought the business would be more like a hunt than a war, but after Redbank he was compelled to 'lay aside

[42] Moultrie, *Memoirs of the American Revolution*, II, p. 234; Henry Lee, *Memoirs of the War in the Southern Department of the United States* (New York, 1869), pp. 277–8.
[43] StaMarburg 13 Acc: 1930/5 Nr. 209, fol. 7, Extract Schreibens Capt. Joh: Cap: Ries, 19 Nov. 1776.
[44] *The Annual Register* (1766), p. 174, 'Reflexions on the general principles of war; and on the composition and character of the different armies in Europe. By a general officer, who served several campaigns in the Austrian Army'. (The author was Henry Lloyd.)
[45] StaMarburg 4h.413. nr. 4, fol. 19, letter of Capt. Wagner, 3 Sept. 1776; Ochs, *Betrachtungen über die Kriegskunst*, p. 30; Stevens, *Facsimiles*, XIX, nr. 1756.

the Hessian prejudices that rebels are not brave soldiers. Our losses prove that we were wrong. . .'[46] And the alacrity with which a number of Hessian soldiers accepted the American invitation to leave the ranks showed that the corps was not without the weaknesses of a despotic prince's army.

The Hessian defeats at Trenton and Redbank are cited as evidence of their total failure in America. But each army suffered disastrous and humiliating defeats. The British lost Stony Point and Paulus Hook through carelessness, and Tarleton's corps was destroyed by his own recklessness at Cowpens. The French were beaten off at St Lucia, Gates's ill-directed army routed at Camden, and the two allies failed at Savannah with losses sixteen times those of the British defenders. Although the Germans lacked the impetuosity in assault of the Light Infantry and Highlanders and the flexibility of the American militia, they were more careful in their means of security at Germantown and Paulus Hook than the British,[47] and certainly less vindictive in their treatment of American prisoners, no small cause of increasing American hostility to the King's troops.

When the Hessians first came to America, John Adams warned his countrymen, 'They are masters of rules for guarding themselves in every situation and contingency. The old officers among them are full of resources, wiles, artifices, and stratagems, to deceive, decoy, and overreach their adversaries.'[48] Despite Rall's carelessness at Trenton, contrary to the advice of his own subordinates and of Donop, the Hessians generally demonstrated skill in their trade. Ambrose Serle recorded,

One Observation, made by Hessian officers in Battle, is worth remembering. They watch steadily the Arms of the Enemy. If they see them moved & waving much about in the Ranks, they are sure the men who bear them are dismayed & without Courage, and that a vigorous Attack will break them. This remark is well founded in nature. I myself can justify the Truth of it; for when the Rebels were drawn up to oppose our Troops both on Long Island & Fort Washington, I well remember to have seen this Tremulation of the Arms among them, and that they did not hold them steadily. The Consequence was, they ran as soon as they were attacked.[49]

Henry Lee reported of his capture of Paulus Hook, achieved while

---

[46] Kipping, *The Hessian View of America*, p. 21.
[47] Ewald, *Belehrungen*, II, pp. 32–3; Münchhausen, fasc. 4, fols. 53–5, note 30; 'Tagebuch des Capt. Wiederholdt', pp. 68–9. For Germantown, see above, p. 136.
[48] Quoted in Alfred Hoyt Bill, *The Campaign of Princeton 1776–1777* (Princeton, NJ, 1948) pp. 16–17.
[49] Serle, *Journal*, pp. 220–1. The comments were made by Col. Sir George Osborne.

the bulk of the garrison, Buskirk's Loyalists, were absent, 'A company of vigilant Hessians had taken their place in the fort, which rendered the secrecy of the approach more precarious, and at the same time diminished the object of the enterprise by a reduction of the number of the garrison.'[50] The only part of the garrison Lee failed to capture was this company of Hessians; of the troops he took, the only ones to wake in time to resist and thus give the alarm was a party under Sergeant Hepe of the Regiment Erbprinz.[51] At the attack on Savannah by Lincoln and D'Estaing, it was Lieutenant Colonel Friedrich von Porbeck of Wissenbach's who recommended to Prevost that a sortie be made at the critical moment, helping to frustrate the attackers.[52]

The Hessians had two distinct weaknesses. The first of these was their undoubted slowness in attack.[53] Despite Heister's optimistic report to Friedrich II at the end of the 1776 campaign,[54] the close Prussian order was not the best way to close with a mobile enemy. Lieutenant Hale of the 45th wrote:

the Hessians, who are allowed to be the best of the German troops, are by no means equal to the British in any respect. I believe them steady, but their slowness is of the greatest disadvantage in a country almost covered with woods, and against an Enemy whose chief qualification is agility in running from fence to fence and thence keeping up an irregular but galling fire on troops who advance with the same pace as at their exercise. . . . At Brandywine when the first line formed, the Hessian Grenadiers were close in on our rear, and began beating their march at the same time with us; from that moment we saw them no more till the action was over, and only one man of them was wounded by a random shot which came over us.[55]

This is borne out by the account of Captain Max O'Reilly, who claimed to have manoeuvred the Lengerke battalion up on the flank of the first line of British grenadiers just as the firing began, 'but those devils of English opened such a hot fire on the enemy and attacked them with the bayonet in such a lively manner, that the rebels thereupon fled before we could get into action'.[56] Lengerke's men clearly could not keep pace.

Similar was the fight outside Savannah in December 1778. The

[50] *New Jersey Archives*, 2nd series, III, pp. 627–8.
[51] StaMarburg 4h.411. nr. 1, fols. 142–3, Report of Capt. von Schallern.
[52] Ibid, 12.11 I Ba 3 (Journal of the Grenadier Regiment von Bischhausen), fol. 40, 9 October 1779. Prevost commended Porbeck in his official dispatch, but did not state specifically how the Hessian was able 'to signalize himself in a most gallant manner'.
[53] Not to be confused with general slowness throughout the campaigns as Howe charged them with.
[54] See Above, p. 82.
[55] Wilkin, *Some British Soldiers*, p. 245.
[56] Schweinburg, 'Briefe eines hessischen Offiziers', *Hessenland*, XVI (1902), p. 308.

flanking movement of the active light infantry and the Highland charge of the 71st, far more than the steady advance of Woell-warth's regiment with closed ranks, routed Major General Robert Howe's continentals and militia. Lieutenant Colonel Archibald Campbell reported, 'I commanded the line to move briskly for-ward: the well directed Artillery of the line, the rapid advance of the 71st Regiment, and the forward Countenance of the Hessian Regiment of Wellworth, instantly dispersed the enemy.'[57]

This shortcoming was appreciated by the Hessians for, in April 1781, Knyphausen wrote to the Landgraf suggesting a more open order with space between each man in the ranks and his neigh-bour. 'I have found through experience that this method is of benefit here, for our troops, when they are fully closed up, are not able to march in line with the English, but lose thirty paces in every hundred.' He recommended immediate use of the new open order, both for tactical movements as well as exercising the regi-ments.[58] With pedantic insistence on form, Friedrich II, whose military theory was limited to the evolutions of his Guards on the drill square at Kassel, replied that the established method was to be observed on all occasions 'because the whole force of the infantry and of every attack obtains solely from good order with fully closed up ranks and lines'.[59]

The second failing was a ceiling on the abilities of the Hessian officers, Knyphausen alone probably excepted. Lieutenant Piel's comment on Rall, that he was made to be a soldier, but not a general,[60] applies through the corps. No great leader emerged among the Hessians during the war. Donop, Scheffer, Friedrich von Wurmb, du Buy, Minnigerode, and Rall were all able enough as battalion commanders. Those with responsibilities above that level were out of their depth, as witness Rall and Donop in December 1776, and then Donop again at Redbank. O'Reilly, Stamford, Philip von Wurmb, Altenbockum, and others were first-rate company commanders. Ludwig von Wurmb, Wreden,

---

[57] CO5/182, fol. 33, Campbell to Germain, 16 Jan. 1779. Whatever 'forward countenance' may mean, it is not a brisk advance. A Scots officer, however, flattering the Hessians, lauded Woellwarth's battalion to Baurmeister. Baurmeister *Journals*, pp. 253–4.

[58] StaMarburg 4h.411. nr. 2, fols. 89–90, 30 April 1781.

[59] StaMarburg 4h.411. nr. 2, fol. 140, 13 Sept. 1781. It does appear, however, that the Hessians in America did become quicker than other German armies. Cornwallis reported of the Prussians in 1785, 'the infantry is exactly like the Hessians, only taller and better set up, but much slower in their movements'. Yet Hessian drill before they left for America was essentially that of the Prussians. Charles Ross, ed., *Correspondence of Charles, First Marquis Cornwallis* (3 vols. London, 1859), I, p. 205.

[60] LB Kassel, 4° Ms. hass. 188, fol. 26.

Hinrichs, and especially Ewald were outstanding leaders of light troops. Knyphausen was universally esteemed, but more for loyal competence as a divisional commander and his good personal relations than for any particular genius. His only expedition as an independent commander was an embarrassing failure.[61]

The historic role of the Hessians as a mercenary contingent hindered the emergence of a great general. A Marlborough or Frederick was unlikely to appear in a corps which always served as subordinate auxiliaries in a larger army. Although Knyphausen took part in Clinton's councils of war, there is no indication he helped to form strategy. Heister was scarcely consulted. The Hessians merely carried out their paymasters' orders. For that, good battalion and company officers were required, not men of independent genius.[62]

DEBITS AND CREDITS

When the Hessians returned from an arduous and unsuccessful war, many doubtless felt as Riedesel did when he wrote to Haldimand, 'rien que l'attachement et reconnaissance m'empêche d'aller sur le Vogelsberg planter mes choux, et de recapituler à mon aise le temps passé'.[63] As participants, and then more and more as mere observers, they learned in America lessons to take back to Europe. When the nations of Europe went to war again in 1792, by common consent the Hessians were the best soldiers. Even French prisoners at Mainz praised them as decidedly the best troops.[64] A Prussian officer noted Hessian skill and experience as a reproach to his own army:

the warlike spirit of this very small people, who brought out a whole host of gallant warriors under arms with remarkable speed and almost single-handed contributed to throw back these latest French expeditions to their own borders, was gained in that very practical school of war [America]. The talents of the higher ranking officers had also developed there. We must answer for the fact that in any situation in the face of the enemy, the Hessian officers knew more of the

[61] It scarcely requires saying that the officers were personally brave. I have discovered only one case of cowardice in the face of the enemy in six campaigns: Ensign Werner of Rall's who abandoned his piquet near Monmouth on 27 June 1778. He was cashiered *mit infame*. Krafft, *Journal*, p. 46; StaMarburg 12.11 1 Ba 3 (Journal of the Grenadier Regiment von Bischhausen), fol. 64.

[62] It was unfortunate for the Hessians that the only men who did show any spark of genius – Ewald, Bernhard Wilhelm Wiederholdt, and Adam Ludwig Ochs – were junior in rank.

[63] Add. MS. 21812, fol. 176, 21 March 1784.

[64] Charles Este, *A Journey in the Year 1793 through Flanders, Brabant and Germany to Switzerland* (London, 1795), p. 272.

business than ours did. Whether it was a piquet to be posted, a patrol to be briefed, or a decision to be fixed upon at an unexpected occurrence, we could make use of the sure skill in war which these gallant people had acquired in all quarters of the world, while our peaceful Europe had denied to us both education and training, or indeed had allowed both to stray into ways of error.[65]

It is remarkable, considering the enormous public debate over the mercenaries in Germany in the years following 1776, how little war-making had changed by 1792–3. In 1787 the younger Pitt concluded an old style subsidy treaty with Landgraf Wilhelm IX, paying as Walpole had done before an annual retainer for first call on the Hessians' services.[66] Burke, an opponent of the American war, supported the treaty in the Commons.[67] The usual pledge of mutual aid and friendship was included, and the opposition raised the bugbear of having to come to Hessen's aid. The only noteworthy variant in the new treaty, a sop to public opinion, Article XIII made a specific point of substituting twelve crowns for each man furnished instead of a sum paid for each man killed or three wounded, 'what was formerly paid for recruiting'. The treaty of 1793 under which the Hessians served with the British in Flanders had similar clauses: a subsidy of 225,000 crowns was paid to take 8,000 men into service (later increased to 12,000). The British also hired 3,000 Hessen-Darmstadt troops and 754 from the Margrave of Baden, and took 18,000 Hannoverians into their pay.[68]

Taking a leaf from the Americans' copybook, the French republicans appealed to the Hessians to leave the colours and join the new brotherhood of man. General Custine's proclamation *An die hessen-casselschen Soldaten* invited them, as the Landgraf had sold their blood, to desert. Hessian captives were once again pressured either by neglect or by promises (or again, by offers of marriage) to renounce their allegiance to 'the seller of souls'. Over three hundred died from hunger and illness as prisoners, while only seventy married and settled in France. As in the American war, it was long-serving NCOs, particularly a Sergeant Major Schneider of the Regiment Erbprinz, who fought against these blandishments.[69]

However, as a more radical republic the French nation was able to go one better than the Americans in their stories of bloodthirsty

[65] George Wilhelm, Freiherr von Valentini, *Erinnerungen eines alten preussischen Officers aus den Feldzugen 1792, 1793, und 1794 in Frankreich und am Rhein* (Glogau and Leipzig, 1833), p. 17.
[66] *Journals of the Commons*, XLIII, pp. 9–12.
[67] *Parliamentary History*, XXVI, pp. 1273–5.
[68] *Journals of the Commons*, XLVIII, pp. 940–2 and XLIX, p. 67.
[69] Ditfurth, *Die Hessen in der Champagne*, pp. 430–7.

Conclusion

Hessians. On 18 December 1792 *Le Moniteur* reported: 'A fact which will cause horror, but which is most certain, is that the Landgraf of Hessen has promised 12 francs to each Hessian soldier who brings him the head of a Frenchman, and 24 livres for those who bring him a living one. For what torment does this monster reserve those prisoners?'[70]

In the interval between the wars the Hessians made tactical innovations: the infantry pace was increased from 75 to 108 paces in the minute, a light infantry battalion was formed to support the *Jäger* as the grenadiers had done in the first two American campaigns, both of these units commanded by former Hanau officers who had served in America, Lentz and Creutzbourg. However, the troops retained the traditional line three ranks deep, two ranks being unsuitable for European battlefields. The infantry manuals of 1796 and 1802 were written mainly by American veterans, Bernhard Wiederholdt and Ochs.[71] The Prussians used the Hessian *Reglement* of 1802 as a basis for their later reforms. Hessian regiments in 1802 included 120 sharpshooters among their 1,440 privates; grenadiers were also to make efforts to learn to shoot well and fight as individuals.[72]

The Hessian *Jäger* were exceptionally mobile, carrying the minimum of kit. Their most important lesson acquired in America was the individual use of cover. At the siege of Frankfurt in 1792 *Jäger* and fusiliers made use of walls and garden houses surrounding the city to escape the fire of French *tirailleurs* while providing fire cover for the advance of the regular columns against the city gates. One column was led by Bernhard Wiederholdt, former ensign of the Leib-Regiment, who was awarded the order *Pour le mérite* from the Prussian King for his part in the capture of the city.[73]

The tactics of the Hessian *Jäger* were ahead of those of both the French and other allies. In April 1793 the Prussian Prince of Hohenlohe observed with astonishment the successful attack of a Hessian *Jäger* company, and afterwards congratulated the men. 'Each one had without orders taken the utmost advantage of even

[70] Ditfurth, *Die Hessen in der Champagne*, p. 437.
[71] Strieder, *Hessischen Gelehrten Geschichte*, XVIII, p. 39; Paret, *Yorck and Prussian Reform*, p. 83.
[72] *Militär-Reglement für die Infanterie* (2 vols. Kassel, 1802), I, pp. 4 and 11.
[73] Georg Wilhelm Freiherr von Valentini, *Erinnerungen eines alten Preussischen Officiers aus den Feldzügen 1792, 1793 und 1794 in Frankreich und am Rhein* (Glogau and Leipzig, 1833), p. 22; Ditfurth, *Kurhessische Leibgarde-Regiment*, p. 56; Strieder, *Hessischen Gelehrten Geschichte*, XVII, p. 37.

the smallest feature of terrain, something he had never seen before, indeed never believed possible.'[74]

In August of the same year the *Jäger* and Lentz's light infantry battalion assaulted a French entrenchment using their new tactics. Aided by an Austrian *Freikorps*, the *Jäger* advanced to left and right of the main road in groups of skirmishers, using cover and shooting back as they came under grapeshot fire from the French. The Lentz battalion followed in close order, with two additional companies in column as reserve, firing the regimental guns and small arms. The French troops defended their position in the traditional manner, firing unaimed volleys. They could not maintain their position against the fire tactics of the *Jäger*, and were driven back when Lentz's troops attacked with the bayonet, leaving a hundred dead, a hundred captives, and five guns.[75]

At Oost Kapelle in Flanders, Ochs, now a captain-lieutenant, led his *Jäger* company in an unexpected attack upon the enemy's rear, thereby greatly facilitating the capture of an important post, and taking three guns with several ammunition carts himself. When his colonel was incapacitated, Ochs took the *Jäger* battalion in that September (1793): 'I ... now had the opportunity to employ the skills gained in Amerika in the previous war in the outpost duties. A command in the outposts out of all proportion to my rank was constantly entrusted to me; I had, besides the *Jäger*, several Imperial and other light troops under my orders, and was commissioned to attend to secret reports on the Duke of York's flank of the army.'[76]

As Ochs wrote later, the failure of the allied campaigns of 1792–5 against revolutionary France was due to no lack of 'pluck and tactical skill' [*Muth und Taktik*] on the part of the Hessians. Rather, it was the lack of a cohesive strategy and common aims which frittered away any advantages won locally by skill and courage.[77]

There is no denying that in military prowess, Hessen-Kassel profited by participation in the American war. But were the results as a whole beneficial? Liberals, pointing to the inevitable suffering borne by the populace in the absence of so many young men, have

[74] Ditfurth, *Die Hessen in der Champagne*, p. 318.
[75] Ibid., pp. 329–33. Both these actions are described in Paret, *Yorck and Prussian Reform*, pp. 70–1, pointing out their tactical significance.
[76] Och's own account, quoted in Strieder, *Hessischen Gelehrten Geschichte*, XVIII, p. 423.
[77] Ochs, *Betrachtungen über die Kriegskunst*, pp. 71 and 77.

Conclusion

not hesitated to answer in the negative. German nationalists like Kapp and Treitschke were indignant that Germany's military capacities were employed in a cause not her own. Contemporary sources are not so clear cut. Du Ry, the architect, thought Hessen had profited. To Erasmus Ritter he wrote:

Our battalions which have served in America are progressively arriving here. . . . Several officers and likewise a number of soldiers have made their fortunes in money in America, and return more or less laden with guineas, others have taken the pains to have passed on to their families sufficiently large sums during the 7 years which the war has lasted, fruits of the savings which they have made, perhaps also booty which they have taken in the little war; a good number of people claim that, without counting the subsidies of the Landgraf, Hessen has gained about a million crowns in the American war.[78]

This is supported by Ewald's assertion that no army in the world was paid so well as the British and their auxiliaries in America, that married subaltern officers who managed their affairs well could generously support the families they had left behind and yet still live handsomely in America; and that the majority of company chiefs, field officers, and generals had made considerable sums.[79]

Financial success was not equally shared among the officers. After the war, Schlieffen, who never went to America, and Knyphausen both drew annual pensions of £300 from the British Crown, good money by Hessian standards.[80] The officers and men of the Regiment Prinz Karl did well out of prize money from Major General Mathew's Virginia expedition of May 1779. Shares varied from Colonel Schreiber's £1166 13s 4d and £700 for his second-in-command, to £87 10s for an ensign and £3 3s 2½d for each private soldier.[81] Captain Wreden ran a faro bank at Philadelphia, 'which has not a little disordered the finances of several officers who have been imprudent enough to endeavour at carrying away two thousand guineas' reported Lieutenant Hale of the 45th. Ewald noted that Wreden and his associates won

---

[78] Burgerbibliothek Bern, Ms. hist. helv. xxv 71, Erasmus Ritter Nachlass, S. L. du Ry to Ritter, 4 Nov. 1783.

[79] Ewald, 'Tagebuch', II, p. 4 (early 1778), quoted in Kipping, *Hessen-Kassel Truppen*, p. 51.

[80] Kapp, *Soldatenhandel*, p. 214; StaMarburg 4h.411. nr. 1, fol. 85, Knyphausen to the Landgraf, 3 May 1779. They continued, of course, to draw their other emoluments as company chiefs etc.

[81] StaMarburg 4h.412. nr. 2 (Journal of the Regiment Prinz Karl), fol. 10. Knyphausen gave slightly higher figures of £2,000 for Schreiber and £5 6s 6½d for each private. Ibid., 4h.411. nr. 1, fol. 214.

249

£100,000. This prompted Wreden to seek his discharge, and the King's army lost one of its ablest leaders of light troops.[82]

The majority of officers, however, did not do so well. Knyphausen reported to his sovereign in May 1778 that, even with generous British allowances of forage money, prices were so high that the captains and subalterns were all falling into debt.[83] Shortly before embarkation, his successor, Lossberg, wrote that, despite all warnings, many of the officers had contracted debts. He withheld payment of forage money to those who could not settle their accounts.[84] Even after the return to Germany, these debts kept cropping up. Lieutenant General Anton von Lossberg reported that the officers of his regiment returned from Canada to Rinteln owed money to the Quartermaster of the Anhalt-Zerbst Regiment.[85] Officers' complaints of high prices are legion in their journals. Some of those who had to live off their pay, not organizing their finances as well as Ewald, had nothing left. Company chiefs, instead of making a tidy little profit from 'off-reckonings' of kit and clothing allowances, had to dip into their own funds to pay for repairs and replacement. Each company chief received an annual allowance for *kleine Montirungs-Stücken* (shirts, socks, shoes) as well as money to maintain weapons, drums, and leather articles. As in the British army, he received this sum for each man in his company plus a number of fictitious men. Thus if he were careful with his holdings, he could make a profit each year. Due to the arduous campaigning and wear and tear on the kit, with high prices, it does not appear they made such a profit in America.[86]

Of the common soldiers, it is more difficult to speak with certainty. Even those who made money might have asserted that their savings in no way made up for the seven year absence from homes and families. However Schlieffen reported to Friedrich II in December 1779, when the latter was considering terminating the treaty and bringing his corps back to Germany, that the soldiers

---

[82] Wilkin, *Some British Soldiers*, p. 240; Kipping, *Hessen-Kassel Truppen*, p. 60 n.13. Ewald wrote this comment in the margin of his copy of Stedman's *History*. Wreden subsequently entered Hessen-Darmstadt service, and died there as a colonel in 1791. Schwank, 'Hessische Offiziere', *Hessenland*, II (1888), p. 99.

[83] StaMarburg 4h.410. nr. 2, fols. 204–5, 23 March 1778.

[84] Ibid., 4h.411. nr. 3, fols. 33–4, 6 Aug. 1778; Krafft, *Journal*, p. 184

[85] Ibid., 11 Militärkabinet T 2 III Pak. 3, Lossberg to the Landgraf, 3 June 1785.

[86] StaMarburg 4h.413. nr. 4, fol. 87, letter of Captain Wagner, 29 May 1777; 4h.411. nr. 2, fols. 88–9, Knyphausen to the Landgraf, 30 April 1781; T38/814, nr. 7, bill for kit damaged in transit; especially, Joachim Fischer, *Eisern Gespartes 1776 bis 1783 aus Amerika* (Sonderdruck: Veröffentlichungen der Historischen Kommission für Hessen 40. Marburg, 1979.)

Conclusion

had already sent back 591,721 talers via the *Kriegskasse* and the country was profiting by this.[87] It is also possible that other sums were sent home with returning officers. Schubart in his *Deutsche Chronik* reported in 1777 that large amounts had been sent back by the Hessian soldiers.[88] Besides the good wages, soldiers were also paid for gathering firewood and some ran illicit refreshment stalls in the garrisons.[89] A number of soldiers and their wives, probably relatively few, brought back far greater wealth than they could have acquired in Germany. As evidence we have the testimony of Stephen Popp, a Bayreuth soldier, that on 8 October 1783 at Bremerlehe, one of the soldiers' wives carrying 400 Spanish dollars fell into the water and was drowned.[90]

However much the financial success of his subjects varied, the Landgraf himself did very well out of the treaty. By the best reckoning available, his profits after all expenses were 12,650,000 talers.[91] Calculating the pound sterling at five and a half talers, this is perhaps eight times what Clive of India brought back from Bengal. A modern democracy would doubtless have spent such sums on education and social services. That the Landgraf disbursed much of this money on conspicuous consumption was only to be expected by the standards of the time. Nevertheless, much of Friedrich's expenditure was beneficial to his country. He founded sixteen new villages, as agricultural colonies, each of ten families; each settler receiving thirty acres and 300 talers for building, a loan of 100 talers to purchase livestock, and three years' exemption from taxes and military service.[92] The old fortifications of Kassel were demolished, and modern buildings raised and squares and parks laid out to make the residence the rival of Weimar, Hannover, and Stuttgart.[93] Among Friedrich's accounts appear the following items:[94]

---

[87] Friedrich Kapp, 'Friedrich II und die neuere Geschichtsschreibung', *Historische Zeitschrift*, XLII (1879, nr. 2), pp. 321–2.

[88] Losch, *Soldatenhandel*, p. 26 n. 29.

[89] Krafft, *Journal* pp. 157–9, 163, 172, and 175; James Pattison, *Official Letters of Major General James Pattison* (Collections of the New York Historical Society for the Year 1875. New York, 1876), p. 398.

[90] Stephen Popp, 'Popp's Journal, 1777–1783', J. G. Rosengarten, ed., *PMHB*, XXVI (1902), p. 254.

[91] Sauer, *Finänzgeschäfte der Landgräfen*, pp. 31–2.

[92] Both and Vogel, *Landgraf Friedrich II*, p. 43.

[93] Georg Sante, *Hessen* (Handbuch der Historischen Städten Deutschlands, vol. IV. Stuttgart, 1960), p. 240.

[94] StaMarburg 6b, 254, Acta die zugestandene Einsicht der Landstände in die Kriegs- und Oberrathkammercasse-Rechnungen ... (1815).

251

The Hessians

For laying out agricultural colonies   58,544 talers
For completing the Foundling Hospital   2,000 talers
To establish the colony *Philippinenhof*   8,532 talers
For transporting the library of the *Museum Friedericianum*
                                                                         1,000 talers
For fully establishing the *Lyceum Friedericianum*   5,078 talers
For buying a house for a garrison hospital   3,800 talers
For establishing a women's foundation   20,000 talers

There was also a remission of taxes to the amount of 2,170,140 talers, and pensions for widows of officers who died in America. In 1784 pensions to officers, widows, and various other persons for services rendered totalled 56,633 talers 26 albus 8 heller. Among those who benefited from the profits of the soldier trade was Voltaire who in 1777 received 324 talers 17 albus 5 heller under 'extraordinaries by gracious command'.[95] In addition, the Landgraf's officials who administered the funds of the Karlshafen Military Hospital began to lend money at 4 or 5 per cent. Throughout the 1760s this business was extended by using the holdings of the military treasury (*Kriegskasse*), first to private individuals and then to other princes. The success of this business and the British subsidies made the Landgraf independent of the Hessian parliament, the Landstände, so that at the death of Friedrich II in 1785 his son inherited an absolutism and a capital holding of nearly 10 million talers.[96] Wilhelm IX became a princely banker, lending throughout Europe, aiding the rise of the Rothschilds, and amassing an enormous treasure.[97] This most considerable memorial to the soldier trade of the Hessian princes lasted until the inflation that followed World War I, when the 39.5 million marks of the Hessen-Nassau treasury fell in real value to the equivalent of some 742,000.[98]

After that only the palaces and private houses of the generals and artists of the Landgraf's court, in the upper town above the Fulda, built in part on the lucrative profits of subsidy treaties, served to remind the people of Kassel of the *Blutgeld*. But that reminder of the unique Hessian vocation was not to survive either. On the night of 22 October 1943, massive air raids shattered the

[95] Kapp, 'Friedrich II und die neuere Geschichtsschreibung', p. 327; StaMarburg 12. nr. 8312, Kriegspfennigzahlamt (1777), fol. 489 and 12. nr. 8319 (1784), fol. 327.
[96] Sauer, *Finanzgeschäfte der Landgräfen*, pp. 23–6, 29–30, 45, passim.
[97] Count Egon Corti, *The Rise of the House of Rothschild* (London, 1928), pp. 19–31.
[98] Losch, *Soldatenhandel*, p. 59.

Conclusion

centre of Kassel, destroying the marble and stucco buildings. There is a certain grim irony, that the bombs were dropped by descendants of the men with whom the Hessians had stood winter vigil on the banks of the Delaware. Only Wilhelm IX's palace at Wilhelmshöhe, the former Weissenstein, with its magnificent collection of Renaissance paintings and antique sculpture, gathered by his father and grandfather, remains as proof of the Hessians' prowess at enriching the coffers of their princes.

APPENDIX A
Hessians mustered into British service 1776–82

1st division, Bremerlehe, 12 April 1776	8,647[1]
2nd division, Ritzbüttel, 6 June 1776	4,327[2]
Jäger, Bremerlehe, 26 March 1777	352[3]
Recruits and *Jäger*, Dordrecht, 12 April 1777	497[4]
Recruits and *Jäger*, Bremerlehe, 27 May 1777	604[5]
Recruits and *Jäger*, Bremerlehe, 10 December 1777	398[6]
Recruits, Bremerlehe, 5 April 1778	283[7]
Recruits, Bremerlehe, 2 May 1779	960[8]
Recruits, Bremerlehe, 1 June 1780	931[9]
Recruits, Bremerlehe, 26 April 1781	937[10]
Recruits, Bremerlehe, 31 May 1782	1,034[11]
Total	18,970

[1] SP81/183; StaMarburg 4h.410. nr. 1, fol. 157.
[2] SP81/185.
[3] C05/140, fol. 109.
[4] Ibid, fol. 91.
[5] Ibid, fol. 159.
[6] Ibid, fol. 264.
[7] C05/141, fol. 58.
[8] C05/142, fol. 103.
[9] C05/143, fol. 93.
[10] C05/144, fols. 60 and 74.
[11] SP81/195. There is some variation between Faucitt's returns and those of Hannoverian officers in StaHannover, depending upon dates. To be consistent, I have used Faucitt's returns, which do not include men whom he rejected. The returns in C05 are copies of those in SP81, but since the latter have unnumbered folios, I have cited the former wherever possible.

APPENDIX B
Hessian casualties in America

	Killed[1]	Wounded[1]	Captured[2]	Dead from all causes[3]
1776	168	426	1,012	516
1777	180	346	341	1,477
1778	26	98	41	368
1779	14	64	242	560
1780	42	175	30	721
1781	104	198	936	496
1782	1	2	26	447
1783	—	—	—	355
1784	—	—	—	43
Total	535	1,309	2,628	4,983

[1] T38/814, nr. 3, fol. 19. This list of killed and wounded, signed by Knyphausen and Lossberg on 10 June 1788, gives a higher number of killed than StaMarburg 13 Acc: 1930/5 Nr. 232, fol. 2, which shows only 357. By comparison with casualty figures in journals for various actions, I find the PRO figure more accurate. The Marburg return of 71 killed in 1776, for example, is exceeded by combined dead at Trenton and Ft. Washington alone.

[2] Again the Marburg return is misleading, giving 8,029 prisoners, nearly 50 per cent of total strength. This is caused by prisoners, taken one year and still captive the next, being shown twice in the return. Thus those of the regiments of Knyphausen and Lossberg, taken at Trenton, are recorded for three consecutive years, those of Rall's for two, 1776 and 1778. The Regiment Erbprinz is shown as having 400 or more prisoners for years 1781–3 inclusive, when the number should be reckoned only once. My estimate is based on the Marburg return corrected by figures in various journals.

[3] This figure is obtained by adding together the columns *Todtgeschossen* and *Gestorben* in Marburg, assuming that the larger number of killed in the PRO return is included within the two.

The following battalions record the largest totals of killed and wounded: Linsing's 169, Minnigerode's 162, Bose's 150, Rall's 138.

APPENDIX C
Calculation of total Hessians remaining in America

Mustered into British service	18,970[1]
Killed and died	4,982[2]
Settled in Nova Scotia	190[3]
Returned during the war	292[4]
Returned in 1783–4	10,492[5]
Total accounted for	15,956
Total remaining	3,014

[1] Appendix A.

[2] StaMarburg 13 A 6 Nr. 232, fol. 2.

[3] The Carleton papers and Hessian correspondence list the number of officers given permission to settle in Nova Scotia, but not the rank and file. Even by comparing names of 'Loyalist' settlers in the article, Marion Gilroy, 'Loyalists and Land Settlement in Nova Scotia', *Public Archives of Nova Scotia*, publication nr. 4 (Halifax, 1937) with those on Hessian muster lists, I was unable to calculate the number of Hessian soldiers settled in Nova Scotia, particularly because of Anglicization of names. I therefore used a simple expedient. Of Platte's grenadier battalion 2 officers and 17 other ranks were permitted to settle. I calculated the number of other ranks in the proportion of eight and a half to one, to the 19 officers and one chaplain who went to Nova Scotia.

The question is further complicated by some officers like Henckelmann first transferring into Loyalist units and then obtaining land. Others later moved to the United States or, like Henckelmann, returned to Germany. There is some information on German auxiliaries who settled, in Maxwell Sutherland, 'Case History of a Settlement', *The Dalhousie Review*, XLI (Spring, 1961), 65–74. The settlement in Ontario's Eastern Townships discussed in Alexander Smith, 'Some Hessians of the U.E.L. Settlement in Marysburgh', *Ontario Historical Society*, paper nr. 21 (1924), 259–61, included only Brunswickers, not Hessians.

[4] Based on references in dispatches to returning groups or individuals. For each officer I have added one servant.

[5] StaHannover 41 V Nr. 39, fols. 3–4, 249–50.

APPENDIX D
German auxiliaries as a proportion of British strength in America[1]

RANK AND FILE, EFFECTIVES, 23 MAY 1778[2]

Philadelphia	11,432 British	4,829 Germans	1,240 Provincials
New York	3,246	3,482	3,267
Rhode Island	1,521	2,111	82
Total	16,199	10,422	4,589

RANK AND FILE, EFFECTIVES, 25 OCTOBER 1778/1 JANUARY 1779[3]

New York	8,045 British	7,076 Germans	2,750 Provincials
Rhode Island	2,538	3,305	738
Halifax	2,848	502	550
Florida and Georgia	3,751	1,791	2,333
Total	17,182	12,674	6,371

RANK AND FILE, EFFECTIVES, 1 MAY 1780[4]

New York	7,094 British	6,451 Germans	2,004 Provincials
South Carolina	6,442	2,593	2,534
Georgia	—	790	905
East and West Florida	972	504	289
Total	14,508	10,338	5,732

RANK AND FILE, FIT FOR DUTY, 1 SEPTEMBER 1781[5]

New York	4,577 British	7,437 Germans	1,316 Provincials
Virginia	3,990	1,783	708
South Carolina	3,886	1,379	1,983
Georgia and East Florida	485	359	276
Halifax	1,590	497	959
Total	14,528	11,455	5,242

GERMAN AUXILIARIES AS A PERCENTAGE OF THE WHOLE

1778: 33   1779: 33   1780: 34   1781: 37

[1] Note including troops in Canada or the 'Convention army'. [2] C05/96, fol. 19.
[3] C05/171, fol. 55. The British returns are dated 1 Jan. 1779, except that for Florida & Georgia, dated 1 Nov. 1778. German & Provincial returns are dated 25 Oct. 1778. [4] C05/99 fol. 254.
[5] C. T. Atkinson, 'British Forces in North America, 1774–1781: their Distribution and Strength', *Journal of the Society for Army Historical Research*, XVI (1937), pp. 22–3.

APPENDIX E

——————

	Chief	Commanding officer
Linsing's Grenadier Battalion (Grenadier Companies of 2nd and 3rd Battalions of the Guards, the Leib-Regiment and Mirbach's)	LtCol (later Col) Otto Christian Wilhelm von Linsing	Linsing
Block's/Lengerke's Grenadier Battalion (Grenadier Companies of Prinz Karl's, Wutginau's, Donop's and Trumbach's)	LtCol Justus Henrich von Block (until 1 April 1777)	Block
	LtCol Georg Emanuel Lengerke	Lengerke
Minnigerode's/Loewenstein's Grenadier Battalion (Grenadier Companies of the Erbprinz's, Ditfurth's, Lossberg's, Knyphausen's)	LtCol (Later Col) Friedrich Ludwig von Minnigerode (until 16 October 1779)	Minnigerode
	LtCol Wilhelm von Loewenstein	Loewenstein
Koehler's/Graf's/Platte's Grenadier Battalion (Companies of Rall's Wissenbach's, Bunau's, Stein's)	LtCol Johann Christoph Koehler (until 27 January 1779)	Koehler

258

Hessian battalions and Jägercorps *serving in America*

Garrison locations and battles

The first three grenadier battalions were brigaded together under Col Karl von Donop until the latter's death at Redbank; subsequently all four were brigaded under Colonel Kospoth.

The first three served at Long Island, White Plains, New Jersey 1776–7, Brandywine, Germantown, Redbank, Philadelphia 1777–8, Monmouth, and then at New York 1778–83 during which period they were on a number of expeditions, notably Clinton's against Charleston in March–May 1780.
Minnigerode's battalion distinguished itself particularly at Metuchen Court House (25 June 1777).

Koehler's battalion landed with the second division, served at Fort Washington and in the New Jersey campaign 1777, and after August 1778 served with the combined grenadier brigade, mainly at New York.

Diarists and correspondents

None

Regimental Journal by (?) Quartermaster Spangenberg

Captain Max O'Reilly

Quartermaster S. A. Ungar
Grenadier Johann Buettner
Captain Karl Ludwig von Dörnberg

Quartermaster Carl Bauer

259

	Major (later LtCol) Wilhelm Graf (until 23 September 1781)	Graf
	Major (later LtCol) Friedrich Platte	Platte
Leib-Regiment (The Prince's Own)	The Landgraf (On 23 March 1783 transferred to the Erbprinz Wilhelm, Count of Hanau, the Landgraf's son)	Col Friedrich Wilhelm von Wumb
Wutginau's/Landgraf	LtGen Henrich Wilhelm von Wutginau (until 10 October 1776)	Col Henrich Julian von Kospoth (until 1778)
	The Landgraf (renamed Leib-Regiment 13 March 1783)	LtCol Caspar Friedrich von Hanstein
The Erbprinz's	Erbprinz Wilhelm, ruling Count of Hanau (on 13 March 1783 transferred to his son Prince Friedrich and renamed Prinz Friedrich's)	Col Carl Wilhelm von Hachenberg (until 1781)
		Col Johann Friedrich von Cochenhausen
Prinz Karl's	Prinz Karl (the Landgraf's second son)	Col Johann Wilhelm Schreiber
Ditfurth's	LtGen von Ditfurth	Colonel Carl von Bose (until 1778) Colonel von Westernhagen
Donop's	LtGen Wilhelm Henrich August von Donop	Col David Ephraim von Gosen, (until 2 September 1780) Col Erasmus Ernst Hinte
Lossberg's (later called alt-Lossberg or Lossberg senior)	LtGen Anton Henrich von Lossberg	Col Henrich Anton von Heringen (until 23 September 1776)

Appendices

White Plains, Newport 1776–7, Brandywine, Germantown, Philadelphia 1777–8, Monmouth, at New York 1778–83 including Tryon's expedition to Horseneck February 1779 and Knyphausen's Springfield expedition

Quartermaster Lotheisen
Captain August von Dinklage
Ensign von der Lith
Captain Friedrich von Münchhausen
Ensign Bernhard Wilhelm Wiederholdt

New York 1776, Newport 1776–9, New York 1779–83 including Tryon's expedition to Newhaven and Fairfield

Quartermaster Bockewitz

Long Island, White Plains, New York 1776–81, Yorktown

White Plains, Newport 1776–7, New York 1777–83 including Leslie's raid into Virginia September 1779

Quartermaster Johann Henrich Pfaff

White Plains, Newport 1776–9, Charleston 1780–2

Quartermaster Christian Cornelius Wende

Captain Friedrich von der Malsburg

Long Island, New York 1776–7, Brandywine, Germantown, Philadelphia 1777–8, Monmouth, New York 1778–1783 including Knyphausen's Springfield expedition

Quartermaster Zinn
Lt Johann Henrich von Bardeleben
Captain Christian Moritz von Kutzleben (in London)
Sergeant (later commissioned) Johann Carl Philipp von Krafft
Chaplain Cöster

Long Island, White Plains, Fort Washington, Trenton (in the Combined Battalion, New Jersey 1777,

Quartermaster Heusser
Lt Jacob Piel
Captain Johann Caspar Ries

261

The Hessians

		LtCol Franziskus Scheffer (until 26 January 1776) (in combined Battalion until 23 July 1778) Col Johann von Loos
Knyphausen's	LtGen Wilhelm von Knyphausen	Colonel Henrich Christian von Borck (in combined battalion 26 December 1776 until 23 July 1778)
Mirbach's/Jung-Lossberg's	MajGen Werner von Mirbach (until 1780) LtGen Friedrich Wilhelm von Lossberg	Col Johann von Loos (until January 1777) LtCol von Schiek (until October 1777) Col von Romrod (from 24 December 1777)
Trumbach's/Bose's	MajGen Carl Levin von Trumbach (until 19 October 1778) LtGen von Bose	Col Carl Ernst von Bischhausen LtCol Johann Christian du Buy (October 1780 to August 1781) Major Max O'Reilly (at Yorktown only)
Rall's/Woellwarth's/ Trumbach's/d'Angelleli's	Col Johann Gottlieb Rall Col Wolfgang Friedrich Woellwarth (from 16 June 1777) MajGen Karl Levin von Trumbach (from 19 October 1778) LtGen the Marquis d'Angelleli	Rall (until 26 December 1776) (in Combined Battalion until 23 July 1778) LtCol Johann Koehler was ordered to take command in 1778, but Major (later LtCol) Johann Wilhelm von Endemann was actually in charge from July 1778
Feldjägercorps	Col Karl von Donop (until October, 1777) Col Ludwig von Wurmb (took command 23 July 1777, although Donop was still Chief.)	First companies were commanded by Captains Wreden and Ewald, the subsequent companies by Wurmb, Major von Prueschenk, Rittmeister von Rau,

262

Brandywine, Germantown, Philadelphia
1777–8, Monmouth), New York until
June 1780, Canada June 1780–83

Same service as Lossberg's until winter   2Lt Ritter
1779–80 when most of Regiment spent   Lt Andreas Wiederholdt
Winter on Prince Edward Island while en
route to Canada; Canada June
1780–October 1781; New York 1781–3

Long Island, White Plains, New York   Quartermaster August
1776–7, Brandywine, Germantown,   Schmidt
Redbank, Philadelphia 1777–8, New   2Lt Carl Friedrich Rüffer
York 1778–83   Major Carl Baurmeister

Fort Independence (Kingsbridge) January   Regimental Journal re-written
1777, New York 1776–1780 except for   after Yorktown
Clinton's Highlands expedition October   Surgeon Fritz Maurer
1777, raid on Paramus April 1780;   Sgt Berthold Koch
October 1780 with Leslie to Hampton
Roads, joined Cornwallis, served at
Guilford Court House, Green Spring
and Yorktown

Long Island, White Plains, Fort   Major (later LtCol) Endemann
Washington, Trenton, (in Combined   Grenadier Johannes Reuber
Battalion, New Jersey 1777, Brandywine,   Sergeant Major Martin Appell
Germantown, Philadelphia 1777–8,
Monmouth, reconstituted 23 July 1778),
Savannah expedition with Archibald
Campbell December 1778, Augustine
Prevost's Charleston expedition 1779,
Stono Ferry, siege of Savannah,
Charleston 1780–82, New York 1782–3

Detachments participated in nearly all   Fourier/Ensign Adam Ludwig Ochs
actions of the war; particularly distin-   Captain Johann Ewald
guished at Iron Hill (20 September   Captain Johann Hinrichs
1777), Brandywine, the siege of
Charleston (March–May 1780), against
Gen. Muhlenberg in Virginia (May
1781), and at Philip's House (July 1781).

The Hessians

		Captain Hinrichs, Captain von Wangenheim. The Ansbach-Bayreuth Company was commanded by Captain von Cramon
Wissenbach's/Knoblauch's Garrison Regiment	LtGen Moriz Adolf von Wissenbach (d. 14 November 1779) MajGen Hans von Knoblauch from 19 February 1780)	Col Ludwig von Horn (until February 1777) LtCol Schlemmer (Feb.-May 1777) Col Friedrich von Porbeck (from May 1777)
Stein's/Seitz's/Porbeck's Garrison Regiment	LtGen von Stein (until 1778) Col. Franz Carl Erdmann von Seitz (d. 19 December 1782) Col. Friedrich von Porbeck (from 1783)	Col v. Seitz (until December 1782) Col Kitzel
Bunau's Garrison Regiment	Col Rudolf Bunau	Bunau
Huyn's/Benning's Garrison Regiment	Col (later MajGen) Johann Christoph von Huyn (d. August 1780) Col Ferdinand Ludwig von Benning	Huyn (until January 1777 when he took over a brigade) Col Kurz (until August 1781) LtCol Johann Philip Hillebrand

Appendices

New York 1776–8, including Heath's attack on Fort Independence (January 1777), expedition to Savannah (December 1778), against Charleston (1780), siege of Savannah; garrisoned Savannah 1780–2.	Quartermaster Pflüger
Fort Washington, New York 1776–8, Halifax October 1778–83	Ensign von Langenscharz Lt Johann Henrich Henkelmann
Fort Washington Newport 1776–79, New York 1779–1783 Fort Washington, Newport 1776–1779 including attack on Windmill Hill August 1778, Charleston 1780–82, New York 1783	None Quartermaster Friedrich Jacob Kleinschmidt Musketeer Valentin Asteroth Chaplain Henrich Kümmel

265

Bibliography

MANUSCRIPT SOURCES

STAATSARCHIV MARBURG

Bestand 4h. Politische Akten nach Landgraf Philipp: Kriegssachen
4h.328. nrs. 100, 106, 108–20, 139–41, 151–4, 157, 158, 159.
4h.409. nrs. 2 and 3.
4h.410. nrs. 1 and 2.
4h.411. 1, 2 and 3.
4h.412. nrs. 1, 2, 4 and 5.
4h.413. nr. 4.
4h.414. nr. 4.
4h.415. nr. 5.

Bestand 11: Militärkabinett mit General- und Flugeladjutantur
11. Conduitenlisten 1788
11. nr. 74.
11. Militärkabinett T 2 III Pak. 3.
11. F 1 d.
11. nr. 398.

Bestand 12. Kriegsministerium
12. nrs. 203, 212, 213, 296, 454, 470, 483, 512, 513, 554, 556, 831, 858, 8084, 8529, 8539, 8841, 8843, 8853, 8826, 8834–5, 8304–8320.

Bestand 12. Verzeichnis 11: Truppentagebücher. I. Feldzug in Amerika.

Bestand 13. Generalstab. A. Kriegsakten. 6. Nordamerikanisches Freiheitskrieg
Nrs. 195–8, 209, 232, 234, 891.

Bestand 6b. Akten des kürfurstlichen Hauses, 254.

Kirchenbücher.

300 Phillipsruhe E11/6. Vols. I-IX.
340 von der Malsburg, Escheburg.

E195/2.

H20.

40b, Rubr. 36, Gen. 59.

Bibliography

MURHARDSCHE BIBLIOTHEK DER STADT KASSEL UND
LANDESBIBLIOTHEK

2° Ms. hass. 247. Brigade von Mirbach.
4° Ms. hass. 186. Dinklage.
4° Ms. hass. 188. Lieutenant Jakob Piel.
4° Ms. hass. 216. Andreas Wiederholdt.
4° Ms. hass. 228. Journal of the Regiment Jung von Lossberg.
4° Ms. hass. 293/3. Martin Appell.
8° Ms. hass. 16a. Bopp.
8° Ms. hass. 123. Heft 1. Gen. von Langenscharz.
8° Ms. hass. 127. Valentin Asteroth.

STADTARCHIV BAYREUTH

MS. 100. Tagebuch des markgräflichen Jäger-leutnants Carl Philipp von
Feilitzsch.

STAATSARCHIV HANNOVER

Hannover 52 III Nr. 29. Münchhausan.
Hannover 41 V Nrs. 3, 4, 8, 9, 22, 23, 24, 30, 35, 37, 38 and 39.
Hannover 47 II Nrs. 113–16. Col v. Scheither.

STAATSARCHIV WOLFENBÜTTEL

337N46–115. Briefschaften und Akten des Generalleutnants Friedrich Adolf
Riedesel, Freiherr zu Eisenach.

STADTARCHIV FRANKFURT-AM-MAIN

Depositum Adolf Reuber Nr. 1: Tagebuch des Grenadiers Johannes Reuber.

STAATSARCHIV BAMBERG

C 18, 1 Collectanea Spiess Nr. 26. Die in Kgl. Grossbritannischen Sold nach
Amerika überlassenen hochfürstl: Brandenburgischen Kriegsvölker betr:
1777ff.

BURGERBIBLIOTHEK BERN

Mss. hist. helv. xxv 71. Erasmus Ritter Nachlass. One item: letter of S. L. du Ry
to Ritter, 4 November 1783.

WILLIAM L. CLEMENTS LIBRARY, ANN ARBOR, MICHIGAN

Selected items from the von Jungkenn papers: letters of Franziskus Scheffer
Johann Friedrich von Cochenhausen, Maximilian Michael O'Reilly, Andreas
Wiederholdt.

Bibliography

THE PUBLIC RECORD OFFICE

Various correspondence dealing with the Hessians: SP81/154–8, 165, 181–96; SP82/94–8; SP84/547, 552–8, 561; SP87/26, 28, 37, 39, 48; FO353/2.
The Carleton papers: PRO3O/55.
Correspondence dealing with the American war: CO5/93–104, 139–44, 168, 169–74, 182–4, 236, 243.
Accounts of the Hessian claim for extraordinaries: T38/814, AO3/55.
Items relating to the Hessians: WO4/96–9, HO5/452.

THE BRITISH LIBRARY

Add. MSS. 21680, 21807–8, 21811–2. Haldimand.
Add. MSS. 23648–51. Rainsford.
Add. MS. 23680 Nr. 1. Colonel Felix Frederick.
Add. MSS. 34413–6. Auckland.
Egerton MS. 2135. The war in America.

THE BEDFORD COUNTY RECORD OFFICE

The Lucas Collection: L29/213 and L29/214.

THE NATIONAL MARITIME MUSEUM GREENWICH

Journal 35. MS. 0085. The War in America 1776: original manuscript Journal by Admiral Sir George Collier.

PRINTED SOURCES

For a full bibliography of published work on the Hessians, see Emil Meynen, *Bibliography on German Settlements in Colonial North America 1683–1933* (Leipzig, 1937), pp. 258–70, and Karl Demandt, *Schifttum zur Geschichte und geschichtlichen Landeskunde von Hessen.* 3 vols. Wiesbaden, 1965–8, I, pp. 448–52, and its supplement for 1965–7 by Winfried Leist, Marburg, 1973.

Almon, John, ed., *The Remembrancer; or Impartial Repository of Public Events.* London, 1775–84.
André, John, *Major André's Journal: an Authentic Record of the Movements and Engagements of the British Army in America from June 1777 to November 1778 as Recorded from day to day by Major John André.* Henry Cabot Lodge, ed., 2 vols. Boston, 1903.
Bardeleben, Heinrich von, 'Tagebuch eines Hessischen Offiziers, Heinrich von Bardeleben', Julius Göbell, ed., *DAGeschBl,* XXVII–XXVIII (1927–8), 7–119.
Baurmeister, Carl L., *Revolution in America: Confidential Letters and Journals 1776–1784.* Bernard A. Uhlendorf, ed. and trans., 2nd edn, Westport, Conn., 1973.
Biddulph, Violet, ed., 'Letters of Robert Biddulph', *AHR,* XXIX (1923), 87–109.
Boswell, James, *Boswell on the Grand Tour: Germany and Switzerland, 1764.* F. A. Pottle, ed., London, 1953.

Bibliography

Buettner, Johann Carl, *Buettner, der Amerikaner: eine Selbstbiographie*. Camenz, 1828. English translation, *Narrative of Johann Carl Buettner in the American Revolution*. Heartman's historical series nr. 1. New York, 1913.

Büsching, Anton Friedrich, *Erdbeschreibung*. Vol. VII. Hamburg, 1790.

Chastellux, the Marquis de, *Travels in North American in the Years 1780, 1781, and 1782*. 2 vols. London, 1837.

Clarke, Walter, ed., *The State Records of North Carolina*. Vol. XIV. Raleigh, NC, 1896.

Clinton, Sir Henry, *The American Rebellion: Sir Henry Clinton's Narrative of his Campaigns, 1775–1782, with an Appendix of Original Documents*. William B. Willcox, ed., New Haven, 1954.

Collins, Varnum Lansing, ed., *A Brief Narrative of the Ravages of the British and Hessians at Princeton in 1776–1777*. Princeton, N J, 1906.

Commager, Henry Steele, and Morris, Richard B., eds., *The Spirit of 'Seventy-Six: the Story of the American Revolution as told by Participants*. New York, 1967.

Cresswell, Nicholas, *The Journal of Nicholas Cresswell 1774–1777*. London, 1925.

Doehla, Johann Conrad, 'The Doehla Journal', Robert Tilden, ed., *WMQ*, 2nd series, XXII (1942), 241–74.

—'Tagebuch eines Bayreuther Soldaten aus dem Nordamerikanischen Freiheitskrieg 1777–1783', *Archiv für Geschichte und Altertumskunde von Oberfranken*. XXV (1912), nrs. 1 and 2.

Dörnberg, Karl Ludwig, *Tagebuchblätter eines hessischen Offizier aus der Zeit der nordamerikanischen Unabhängigkeitskrieg*. Gotthold Marseille, ed., 2 vols. Pyritz, 1899–1900.

Downman, Francis, *The Services of Lieut. Colonel Francis Downman in France, North America, and the West Indies, between the Years 1758 and 1784*. F. A. Whinyates, ed., Woolwich, 1898.

Droysen, Hans, 'Die Braunschweigischen Truppen in Nordamerikanischen Unabhängigkeitskrieg: aus den Briefen der Herzogin Philippine Charlotte von Braunschweig', *Jahrbuch des Geschichtsvereins für das Herzogtum Braunschweig*, XIII (1914), 145–59.

Ewald, Johann, *Abhandlung über den kleinen Krieg*. Kassel, 1785.

—*Belehrungen über den Krieg, besonders den kleinen Krieg, durch Beispiele grosser Helden und kluger und tapferer Männer*. Vols II and III. Schleswig, 1800–3.

Force, Peter, ed., *American Archives*: Fifth series, *Containing a Documentary History of the United States of America from the Declaration of Independence*. 3 vols. Washington, DC, 1848–53.

Forster, Johann Georg, *Briefwechsel*. Vol. I. Leipzig, 1829.

Fortescue, Sir John, ed., *The correspondence of George III from 1760 to December 1783*. 6 vols. London, 1928.

Frederick the Great, *Politische Correspondenz Friedrich's des Grossen*. 46 vols. Berlin, 1879–1939.

Gerland, Otto, 'Kasseler Tagesneuigkeiten aus dem 18. Jahrhundert', *Hessenland*, VII (1893), 71–3.

Gilsa, F. von, 'Aus dem Stammbuche des landgräflich hessischen Capitain im Leibregiment Christian Friedrich von Urff 1774–1792', *Hessenland*. XIII (1899), 108–10, 124–6.

Günderode, Friedrich Justinian, Freiherr von, *Briefe eines Reisenden über den gegenwärtigen Zustand von Cassel*. Frankfurt and Leipzig, 1781.

269

Bibliography

Hanger, George, Baron Coleraine, *The Life, Adventures, and Opinions of Colonel George Hanger*. 2 vols. London, 1801.

Harnier, Erasmus, 'Der Überfahrt des letzten hessischen Rekruten-transports nach Amerika', *Mitteilungen* (1909–10), 147–70.

Heath, William, *Memoirs of Major-General Heath. Containing Anecdotes, Details of Skirmishes, Battles, and other Military Events during the American War*. New York, 1901.

Heister, Lieutenant [Carl Levin] von, 'Auszüge aus dem Tagebuch eines vormaligen kurhessischen Offiziers über den Nordamerikanischen Freiheits-krieg 1776 und 1777', *Zeitschrift für Kunst, Wissenschaft, und Geschichte des Krieges*, III (1828), 223–70.

Heringen, Oberst [Henrich Anton] von, 'Einige Briefe aus dem amerikanischen Krieg', *Militär Wochenblatt*, XVIII (1833), 4854–6, 4858–9.

HMC: *Report on American Manuscripts in the Royal Institution of Great Britain*. 4 vols. London and Dublin, 1904–9.

HMC: *Report on the Manuscripts of the late Reginald Rawdon-Hastings*. Vol. III. London, 1934.

HMC: *Report on the Manuscripts of Mrs. Stopford-Sackville of Drayton House, Northamptonshire*. Vol. II. London, 1910.

Hinrichs, Captain [Johann], 'Extracts from the Letterbook of Captain Hinrichs', *PMHB*, XXII (1898), 137–70.

Hochfürstlich Hessen-Casselischer Staats- und Adress-Calender. 34 vols. Kassel, 1764–1802.

Howe, Sir William, *The Narrative of Lieut. General Sir William Howe in a Committee of the House of Commons*. London, 1780.

Huth, Hans, 'Letters from a Hessian Mercenary', *PMHB*, LXII (1938), 488–501.

Jackson, Robert, *A View of the Formation, Discipline and Economy of Armies*. 3rd ed, London, 1845.

Justi, Karl W., 'Johann Ludwig Friedrich von Stamford', *Hessische Denkwürdigkeiten*, VI (1805), nr. 2, 73–87.

Kemble, Stephen, *Journals of Lieut.-Col. Stephen Kemble, 1773–1789; and British Army Orders: Gen. Sir William Howe, 1775–1778; Gen. Sir Henry Clinton, 1778; and Gen. Daniel Jones, 1778*. Boston, 1972.

Krafft, John Charles Philip von, *The Journal of Lieutenant John Charles Philip von Krafft 1776–1783*. Thomas H. Edsall, ed. Collections of the New York Historical Society for 1882. New York, 1883.

Kröger, Alfred, *Geburt der USA: German Newspaper Accounts of the American Revolution 1763–1783*. Madison, Wisc., 1962.

Kümmel, Heinrich, 'Aus dem Tagebuch eines hessischen Feldpredigers in amerikanischen Krieg', *Hessenland*, VIII (1894), 72–6, 87–91.

Lith, Friedrich, Freiherr von der, 'Amerikanische Anekdoten', *Journal von und für Deutschland* (1788), 563–6.

—'Feldzug der Hessen nach Amerika', *Ephemeriden über Aufklarung, Literatur und Kunst*, II (Marburg, 1785), 1–60.

—'Wilhelm, Freiherr von Knyphausen', *Hessische Denkwürdigkeiten*, III (1802), 442–6.

Lydenberg, Henry Miller, ed., *Archibald Robertson, Lieutenant Colonel Royal Engineers. His Diaries and Sketches in America 1762–1780*. New York, 1930.

Bibliography

Mackenzie, Frederick, *The Diary of Frederick Mackenzie as an Officer of the Regiment of Royal Welch Fusiliers during the years 1775–1781.* 2 vols. Cambridge, Mass., 1930.

Martin, Samuel, *Deliberate Thoughts on the System of our late Treaties with Hesse-Cassel and Russia in regard to Hannover.* London, 1756.

Maurer, Fritz, 'Brief eines Hessen aus der Zeit der englisch-nordamerikanischen Kriegs', *Hessenland*, XX (1906), 48–50.

Memoirs of the House and Dominions of Hesse Cassel: giving an Account of the Origin and History of that illustrious Family. London, 1740.

Militär-Reglement für die Infanterie. 2 vols. Kassel, 1802.

Mirabeau, Honoré Gabriel, 'Avis aux Hessois et Autres Peuples de l'Allemagne vendus par leurs Princes à l'Angleterre', J. G. Rosengarten, ed., *Proceedings of the American Philosophical Society*, XXXIX (April 1900), 150–4.

Moore, Frank, *Diary of the American Revolution, from Newspapers and original Documents.* 2 vols. New York, 1860.

Moore, John, *A View of Society and Manners in France, Switzerland and Germany.* 2 vols. London, 1779.

Morton, Robert, 'The Diary of Robert Morton, kept in Philadelphia while that city was occupied by the British Army in 1777', *PMHB*, I (1877), 1–39.

Müller, Johannes von, *Sämtliche Werke.* 27 vols. in 15. Tübingen, 1810–19.

Münchhausen, Friedrich von, *At General Howe's Side 1776–1778: The Diary of General William Howe's aide de camp, Captain Friedrich von Muenchhausen.* Translated by Ernst Kipping, and annotated by Samuel Smith, Monmouth Beach, NJ, 1974.

Naval Records of the American Revolution. William Bell. Clark, ed., 7 vols. to date. Washington, DC, 1964–76.

New Jersey, *Archives of the State of New Jersey.* W. S. Stryker, ed., 2nd series. 6 vols. Trenton, NJ, 1901.

North Carolina, *The State Records of North Carolina.* Walter Clarke, ed., Vol. XIV. Raleigh, NC, 1896.

Ochs, Adam Ludwig von, *Betrachtungen über die neuere Kriegskunst, über ihre Fortschritte und Veränderungen und über die wahrscheinlichen Folgen welche für die Zukunft daraus entstehen werden.* Kassel, 1817.

—'Das hessische Militär. Eine Skizze', *Neue Bellona*, II (1802), part iii, 193–234.

Pettengill, Roy W., *Letters from America 1776–1779: Being letters of Brunswick, Hessian and Waldeck Officers with the British Armies during the Revolution.* Cambridge, Mass., 1924.

Popp, Stephen, 'Popp's Journal, 1777–1783', J. G. Rosengarten, ed., *PMHB*, XXVI (1902), 25–41, 245–54.

Powell, William S., ed., 'A Connecticut Soldier under Washington: Elisha Bostwick's Memoirs of the First Year of the Revolution', *WMQ*, 3rd series, VI (1949), 94–107.

Reglement vor die hessische Infanterie. Kassel, 1767.

Reinhardt, Max, 'Aus dem Tagebuch eines hessischen Feldpredigers im amerikanischen Freiheitskrieg 1776–1783', *NGFKW*, XVI (1941), nr. 1, 1–16.

Reuber, Johannes, 'Tagebuch des Grenadiers Johannes Reuber aus Niedervellmar vom amerikanischen Feldzug', F. W. Junghans, ed., *Hessenland*, VIII (1894), 155–7, 167–8, 183–6.

Riesbeck, Johann Caspar, *Travels through Germany in a Series of Letters written in German by the Baron Riesbeck.* 3 vols. London, 1787.

271

Bibliography

Rogge-Ludwig, K., 'Über Berthold Koch und seine Erlebnisse in amerikanischen Freiheitskrieg 1776–1782', *Mitteilungen* (1876), part i, 1–2.

Russell, Peter, 'The Siege of Charleston: Journal of Captain Peter Russel, December 25, 1779, to May 2, 1780', *AHR*, IV (1898), 478–501.

Schoepf, Johann David, *Reise durch einige der mittlern und sudlichen Vereinigten Nordamerikanischen Staaten . . . in den Jahren 1783 und 1784*. 2 vols. Erlangen, 1788.

Schweinsburg, Karl Alexander, Freiherr Schenk zu, 'Briefe eines hessischen Offiziers [Maximilian Michael O'Reilly] aus Amerika', *Hessenland*, XVI (1902), 288–91, 308–11.

Serle, Ambrose, *The American Journal of Ambrose Serle, Secretary to Lord Howe 1776–1778*. E. H. Tatum, ed., San Marino, Calif., 1940.

Simcoe, John Graves, *A History of the Operations of a Partisan Corps called the Queen's Rangers commanded by Lt. Col. J. G. Simcoe during the American Revolution*. London, 1844.

—*Remarks on the Travels of the Marquis de Chastellux in North America*. London, 1787.

Staatsarchiv Marburg, *Hessische Truppen im amerikanischen Unabhängigkeitskrieg (HETRINA). Index nach Familiennamen*. Eckhardt G. Franz, Inge Auerbach, and Otto Frohlich, eds., 4 vols. Marburg, 1972–6. (Computer print of all Hessian soldiers and officers, based on muster lists.)

Stedman, Charles, *The History of the Origin, Progress, and Termination of the American War*. 2 vols. London, 1794.

Stevens, Benjamin F., ed., *Facsimiles of Manuscripts in European Archives relating to America 1773–1783*. 25 vols. London, 1889–1895.

Strieder, Friedrich Wilhelm, *Grundlage zu einer hessischen Gelehrten und Schriftsteller Geschichte*. 18 vols. Kassel, 1781–1819.

—*Grundlage zur Militär Geschichte des Landgräflich Hessische Corps*. Kassel, 1798.

Stryker, William S. *et al.*, eds., *Archives of the State of New Jersey*. 2nd series. 6 vols. Trenton, NJ, 1901.

Stuart-Wortley, the Hon. Mrs. E., *A Prime Minister and his Son: from the Correspondence of the 3rd Earl of Bute and of Lt.-General the Hon. Sir Charles Stuart, K. B.* London, 1925.

Thacher, James, *A Military Journal during the American Revolutionary War from 1775 to 1783*. 2nd edn, Boston, 1827.

Uhlendorf, Bernhard A., ed., *The Siege of Charleston, with an Account of the Province of South Carolina: the von Jungkenn Papers in the William L. Clements Library*. Ann Arbor, Michigan, 1938.

Valentini, Georg Wilhelm, Freiherr von, *Erinnerungen eines alten preussischen Officiers aus den Feldzügen 1792, 1793 und 1794 in Frankreich und am Rhein*. Glogau and Leipzig, 1833.

—*Abhandlung über den kleinen Krieg und über den Gebrauch der leichten Truppen mit Rucksicht auf den französischen Krieg*. Die Lehre vom Krieg, part I. Leipzig, 1820.

Wainwright, Nicholas B., ed., 'A Diary of Trifling Occurrences, Philadelphia, 1776–1778', *PMHB*, LXXXII (1958), 411–65.

Walpole Horace, *Journal of the Reign of King George III from the Year 1771 to 1783*, 2 vols. London, 1865.

Walpole, Horatio, first Baron, *The Case of the Hessian Forces in the Pay of Great Britain*. London, 1731.

Washington, George, *The Writings of George Washington*. John C. Fitzpatrick, ed., 39 vols. Washington, DC 1931–44.

Wiederholdt, Andreas, 'Tagebuch des Capt. Wiederholdt von 7 October 1776 bis 7 December 1780', M. D. Learned and C. Grosse, eds., *Americana Germanica*, IV (1901), 1–93.

Bibliography

Wiederholdt, Bernhard Wilhelm, 'Über den kriegerischen Charakter der Deutschen und die Vorzüge des deutschen Militärs', *Neue Bellona*, III (1802), part ii, 33–94.

Woelfel, Margarete, trans., 'Memoirs of a Hessian Conscripts: J. G. Seume's Reluctant Voyage to America', *WMQ*, 3rd series, V (1948), 553–670.

Woringer, August, 'Auszüge aus Tagebuchern und Aufzeichnungen hessischer Offiziere und Regiments-Chroniken im Amerikanischen Befreiungskrieg', *DAGeschBl*, XX-XXI (1920–1), 251–80.

—'Protocoll der Amtshandlungen, die der Feldprediger G. C. Cöster bei den beiden löblichen Regimentern von Donop und von Lossberg und andern verrichet', DAGeschBl, XX-XXI (1920-1), 251–280.

—'Zwei Briefe hessischer Offiziere [Johann Heinrich Henkelmann and Philipp Schirmer]', *Hessenland*, XX (1906), 339–41.

SECONDARY WORKS

Allgemeine Deutsche Biographie. 55 vols. Leipzig, 1875–1910.

Friedlander, Ernst, 'Martin Ernst von Schlieffen', XXI, 516–17.

Liliencron, V., 'Johann von Ewald', VI, 443–4.

Poten, B., 'Wilhelm, Freiherr von Knyphausen', XVI, 343–4.

Ibid, 'Adam Ludwig von Ochs', XXIV, 128–30.

Ibid, 'Johann Gottlieb Rall', XXVII, 151–3.

Ibid, 'Wilhelm Dietrich von Wakenitz', XL, 635–8.

Wyss, A., 'Friedrich II von Hessen-Kassel', VII, 524–8.

Anderson, Troyer S., *The Command of the Howe Brothers during the American Revolution*. London, 1936.

Apel, Karl, 'Regiment Prinz Karl im Amerikanischen Unabhängigkeitskrieg 1776–1783', *Mein Heimatland* (monthly supplement to the *Hersfelder Zeitung*), XVII, nr. 6 (23 August 1956), 21–3.

Bancroft, George, *History of the United States of America from the Discovery of the Continent*. Vol. V. London, 1876.

Berger, Carl, *Broadsides and Bayonets: the Propaganda War of the American Revolution*. Philadelphia, 1962.

Bill, Alfred Hoyt, *The Campaign of Princeton 1776–1777*. Princeton, NJ, 1948.

Boehme, Hans George, 'Zur Wehrverfassung in Hessen-Kassel im 18. Jahrhundert bis zum Siebenjahrigen Krieg', *Hessisches Jahrbuch für Landesgeschichte*, I (1951), 206–9.

Both, Wolf von, and Hans Vogel, *Landgraf Friedrich II von Hessen-Kassel*. Munich, 1973.

—*Landgraf Wilhelm VIII von Hessen-Kassel*. Munich, 1964.

Bowie, Lucy Leigh, 'The German Prisoners in the American Revolution', *Maryland Historical Magazine*, XL (1945), 185–200.

Braubach, Max, *Die Bedeutung der Sudsidien für die Politik im spanischen Erbfolgekrieg*. Bonn, 1923.

Bruford, W. H., *Germany in the Eighteenth Century*. Cambridge, 1935.

Butterfield, Lyman H., 'Psychological Warfare in 1776: the Jefferson–Franklin Plan to cause Hessian Desertions', *Proceedings of the American Philosophical Society*, XCIV (1950), 233–41.

Carrington, Henry B., *Battles of the American Revolution 1775–1781*. New York, 1876.

Carsten, F. L., *Princes and Parliaments in Germany*, Oxford, 1959.

273

Bibliography

Dalwigk, Freiherr von, zu Lichtenfels, 'Der Feldzug des Regiments Bose in den Karolinas im Jahre 1781', *Hessenland*, XXI (1907), 93–7.

—*Geschichte der Waldeckischen und Kurhessischen Stammtruppen des Infanterie-Regiments von Wittich (3 Kurhessiches) Nr. 83 1681–1866.* Oldenburg, 1909.

Danckelmann, L. von, 'Die Einschiffung und Überfahrt der hessischen. Brigade von Mirbach nach Nordamerika in Jahr 1776'. *Mitteilungen* (1881), part i, 1–2.

Davidson, Philip, *Propaganda and the American Revolution 1763–1783.* Chapel Hill, 1941.

Dawson, Henry Barton, *Battles of the United States.* Vol. I. New York, 1858.

Delancey, Edward Floyd, 'Mount Washington and its Capture November 16, 1776', *Magazine of American History*, I (1877), 65–90.

Demandt, Karl, *Geschichte des Landes Hessen.* 2nd edn, Kassel, 1972.

Ditfurth, Maximilian, Freiherr von, *Die Hessen in den Feldzügen in der Champagne, am Maine und Rheine während der Jahre 1792, 1793, und 1794.* Marburg, 1881.

—*Das Kurhessische Leibgarde-Regiment.* Kassel, 1882.

Dülfer, Kurt, 'Fürst und Verwaltung: Grundzüge der hessischen Verwaltungsgeschichte 16–19. Jahrhundert'. *Hessisches Jahrbuch für Landesgeschichte*, III (1953), 150–223.

Eelking, Max von, *Die deutschen Hilfstruppen im nordamerikanischen Befreiungskriege 1776 bis 1783.* 2 vols. Hannover, 1863. English translation, J. G. Rosengarten, *The German Allied Troops in the North American War of Independence 1776–1783.* Albany, 1893.

—*Leben und Wirken des herzoglich Braunschweigischen General Lieutenants Friedrich Adolph Riedesel Freiherrn zu Eisenach.* 3 vols. Leipzig, 1856. English translation, W. L. Stone, *Memoirs and Letters and Journals of Major-General Riedesel.* 2 vols. Albany, 1868.

Eisentraut, G., 'Johann Gottfried Seume's Rekrutenzeit 1781–1783', *Hessenland*, XXIV (1910), 57–9, 89–91, 107–9, 122–4.

Field, Thomas W., *The Battle of Long Island.* Long Island Historical Society Memoirs. Vol. II. Brooklyn, NY, 1869.

Fortescue, Sir John, *A History of the British Army.* 13 vols. London, 1899–1930.

Fuller, Major-General J. F. C., *British Light Infantry in the Eighteenth Century.* London, 1925.

Has, Wilhelm, *Geschichte des 1. Kurhessischen Feldartillerie-Regiments Nr. 11 und seiner Stammtruppen.* Marburg, 1913.

Higginbotham, Don, *The War of American Independence: military Attitudes, Policies and Practice 1763–1789.* New York, 1971.

Hoffmeister, Jacob Christoph Carl, *Historisch-Genealogisches Handbuch über alle Linien des hohen Regentenhauses Hessen.* Kassel, 1861.

Hohenhausen, Leopold, Freiherr von, *Biographie des Generals von Ochs.* Kassel, 1827.

Johnston, Henry P., *The Battle of Harlem Heights.* New York, 1897.

Kapp, Friedrich, 'Friedrich II und die neuere Geschichtsschreibung. Ein Beitrag zur Widerlegung der Märchen über angeblichen Soldatenhandel hessischer Fürsten', *Historische Zeitschrift*, XLII (1879, nr. 2), 304–30.

—*Der Soldatenhandel deutscher Fürsten nach Amerika.* Berlin, 1864.

Kipping, Ernst, *The Hessian View of America 1776–1783.* Monmouth Beach, NJ, 1971.

—*Die Truppen von Hessen-Kassel im Amerikanischen Unabhängigkeitskrieg 1776–1783.* Darmstadt, 1965.

Bibliography

Lettow-Vorbeck, Friedrich von, *Geschichte des Fusilier Regiments von Gersdorff (Kurhessisches) Nr. 80 und seines Stamm-Regiments von 1631 bis 1830*. Marburg, 1913.

Losch, Philipp, *Soldatenhandel: Mit einem Verzeichnis der Hessen-Kasselischen Subsidienverträge und einer Bibliographie*. Kassel, 1933.

Lowell, Edward J., *The Hessians and the Other German Auxiliaries of Great Britain in the Revolutionary War*. New York, 1884. German translation, Verschuer, O. C., Freiherr von, *Die Hessen und die anderen deutschen Hilfstruppen im Kriege Grossbritanniens in America 1776–1783*. Braunschweig and Leipzig, 1901.

Lundin, Leonard, *Cockpit of the Revolution: the War for Independence in New Jersey*. Princeton, NJ, 1940.

Mackesy, Piers, *The War for America, 1775–1783*. Cambridge, Mass., 1964.

Paret, Peter, 'Colonial Experience and European Military Reform at the end of the Eighteenth Century'. *Institute of Historical Research*, XXXVI (1964), 47–59.

—*Yorck and the Era of Prussian Reform 1807–1815*. Princeton, NJ, 1966.

Peckham, Howard H., ed., *The Toll of Independence: Engagements and Battle Casualties of the American Revolution*. Chicago and London, 1974.

Perry, Walter Copeland, 'On the Employment of Mercenaries in Ancient and Modern Times '. *The Nineteenth Century*, LXI (1907), 320–55.

Pfister, Ferdinand von, 'Über die Heerverlassung hessischer Soldaten im nordamerikanischen Unabhängigkeitskrieg', *Zeitschrift des Vereins für Hessische Geschichte und Landeskunde*, X (1865), 361–73.

Preser, Carl, 'Der angebliche Verkauf der Hessen nach Amerika', *Allgemeine Militär-Zeitung*, LXV (1890), 410–13, 418–19, 426–8, 434–6, 442–4, 450–2, 458–60.

—*Der Kurfürst von Hessen, seine Dynastie und seine Gegner*. Vienna, 1869.

Redlich, Fritz, *The German Military Enterpriser and his Work Force: a Study in European Economic and Social History*. I and II. Vierteljahrschrift für Sozial- und Wirtschaftsgeschichte, nrs. 47 and 48. Wiesbaden, 1964–5.

Rosengarten, J. G., 'American History from German Archives', *Proceedings of the American Philosophical Society*, XXXIX (April, 1900), 129–50.

—'A Defense of the Hessians', *PMHB*, XXIII (1899), 157–83.

Sante, Georg Wilhelm, *Hessen*. Handbuch der Historischen Städten Deutschlands, vol. IV. Stuttgart, 1960.

Sauer, Josef, *Finanzgeschäfte der Landgrafen von Hessen-Kassel*. Fulda, 1930.

Savory, Sir Reginald, *His Britannic Majesty's Army in Germany during the Seven Years War*. Oxford, 1966.

Scheer, George F., and Rankin, Hugh, *Rebels and Redcoats*. New York, 1957.

Schmidt, H. D., 'The Hessian Mercenaries, the career of a political cliche', *History*, XLIII (1958), 207–12.

Shy, John, 'The American Revolution: the Military Conflict considered as a Revolutionary War', in Stephen G. Kurtz, and James H. Hutson, eds., *Essays on the American Revolution*. Chapel Hill and New York, 1973.

Smith, Samuel S., *The Battle of Trenton*. Monmouth Beach, NJ, 1965.

—*Fight for the Delaware 1777*. Monmouth Beach, NJ, 1970.

Speier, Hans, 'Militarism in the Eighteenth Century', *Social Research*, III (1963), 304–35.

Städtler, Erhard, *Die Ansbach-Bayreuther Truppen im Amerikanischen Unabhängigkeitskrieg 1777–1783*. Nürnberg, 1956.

Staatsarchiv Marburg, *Hessen und die Amerikanische Revolution: Austellung der hessis-*

Bibliography

chen Staatsarchive zum Hessentag 1976. Marburg, 1976.

Stryker, William S., *The Battles of Trenton and Princeton*. Boston and New York, 1898.

Sunkel, W., *Geschichte des 2. hessische Infanterie Regiments Nr. 82*. Berlin, 1876.

Treitschke, Heinrich von, *History of Germany in the Nineteenth Century*. Eden and Cedar Paul, translators. Vol. VI. London, 1918.

Trevelyan, Sir George Otto, *The American Revolution*. Vols. II–IV. London, 1905.

Wallace, Willard M., *Appeal to Arms: a Military History of the American Revolution*. New York, 1951.

Ward, Christopher, *The War of the Revolution*. John Alden, ed., 2 vols. New York, 1952.

Wilkin, W. H., *Some British Soldiers in America*. London, 1914.

Willcox, William B., *Portrait of a General, Sir Henry Clinton in the War of Independence*. New York, 1964.

Zwenger, Ferdinand, 'Johann Ewald in hessischen Dienst', *Hessenland*, VII (1893), 142–4, 158–60, 194–7, 207–9.

UNPUBLISHED DISSERTATIONS

Dippel, Horst, 'Deutschland und die amerikanische Revolution. Sozial-geschichtlichen Untersuchung zum politischen Bewusstsein im ausgehenden 18. Jahrhundert', Cologne, 1972. (Since this was written, Dippel's work has been published in English translation as *Germany and the American Revolution 1770–1800: A Sociohistorical Investigation of Late Eighteenth-Century Political Thinking*. Bernhard A. Uhlendorf, trans. Chapel Hill, 1977.)

Slagle, Robert Oakley, 'The von Lossberg Regiment: a Chronicle of Hessian participation in the American Revolution'. The American University, 1965.

Index

Adams, John 31, 242
Admiralty Board 207
Altenbockum, Captain Ernst Eberhard von 74, 89, 93 and n48, 96, 115–16, 244
Amboy, N. J. 112, 144
Amelung, Chief Surgeon Johannes 239
American army,
  British contempt for 58, 91
  Campaigns: Long Island 66–70, 242; Kip's Bay 70–1; Harlem Heights 71; Pell's Point 72–3; White Plains 73–4, 179, 240; Fort Washington 76–9, 242; New Jersey (1776) 80, 84, 86, 87, Trenton 92–5; Fort Independence 101; New Jersey (1777) 38–9, 101–2, 111–12, 138–9; Philadelphia 117–28, 133; Virginia 135; Guilford Court House 140–1, 240; Yorktown 142
  desertion from 102, 188, 192, 206
  Hessian opinion of 60, 68, 70, 89, 90, 158–9, 240–1
  militia 71, 139, 171, 177, 178, 240–1, 242
  prisoners, Hessian treatment of 182, 242
  regiments:
    artillery 70, 92
    dragoons 178, 191
    Connecticut 70–1
    Delaware 69, 73
    'Flying Camp' 188 n21
    Marblehead 72
    Maryland 69
    Ottendorf's 177 and n37
    Pennsylvania 73, 76
    riflemen 59, 61, 65, 70, 72–3, 78, 132
  relations with French 155–6
  tactics of 97, 130–1
  trained by Steuben 240
  plundering and 176–9
Americans as warlike people 240
Amsterdam 221
André, Major John 111 n143, 172
Andresohn, Lt Ernst Wilhelm von 143
Angelelli, Lt Gen. Marquis Luigi d' 51, 262

Anhalt-Zerbst, troops of 40, 155 n74, 157 n82; treaty 227
Ann Arbor, Michigan 4
Ansbach-Bayreuth, troops 102, 117 n2, 134, 137 and n88, 142–3, 144–5, 157 n82
  their letters 4
  Margrave 208, 209
  treaty 227
Appell, Sgt Maj Martin 41, 161, 237–8 and n21, 263
Arnold, Benedict 58, 102, 135
Assunpinck creek 93, 95, 96 n59, 114, map 94
Austria 2, 8, 23, 210
  troops 51, 122 n16, 131, 215, 248
  desertion 192, 204, 205
  recruiters 10, 34
Austrian Succession, war of 16, 45
auxiliaries 1, 4, 32
  legal position of 22–3

Baden 24, 246
Bad Hersfeld – see Hersfeld
Balfour, Major Nisbet 104–6
Bamberg 4
Bancroft, George 2, 5 and n5, 216 n3, 233
Bardeleben, Lt Johann Heinrich von, 4, 5, 37, 62 n22, 68, 69, 107, 151, 158, 174 n22, 179, 261; brother 204
Bardeleben, Gen. von, 163 n20
Barton, Miss, 151
Bauer, QM Carl 56, 218–19, 259
Bauer, surgeon 143
Baumbach, Landrat, 210, 224, 225–6
Baurmeister, Major Carl Leopold 51, 71, 90–1, 128, 130, 179, 181, 199 n87, 200–1, 222 n33, 244 n57, 263
Bavaria 1, 8, 11, 16, 173
  war of succession 205, 230
Beaumarchais 129 n11
Beckwith, Capt. George 156
Bedford Record Office 5
Benning, Col Ferdinand Ludwig von 146, 197 n71, 209, 264

Index

Benning, Capt. Friedrich Wilhelm von 74
Bennington, battle (1777) 107 n126
Berdot, Lt Friedrich von 118–19
Bergen, battle (1759) 42
Bergen Neck, NJ 139
Bern, *Burgerbibliothek* 5
Berlin 24, 229
Bethlehem, Pennsylvania 199
Bevern, Duke of 83 n118
Bickel, *Jäger* 134
Biddle, Nicholas 182
Biddulph, Robert 152
Bielefeld 41, 213 and n37
Biesenrodt, Capt 114–5
Billingsport, NJ 120
Bischhausen, Col Carl Ernst von, 53, 139
   n98, 262
Bishop, Thomas 26
Black Horse, NJ 87
Blackmore, Capt 118–19
Block, Col Justus Henrich von 55, 112,
   151, 258
Bloomingdale, NY 236
Bockewitz, QM 236, 261
Bode, Major 222
Bohemia 131
Bopp, *Kammerdirektor* Heinrich Christian
   Ernst 231–3 and n77
Borck, Col Henrich Christian von, 51, 90,
   262
Bose, Col Carl Ernst Johann von 203
   n112, 260, 262
   distinguished 64, 151
   ill 82, 90
   promotion 138 n93, 145
   seeks discharge 129
Bordentown NJ 87, 137
Boston, Mass. 31, 58, 155, 183
   Massacre 31
   tea party 216
Boswell, James 35 and n78
Bostwick, Elisha 92 n47, 97
Boudinot, Elias 200
Boundbrook, NJ 5, 195 n63
Brandenburg, troops of 13
Brandywine, battle (1777) 117–18, 135,
   147, 234, 243, 259, 261, 263
Braunschweig-Wolfenbüttel
   convention with Hessen-Kassel 42
   lands of 163
   Dukes of 10, 13
   public opinion of 227
   recruiters of 11
   subsidies and 23
   treaty with Britain 25, 28, 31, 186, 227,
      230
   troops of 2, 16, 18, 59, 155 n74, 156, 240;
   their strength 157 n82; foreigners dis-
      charged 205; prisoners 199, 201
   seized by Prussia (1866) 229
   see also Karl Wilhelm Ferdinand,
      Riedesel
Breed's Hill, battle (1775) 24, 58–9, 76,
   241
Bremen 19, 207, 208
Bremer barges (*Bremerböcke*) 207, 211
Bremerlehe (now Bremerhaven-Lehe) 36,
   37, 38, 43, 52, 53, 55, 63, 128, 207,
   226, 251, 254
Breslau 51
Bretthauer, Lt Col Balthasar 90, 235
Briede, Lt 75
Brinkmeyer, Henrich 213 and n37
British army
   'Britannic Majesty's Army in Germany'
      16, 18, 144
   command structure of 144–6
   desertion from 188, 192
   dragoons 73
   regiments:
      4th (King's Own) 24
      10th 118
      16th 156 n80
      16th dragoons 56
      23rd 141
      33rd 141
      42nd highlanders 68 n43, 77–8 and
         n90, 87, 101, 120, 123
      45th 6, 106, 243
      53rd 152
      54th 155
      60th (Royal Americans) 10, 69, 138
         n96, 210
      71st highlanders 68 n44, 140, 242
      Diemar's Hussars 138
      Georgia Loyalists 155
      Guards 52, 53, 59, 64, 111, 140–1
      Provincial Light Horse 155
      Queen's Rangers 101, 132, 135
      Volunteers of Ireland 155
   German recruits 10, 11, 153
   grenadiers 82, 84, 115–20, 243
   highlanders 242
   light infantry 71, 82, 84, 132, 180, 242,
      244
   relations with Hessians 1, 55, 60, 61–4,
      69, 74, 76, 79, 87–8, 103–12, 122–3,
      124, 144–57, 245
Broescke, QM 196
Bronx river 74
Brooklyn, NY 82
Bruce, Lt Col 145
Brunswick and Brunswickers – *see*
   Braunschweig-Wolfenbüttel

Index

Brunswick, NJ 84, 87, 101
Bückeberg 42
Buettner, Johann Carl 177 and n37, 259
Bulow, MajGen. von 213 n37
Bunau, Col Rudolf 264
Bunker Hill – *see* Breed's Hill
Bunn, Sally 197
Burgoyne, Gen. John 102, 103, 107 n126, 138 n96, 240
Burke, Edmund 246
Burlington, NJ 86
Burr, Aaron 183
Buskirk's Loyalists 243
Byles, Major Thomas 138–9
Byng, Adm John 115

Cadenberg 45
Caldwell, Mrs James 149
Camden, S. C. 139
  battle (1780) 240, 242
Camden, Charles Pratt, Earl of 32
Campbell, Col Archibald 197 n71, 235, 244, 263
Campbell, Gen. John 145
Campbell, Col William 140–2
Canada 5, 58, 102, 144, 145, 151, 191, 195, 240, 262
Carleton, Gen. Sir Guy 58, 150, 198 n79
Carlisle, Frederick Howard, 5th Earl of 29
Carter, Landon 31
Cartheuser, Corporal 221
Catherine, Empress of Russia 24
Cavendish, Lord John 30
Chad's Ford, Pennysylvania 147
Charleston, South Carolina 139, 146, 148, 151, 152, 183, 193
  attacks on (1776) 58, (1779) 235, (1780) 76, 135, 147 168, 217
  disagreement at, 156
  Hessian regiments at, 169, 197 and n71, 193, 259, 261, 263, 265
  Hessian school at, 239
  sickness at, 169
  slaves at, 165–6
Charleston Neck 168
Chase, Samuel, 182
Chastellux, Marquis de, 127
Chatham, Kent 30, 155, 198 n70
Chatterton Hill 74–5, 101; *see also* White Plains
Chesapeake Bay 117
Chesterfield, Philip Stanhope, 4th Earl of, 30
Clarke, Gen. Alured 197, 200
Clavering, Col John 19, 34, 35 n78, 146
Clinton, Gen. Sir Henry 6, 49, 61, 66, 79–80, 103, 145, 146, 165, 197, 205, 240, 245

comments on Hessians 24, 150, 156, 186 n11
comments on the war 58–9, 99, 102, 140, 148
  Hessian view of 144 n3
  intelligence misinterpreted 137–8
  relations with Howe 75–6
Clive, Sir Robert 251
Closen, Baron Ludwig von 143
Cochenhausen, Col Johann Friedrich von, 142, 163, 167, 260
Collegium Carolinum – *see* Kassel
Collier, Captain Sir George 5, 54–5, 56 n180
Cologne 208, 228
Concord, Mass. 31, 58
Congress – *see* Continental Congress
Connecticut Coast raid (1779) 181–2 and n57
Connecticut Farms 149
Constitutional Gazette 59
Convention Army 138 n96, 144
Cork, mutiny among recruits at 213–14
Cornwallis, Gen. Charles, Earl 49, 74, 79, 84, 99, 103. 119, 145, 147, 171, 217, 244 n59
  and Ewald 134–5
  and Redbank 122–3, 128, 130, 146
  southern campaigns 139–41
  Yorktown 136, 142–3
Cöster, Chaplain G. C. 196, 237 and n. 18, 261
Cowpens, battle (1781) 154, 242
Cramon, Captain 137, 264
Cressener, George 228
Cresswell, Nicholas 84, 100, 156
Creutzbourg, Col Carl Adolph Christoph von 247
Crosswicks creek 99
Cumberland, William Augustus, Duke of 17
Custine, General 246

Darmstadt – *see* Hessen-Darmstadt
Deane, Silas 31
Dechow, Major Friedrich von 89, 90, 92–5, 114
debts, of Hessian officers, 20–1, 201, 203 n112, 250
Delaware river 86, 92–3, 97, 107, 123, 175, 176, 252
  fighting for (1777) 118–28
  map 125
Demont, Captain William 76 and n82
Denmark 13, recruiters from 210
desertion, Hessian – *see under* Hessen-Kassel, army

Index

Deutsche Chronik 190, 251
Diemer, Capt. 138 and n93
Dietzel, Lt Christian Henrich 237
Dilkes, Sir Thomas 82–3
Dinklage, Captain August Eberhardt von
  48, 54, 80, 151–2, 154, 160, 166, 167,
  169, 234, 236, 261
Dippel, Horst 5, 231 n77
Ditfurth, LtGen. von, 260
Doehla, Conrad 152 and n55
Döhm, Wilhelm 33
Donkin, Major Robert 131
Donop, August Moritz von, 34
Donop, Col Karl Aemilius Ulrich von 37,
  102–3, 106, 133, 134, 157, 180, 217,
  259, 262
  1776 campaign 64, 65, 71, 75–6, 79, 84,
  86
  Trenton 87ff, 91–2,99, 106, 242, 244
  Redbank 122–7, 146, 244 and death
  127, 157
Donop, LtGen. Wilhelm Henrich August
  von, 37 n86, 260
Donop, Captain Carl Moritz von, 70
Dorchester Heights, Mass. 58, 76
Dordrecht 212, 254
'Dormant Commission' 145
Dörnberg, Capt.-Lt Karl Ludwig von 48,
  165, 168, 211, 217, 259
Dover 30, 198 n79
Dresden 138, 173
du Buy, LtCol Johann Christian 138-142
  and n105, 244, 262
Dumfries, Virginia 168, 169
Duncan, Capt Henry 69
du Ry – *see* Ry

East river 69, 70, 72, 73, 167
Eelking, Max von 4, 123 n19
Eisenach 210, 231
Eisenard, Johann Friedrich 22
Eisentraut, MajGen. von 3
Elberfeld (now Wuppertal-Elberfeld) 219
Elizabethtown, NJ 148–9, 234
Emmerich, Andreas 133, 191
Empire, Holy Roman 15, 16, 30, 228;
  Emperor – *see* Habsburgs
Endemann, Major Johann Wilhelm von
  262–3
Engelhardt, Lt 93, 114
Erbach, Count of 208
Erbprinz, of Hessen-Kassel, *see* Wilhelm
  IX; of Braunschweig-Wolfenbuttel, *see*
  Karl Wilhelm Ferdinand
Eschwege (town) 224
Eschwege, Major Karl von 71, 128
Eschwege, *L andrat* von 225–6

Eskuche, August Wilhelm 238
Estaing, Comte d' 155, 235, 243
Eugene of Savoy 14, 21
Evelyn, Capt William Glanville 24, 186
  n11
Ewald, Capt. Johann
  commands *Jäger* company 262
  desertion in his company 194–5
  engagements 73, 117, 133–7, 142
  letters to Misses Van Horne 5, 195 n63
  outstanding leader 134–5, 245 and n62
  Redbank 123, 126
  Simcoe on 151, 153
  sickness 168
  war profits 249–250
  writings and comments 50, 81, 86, 89,
  103, 132–3, 136 n84, 174 n82, 176,
  180, 212, 215, 263
Eyb, Col. von 144 and n4

Faesch, Jakob 199–201
Fairfield, Conn. 173, 181. 182 n57, 261
Faucitt, Col Sir William 36, 53, 69 n47,
  113, 207, 210, 212 and n25, 213, 254
  negotiates subsidy treaty 25–8, 38
  offers bribe 61–2, 104 and supreme com-
  mand 145
  reports on Hessians 43, 45 and n128,
  62–3, 77, 169, 223–4 254 n77
  Scheither's recruits 10–11
  son 105 n113
Feilitzsch, Lt Carl Philipp von 134, 167,
  193
Feldjägercorps – *see* Hessen-Kassel, army,
  Jäger
Ferdinand of Braunschweig, Prince 18,
  105, 108, 131, 144, 154
Ferguson, Capt. Patrick 203
Fielding, Capt. 56
Finck, General 141
Fischer, Joachim 5, 127 n34
Fischer, basketmaker 218
Flanders, allied campaign in (1793–4) 146,
  246, 248
Flatbush, NY 66, 68, 69, 132, 158
  burnt by Americans 179
Florida 257
Flueck, Lt Claudius 49
Force, Peter, *American Archives* 5
Forrest, Capt. 93
Forster, George 3, 154, 228–9
Fortescue, Sir John 78n90
Fort Independence 76, 101, 265
Fort Knyphausen 79, 138, 236
Fort Lee 76, 79, 80, 84, 139
Fort Mercer 120–1 *see also* Redbank
Fort Mifflin 118, 120, 127–8

Index

Fort Washington 76–9, 80, 81, 84, 90, 106, 107, 130, 174, 186, 188, 241, 242, 255 n1, 259, 261, 263, 265
Foundling Hospital – see Kassel
France
  Americans seek alliance 31–2
  campaigns 1792–5, 245–8
  desertion in the army 115, 192
  officers join Hessians 51, 202–3
  propaganda 229, 246–7
  revolution 2, 228
  threatened invasion of England 17
  troops in America 102, 103, 142–3, 155
  troops in Hessen-Kassel 17–18, 21, 30, 34, 131, 172, 183, 216, 233
  troops at St Lucia 242
  War of Spanish Succession 14
Frankfurt-am-Main 5 and n5, 35 n78, 208–10, 216, 217, 247
Franklin, Benjamin 186, 204
  Uriasbrief 229
Frederick (Friedrich) II of Prussia ('the Great') 3, 15, 17 and n44, 19, 131, 205, 211, 245, and soldier trade, 18, 24, 229–30
Frederick, Col Felix 11
Fredericksburg, Virginia 195, 204
Freehold, NJ 181
Freeman's Journal 60 n 14
French army – *see* France
Friedrich I, Landgraf of Hessen-Kassel (1730–1751) and King of Sweden 14, 16
Friedrich II, Landgraf of Hessen–Kassel (1760–1785) 19, 50, 59, 63, 68, 81, 82, 90 and n32, 120, 127, 146, 147, 189, 204, 222, 235, 243, 253, 260
  character of 35–6 and n78, 230, 'Seller of Souls' 228, 230
  death of 252
  domestic policy of 2, 33–6, 216–20, 231–3, 251–2, *Pensées diverses sur les Princes* 230 n70, 232
  family of 3, 34
  finances of 26, 33, 34–5, 250–2, British mistake regarding 6
  military policy of 21, 30, 31, 38, 43, 47, 51, 104, 163–4, 169, 174, 224, 244
  pub named in honour of 79
  recruiting by 21, 35, 207–8, 213, 223–4
  subsidy treaty 25–8, 34–5, 227
  Trenton court-martial 103, 108–110, 112, 113, 115–6
  views on Knyphausen 149–150
Friedrich Wilhelm, Prince of Prussia 103
Fritzen, Capt. 226
Führer, Lt Carl August 201–2
Fulda river 252

Gage, Gen. Thomas 24
Gaine, Hugh 99
Galloway, Joseph 77, 84, 86, 87, 88 n18, 89 n28, 153
Gardner, Major 120
Gärtner, Friedrich 227 n56
Gates, Horatio 242
Gechter, surgeon 129
Gerland, Conrad 221–2
Gerland, Otto 3
Germain, Lord George, 25, 86 n11, 102, 104, 106, 112–3, 144, 154
Germantown, Pennsylvania, 118, 191, 203
  battle (1777) 117, 136, 234, 242, 259, 261, 263
Germany
  map 9
  and soldier trade 5, 7–8, 29–30
  German character 7, 92, 152–3
  German troops in British service 5, in French 11, 142–3
  emigrants to America 32, 169, 186–7 and n10, 152–3, 160, 169
  martial spirit 1, 162
  military arrangements 13, 164
  nationalism 2–3, 6
  public opinion in 5, 100, 170, 227–30
  princes 8, 11, 24, 208, 212 n25
George I 14
George II 34
George III 3, 11, 23, 24–5, 26, 27, 28, 60, 63, 158
George, surgeon 199
Georgia 145, 169, 238, 257
Gibbon, Edward 29
Gibraltar 25
Girancourt, Lt de 46
Glover, Gen. John 72 and n61, 73, 93, 95
Goebel, Johann 51
Gohr, Lt. Gen. Johann Henrich von 45
Gooch, G. P. 2
Gosen, Col David Ephraim von 260
Gotha 231
Gotschall 128
Governor's Island 70
Graf, Lt Col Wilhelm 260
Grafton, Duke of 31 and n54
Grant, Gen James 66, 87, 91–2, 101, 103
Grasse, Adm de 103
Gravesend, Kent 11
Grenadiers – *see under* British army and Hessen–Kassel army
Greene, Col Christopher 126
Greene, Gen Nathaniel, 77, 93, 97, 140–1, 192
Green Spring, Virginia 263
Greenwich, National Maritime Museum at, 5

Index

Grim, Miss Peggy 195 n63
Groening, Lt Friedrich Henrich 118, 120
Groening, Capt. 128
Grothausen, Lt 114, 134
Grotius, Hugo 170
Grouchy 95
Gruber, Ira D. 5
guerilla warfare – see 'Little War'
Guibert, G. A. H. 7, 17
Guilford Court House, battle (1781)
    140–1, 217, 263
Günderode, Friedrich Justinian, Freiherr
    von 212

Habsburgs 15, 16
Hachenberg, Col Carl Wilhelm von 260
Hackensack, NY 84, 139
Haddonfield, NJ 123
Hague, Prussian minister at 230
Haldimand, Gen Frederick 5, 101, 151,
    240, 245
Hale, Lt William John 6, 116, 147, 243,
    249
Halifax 54, 55, 145, 151, 234, 237, 257,
    265
Hamburg 10, 19, 56 n183, 208, 209
Hampton, Virginia, 139
Hanau 191, Hessians garrisoned at, 17; see
    also Hessen-Hanau
Hanau, Count of see Wilhelm IX
Hanbury-Williams, Sir Charles 29
Hancock, John 186, 188
Hand, Edward 65, 73, 137
Hanger, Captain George, Lord Coleraine
    96, 156 and n80.
Hannover 10, 15, 25, 28, 29, 37, 42, 163,
    208, 216, 226, 229
    sources at, 4
    troops of, 11, 16, 17, 18, 40, 41, 42, 44,
    59, 60, 246
    Hessian recruits from, 211
Hanstein, Lt Col Caspar Friedrich von 260
Hanstein, Major von 74, 42 n113
Harcourt, Col William 101, 123, 156–7
Harlem 70
Harlem Heights 71–2, 179
Harlem river 77
Harris, Captain George 100
Hartung, Corporal Wilhelm 41
Harvey, General Edward 63
Haslet, Colonel John 73
Hastenbeck, battle (1757) 17
Hatzfeld, Colonel Maximilian 213–14,
    217 n11
Haussmann, Jacob 221–2
Hazen, Brigadier General Moses, 200
Heath, General William 6, 79, 101

Heilbronn 208
Heister, Lieutenant Carl Levin von 48, 69,
    76, 81, 124, 151
    subsequent career 164
Heister, Lieutenant General Leopold von
    161, 217
    character of 5, 49, 50, 62–3, 65
    commands first Hessian division 36
    respected by troops 109
    relations with Howe 54–5, 56, 61–4, 82,
    103–112, 145, 146, 147, 245
    in 1776 campaign 66, 68, 69, 73, 133,
    243
    and Trenton 89, 90, 107
    correspondence quoted in Stryker 110
    n140
    plundering 60, 111–2, 106, 147, 174,
    180–1
    and prisoners 158 and n2
    and desertion 41, 187–8
    relieved of command and death 112–3,
    164, 161, 217
Heister, Madame von 62, 113
Helmstedt 15, 22, 36
Henckelmann, Lieutenant Johann Henrich
    159, 161, 256 n3, 265
Henry (Henrich) Prince, of Prussia 230
Hepe, Sergeant 243
Heringen, Colonel Henrich Anton von
    41–2, 69, 70, 161, 260
    death 74, 82, 90
Hersfeld 13, 217, 233
Herz, Henriette 227 n55
Hessen-Darmstadt 13, 16, 24 and n16, 35,
    187 and n13, 208, 224, 246, 250 n82,
    map 9
Hessen-Hanau 35 n78
    Hessen-Kassel claim to 16–17 and n43
    subsidy treaty (1776) 24–5, 28, 186, 227
    troops 144, 157 n82, 247
    recruiters 210, 212
    prisoners 199, 201
Hessen-Kassel
    map 9
    described 4, 19, 220 n26
    people 12, 19–20, 33 n64, 189, 218–9,
    220, 240, flee abroad 216, 219, 222,
    225–6; suffering 222–3
    population size 66, 216, 220 and n27,
    233
    government 18, 20, 34, 38, 231–2, 252;
    Landstände 18, 34, 252, *Kriegs- und
    Domänen Kammer* 48, 231–2 and n82;
    Kriegscollegium 38, 114 n159, 209, 221,
    225; *Policey Commission* 226
    princes and Landgraf *see under individual
    names*

Index

finance and taxes 13–18, 20, 26, 28, 33,
34–5, 217, 227, 230, 232 and n82,
249–252; *Kriegskasse* 18, 20, 34–5, 38,
227, 251, 252; *Kammerkasse* 34;
Kontribution 20, 221–3
industry and agriculture 217, 218, 219,
231–3; 251; Labour shortage 224–5,
impact of war 17–18, 172–3, 183,
216–33, 248–52
the soldier trade 12–21, 24–8, 218–19,
231–3, 248–52
subsidy treaties: total concluded 35; with
Denmark (1677) 13; with Venice
(1687) 13; with Holland (1688) 14;
with Sweden (1714) 14; with Bavaria
(1744) 16; with Britain (1726) 14,
(1727) 14, (1745) 17, (1755) 15,
(1759) 18, (1776) 27–8, 186, 189, 216
(1787) 246, (1793) 247
army: strength 14, 16, 18–19, 20, 39–40,
51–2, 59, 87, 117, 122 and n13, 138,
139, 157 and n82, 254, 257; described
17, 19–20, 39–51, 61, 65–6, 73, 77,
205, 215, 240, 256, 267; battalion and
regiment, defined 27 n32, 39, 44; leadership 47–51, 63 n25, 65–6, 244–5,
and n62; recruiting and recruit transports 1, 21, 205, 207–213, 215,
218–19, 223–5, 226, 232, 254; morale
109, 235–6, 237; mobilisation 38–40;
crossing to America 52–7; attitudes to
America 60, 69–70, 158–170; discipline 42–3, 45, 136, 172, 173, 180–1,
192–3, 205, 212–13, 215, 235; sickness
54–6, 61, 81–2, 168–9, 235, 238 and
n26; medical care 27, 39, 213 n37,
217–8, 238; desertion from 19, 41–2,
45, 51, 81, 184–206, 216, 242; tactics of
61, 66 and n35, 68, 82–3 and n118,
95–7, 111, 242–4, 245–8; casualties in
13, 17, 56–7 and n187, 68, 72, 73
n67, 75 n77, 81, 95, 117, 120, 127,
128 n38, 141, 142–3, 149, 197, 233,
235, 238 n22, 255; relations with
British *see under* British army; plundering and 106, 111–12, 147, 149, 153
and n60, 171–83; pay and emoluments of 27–8, 50, 51 n155, 133,
213–4, 227, 249–51 language difficulties of 152, 177; prisoners of 97–9,
159, 190–1, 194, 195, 198–201, 204,
246; wives and children of 52, 238–9,
'Amazons' 133; uniforms of 45, 81, 97
and n67, 141, 217, 250; muskets of
217
regiments
  Angelelli 197 n71, 198 n79, 234 n3, 262

Balecke 224 n42
Benning 197 and n71, 198 n79, 239,
264
Block 37 n87, 65, 71, 102, 258
Bose 130, 138–43, 194, 198 n79, 202,
217, 236, 255 n3, 262
Bunau 37 n89, 198 n79, 258, 264
combined 234 and n4, 261–2
Ditfurth 37 n87, 74, 82, 156 n80, 184,
197 n71, 198 n79, 223n 36, 258, 260
Donop 37 n87, 43, 46, 84, 196, 198
n79, 221, 223 n36, 258, 260
Erbprinz 37 n87, 71, 142–3, 163, 192,
194, 198 n79, 223 n36, 234, 243, 255 n2,
258, 260
Graf 258
Guards 12, 21, 35, 38, 46, 129, 209,
243, 258
Hornumb 13
Huyn 36 n84, 37 n89, 46, 51, 59,
161, 167–8, 187, 197 and n71, 198
n77, 223 n36, 239, 264
Knoblauch 193, 197, 264
Knyphausen 37 n87, 40, 41, 46, 49,
51, 72, 74–5, 89–90, 93–5, 114, 190,
193, 198–201 and n79, 223 n36, 234,
240, 255 n2, 258, 262
Koehler 37 n89, 56, 78, 218, 258–9
Landgraf 181–2, 185 n6, 198 n79,
203, 236, 260
Leib 37 n87, 43–4, 48, 74, 79–80, 105,
150, 167, 184–5, 187, 198 n79, 234,
258, 260
Leib Dragoons 222
Lengerke 122, 126, 128, 243, 258
Lentz 247–8
Linsing 37 n87, 41 n112, 120, 122,
126, 196, 199, 255 n3, 258
Loewenstein 165, 258
Lossberg 37 n87, 40, 41–2, 51, 60,
74–5, 82, 89–90, 93, 105, 114, 150,
151, 191, 196, 205 n121, 209, 217
n11, 234, 241, 250, 255 n2, 258, 260
jung-Lossberg 150, 198 n79, 262
Mansbach 17, 43
Minnigerode 37 n87, 65, 111, 122,
124, 126, 255 n3, 258–9
Mirbach 37 n87, 122, 126–7, 128,
138, 150, 198 n79, 223 n36, 234, 235,
239, 258, 262
Platte 256 n3, 258
Porbeck 264
Prinz Friedrich Dragoons 225, 227
Prinz Karl 13, 37 n87, 74, 80, 198
n79, 234, 239, 249, 258, 260
Rall 37 n87, 40, 41, 43, 69, 74–5,
89–90, 93, 115, 161, 190, 191, 197

283

n71, 199, 234–5, 237, 239, 245 n61, 255 n2 258, 262; 2nd battalion 213

Seitz 234, 264

Stein 37 n89, 47, 101, 159, 174 n20, 234, 258, 264

2nd battalion 225

Trumbach 37 n87, 41, 52, 101, 194, 223 n36, 234 n3, 236, 258, 262

Ufm Keller 13

White 12

Wissenbach 37 n89, 45, 46, 82, 101, 181, 197 n71, 243, 258, 264

Woellwarth 197 n71, 234 n3, 244, 262

Wutginau 37 n89, 45, 77, 223 n36, 239, 258, 260

artillery 21, 37 n87 and n89, 45, 114, 223 and n36

dragoons 44, 45, 209, 210, 223

engineers 46

garrison regiments 36, 38–9, 44–5, 77, 79, 132, 241; 2nd battalions still in Hessen 224–5 and n42

field regiments 37 n87 and n89, 39, 66, 132, 224

grenadier 27 n 32, 37 n87 and n89, 39, 71 n57, 117, 199, 171, 188, 189 n79, 196, 217, 235, 243, 247, 258–9; in 1776 campaign 64–5, 68, 70–2, 74, 79, 82–4, 87; at Redbank 122, 126–7, 130

Jäger: 37 n87 and n89, 45, 48, 59, 61, 114, 132, 142; in 1776 campaign 64–5, 68–70, 72, 73, 84, 87; distinguished service 117–8, 130–7; at Redbank 122, 123, 126; at Springfield 148–9; new companies 102, 111 n145, 133–4, 212, 219, 262; plundering and discipline 180–1; desertion 188, 193, 194, 195, 199, 202, 206; recruiters 209–10; recruits 211–5, 219; service in America 235, 240, 262; in 1792–4 247–8; ghost 99

Landgrenadier 43

Landmiliz 43

cadet corps 47, 163

Hessen-Nassau 252

Hessians – *see* Hessen-Kassel, army

Hessische Morgenzeitung 229

Heusser, Quartermaster Christian 60, 89 and n27, 261

Heymel, Colonel Carl Philipp 62 n22

Hildesheim 42

Hillebrand, Freikorporal Carl 46–7

Hillebrand, Lieutenant Colonel Johann Philip 46, 264

Hinrichs, Captain Johann 72, 135, 136, 154, 159–60, 165, 169–70, 179, 244, 245, 263, 264

Hinte, Major Erasmus Ernst 46, 260

Hochkirchen, battle (1758) 51

Höchst 216

Hoepfner, Lieutenant 53

Hohenlohe, Prince of 147

Hohenstein, Captain George 78

Holland 8, 14, 24

  Dutch East India Company recruiters 10, 11, 210

  Hessian flight to 216, 222, 226

Homberg 37

Hopkinson family 136

Hopperstown, NJ 139

Horch, Johannes 221

Horn, Colonel Ludwig von, 82, 264

Horne, Misses van, of Boundrook, NJ 5, 195 n63

Horseneck, Mass. 261

Hosbach, Caterina Maria 219 n20

Hotham, Commodore William 54–5

Howe, Admiral Richard, Viscount 5, 55, 60, 63, 69, 106, 129

Howe, General Robert 244

Howe, General Sir William 4, 5, 49, 144 n3, 166–7

  character and generalship 86–7, 97, 100

  complements *Jäger* 135

  plundering 172, 176 and n30, 177, 179, 180

  receives Hessians 55–6, 58

  relations with Heister 62-4, 103–12, 146–7

  1776 campaign 54, 66–9, 70–3, 76, 84–6, 133

  Trenton 87–8 and n18, 90, 91, 98–9, 102, 107 and n126, 154

  1777 campaign 117–8, 120

  Redbank 122, 126, 129, 132

Hudson river 76, 79, 138, 139, 148, 185, 236

Hughes, Ensign Thomas 149, 152

Hunold, Philipp 239

Hutcheson, Captain Francis 69, 101

Hungary 21, 216

Huyn, Major General Johann Christoph von 80, 145, 180 death 197 n71, 264

Immenhausen 224

Ingolstadt 16

Ireland, reaction to introduction of German troops 25 n18

Iron Hill, skirmish (1777) 117, 134, 263

Iroquois 148, 177 n33

Jackson, Dr Robert 130 and n46, 175, 238

Jäger – *see* Hessen-Kassel, army

Index

Jamaica pass (Long Is.) 66
Jefferson, Thomas 165, 204
Jews in Hessen 165, 231
Johann Friedrich, Duke of Braunschweig-Wolfenbüttel 13
John's Island, South Carolina 168
Johnson, Elizabeth 236
Juliad, Lieutenant Carl 203 and n112
Junghans, Pastor 3
Jungkenn, Lieutenant General Friedrich Christian Arnold von letters to 4–5, 112 n152, 130, 163, 167
letters to 4–5, 112 n152, 130, 163, 167
interest in botany 167 n38
Prussian 'junta' 36

Kapp, Friedrich 2–4, 25–6, 229 and n69, 231 n77, 249
Karl VII of Bavaria 16–17
Karl, Landgraf of Hessen-Kassel (1670–1730) 12–14, 16, 35
Karl, son of Friedrich II of Hessen-Kassel 230, 260
Karl Eugen, Duke of Württemberg 2, 19, 211
Karl Wilhelm Ferdinand, Erbprinz of Braunschweig-Wolfenbüttel 24, 230
Karlshafen 207
Military Hospital 50, 150 n31, 252
Trading Company 217
Kassel 30, 35, 36, 49, 68, 81, 110, 141, 154, 164, 198 n79 212, 219, 220 and n27, 226, 228, 229, 231, 244
described 36, 220, 251–2
court at 25, 33, 34, 220, 252
Foundling Hospital 2, 33, 252
Murhardsche Bibliothek 4, 5 n5, 49 n149
Collegium Carolinum 33, 47, 48, 63 n25, 239
Bowling Green and Rennbahn 207 and n1, 213, 235
Weissenstein 34, 218, 253
other buildings 38, 218, 232, 251–2
bombed in 1943 252–3
recruiting 21, 45, 207, 212
captured by the French 17, 30
occupied by Hannoverians 34
Kemble, Major Stephen 111, 153, 172, 173
Keudell, Colonel 211, 213
Kingsbridge, NY 70, 73, 77, 137, 167
Kipping, Ernst 4, 181
Kip's Bay, NY 70–1, 130
Kistner, Corporal 200
Kitz, Quartermaster 199
Kitzel, Colonel Carl von 264
Kleinschmidt, Quartermaster Friedrich Jacob 152, 187, 265

Kleinschmidt, Lieutenant Carl Wilhelm 201–2
Knight, Captain 151
Knoblauch, Major General Hans von 264
Knox, William (Undersecretary of State) 113
Knyphausen, Lieutenant General Wihelm, Freiherr von 74 n75, 135, 138, 255 n1
character and leadership 49, 50, 77, 147, 244–5
with second division 37, 73
captured Fort Washington 76–9, 107
takes over command 110; his successor 129
convenes court-martial 114
Brandywine 118, 147
Springfield expedition 147–9, 261
relations with British 61–2, 104, 144 n3, 145, 147, 156, 157, 245; pension 249
discipline 174, 175, 187
desertion 191, 194, 201–2, 204
recruits 211, 212
wife's death 147 n23
returns to Hessen 150; made Governor of Kassel 164
Koch, Sergeant Berthold 41, 263
Koehler, Lieutenant Colonel Johann Christoph 258
Kontribution – see Hessen-Kassel, finance and taxes
Kospoth, Major General Henrich Julian von 114 and n160, 145, 259, 260
Krafft, Sergeant Johann Karl Philipp von, 155, 175, 181, 198, 212, 261
Kriegscollegium – see Hessen-Kassel, government
Kriegskasse – see Hessen-Kassel, finance and taxes
Kümmel, Chaplain Henrich 52 n160, 159, 265
Kuntzin, widow, 218
Kurz, Colonel Lubert Franz 159, 264
Kutzleben, Captain Christian Moritz von 26–7, 96 n59, 109, 180, 261

Lally, Comte Thomas Arthur de, 115
Lafayette, Marquis de 133, 136
Lancaster, Pennsylvania 98, 191, 199
Landstände – see Hessen-Kessel, government
Langenscharz, Freikorporal George Julius von 37, 47, 151, 220, 237, 265
Laudon, Baron Gideon Ernst von (Austrian general) 131
Lee, Arthur 59
Lee, General Charles 79, 80, 86, 97, 100, 115
Lee, Henry ('Light-Horse Harry') 140–1, 242

Index

Lee, Richard Henry 31
Leesburg, Virginia 100
Leiden Gazette 229
Leigh, Egerton 184
Leinhos, *Jäger* 214
Lengerke, Colonel Georg Emanuel von 198, 236, 258
Lentz, Colonel 247, 248
Leopold, Colonel 210
Leslie, General Alexander 74, 87, 139, 145, 146, 151, 197, 261, 263
Leuthen, battle (1757) 19
Lexington, Mass. 58
Lincoln, General Benjamin 200, 235, 243
Linsing, Colonel Otto Christian Wilhelm 258
Lippe-Detmold 208, 209
Lippe-Schaumberg 41 and n112, 233, map 9
Lith, Friedrich, Freiherr von der 48, 51, 152–3, 165, 182, 196, 236, 237, 261; subsequent career and death 184–5 and n6
Little Egg Harbour, NJ 203
'Little War' 130–1
Livingston, Governor William 179
Loewenstein, Colonel Wilhelm von 258
Loewenstein, Captain 114
London Chronicle 218, 240
Long Island 55, 144
  battle (1776) 60, 64–70, 80, 96, 106, 107, 161, 182, 186, 230, 241, 242, 259, 261, 263
Loos, Colonel Johann von 64, 127, 151, 234 n3, 241–2, 262
Lorentz, Richard 238
Lorey, Captain Friedrich Henrich 123, 132
Losch, Philipp 4, 229 n69
Lossberg, Lieutenant General Anton Henrich von 42, 161, 250, 260
Lossberg, Lieutenant General Friedrich Wilhelm von 80, 198 and n79, 255 n1, 262
  battalion commander 64, 250
  Hessian commander 129, 145, 150, 212 and Heister 109
  desertion 187, 191, 192, 200, 205
Lotheisen, Quartermaster and *Stabsauditeur* 114, 167, 187, 261
Lowell, Edward J. 3, 115
Lowry, James 129
Loyalists 58, 80, 84, 87, 91, 130, 131, 135, 138, 148, 155, 159, 178, 199, 206, 217
  Hessian view of 166–7
  their view of Hessians 153
  and plundering 149 and n33, 172, 181–2 and n57

Lübeck 19, 208
Ludwick, Christopher 186–7 and n13, 188
Luttrell, James 32, 186
Lützow, Ensign von 147 and n25

Macdougall, General Alexander 73
Maclean, Brigadier General Francis 145
Mackenzie, Major Frederick 6, 44, 58, 71 n57, 78 n91
Magaw, Colonel Robert 77, 78, 174
Magdeburg, Concert of (1688) 14
Mainz, 208, 209, 245
Maitland, Lieutenant Colonel John 145
Malsburg, Captain Friedrich von der 187 n13, 261
  and career and marriage 184
  on Rhode Island 96, 151–2, 180, 184
Manhatten Island 76, 159, 179
Marblehead, Mass., American regiment from 72 and n61, 73
Marburg
  sources at 3, 169 n46
  occupied by French 17, 30
  recruiting 21, 45
  university of 220, 239
Marlborough, 1st Duke of 63, 245
Martin, Joseph Plumb 70–1
Martin, Captain Wilhelm Reinhard Jakob 46
Mary, first wife of Landgraf Friedrich II 34
Massachusetts Spy 68 n44
Mathias, Emanuel 11
Mathew, Brigadier General Edward
Matthaus, Major J. Jost, 96 n59, 115, 235 son 115
Mauduit – see Plessis
Maurer, Surgeon Fritz 52, 263
Mauvillon, Jacob 33, 47, 63 n25
Mawhood, Colonel Charles 99
Maxen, battle (1759)
Maxwell, General William ('Scotch Willie') 117
May, Sebastian 226
Melsungen 222
mercenaries 1 and n1, 32, 40, 45 n128, 144, 186, 191, 192, 204, 248 British attitude to, 152; *see also* Hessen-Kassel, army
Mercer, General Hugh 93
Mercure de France 229
Mertz, Lieutenant 181
Metuchen Court House, NJ (skirmish) 259
Michaelis, Dr 238
Micklaskewicz, Ensign von 203–4
Minden 41, 144, 207, 211

Index

Minnigerode, Colonel Friedrich Ludwig
von 84
  battalion commander 64, 99, 111, 244,
258
  wounded 127
  death of 150–1
Minorca, 25
Mirabeau, Honoré Gabriel, Comte de 229
Mirbach, Major General Werner von 55,
63, 65, 77 n83, 82, 109, 262
Mohawk river 186 and n10
Möller, Caspar 222
Moncrieff, Captain James 118
Moniteur, Le 247
Monmouth, NJ 245 n61
Monroe, James 93
Montgomery, General Richard 58
Montluisant, Lieutenant 202–3
Moore, Frank, newspaper collection 5
Moravia 172
Morristown, NJ 148
Morton, Robert 176, 177
Moser, Friedrich Karl von 29, 228
Moser, Johann Jacob von 23
Mount Holly, NJ 92, 106
Mount Hope, NJ 199–201
Mud Island 120, 122, map 121
Muhlenberg, General Peter 135, 142, 159
n4, 263
Mülhan, *Jäger* 214
Mulhausen 208
Müller, Johannes von 21, 141, 227, 228
Müller, Quartermaster 49, 198
Münchhausen, Captain Friedrich von 64
n46, 151, 181, 195, 236, 261
  appointed Howe's ADC 80
  on Trenton 86, 87, 88 and n18, 91
  on Heister 105, 146
  on 'Loyalists' 87, 166–7, 176
  as ADC 110, 112
  on casualties 111 n145
  on Redbank 123, 124
  subsequent career of 163 and n20
Münchhausen, Major Hilmar Borries 236

Nassau-Saarbrucken 51
Natural Law 1, 23
Negroes, treatment of, viewed by Hessians
165–6
Netherlands – *see* Holland
Neu-Isenberg 208
Newark, NJ 79, 84
New England 59, 76
Newfoundland 54
New Haven, Conn. 173, 261
New Jersey
  map 85

winter campaign (1776–7) 84–95,
99–102, 106
spring campaign (1777) 111–12, 128,
261, 263
Knypausen's expedition (1780) 147–9
German settlers 186
'Little War' 176–7
Hessian prisoners 191, 201
Hessian brutality 229
Newport, Rhode Island 80, 103, 183, 192,
239, 261, 265
Newport News, Virginia 139
New Rochelle, NY 73, 159
newspapers, American
  on Hessians 59, 60 n14, 68 n44, 98–9,
133, 149, 156, 158 n2, 161, 171
  Hessian opinion of, 161
newspapers, French and Dutch 229
Newton's Creek 123
Newtown, Pennsylvania 159
New York (state) 148
New York city 2, 86, 102, 148, 151, 161,
165
  map 67
  capture (1776) 2, 70, 80, 107, 143
  Hessians at 90, 114, 117, 147, 150, 185,
193, 194, 196, 200, 201, 202, 227,
235, 236, 237, 240
  fire 183, 189
  evacuation 198 and n79
  Hessian hospital at 239
  Hessian strength at 257, 259, 261, 263,
265
  religion at 169
  German society 184
  Public Library 5 n5
  pub renamed 79
Niedervellmar 220, 222
Nooth, Dr Mervin 238 n24
North Carolina 142, 221
Nova Scotia, German soldiers settle in 256
n3

Ochs, Adam Ludwig 263
  joins Hessians 48, promotion 134
  on Hessian military 47, 217
  on war in America 124, 183, 235, 238
n22
  on Ludwig von Wurmb 137
  outstanding leader 245 n62, 247, 248
Oetker, Friedrich 229
Offenbach 208, 209
Ogilvie, Mrs John 72, 179
Olmutz, siege (1758) 122 and n16, 131
Oost Kapelle 248
O'Reilly, Captain Maximillian Michael
188, 244, 259

Index

background to 51
at Long Island 65, 70
at Kip's Bay 71
at Redbank 122–4, 128–9
at Brandywine 243
at Yorktown 142–3
Orlov, Gregory 43
Osborne, Colonel Sir George 6, 52, 57
n187, 63, 79, 127 n32, 172–3, 188 and
n22, 238, 242 and n49
Ottendorf, Nicholas Dietrich, Baron von
177 and n37

Paderborn 224
Paine, Thomas 33, 165 and n29
Palatinate 11
emigrants to America 32, 70, 169, 186–7
and n10,
Paramus, NJ 139, 263
Paris
treaty of (1783) 193, 200
Landgraf Friedrich II visits 31
Parker, Commodore Sir Peter 58
Parliament, British, debates in, 15, 30, 91,
161, 186, 246, 11, 18, 102
Pauli, Captain George 46, 88, 93
Paulus Hook, NJ 155, 242–3
Pausch, surgeon 49
Pell's Point, NY skirmish (1776) 72–3
Pembroke, Lieutenant Colonel the Earl of,
173
Pennsylvania
map 121
German settlers 70, 186
Hessian prisoners 97, 191
Council of Safety 98
Pennsylvania Packet (newspaper) 184, 201
Percy, General Hugh, Lord, 76, 77, 80,
151
Pestalozi, Johann Heinrich 228
Pfaff, Quartermaster Johann Henrich 261
Pflüger, Quartermaster 265
Pfremel, *Jäger* 193
Philadelphia 84, 86, 117, 134, 147, 161
181, 203, 235, 249
British occupation of 118, 132, 171, 175,
176, 183
Hessian prisoners at 98, 188, 199–200,
202
desertion to 191
retreat from 193, 221, 234
college of 136
academy at 151–2
Hessian view of 165, 166, 169
Philip the Magnanimous, Landgraf of
Hessen 12 n16
Philip's House, NY 263

Phillips, General William 142, 173
Piel, Lieutenant Jacob 89 and n27, 93, 96
n59, 97, 168 n41, 244, 261
Pitt, William, the Elder 15–16
Pitt, William, the Younger 29, 246
Platte, Lieutenant Colonel Friedrich 260
Plessis, Mauduit du, 126
Poland 216
Pomerania 14
Popp, Stephan 251
Pour la vertu militaire 90, 96, 116, 120, 134,
143, 163, 184
Pour le mérite 247
Porbeck, Colonel Friedrich von 46, 145,
168, 193, 197, 264
distinguished at Savannah (1779) 243
and n52
Portsmouth, England 10, 30, 52, 53, 63,
112, 156, 198 n79, 214
Portsmouth, Virginia 135, 139, 140 n103
'Potato War' 205
Potsdam 34
Prague, Battle (1757) 51
Prevost, General Augustine 145, 197 n71,
235, 243 and n52, 263
Prevost, Lieutenant Colonel Mark 145
prices
in Hessen-Kassel 51 n155, fixed 232
in America 201, 250
Prince Edward Island 262
Princeton, NJ 84, 87, 175–6, 185
battle (1777) 99, 102, 190
propaganda 59, 98, 149, 171, 191–2, 229,
246–7
Providence, Rhode Island 203
Province Island, skirmish (1777) 118–120,
map 125
Prueschenk, Colonel Adam Ernst Carl von,
134, 262
Prussia 2, 14, 15, 16, 20, 21, 36, 163, 207,
229, 231, 232
troops 41, 51, 131, 172, 215, 232, 245,
247; compared with Hessians 244 n59
desertion 42, 204, 205, 211, 212, 213
n37
recruiters 10, 210
Pulaski, Casimir 203
Putnam, General Israel 77, 179, 191

Quakers 160
at Philadelphia 169–70 and n50
their view of Hessians 176
at Rhode Island 80
Quebec 58
Quibbletown, NJ, 111

Rainsford, Colonel Charles 213

Index

Rall, Colonel, Johann Gottlieb 262
 character of 43, 64, 89 and n28, 244
 and Long Island 69
 and White Plains 74–5
 and Fort Washington 77–8 and n83,
 and Trenton 86–95, 101, 106, 107, 112,
  130, 242
 death of 95, 114, 115, 235
 defence of 96 n59
Ramseur's Mill, NC 140
Rau, Lieutenant 137, 262
Rauschenberg 173
Rawdon, Francis, Lord 6, 60, 61, 71, 76,
  151, 155
Rawlings, Colonel Moses 78
Raynal, Abbé 229
Reading, Pennysylvania 199
Redbank, Hessian defeat at (1777) 122–9,
  157, 206, 241, 242, 244
 name of 120 n11
 map of 125
 and prisoners 199
Reed, Colonel Joseph 66
Reichenbach, battle 83 n118
Remembrancer 171
Reuber, Grenadier Johannes 5 and n5, 40,
  43, 53, 78, 89, 190, 191, 220, 263
Rheider, Barbara 237
Rheinfels
 recruit depot at 207 and 209
 surrendered to French (1794) 115, 184
Rhine, recruiters along, 10
Rhode Island 161, 169
 British occupation (1776) 79–80, 234,
  237
 Franco-American siege (1778) 96, 155,
  184
 Hessians at 151, 152, 180, 191, 192, 203
 and n12
Richebitter, Friedrich 213
Richmond, Duke of 30
Riedesel, General Friedrich Adolf 4, 62
 n20, 142, 144, 145, 149, 164, 228,
  245; Madame Riedesel 4
Ries, Captain Johann Caspar 74, 75, 241,
  261
Riesbeck, Johann Caspar 216 and n2
riflemen – see American army and Hessen-
  Kassel, army, *Jäger*
Rights of Man 6, 159, 162, 165
Rinteln 36, 41–2, 74, 150, 209, 238, 250
Ritter, Erasmus 249
Ritter, 2nd Lieutenant 263
Ritzebüttel 37, 56 and n183, 254
Robertson, Lieutenant Colonel Archibald 6
Robertson, General James 148, 153, 172,
  173

Rochambeau, Comte de 137, 142, 143
Rocoux, battle (1746) 17
Roeder, Corporal 200
Roll, Captain 143
Romrod, Colonel Christian von
  262
Rosengarten, J. G. 4, 136
Rostock 36
Rothschild, 252
Rousseau, Jean-Jacques 185
Royal Gazette 149, 150 n42, 204
Ruffer, 2nd Lieutenant Carl Friedrich 263
Russia 2, 15, 23
 troops 24, 29, 43, 172, 183
Ry, Simon Louis du 5, 36, 50 n152, 63
 n25, 249

St Clair, Brigadier General Arthur 93, 95
St Eustatius 221
Saloman, Haym 187
Sachsen-Gotha 24
Sackville – see Germain
Sandy Hook, NY 54, 55, 63, 151
Sangerin, widow 217
Saratoga, battle (1777) 103
Sargent, Colonel Paul 93
Savannah, South Carolina
 capture (1778) 181 and 182 n57, 235,
  243–4, 263, 265
 siege (1779) 103, 154, 235, 243, 263, 265
 Hessians at 114, 155, 169, 183, 193, 194,
  197 and n71
Saxe, Maurice de 174
Saxony 172, Hessian recruits from 211
Scharnhorst, General von, on Ewald 136
 n84
Schaumberg enclave – see Lippe-
  Schaumberg
Scheffer, Lieutenant Colonel Franziskus
 1776 campaign 74, 90 and n32
 Trenton 87, 89–90, 93, 96 n59, 114
 career 116
 battalion commander 244, 262
Schellhausen, gardener 226
Schenk zu Schweinsburg 222–3, 224
Scheither, Colonel Georg Heinrich
 Albrecht von 10–11, 23, 25, 153
Schiek, Lieutenant Colonel Ernst Rudolph
 von 127, 262
Schiller, Johann Christian Friedrich 229
Schlemmer, Lieutenant Colonel 264
Schlieffen, Lieutenant General Martin
 Ernst von 52, 133, 207
 character 25, 35
 negotiates treaty 27, 227, 250–1
 'Prussian Junta' 36
 and Heister 63, 108–10

Index

'Les Hessois en Amerique' 229
English pension 249
Schlözer, August Ludwig von 4, 72 n59, 160, 179, 229
Schmalkalden 217, 225
Schmidt, Major General Martin 77, 82
Schotten, Captain 128–9, 222
Schreiber, Colonel Johann Wilhelm 249 and n81, 260
Schrecker, Chaplain 239
Schubart, Christian 170, 190, 251
Schumann, Musketeer Benedictus 193
Schuykill river 118, 119, 132, 181, 125
Schweinsburg – see Schenk
Schwein, Lieutenant von 174
Seitz, Colonel Franz Carl Erdmann von 145, 264
Sellwitz, von (fictitious member of Congress) 161
Serle, Ambrose 60, 63, 79, 115, 177, 178, 179, 242
Seume, Johann Gottfried 228
Seven Years War 10, 15, 17–19, 20–1, 30, 32–3, 35, 144, 154, 210, 216, 233;
  Hospital account outstanding 26
S'Gravendael 213
ships
  Augusta 127
  Merlin 127
  Niger 112
  Perry 54
  Rainbow 54–5
  Rattlesnake 156 n80
  South Carolina 199
Short Hills, NJ 148, action at (1777) 111
Simcoe, Colonel John Graves 132, 135–6, 151, 153, 183
Smith, Samuel S. 4
Sobbe, Lieutenant 166
soldier trade, international jurists on 22–3
Solms-Braunfels 208
Sontra 224
Sotheby's, sale of Reuber ms 5 and n5
South Carolina 184
Spain 183
Spangenberg (town) 104, 115, 220
Spangenberg, Captain 225
Spangenberg, Ensign 204
Spangenberg, Quartermaster 259
Spencer, General Joseph 74
Speyer 208
Springfield, NJ 148–9, 260
Städtler, Erhard 4
Stamford, C. von 22
Stamford, Captain Friedrich von 51, 120, 127, 244; letters to Misses Van Horne 5, 195 n63

Staten Island, NY 54, 55–6, 60, 104, 111, 112, 117, 138, 148, 152, 160, 186, 187
Steding, Captain 74
Stedman, Charles, 86 n7, 119 n8, 250 n82
Steuben, Friedrich von 142, 184, 240
Stephen, General Adam 93
Stirling, William Alexander, 'Lord' 67–8, 92, 93, 158 n2
Stirn, Major General Johann Daniel 54, 56, 65, 82, 111, 155
Stockhausen, *Landrat* von 219, 224–5
Stockholm 13, 51
Stono Ferry, South Carolina, battle (1779) 235, 238 n21, 263
Stony Point, NY 242
Stormont, Lord (Secretary of State) 11, 210
Stuart, Colonel Charles 123 n22, 124
Stuttgart 251
Suffolk, Earl of (Secretary of State) 146
  subsidy treaty 26–7, 30,
  and Heister 52, 61–2, 108–110, 112, 113, 207, 212 n25
subsidies – see Hessen-Kassel, finance and taxes
Sullivan, General John 92, 148, 179, 181, 184
Susquehanna river 97
Sweden 97
Switzerland 208

Tarleton, Colonel Banastre 140, 154, 242
Thacher, Dr James 189, 203
Thirty Years War 8, 12, 171
Throg's Point, NY 72
Thuringia 150
Toll, Lieutenant Carl Heinrich 127
Topp's Ferry, NY 76
Treitschke, Heinrich von, 2–3, 231 n77, 249
Trendelburg, bailiwick in Hessen-Kassel 219
Trenton, NJ 86, 112, 134, 138, 255 n1
  map 94
  Hessian occupation 87–92
  battle (1776) 92–7, 227, 242
  effects of Hessian defeat 100–3, 106–7, 109–10 and n140, 128, 130, 154, 228
  court-martial 103, 114–5, 196 n59
  'wagon-loads of plunder' 153 and n60
  captives 159, 160, 190, 198–9, 201
Trevelyan, Sir George Otto 2, 45 n128, 68, 101
Treves 209
Treysa 38, 226
Troup, Lieutenant Robert 182

Index

Trumbach, Major General Carl Levin von
138 n93, 262
Tryon, Governor William 181–2 and n57,
261
Turkey 216
Tybee Island, South Carolina 168

Uhlendorf, Bernhard A. 4
Ungar, Lieutenant 201
Ungar, Quartermaster S. A. 124, 259
Urff, Lieutenant Christian Friedrich von
195 n63

Valentine's House, NY 101
Varnum, Brigadier General James 191
Vatas, Major 118–19
Vattel, Emer de 22
Venice 13, 14
Vergennes, Comte de 31, 129 n11
Virginia 202, 257
campaigns in 135–6, 138, 142–3, 261
Hessian prisoners in 169, 195
Voit, Colonel von 144 n4
Voltaire, Marie Arouet de 3, 230 n70, 252

Wagner, Captain 70, 128, 179, 183
Wakenitz, Dietrich-Wilhelm von 36
Waldeck 56, 59, 73, 77, 102, 180, 227,
229, map 9
troops 144, 157 n82, 189, 205
Waldenberger, Captain 151
Wallenstein, Albrecht von 8
Wallop, Captain Bennett 155 n80
Walpole, Horatio, 1st Baron 14
Walpole, Sir Robert 15, 246
Wangenheim, Captain von 264
Wangenheim, General von 44
Washington, George 49, 111 and n145,
136, 148
correspondence 4, 5
1776 campaign 70–1, 73, 76–9, 84–6,
107
Trenton 91–3, 227
generalship and tactics 97, 100, 102,
131, 240
Yorktown 137–8
plundering 176–7, 179
on Hessian treatment of prisoners 182
desertion 186, 188, 193 n53, 198, 202,
204
Washington, William 93
Waterloo, battle (1815) 95
weather, American, Hessian comments on
81, 140, 168–9
Weedon, Colonel George 192
Weimar 251
Wekhrlin, Wilhelm Ludwig 229

Wende, Quartermaster Christian Cornelius
261
Wesel 230
Weser river 207
Westphalia, treaty of (1648) 22
Westphalian troops 183
Westerhagen, Captain 132
Westernhagen, Colonel Maximilian von
146, 260
West Indies 169, 197, 221
Wetzlar 209
White Plains, NY 79, 191, 201, map 67
battle (1776) 73–5, 90, 104–6, 130, 234
Wiederholdt, Lieutenant Andreas
character and career 49, 116, 174 n22
at Pell's Point 72–3
White Plains 75
Fort Washington 107
Trenton 89–90, 92, 93, 95, 97
views on America 166, 169
and desertion 195, 202
diarist 263
Wiederholdt, Ensign Bernhard Wilhelm
48, 245 n62, 247, 261
Wied-Neuwied 208
Wied-Runkel 208
Wiegand, Fusilier Abraham 39 n100
Wilhelm VIII, *Statthalter* (1730–1751) and
Landgraf (1751–60) of Hessen-Kassel,
16–7 and n43, 20, 30, 35, 46, 253
Wilhelm IX, Landgraf of Hessen-Kassel
(1785–1821, Elector from 1803) for-
merly Count of Hanau, 3, 24, 35, 57
n187, 230, 231, 246, 247, 253, 260,
'the seller of souls' 246
William III 29
Willichs, Lieutenant 210
Wilmington, North Carolina 141
Wilmowsky, Captain 101
Wilson, Colonel James 188 n21
Wimpfen 208
Winchester, Virginia 169
Windmill Hill, Rhode Island 265
Winzingerode, Colonel von 228
Wissenbach, Lieutenant General Moriz
Adolf von 264
Wittgenstein 208
Wittorf, Julius-Jürgen von 57 n182
Woellwarth, Colonel Wolfgang Friedrich
von 235, 262
Wolff, Captain 156 n80
Wolff, Sergeant Major Carl 151
Wolff, Christian 23
Wolfhagen 36, 37, 225
women in America, attraction for Hessians,
80, 195–7, 236–7
Worms 208

Index

Woringer, *Zolldirektor* August, 3, 49 n149
Wraxall, Sir Nathaniel 3
Wreden, Captain August von 195, 262
  Jäger leader 117, 132–7, 244
  profits and career 249–50 and n82
Wumme river 37
Wurumb, Lieutenant Carl von 48–9, 127
Wurmb, Friederike von 48–9
Wurmb, Colonel Friedrich Wilhelm von
  44, 64, 244, 260
Wurmb, Colonel Ludwig von
  Jäger leader 134, 137–8, 149, 180, 244, 262
  comments on war 130, 141, 154
Wurmb, Captain Philip von 101–2,
  118–20, 134, 244
Württemberg 2, 8, 11, 19, 24, 36, 208,
  211–12 and n25, 216 n2
Wutginau, Lieutenant General Henrich

Wilhelm von 260

York, Frederick Augustus, Duke of 248
Yorke, Sir Joseph 24, 129
York Neck, NY 76
Yorktown, Virginia, battle (1781) 103,
  136, 142–3, 154, 202, 234, 261, 263
  prisoners 194, 204
Ysenburg, Prince of 50

Ziegenhain 36, 37, 38, 49,
  recruit depot 207, 209, 210, 213 n37,
  221 n39
Zinn, Quartermaster 261
Zorndorf, battle (1758) 172
Zulauff, Helwig 213
Zweibrucken (Deuxponts) 11
  regiment at Yorktown 142